Fifth Edition

ORGANIZATIONS
Structures,Processes, and Outcomes

RICHARD H. HALL
Distinguished Service Professor
State University of New York—Albany

PRENTICE HALL, *Englewood Cliffs, New Jersey 07632*

Library of Congress Cataloging-in-Publication Data

Hall, Richard H., (date)
Organizations : structures, processes & outcomes / Richard H.
Hall. -- 5th ed.
p. cm.

Includes bibliographical references and index.
ISBN 0-13-642562-3 (case)
1. Organization. 2. Organizational change. I. Title.
HM131.H237 1991
302.3'5--dc20   90-39915
                                                         CIP

Editorial/production supervision and
  interior design: ELIZABETH BEST
Cover design: BARBARA SINGER
Prepress buyer: DEBRA KESAR
Manufacturing buyer: MARY ANN GLORIANDE
Page makeup: AUDREY KOPCIAK

Prentice Hall-International (UK) Limited, *London*
Prentice-Hall of Australia Pty. Limited, *Sydney*
Prentice-Hall Canada, Inc., *Toronto*
Prentice-Hall Hispanoamericana, S.A., *Mexico*
Prentice-Hall of India Private Limited, *New Delhi*
Prentice-Hall of Japan, Inc., *Tokyo*
Simon & Schuster Asia Pte. Ltd., *Singapore*
Editora Prentice-Hall do Brasil, Ltda., *Rio de Janeiro*

Contents

Preface   *vii*

PART I   THE NATURE OF ORGANIZATIONS

1—The Outcomes of Organizations   *1*

Why Study Organizations? *1*
Organizations and the Individual, *2*
Organizations and the Community, *10*
Societal Outcomes, *11*
Organizations and Social Change, *17*
Organizations Across Societies: The Multinational Corporation, *24*
Why Study Organizations? *26*
Summary and Conclusions, *27*

2—On the Nature and Types of Organizations   *28*

Definitions from the Past, *28*
Are Organizations Real? *33*
Types of Organizations, *37*
The Voluntary Organization, *45*
Summary and Conclusions, *47*

PART II   ORGANIZATIONAL STRUCTURE

3—Organizational Structure: Forms and Outcomes   48

Complexity, *50*
Formalization, *62*
Centralization, *74*
Summary and Conclusions, *83*

4—Organizational Structure: Explanations   84

Contextual Factors, *87*
Organizational Design Factors, *100*
Explaining Organizational Structure, *106*
Summary and Conclusions, *107*

PART III   ORGANIZATIONAL STRUCTURE

5—Power   108

The Nature of Power in Organizations, *109*
Horizontal Power Relationships, *113*
A Perspective on Power in Organizations, *118*
Power in Voluntary Organizations, *122*
Power of Lower Participants, *122*
Summary and Conclusions, *123*

6—Conflict and Other Outcomes of Power   125

Outcomes of Power Relationships, *125*
Conflict, *127*
The Social Outcomes of Power, *131*
Summary and Conclusions, *133*

7—Leadership   134

What is Leadership? *135*
The Outcomes of Leadership for Organizations, *140*
Leadership for the Voluntary Organization, *152*
Summary and Conclusions, *153*

8—Decision Making   154

Strategic Decisions, *154*

The Decision-Making Process, *161*
Summary and Conclusions, *162*

9—Communication 163

The Importance of Communication, *164*
Individual Factors, *167*
Organizational Factors, *169*
Horizontal Communication, *174*
Communication Problems, *177*
Communication from Outside the Organization, *179*
Summary and Conclusions, *181*

10—Change 182

The Nature of Organizational Change, *182*
The Change Process, *185*
Summary and Conclusions, *198*

PART IV   ORGANIZATIONAL ENVIRONMENTS

11—Organizational Environments 199

Some Research Findings, *199*
Environmental Dimensions, *203*
Analytical Dimensions, *210*
The Perception of the Environment, *213*
The Impact of the Environment on the Organization, *214*
Summary and Conclusions, *215*

12—Interorganizational Relationships 216

IOR: Forms and Levels, *217*
A Framework for IOR Analysis, *223*
IORs in the Private Sector, *238*
Outcomes of IOR, *242*
Summary and Conclusions, *243*

PART V   ORGANIZATIONAL EFFECTIVENESS
AND ORGANIZATIONAL THEORY

13—Organizational Effectiveness 244

An Orientation Toward Effectiveness, *246*

Models of Organizational Effectiveness, *248*
Goals and Effectiveness, *254*
The Contradiction Model, *265*
Summary and Conclusions, *272*

14—Organizational Theory   *273*

The Population-Ecology Model, *274*
The Resource-Dependence Model, *277*
The Rational-Contingency Model, *282*
The Transaction-Cost Model, *285*
The Institutional Model, *287*
Summary and Conclusions, *291*

References   *292*

Index   *331*

Author Index, *331*
Subject Index, *337*

Preface

Why a fifth edition? Colleagues, friends, and relatives have asked that question repeatedly. I give them several answers. Since the Fourth Edition was written, I had the opportunity to visit and teach in the People's Republic of China in 1986 and 1987 and observe organizations there. I also spent a summer at the University of New England, Armidale, New South Wales, Australia, and had extensive conversations with Stewart Clegg about national cultures and organizations. David Hickson has visited Albany twice over the past two years, and we explored cultural differences also during these visits. These experiences have contributed to a much greater awareness on my part of how national cultures do and do not influence what happens in and about organizations. This awareness will, I hope, be evident in many of the interpretations in this volume.

There have been recent "plate tectonic" changes in world events, particularly in Eastern Europe. While only a few aspects of these events are captured here, it should be evident that old truths about organizations and their environments may just no longer be relevant. It is increasingly hard to know what is certain and what is not.

There also have been major changes in the narrower world of organizational theory. The major one is the widespread recognition that our understanding of organizational phenomena will only be advanced when theoretical perspectives are used in *combination*. The most outspoken proponents of specific theoretical positions ("paradigm warriors" in Howard Aldrich's term) now openly urge that their perspectives be used in combination with other perspectives. Sociologists appear to be quite a bit in front of our colleagues in economics and psychology who continue to test one theory against another. This would appear to be a fruitless exercise when complex phenomena are being considered. Other changes include more attention being paid to national cultural differences *and* the outcomes of organizations and interorganizational linkages for the state.

What do these changes mean in terms of this book? There are two new chapters. The first new chapter deals with decision making, which was buried in the chapter on leadership in earlier editions. My own students convinced me that this was needed. The second new chapter deals with conflict. My friend and colleague, John P. Clark, publicly chided me for dropping this topic in the chapter title of the Fourth Edition. In this edition there is a full chapter devoted to the topic. Other changes appear in each chapter to reflect developments in research and theory.

As in the past editions, the approach taken is essentially sociological and inductive. I have tried to capture the essence of where organizational theory is in mid-1990. My intellectual debts are documents in the references cited. I would like to thank Nancy Roberts of Prentice Hall for her encouragement and Elizabeth Best for her editorial help. As in past editions Eileen Pelligrino provided expert help with references and other matters. And, as in all matters, Sherry gave me continuing love and support.

Richard H. Hall
State University of New York—Albany

The Outcomes
of Organizations

WHY STUDY ORGANIZATIONS?

There are two answers to this question. The first answer is obvious. Organizations surround us. We are born in them and usually die in them. Our life space
in between is filled with them. They are just about impossible to escape. They
are as inevitable as death and taxes.

A simple exercise will illustrate the pervasiveness of organizations in our
lives. Simply think of all the activities that we engage in during a day. Which,
if any, are not influenced by an organization in one way or another? If you are
reading this book by yourself, it may seem to be an individual matter, but, after
all, the book was prepared and published by an organization and the fact that you
are reading it is probably based on some kind of organizational demand. I wrote
the book in an organizational context. Our tastes in food and drink (and the
amounts we consume) are shaped by marketing organizations. The products we
come into contact with, such as automobiles, desks, and so on, were made in
organizational settings, and the services we rely upon, such as police, banking,
or insurance are clearly organizational. We work in organizations. Our leisure
activities are typically in some sort of organizational setting. Almost every story
in every newspaper describes the activities of an organization—General Motors,
the FBI, the San Francisco 49ers—or the reactions of organizations to acts of
individuals, such as the fire department to an arsonist or a hospital to an AIDS
patient.

The great social transformations in history have been essentially organizationally based. The Roman Empire, the spread of Christianity, the growth and

development of capitalism and socialism, and the current changes taking place in both capitalism and socialism have been and are accomplished through organizations. Toxic waste disposal, nuclear energy, terrorism, unemployment, abortion, and all the issues facing contemporary society cannot be understood without a consideration and understanding of their organizational contexts.

These simple examples were intended to suggest that the analysis of organizations is not trivial. It is also not just an academic exercise. Organizations are continually analyzed from a variety of perspectives. The stock market is an ongoing organizational analysis. Investors constantly assess how business firms are doing and buy and sell stocks accordingly. As in other forms of organizational analyses, this is not an exact science. If we have the opportunity to choose between potential employers, we are making an organizational analysis. We are attempting to decide which would be a better place to work. When we vote for the president of the United States in an election, it is an assessment of an organization to a surprising extent. There is a large organization which has handled the campaign, and we estimate what kind of organization the individual will bring to office.

Organizational analysis also occurs at other levels. Organizational management has the job of assessing the state of the organization. Labor unions, themselves organizations, analyze the operations of the companies with which they have contracts. As customers or clients, we assess the quality of stores and their merchandise. When I buy a pair of skis, I want to be fairly certain that the manufacturer has the reputation of quality and the likelihood of staying in business. I also want to know that the ski shop can handle any problems which arise. More serious individual concern comes when we select an organization like a hospital.

Hart and Scott (1975, p. 261) have noted that whatever is good for humanity can only be achieved through modern organizations. The reverse is also true, since it is organizations that discriminate, pollute, and wage wars. This brings us to the second answer to the question that was posed at the beginning of this chapter. *Organizations have outcomes.* In this first chapter we will analyze the outcomes of organizations for individuals, for categories of individuals, for communities, and for society. The analyses throughout the book are based on research on organizations and interpretations of that research. They are also based on theoretical analyses which have developed over the years.

ORGANIZATIONS AND THE INDIVIDUAL

The strikingly obvious importance of organizations for individuals is the simple fact that almost all of our work is in organizations. Table 1–1 shows the occupations of employed persons in the United States in 1980. It can be seen that both farm work and private household work comprise very small proportions of the total labor force. These forms of work are typically not organizational. The other occupations are organizational occupations, even that of professional workers who are overwhelmingly organizational employees (Hall, 1986). Another way of demonstrating this point is shown in Table 1–2. Here the industry and class of worker is displayed. The industrial sectors in which employment is concentrated are composed of organizations. The same is true when class of worker is considered. Both private and public employment is organizational employment.

These social patterns can be approached in another way. Danet (1981, p. 382) reports that increasingly goods and services once supplied by solo practitioners or small organizations are now being delivered by large organizations, which are often branches of still larger organizations. While there is a definite tendency for a great deal of work to be carried out in large organizations, Granovetter (1984) cautions that a focus exclusively on large organizations would be a mistake, since approximately 60 percent of the labor force in the private sector is employed in firms of less than 1,000 employees. Granovetter's data indicate that in the wholesale, retail, and service industries, small size is particularly evident. Ritzer (1989) suggests that the actual heart of the American economy is shifting from large firms to smaller ones. He reports that the large *Fortune* 500 companies laid off over 3 million workers between 1980 and 1987. During the same period of time, firms with fewer than 100 employees created 12 million new jobs. When these small organizations are successful, of course there is a strong tendency for organizations to become larger and larger through growth or merger.

The fate of the individual in the organization is a hotly debated topic. Several recent analyses have examined how individuals react to their lives as employees of organizations (Terkel, 1974; Rosow, 1974; Aronowitz, 1973; *Work in America*, 1973; Hall, 1986). These analyses agree that work that is highly routinized, repetitive, and dull is highly alienating for the individual. Whether or not organizational managers seek to routinize work in order to control workers is a major and ongoing debate, which will be considered in later chapters. There is no evidence, of course, that work in preorganizational societies was *not* alienating. Subsistence farming or hunting and gathering is hardly enlightening. Romanticized imageries of preorganizational systems forget that people starved to death and froze to death. Some people were slaves. Early industrialization, with its exceedingly low pay, child labor, and absence of worker protection, was also alienating, but in a truer Marxian sense than the social-psychological alienation felt by today's worker in a routine job.

The studies of individual reactions to work also reveal that work which provides challenge, potential for advancement, and the use of creative or expressive capabilities is enjoyable and even enlightening. The ways in which people react to their work results from their own expectations and the characteristics of the organization (Lorsch and Morse, 1974). Although organizational characteristics will be discussed at length at a later time, at this point it should be noted that there are limits to the variation possible in organizational characteristics, given the constraints of size, the technology employed, the market conditions, and other environmental factors. Organizations cannot change simply to be more pleasant places in which to work.

There is another side to working in organizations. In an important study, Kohn (1971) found small but consistent tendencies for people who work in more bureaucratized organizations to be more intellectually flexible, more open to new experiences, and more self-directed than those working in nonbureaucratized settings. Kohn and Schooler (1978, 1982) suggest that people's occupational

TABLE 1-1 Occupation of Employed Persons by Race and Sex in the United States, 1980

	Total	White	Black	PERCENT Total	PERCENT White	PERCENT Black
Employed persons 16 years and over	97,639,355	84,027,375	9,334,048	100.0	100.0	00.0
Managerial and professional specialty occupations	22,151,648	20,067,464	1,317,080	22.7	23.9	14.1
Executive, administrative, and managerial occupations	10,133,551	9,336,266	487,432	10.4	11.1	5.2
Professional specialty occupations	12,018,097	10,731,198	829,648	12.3	12.8	8.9
Technical, sales, and administrative support occupations	29,593,506	26,150,562	2,352,079	30.3	31.1	25.2
Technicians and related support occupations	2,981,951	2,590,639	247,834	3.1	3.1	2.7
Sales occupations	9,760,157	8,998,463	468,364	10.0	10.7	5.0
Administrative support occupations, including clerical	16,851,398	14,561,460	1,635,881	17.3	17.3	17.5
Service occupations	12,629,425	9,765,973	2,156,194	12.9	11.6	23.1
Private household occupations	589,352	312,472	241,717	0.6	0.4	2.6
Protective service occupations	1,475,315	1,253,799	176,304	1.5	1.5	1.9
Service occupations, except protective and household	10,564,758	8,199,702	1,738,173	10.8	9.8	18.6
Farming, forestry, and fishing occupations	2,811,258	2,437,307	182,190	2.9	2.9	2.0
Precision production, craft, and repair occupations	12,594,175	11,249,214	834,947	12.9	13.4	8.9
Operators, fabricators, and laborers	17,859,343	14,356,855	1,491,558	18.3	17.1	26.7
Machine operators, assemblers, and inspectors	9,084,988	7,242,863	1,256,932	9.3	8.6	13.5
Transportation and material-moving occupations	4,389,412	3,665,245	563,210	4.5	4.4	6.0
Handlers, equipment, cleaners, helpers, and laborers	4,384,943	3,448,747	671,416	4.5	4.1	7.2

Employed Females 16 years and over						
Managerial and professional specialty occupations	41,634,665	35,183,388	4,659,177	100.0	100.0	100.0
Executive, administrative, and managerial occupations	8,954,843	7,876,425	770,809	21.5	22.4	16.5
Professional specialty occupations	3,070,247	2,746,156	219,108	7.4	7.8	4.7
Technical, sales, and administrative support occupations	5,884,596	5,130,269	551,701	14.1	14.6	11.8
Technicians and related support occupations	18,971,458	16,646,739	1,639,737	45.6	47.3	35.2
Sales occupations	1,302,889	1,089,273	155,450	3.1	3.1	3.3
Administrative support occupations, including clerical	4,671,493	4,231,750	283,771	11.2	12.0	6.1
Service occupations	12,997,076	11,325,716	1,200,516	31.2	32.2	25.8
Private household occupations	7,451,845	5,725,271	1,363,664	17.9	16.3	29.3
Protective service occupations	562,886	297,021	233,024	1.4	0.8	5.0
Service occupations, except protective and household	168,861	132,677	30,648	0.4	0.4	0.7
Farming, forestry, and fishing occupations	6,720,098	5,295,573	1,099,992	16.1	15.1	23.6
Precision production, craft, and repair occupations	404,269	347,744	25,368	1.0	1.0	0.5
Operators, fabricators, and laborers	977,950	802,126	108,755	2.3	2.3	2.3
Machine operators, assemblers, and inspectors	4,874,300	3,785,083	750,844	11.7	10.8	16.1
Transportation and material-moving occupations	3,646,237	2,803,586	571,893	8.8	8.0	12.3
Handlers, equipment, cleaners, helpers, and laborers	347,880	293,092	44,147	0.8	0.8	0.9
	880,183	688,405	134,804	2.1	2.0	2.9

Source: *1980 Census of Population*, Vol. 1: *Characteristics of the Population*, Chapter C: General Social and Economic Characteristics (Washington, DC: U.S. Department of Commerce, U.S. Government Printing Office), p. 45.

TABLE 1-2 Industry and Class of Worker of Employed Persons by Race and Sex in the United States, 1980

INDUSTRY	Total	White	Black	PERCENT Total	White	Black
Employed persons 16 years and over	97,639,355	84,027,375	9,334,048	100.0	100.0	100.0
Agriculture, forestry, and fisheries	2,913,589	2,554,976	161,065	3.0	3.0	1.7
Mining	1,028,178	948,911	42,929	1.1	1.1	0.5
Construction	5,739,598	5,105,836	403,992	5.9	6.1	4.3
Manufacturing	21,914,754	18,705,053	2,163,603	22.4	22.3	23.2
Nondurable goods	8,435,543	7,063,668	940,224	8.6	8.4	10.1
Durable goods	13,479,211	11,641,385	1,223,379	13.8	13.9	13.1
Transportation, communications, and other public utilities	7,087,455	6,003,704	827,283	7.3	7.1	8.9
Wholesale and retail trade	19,933,926	17,788,047	1,295,626	20.4	21.2	13.9
Wholesale trade	4,217,232	3,796,001	259,997	4.3	4.5	2.8
Retail trade	15,716,694	13,992,046	1,035,629	16.1	16.7	11.1
Finance, insurance, and real estate	5,898,059	5,231,499	449,853	6.0	6.2	4.8
Business and repair services	4,081,677	3,564,988	340,054	4.2	4.2	3.6
Personal services	3,075,764	2,312,315	571,224	3.2	2.8	6.1
Entertainment and recreation services	1,007,070	889,144	76,419	1.0	1.1	0.8
Professional and related services	19,811,819	16,719,601	2,300,399	20.3	19.9	24.6
Public administration	5,147,466	4,203,301	702,501	5.3	5.0	7.5
Employed females 16 years and over	41,634,665	35,183,388	4,659,177	100.0	100.0	100.0
Agriculture, forestry, and fisheries	522,050	456,765	29,342	1.3	1.3	0.6
Mining	124,173	110,782	8,536	0.3	0.3	0.2
Construction	479,766	438,746	26,234	1.2	1.2	0.6
Manufacturing	6,995,805	5,781,947	810,178	16.8	16.4	17.4
Nondurable goods	3,493,250	2,839,365	437,426	8.4	8.1	9.4
Durable goods	3,502,555	2,942,582	372,752	8.4	8.4	8.0
Transportation, communications, and other public utilities	1,752,965	1,446,084	239,996	4.2	4.1	5.2

Category				
Wholesale and retail trade	9,138,160	588,278	21.9	23.3	12.6
Wholesale trade	1,133,761	67,617	2.7	2.9	1.5
Retail trade	8,004,399	520,661	19.2	20.4	11.2
Finance, insurance and real estate	3,421,717	286,904	8.2	8.5	6.2
Business and repair services	1,380,020	130,241	3.3	3.4	2.8
Personal services	2,165,306	456,693	5.2	4.5	9.8
Entertainment and recreation services	407,324	27,058	1.0	1.0	0.6
Professional and related services	13,144,812	1,682,576	31.6	31.2	36.1
Public administration	2,102,567	373,141	5.1	4.6	8.0

CLASS OF WORKER

Category				
Employed persons 16 years and over	97,639,355	9,334,04	100.0	100.0	100.0
Private wage and salary workers	73,772,204	6,565,487	75.6	76.0	70.3
Federal government workers	3,762,008	693,500	3.9	3.4	7.4
State government workers	4,473,825	617,821	4.6	4.3	6.6
Local government workers	8,453,968	6,915,895	8.7	8.2	13.1
Self-employed workers	6,677,871	1,221,081	6.8	7.5	2.5
In agriculture	1,284,649	223,808	1.3	1.5	0.3
Unpaid family workers	499,479	23,831	0.5	0.6	0.3
In agriculture	139,760	12,351	0.1	0.2	0.1
		2,483			
Employed Females 16 years and over	41,634,665	4,659,177	100.0	100.0	100.0
Private wage and salary workers	31,219,189	3,132,298	75.0	76.0	67.2
Federal government workers	1,484,036	356,032	3.6	3.0	7.6
State government workers	2,363,754	394,681	5.7	5.3	8.5
Local government workers	4,695,676	712,254	11.3	10.9	15.3
Self-employed workers	1,529,190	57,899	3.7	4.0	1.2
In agriculture	135,929	1,709	0.3	0.4	—
Unpaid family workers	342,820	6,013	0.8	0.9	0.1
In agriculture	69,113	623	0.2	0.2	—

Source: *1980 Census of Population*, Vol. 1: *Characteristics of the Population*, Chapter C: General Social and Economic Characteristics (Washington, DC: U.S. Department of Commerce, U.S. Government Printing Office), p. 47.

conditions both affect and are affected by their psychological functioning. In regard to work in a bureaucratized setting, Kohn attributes the findings to the fact that bureaucratized organizations require their work force to be better educated and also provide more job protection, higher salary, and more complex work. The implication of these studies is that work in organizations is not necessarily deadening to the individual. Indeed, it is likely that for exactly the same work some organizations demand more creativity and flexibility than other organizations do. The work of a secretary or an executive can be challenging and have potential for advancement in one organization and not in another. Some jobs have a strong potential for idiosyncratic behavior, while others do not (Miner, 1987). Here again, organizational characteristics are critical variables as they interact with those of the individual.

We not only work in organizations, but we also have extensive contacts with them as customers or clients. The growth of consumer and client-advocacy organizations is testimony to the fact that those who come to organizations for products or services are not totally satisfied with what they receive. Advocacy organizations, of course, are every bit as much organizations as the ones they are advocating against.

A study by Katz et al. (1975) sheds some light on how people react to their encounters with organizations. In a survey of people's reactions to their contacts with government agencies in the areas of employment, job training, worker's compensation, unemployment compensation, welfare services, hospital and medical services, and retirement services, it was found that the majority of these clients were satisfied with the service and treatment they received. Thus, widespread discontent with the "system" in this regard appears to be a myth, because common stereotypes about encounters with government bureaucracies are contradicted by the data. Nevertheless, the fact that most people are satisfied does not mean that the organizations are operating as effectively as possible. Katz et al. note:

> A majority of satisfied clients may leave a sizable minority dissatisfied. Even a 75 percent level of satisfaction may be low for some programs in which 90 percent or higher is desirable and feasible. In a population of 200 million, small percentages are large numbers. (p. 115)

In a related study of the same phenomenon, this time among juveniles who have had contact with the juvenile justice system, Giordano (1974) found "something less than a seething rage against the professionals who staff the juvenile justice system." Apparently even in this population, which is thought to have very negative encounters with the establishment, organizations are not viewed with the distaste that is generally believed to be present.

An element in the Giordano research is worth noting: if a client feels close to an individual in an organization, his or her interpretation of the total organization appears to be affected. Individuals coming to an organization do so as individuals. The person in the organization may or may not be able to respond in a personal way. Many organizations prescribe the manner in which their employees are to respond to outsiders. Even if the prescribed manner is warm and friendly, as is the case of airline cabin attendants, it is still an organizational prescription (see Hochschild, 1983). In the case of the professional staffs with which Giordano dealt, and which formed the bulk of the services studied by Katz et al. (1975), the professional is granted some latitude in interpersonal interactions. Such latitude is less likely at the clerical or retail sales level, where many individual contacts with organizations are made.

The analysis of individuals in organizations must also consider economic factors. Sociologists have a tendency to ignore the economic, but it is a mistake to do so. Focusing on factors such as morale and satisfaction deflects attention away from the fact that economic factors are a major consideration for both management and workers. Hage (1980) notes that "on the one hand managerial elites and owners of capital want to drive costs down by means of policies of low wages and uniform tasks. On the other hand workers want to increase their standard of living and have interesting work. There is an inherent conflict of interest between these two perspectives" (p. 7). Hage goes on to suggest that the inherent conflict can be handled by either fighting or quitting, as suggested by Hirschman (1972). When workers neither fight nor quit, they can engage in patterns of neglect in regard to their work (Withey and Cooper, 1989). People have an obvious economic stake in the organizations in which they work. Organizations affect the economic well-being of workers and hence also their dependents.

Organizations are the context in which people work. The performances of individuals are shaped by that context. For example, Long and McGinnis (1981) found that the productivity of scientists was strongly affected by their work context. The productivity levels of the scientists studied rather quickly conformed to the levels of the organizations where they obtained employment. If expectations were that an individual be highly productive, the behavior would tend to conform to that expectation.

The *most* important outcome of organizations for individuals is in terms of the placement or attainment of individuals within the social stratification system. There has been a dramatic realization that organizations are key actors in stratification. Baron (1984; see also Stolzenberg, 1978; Baron and Bielby, 1980; Kalleberg, 1983; and Pfeffer and Cohen, 1984) has pointed out that the division of labor among jobs (the internal labor market) within an organization and differentiation among organizations results in a situation in which unequal opportunities and rewards are attached to organizational positions. These are present prior to the arrival of any particular incumbent. Organizations also have procedures for filling their positions. Education, skill, or experience of varying levels and intensities are specified in advance. Organizations then match workers with jobs. Organizations are thus the process by which stratification is accomplished. This is a dynamic process. When organizations are growing, there are more promotional opportunities (Rosenbaum, 1979). When organizations are in a decline, the opportunity structure also is diminished.

Categories of Individuals

The recognition that organizations are at the core of the stratification process is incomplete unless it is also recognized that categories or classes of individuals are differentially affected by organizations (Wright 1978, 1979).

Tables 1-1 and 1-2 demonstrate the differential distribution of blacks and women in the occupational, industrial, and class of worker categories used. Alvarez et al. (1979) have documented the fact that an important organizational outcome is discrimination against minority group members and women in terms of access to organizational positions and opportunity structures within organizations.

Miles, Snow, and Pfeffer (1974) and Kanter (1977) have demonstrated the manner in which organizations discriminate against women. These studies suggest that even when women are promoted, there are detrimental consequences. Miller, Snow, and Pfeffer suggest that women who advance lose friendship and respect. Their influence declines as does their access to information. Kanter finds that advancing women face responses to themselves in stereotypical categories. What holds true for women would also hold true for minority group members, perhaps to a greater degree. Thus, organizations reflect the divisions in society and reinforce them. Obviously, organizations are the only means by which women and minorities can advance. Affirmative action policies are organizational policies. If such policies work, then the categories of individuals who have suffered discrimination may be able to experience the same mobility patterns as the dominant white males.

In concluding that affirmative action policies might benefit categories of individuals, the fact that organizations are the mechanisms of stratification should not be forgotten. Organizations sort their members into levels. These levels are the individuals' places in the stratification system.

ORGANIZATIONS AND THE COMMUNITY

Organizations are clearly not benign in their outcomes for individuals and categories of individuals. The same is true for the communities or localities in which they operate. This can be seen dramatically in a study reported by Seiler and Summers (1979). They examined the consequences of the decision by a large steel manufacturing firm to locate a major new plant in a small town in the middle western United States. This company did not want to be identified in the community power structure as such, but their actions clearly had a major impact on the community.

The steel company, Jones and Laughlin, engaged in unilateral actions, such as buying land for their plant through ghost buyers and having a policy of hiring workers from surrounding counties rather than in the home county. The company also co-opted the local community leaders through such means as using key bankers and lawyers as their local representatives. No Jones and Laughlin personnel were active in the community, but their operatives were. The company also directly intervened in plans for a new high school in the community, forcing the building of a less expensive, and more practical, school and thus reducing their tax liability.

Seiler and Summers do not suggest that all of the results of the company's actions were bad for the local community. Indeed, some were recognized as positive and others as negative. The important point is that this organization had a direct and dramatic impact on the local community. The impact of a single powerful organization can thus be great. This is easily seen in other settings. The college or university town is dominated by that organization as much as any "company town" is dominated by a single industry.

Most communities have more than a single dominant organization. This does not dilute the power of organizations in the community, however. Perrucci and Pilisuk (1970) and Galaskiewicz (1979) have examined patterns of interorganizational relationships in local communities. Local power structures reflect interorganizational competition and thus the interests of powerful actors. Interorganizational relationships, which will be considered in detail in Chapter 12, can have both positive and negative consequences for a community. Crittenden (1978) reports that Minneapolis, Minnesota, is blessed with an extraordinarily high level of corporate philanthropy. Much of this is based on the interorganizational linkages among the business firms there. Most other cities are less fortunate. Some have been literally destroyed as businesses move to other areas. Still others receive virtually nothing from their organizational inhabitants. In many ways, communities can be viewed as networks of interorganizational linkages (Galaskiewicz and Krohn, 1984).

There is a more subtle way in which organizations influence the communities in which they are located. Christenson et al. (1988) found that companies vary in the degree to which they encourage their middle managers to participate in community affairs. If communities were filled with organizations that encourage such participation, local life would be enriched. This same study also found that those middle managers who did get involved in community life were less likely to opt for transfers to other communities.

SOCIETAL OUTCOMES

m environments

If organizations have important outcomes for individuals and communities, it is obvious that they also have important outcomes for the wider society or environment in which they are embedded. At the very outset, it must be recognized that there is a *reciprocal* relationship between organizations and their environments. Indeed, the dominant contemporary theories regarding organizations stress the central role of environments for the operations of organizations. As we will see in the chapters that follow, the environments of organizations are viewed as a major determinant of the structure and processes of organizations. In this section I am going to turn this line of reasoning around and consider the impacts of organizations on their environment. The analysis will begin with a consideration of some specific organizational impacts and then move into more broadly based conceptualizations.

Some Specific Organizational Outcomes

Organizations serve the interests of individuals or groups. These controlling interests shape the directions which organizations take. For example, Antonio (1979) examined the organizational context of the Roman Empire. According to Antonio, the Roman bureaucracy was controlled by the ruling class whose orientation was to dominate the masses. Rather than emphasizing production of goods and services, the emphasis on domination "preserved, and even intensified, conditions which contributed to the erosion and eventual destruction of the socioeconomic substructure of the bureaucracy" (p. 906). Short-term success thus contributed to longer-term failure—a theme to which we will return at a later point.

The point of the Antonio study is that the bureaucracy serves the interest of the ruling elite. This has been a point of contention for organizational analysts for some time. In 1932 Berle and Means claimed that the ownership of private corporations had become so widely distributed that ownership per se no longer was of central importance in the control of organizations. Control was passed to corporate management, which in turn, appointed people to boards of directors. Boards of directors were viewed as tools of management rather than of the stockholders.

Aldrich (1979) has noted that this point of view has now been severely challenged on several grounds. First, there is some evidence that families such as the Mellons, who have controlling interests in Gulf Oil, Alcoa, Koppers Company, and Carborundum Company in the manufacturing sector, also have controlling interests in the First Boston Corporation, the General Reinsurance Corporation, and the Mellon National Bank and Trust Company in the financial sector (Zeitlin, 1974). The Mellon National Bank, in turn, owns almost 7 percent of Jones and Laughlin Steel. The Rockefeller family has similar points of linkage among financial institutions and insurance companies. Patterns of interlock like these have also been found outside the United States. Aldrich (1979) suggests that while there is no direct evidence that such family control has direct economic implications, the fact of family ownership indicates the potential for organizational control, rather than control by organizational management or diffused stockholders.

There is also a remarkable degree of interlock among the boards of directors of corporations. This means that members of the board of directors of one corporation are likely to serve on the boards of other corporations. Such interlocks are believed to give a corporation access to capital and to co-opt or control sources of pressure in the environment. Pennings (1980b) states:

> We have investigated one aspect of the 797 largest American corporations: the relationships among the organizations' strategic interdependence on firms in their environment, their economic effectiveness, and their propensity to form interlocking directorates. Our survey of these organizations showed that only 62 of them have no interlocks with the remaining 735 and that financial firms are disproportionately active in interlocking. (p. 188)

In general, the more interlocks, the more effective was the organization. A specific finding of interest in the Pennings study was that firms that are well interlocked with the financial community enjoyed lower interest rates for their debts than did their more poorly interlocked fellow firms. Similar relationships between interlocks and profitability have been found in analyses by Burt and his colleagues (Burt et al., 1980; Burt, 1983).

There are two basic ways in which findings such as these can be viewed. They can be viewed as sound management. Interlocks, with or without family ties, are a means to achieve a competitive edge. The other view is conspiratorial. Such interlocks permit a ruling class to maintain its power and wealth at the expense of the rest of the population.

There are some additional interpretations of the impact of corporate power in society. Useem (1979) notes that an "inner group" of business elites is selected to assist in the governance of other institutions, such as governmental advisory boards, philanthropic organizations, colleges and universities, and so on. The same pattern of interlocking directorates is found in the noncorporate sector of society. Useem concludes that this permits the promotion of the more general interests of the entire capitalist class. This political interpretation could be challenged by the claim that these institutional interlocks are merely a means by which able people are brought to the boards of directors of organizations that provide benefits for society. Whichever interpretation is taken cannot deny the importance or presence of the interlocks.

In yet another examination of the impact of business corporations on society, Hicks, Friedland, and Johnson (1978) examined the consequences of the presence of large business corporations and labor unions for governmental redistribution to the poor. The presence of business corporations was negatively related to such redistribution, while the presence of labor unions was positive. Organizations are thus not inert masses in society. They act in their own or their owners' or members' behalf.

Government organizations also affect society by more than just the coordination and control activities of services that they provide. Altheide and Johnson (1980) have documented the manner in which government agencies present themselves to the public, making statements of "fact" which may well be self-serving interpretations. "Official information" in forms as varied as crime rates or inflation indices can be used to serve the purposes of office holders and civil servants.

Organizations are active participants in the development and implementation of governmental or public policy. Champagne et al. (1981) note that organizations must be concerned with all branches of government—the legislative, the executive, and the judicial. Organizations are viewed as the cause of law and are vital in the selection of judges.

In an analysis of the U. S. State Department, Roy (1981; 1983; see also Carstensen and Werking, 1983) studied the patterns of interests that were represented in State Department actions for the period 1886–1905. He found that core financial and industrial interests became vested interests for the State Department to an increasing degree. American foreign policy came to reflect these organizational interests.

Public policies in the areas of energy and health were examined by Laumann et al. (1985). They found that corporate entities in the form of trade associations, professional societies, public interest groups, government bureaus, and congressional committees were the key actors in the state policy domains. These organizations have a stake in the policies that are enacted and implemented. Individuals or natural persons, unless they act on behalf of, or at the behest of the corporate, have little importance in these policy domains. It is important to note that Laumann et al. found government bureaus and congressional committees as important actors in these policy areas. From the rather frequent revelations in regard to apparent overspending on defense contracts, it is apparent that there are common interests among defense contractors and government agencies, with some congressional organizations also having common interests.

Harmful Impacts   Organizations have a strong potential to harm society or its components. Some aspects of harm are unanticipated. Hall (1981) has pointed out that organizational policies are designed to have anticipated consequences, but that they also can have outcomes that are not anticipated in both the short and long term. A simple example of this is the problems that U. S. automobile manufacturers experienced during the petroleum crises in the 1970s. Earlier decisions in regard to chassis and engine sizes almost led to corporate disasters. For most of the public, high levels of fuel consumption and the resultant crisis of natural resources was another unanticipated consequence. Another example of this sort of thing is the realization that acid rain is caused by technological decisions that were made in regard to waste emissions through smokestacks and other fossil-fuel emission techniques. Potential and actual disasters result from the unanticipated consequences of organizational decisions.

Perrow (1984) coined the term "normal accidents" to describe actual and potential disasters involving nuclear plants, nuclear weapons systems, recombinant DNA production, ships carrying highly toxic or explosive cargos, and chemical plants. His analysis was published prior to the chemical plant disaster in Bhopal, India, in which thousands of individuals were killed, and the Chernobyl nuclear disaster in Russia. Perrow's contention is that highly complex technical systems which are tightly coupled or integrated have the strong potential for catastrophe inasmuch as it is not operator error which is the source of the potential problem, but systemic or organizational problems. Hirschhorn (1985) argues that Perrow does not go far enough in his organizational analyses of technologically related disasters, since in Hirschhorn's view, there are potential organizational solutions to these very real issues. Nonetheless, Perrow's basic point remains valid and frightening—organizational arrangements have the potential to contribute to catastrophes of immense scope.

In keeping with the theme of reciprocity that was introduced at the beginning of this analysis of organizational-societal relationships, organizations can themselves experience disasters from events outside heir own control.   In an analysis of "corporate tragedies," Mitroff and Kilmann (1984) describe how things happen *to* organizations. These include events such as product tampering, as was the case with Tylenol being laced with cyanide, and the projection in the mind of some people that the logo long used by Procter & Gamble was in some way related to evil forces. Organizations can be affected by events far beyond their control, just as activities that are within organizational control can have effects that are not anticipated by society.

Organizations can cause accidents or be accident victims. They can also engage in criminal acts (Sutherland, 1949; Clinard and Yeager, 1980). Needleman and Needleman (1979) have suggested that organizations can contribute to crime in two ways. They argue that some organizations are "crime-coercive." These organizations force their members or customers to engage in illegal activities. Farberman (1975) found, for example, that some franchised automobile dealers are forced into illegal practices such as kickbacks and unrecorded income to survive financially. Needleman and Needleman propose that there are also "crime-facilitative" organizations. Fire insurance companies facilitate the "torching" of buildings by arsonists. The arsonist owns the building, which is rundown and unsalable. After it burns, the arsonist collects the insurance on the building. The insurance companies facilitate the arsonist, but do not benefit themselves. More vigorous investigations of slum ownership and insurance patterns could be conducted, but apparently insurance companies believe that vigorous background investigation might offend or drive away legitimate customers. Organizations thus contribute to these property crimes. In the case of arson, of course, there is the potential for the loss of life, making it more than a simple financial matter.

The well-documented history of crimes committed by corporations (Sutherland, 1949; Clinard and Yeager, 1980) can be interpreted from two basic perspectives. One is that it is simply a case of individual deviance, with people attempting to line their own pockets whether it hurts the organization or not. The alternative perspective brings the organization into the picture. Vaughan (1983), for example, uses the idea of "authority leakage" (p. 74) as a means of indicating that organizational characteristics play a role in crime. Organizational leakages involve long hierarchies and intensive specialization to the extent that subunits cannot be controlled. In Vaughan's view, corporate crimes are more likely to develop in such situations, and this indeed seems to be the case in most instances of such crimes. Seldom is the total organization involved, and seldom do the majority of personnel in organizations participate in such crimes.

One further point regarding the harmful effects of organizations must be noted in order to complete the picture. While the emphasis has been on private business firms, *government* or *public* organizations can also produce harmful outcomes. After all, it is government organizations that wage wars and commit attrocities of the right and left. Government organizations can have harmful effects of a more subtle nature, such as by their inactions. Levine's (1982) analysis of the Love Canal situation in Niagara Falls, New York, is an excellent case in point. In this case toxic wastes were placed in an unused canal, which was later covered with landfill. Homes and a school were built on and near the site. When the homeowners became aware of the situation and its consequences, which included miscarriages, birth defects, and illness, they approached local, state, and federal agencies for help. At each level of government, government organizations such as Departments of Health worked hard to protect their own interests and in so doing prolonged the harmful outcomes for the residents involved.

General Societal Outcomes

The impact of organizations on the societies in which they are imbedded is great. Morris (1972) has pointed out that organizational growth is organizational success. Even in a no-growth economy, private and public organizations try to grow at one another's expense. Growth is a major way in which organizational decision makers or elites demonstrate their contributions to the organization.

In addition to their size, there is another factor that gives contemporary organizations their unprecedented role in contemporary society: the modern organization is a *legal* entity, just like the individual person. In a perceptive set of essays, Coleman (1974) has indicated that organizational legality is granted by the state, itself a legal creation. While the individual is given a set of rights and responsibilities by the state, rights and responsibilities are extended to organizations. These rights, coupled with size, give organizations an enormous amount of power within the state. Coleman also points out that the state or government is more comfortable dealing with other organizations than with individual persons, and thus tends to provide more preferential treatment to organizations in areas as diverse as taxation or rights to privacy.

The recognition of organizations as legal entities is not a trivial matter. Organizations, rather than individuals, can be held responsible for certain actions. Air New Zealand, for example, was held responsible for a crash that killed 257 people (*The New York Times*, 1981). A new flight plan was put into effect which led to a collision course with a volcano. The crew had not been informed. The judge in the case also accused airline officials of attempting to conceal their mistakes. Swigert and Farrell (1980–81) analyzed the case of the Ford Motor Company which was charged with homicide. They found that the mass media shifted its orientation from the recognition of harm based on mechanical defects to an attribution of nonrepentance on the part of the offender. Swigert and Farrell concluded that a shift in public attitudes had occurred in which an organization was believed to have engaged in criminality in a form previously reserved for individuals. The fact that Ford was found not guilty does not alter the importance in the shift in public attitude. Waegel et al. (1981) also note that organizations are viewed as actors to which deviance can be imputed. They also suggest that a frequent organizational response is to try to redefine the situation so that actions are seen as normal and not deviant.

The consideration of the legal status of organizations raises an issue which will be considered directly in the next chapter—can organizations be considered as objects or entities in their own right, apart from the individuals which comprise them? This is a complex question which involves more than their legal status.

At the very broadest level, then, organizations are affected by society and affect it. Even in situations in which efforts are made to reduce the impact of organizations, organizational factors intrude. Shenkar (1984), for example, has shown that bureaucratic rules and specialization were evident during the extreme periods of the Cultural Revolution in the Peoples' Republic of China. Organizational outcomes were inevitable in even that situation. The specific forms of the Chinese organizations, of course, were affected by the Chinese culture and social system, a point clearly punctuated by the events in Tianenmen Square in June 1989. Organizations are thus systems within the wider social system (Abbott, 1989).

ORGANIZATIONS AND SOCIAL CHANGE

Organizations are active participants in society. This becomes abundantly clear when we consider the issue of social change. Paradoxically, organizations both foster and impede social change. In this section we will first examine the ways in which *internal* changes in organizations have social change outcomes. We will then turn to organizations as active change agents. Finally, we will consider organizations as resisters of change.

Internal Change and the Social Structure

Internal organizational changes affect the social structure in two ways. The first is by changing membership patterns. By this I mean alterations in the distribution of types of individuals who compose the organization. For example, many organizations have made the MBA degree a basic entry-level requirement for managerial personnel. This can be based on the actual complexity of the work or simply keeping up with the corporate Joneses, but regardless of the cause, the change has ramifications for the educational system as universities scurry to crank out MBA graduates. Similarly, other changes in the demographic patterns of organizations, whether in regard to age, gender, or racial or ethnic group membership, would have repercussions beyond the immediate organization.

The second way in which internal changes affect the social structure is through altered patterns of work. Although it is unclear whether or not people's attitudes toward their work affect their outlooks on life, or vice versa, there is certainly a relationship (see Hall, 1986). Thus, changes in the manner in which work is performed—such as through programs of participative management, quality circles, or other such mechanisms—would appear to be related to other important social relationships.

Research by Kohn (1971, 1982) and Kohn and Schooler (1973) has presented compelling evidence that work that is self-directed leads to self-direction outside of the work setting and to "ideational flexibility." Thus, if organizations alter their patterns of work toward more or less complexity and self-direction, this would have a carryover effect on the personalities and orientations of their members. As will be seen in Chapter 5 on power, there is an intense debate regarding whether organizations attempt to move in the direction of more or less such self-direction on the part of their members. The point here is that the changes in the ways in which work in organizations is structured would also result in social change.

The Organization as a Change Agent

Besides affecting society (intentionally or unintentionally) through their structuring of social life and impacts on members, organizations are also active participants in the social change process. This can be most readily seen in the political arena, as organizations lobby and fight for legislation and rulings favorable to their own programs. A favorable decision for one organization leads to programs that in turn affect the society. Whenever a government agency is established to carry out a new program, it becomes a social change agent. We will begin the analysis of change agents with this point, moving from this commonly accepted form of social change to a consideration of organizations as revolutionary agents.

A prime example of the organization as a change agent is provided by Selznick's (1966) classic study of the Tennessee Valley Authority (TVA) during its formative years. In addition to its pertinence to the analysis of change, this study is also very important for its contribution to the analysis of the environmental impact on organizations, serving as the forerunner for many subsequent such studies.

The TVA Act was passed by the U.S. Congress in 1933. Selznick notes:

> A great public power project was envisioned mobilizing the "by-product" of dams built for the purpose of flood control and navigation improvement on the Tennessee River and its tributaries. Control and operation of the nitrate properties, to be used for fertilizer production, was also authorized, although this aspect was subordinated to electricity.... A new regional concept—the river basin as an integral unit—was given effect, so that a government agency was created which has a special responsibility neither national nor state-wide in scope. (pp. 4–5)

That the TVA has had an affect on the physical environment is evident. Of greater interest for our purposes here is its effect on the social system into which it was placed. An important consideration in understanding the social effects of the TVA is the fact that the organization was designed to be decentralized. Not only were decisions within the organization to be made at the lowest reasonable levels with participation by members, but local organizations and even local citizens were also to be brought into the decision-making process. For example, the agricultural extension services of the land-grant colleges were intimately involved with the TVA. This, of course, is one of the prime examples of a co-optation, or "the process of absorbing new elements into the leadership or policy-determining structure of an organization as a means of averting threats to its stability or existence" (p. 13).

Co-optation, however, is a two-way process. The organization itself is affected by the new elements brought into its decision-making process; Selznick documents the manner in which some activities of the TVA were deflected from the original goals because of the new elements in the system. At the same time, the co-optation process affects the system from which the elements were co-opted. The presence of the agricultural extension element from the land-grant colleges gave this part of the local system much more strength than it had in the past. The American Farm Bureau Federation was also brought into the process at an early point. In both these cases, the inclusion of one group was associated with the exclusion of another. Black colleges and non–Farm Bureau farm organizations either lost power or did not benefit to the degree that the co-opted organizations did. In addition, the strength of the Farm Bureau in the decision-making process led to the exclusion of other federal government farm programs. Regardless of their merits, these programs were therefore unavailable to the system. Selznick notes, "This resulted in the politically paradoxical situation that the eminently New Deal TVA failed to support agencies with which it shared a political communion, and aligned itself with the enemies of those agencies" (p. 263). This becomes a rather complex analysis when one considers the fact that the other government programs involved were also part of the same larger organization, so that internal politics in one large organization were affected by the external relationships of some of its component parts.

An organization like the TVA affects the surrounding social organization. Some elements prosper while others suffer. New social relationships arise as alliances among affected individuals and organizations are formed. Thus, an organization specifically designed to be a change agent can be exactly that, but perhaps in ways that can be most inconsistent with the original intent of the planners. The dynamics of the interactions with the environment affect both the organization and its environment.

In a later reexamination of the study, Selznick (1966) notes that the TVA has been attacked by conservationists for strip mining. The need for coal for its power productions and the strength of those supporting an expansion of this function within the TVA has led to a further environmental impact. Selznick attributes the current state of the TVA to the internal struggles that occurred in its early history—struggles to obtain environmental support. Since such support is selective, a strong organization such as this rearranges the world around it. If the groups in power in the TVA see the need for a greater capacity for generating electrical power as more important than soil conservation, the internal decision-making process, affected as it is by external pressures, makes a further impact on the social and physical environment.

In another analysis of organizations as change agents, Selznick (1960) studied the Bolshevik revolution in Russia. Here he analyzed the nature and role of the "organizational weapon." In defining what he means, Selznick states:

> We shall speak of organizations and organizational practices as weapons when they are used by a power-seeking elite in a manner unrestrained by the constitutional order of the arena within which the contest takes place. In this usage, "weapon" is not meant to denote any political tool, but one torn from its normal context and unacceptable to the community as a legitimate mode of action. Thus the partisan practices used in an election campaign insofar as they adhere to the written and unwritten rules of the context—are not weapons in this sense. On the other hand, when members who join an organization in apparent good faith are in fact the agents of an outside elite, then routine affiliation becomes "infiltration." (p. 2)

An important component of the organizational weapon is the "distinctive competence to turn members of a voluntary association into disciplined and deployable political agents" (p. xii).

The Organization as the Requisite of Social Change   Before turning to further elements of Selznick's analysis, we must point out that the organizational weapon cannot be regarded as a tactic of the Bolsheviks alone. Indeed, it is the vital component of most major social changes and of change within the organization itself. In other words, in order to achieve change, *there must be organization.* Spontaneous demonstrations or collective emotional

responses may be sincere and well intended, but longer-lasting movements toward change must come about through the organizational mode. The events in Eastern Europe in 1989 and 1990 vividly and ironically illustrate this point.

The scope of the organization as a weapon is determined by its aims. Even if the change sought is a limited one and one that will not upset the basic system under attack, the change agent still must be viewed as a weapon, although of lesser scope than one that seeks total organizational or societal change. The aim of Bolshevism was total societal change. The basic means of accomplishing the movement's goal was the "combat party." Cadres of dedicated people are a basic component of such parties. This dedication requires that the individuals be totally committed to the cause, insulated from other concerns, and absorbed in the movement. Once a core of dedicated personnel is available, the party must protect itself from internal dissension, banning power centers that might threaten the official leadership. The party must be capable of mobilization and manipulation; it must be protected from possible isolation from the people it hopes to convert and also from possible liquidation at the hands of the existing authorities; and it must struggle for power in every possible area of action. This struggle can take place through seeking official recognition, as well as through conspiratorial or illegal practices. And at all times, the basic ideology must be kept at the forefront of the members' minds (pp. 72–73).

The operation of these principles can be seen in the history of the movement that Selznick carefully traces. This manifesto for an organizational weapon is potentially applicable at any point in history, in any social setting, and at either the total societal or more microcosmic levels. Contemporary terrorist groups exhibit many of the same characteristics as the Bolshevik movement, and so does the history of early Christianity. The homeowners in the Love Canal situation described earlier formed an organization as their weapon for their own good.

For our purposes, the important thing is not the cause being advanced, but rather the fact having a cause is not enough for social change. The cause must be organized if it is to be successful. The organization can be a successful change agent if it is capable of maintaining dedication and gaining power in the system. The specific means of gaining power will depend on the situation. Political or military power is successful only where it is relevant. Selznick says:

> We must conclude, therefore, that in the long view political combat plays only a tactical role. Great social issues such as those which divide communism and democracy are not decided by political combat, perhaps not even by military clashes. They are decided by the relative ability of the contending systems to win and to maintain enduring loyalties. Consequently, no amount of power and cunning in the realm of political combat can avail in the absence of measures which rise to the height of the times. (p. 333)

The implication is that the specific tactics used in the Bolshevik movement may not be effective in another setting, but that the need for a dedicated membership and the concern for power are central to the change process.

Societal Support We have stressed the reciprocal nature of the relationship between an organization and its environment. This is seen in clear relief in the consideration of organizations as change agents. The basic processes are the same in all effective change situations: to be successful, an organizational weapon must gain power and support in the society it is attempting to change. The pages of history are filled with abortive efforts that did not gather sufficient support from the society they were trying to change. The basic set of ideas underlying the change effort must therefore be compatible—or become compatible—with the values of the population as a whole. These values of the wider community can be altered during the change process to become more congruent with those of the change agent. At the same time, the change agent itself can become altered as it seeks support from the wider community.

The importance of this form of support can be extrapolated from Joseph Gusfield's (1955, 1963) analysis of the Women's Christian Temperance Union. This organization was highly successful in its attempts to change society through the passage of legislation prohibiting the sale of alcoholic beverages. Its tactics were appropriate for the values of the times, and it succeeded in mobilizing support from a sufficiently large segment of the population. But later, as it became evident that Prohibition was not accomplishing what it was intended to do—and indeed had some unintended consequences that have lasted until the present—and as the originally supportive society changed, the WCTU was faced with a decision regarding its future. It could have altered its stance toward alcohol to keep it in line with the prevailing opinions or maintained its position in favor of total abstinence. The latter course was selected as the result of decisions made within the organization. The consequences of the decision were to isolate the movement from the population, reducing it to virtual ineffectiveness as a force in the wider society.

It is difficult to predict what might have happened to the WCTU if the stance had been altered to one of temperance rather than abstinence. It well might be that the whole antialcohol movement was one whose time had passed. It might also be that the WCTU would have had a greater educational and social impact if its position had shifted with the times. In any event, what was once an important social movement became a small, socially insignificant organization.

The social system around it thus affects the social-change agent as much as it does any other form of organization. While such organizations can appear to be revolutionary, deviant, or martyred or to fit any other emotion-laden category, the fact remains that they are organizations. The critical aspect is the acceptance of the organization by society. This is obviously important for any organization, since to survive it must receive support in one form or another, but for these change-oriented ones it is even more so. Unfortunately (or fortunately in some cases), because organizational analysts, decision makers, and politicians have not figured out exactly how to determine when an idea's time has come, the organization embarking on a change mission is in a precarious position at best.

There are other, more subtle ways in which organizations are change agents. As Perrow (1970b) notes:

> We tend to forget, or neglect, the fact that organizations have an enormous potential for affecting the lives of all who come into contact with them. They control or can

activate a multitude of resources, not just land and machinery and employees, but police, governments, communications, art, and other areas, too. That is, an organization, as a legally constituted entity, can ask for police protection and public prosecution, can sue, and can hire a private police force with considerably wider latitude and power than an individual can command. It can ask the courts to respond to requests and make legal rulings. It can petition for changes in other areas of government—zoning laws, fair-trade laws, consumer labeling, and protection and health laws. It determines the content of advertising, the art work in its products and packages, the shape and color of its buildings. It can move out of a community, and it selects the communities in which it will build. It can invest in times of imminent recession or it can retrench; support or fight government economic policies or fair employment practices. In short, organizations generate a great deal of power that may be used in a way not directly related to producing goods and services or to survival. (pp. 170–71)

Rather obviously, the power potential of organizations is often used to thwart change, as will be seen in the next section. Even when an organization is an active change agent, if the change is accomplished, the organization then tends to resist further changes. The labor union movement, which was once considered revolutionary, is now viewed by some as reactionary. National revolutions lead to established governments that later, in turn, are attacked as opponents of social progress. We commonly think of the American, French, Russian, Chinese, and Cuban *revolutions*. Now, many people inside and outside of those nations view the present regimes as highly conservative and even reactionary.

Before we turn to the discussion of organizations as resisters of change, it should be reiterated that organizations have a wide variety of impacts on the environment. These range from the exciting examples of revolution or pollution to the more mundane but equally important matters of establishing and maintaining equilibrium in the system. In a comprehensive analysis, organizations must be viewed as a major stabilizing factor in society. Each kind of output has an impact on society, from the production of goods to the development of ideas. Since an organizational society contains a multitude of values, it must also be recognized that what is of value to one segment of the society may be violently opposed by another segment. Thus, organizations that provide drugs or prostitutes are still organizations and can only be understood as such.

Organizations as Resisters of Change

Since our concern in this chapter is with organizational outcomes, it is important to go beyond the basic fact of organizational contributions to social change. Organizations also actively *resist* change. This resistance is directed toward change introduced from outside the organization.

Organizations by their very nature are conservative. Lipset's (1960) analysis of populist rural socialism in Saskatchewan, Canada, provides an example of this point. In 1944, the Cooperative Commonwealth Federation (CCF) came to power in that province. The objective was "the social ownership of all resources and the machinery of wealth production to the end that we may establish a Cooperative Commonwealth in which the basic principle regulating production, distribution and exchange will be the supplying of human needs instead of the making of profits" (p. 130). This aim has been only partially realized. One reason was continued political opposition to the movement; another, consistent with the argument here, is that the movement itself apparently became more conservative as power was achieved. An additional important consideration was the fact that the new socialist government utilized the existing government structures in attempting to carry out its program. In explanation Lipset notes:

> Trained in the traditions of a laissez-faire government and belonging to conservative social groups, the civil service contributes significantly to the social inertia which blunts the changes a new radical government can make. Delay in initiating reforms means that the new government becomes absorbed in the process of operating the old institutions. The longer a new government delays making changes, the more responsible it becomes for the old practices and the harder it is to make the changes it originally desired to institute. (pp. 272–73)

The reason for this blunting is quite simple. The new ruling cabinet had to rely on the system already in operation.

> The administratively insecure cabinet ministers were overjoyed at the friendly response they obtained from the civil servants. To avoid making administrative blunders that would injure them in the eyes of the public and the party, the ministers began to depend on the civil servants. As one cabinet minister stated in an interview, "I would have been lost if not for the old members of my staff. I'm only a beginner in this work. B _____ has been at it for twenty years. If I couldn't go to him for advice, I couldn't have done a thing. Why now (after two years in office) I am only beginning to find my legs and make my own decisions.... I have not done a thing for two years without advice." (p. 263)

It is important to note that the aims of a movement can be blunted without malice or intent. It is not a personal matter, but an organizational one. Certainly, personal motivations can also enter the picture in an important way, but the crucial factor is that the new leaders did not understand the organizations they were to head. The organization itself contained rules and procedures that had to be learned along the way, so that the organization became the instrument that deflected the party in power from its goals.

The organization trains its members to follow a system for carrying out its activities. It would require a complete resocialization before the takeover of a new party if this sort of thing were to be prevented. This, of course, is impossible in government organizations. An alternative practice would be to purge the entire system, replacing the original members with ones of the appropriate ideology. This would in essence mean that the organization would have to start de novo and that nothing would be done until the organizational roles were learned and linkages to the society were established. Since the organization has clients and customers, as well as a broader constituency in the case of government organizations, the expectations of nonmembers would also have to be altered. For these reasons, the likelihood of success is slim, regardless of the technique selected. The tendency for the organization to operate as it has in the past is very strong.

Most government organizations in Western democracies operate with a civil service system. An extension of Lipset's analysis suggests, therefore, that changes in the party in power will have less impact on the operation of the government agencies than political rhetoric would suggest. In most societies, the same principles seem to hold. The potentiality for major social change through change in government is therefore modified by the organizational realities that exist. Since social systems do change, of course, the organizations must be viewed as entities that do not change overnight, but will change with time. The changes that occur may not be in phase with the change in political philosophy of the government in power. A liberal or conservative party in power may over time be able to introduce more of its adherents into the civil service system. Nonetheless, in whatever political direction a state, county, or nation is moving, organizational conservatism will remain an important consideration.

Government organizations are not the only example of organizational conservatism. In the United States, automobile manufacturers persisted in making large, fuel-inefficient automobiles, despite several kinds of warnings that the market for these cars would soon dwindle. While much higher profits were made with the large cars in the short run, rapidly shrinking markets soon brought financial losses and layoffs for workers. Janowitz (1969) has documented the manner in which urban educational systems persisted in maintaining traditional academic programs while the population around the schools shifted and the needs of students changed. In later analyses, we will examine some of the reasons why organizations are resistant to change. Their very resistance is a source, desirable or not, of social stability. Social stability must thus be viewed as a major organizational outcome.

ORGANIZATIONS ACROSS SOCIETIES: THE MULTINATIONAL CORPORATION

The analysis of the outcomes of organizations thus far has moved from the individual to the society. It is also clear that organizations can have important outcomes across societies. This is easily seen in the myriad accounts of international spy rings and terrorist groups and in the case of extractive industries that take natural resources away from developing nations and give little in return, aside from low wages to workers. The multinational corporation is less visible, but perhaps more important in the long run.

There have been international organizations for longer than there have been nations. The Roman Empire and the Catholic Church exemplify this as do the imperialist organizations that were at the heart of the British Empire. The multinational corporation is a different matter, however. This organizational form involves much more than simply having branch offices in more than one nation. In the case of the multinational firm, the total operation of things as diverse as the production and sales of automobiles or chocolate candy or banks is in the hands of a subsidiary or equal firm in another nation. German, Dutch,

British, French, Swedish, Canadian, U. S., and Japanese firms are all important parts of this international scene.

There are many explanations for the emergence of the multinational corporation. All have strong elements of truth. The first such explanation is imperialism, or the attempt to expand corporate markets and reduce costs through the use of economic power over a weaker nation. The nation could be weaker in terms of pay scales and thus provide cheap labor; it could be weaker in terms of political dependence and thus give corporations of the more powerful nations tax breaks and incentives. Heilbroner (1974) sees technology as the key to the growth of multinationals. Mass-production systems and computer information handling have pushed all societies to larger and larger units of production. An inevitable consequence of this is expansion to overseas markets and production facilities.

Toynbee (1974) offers another explanation: multinational firms overcome the problem that sovereignty is dispersed over 140 local states, many of which can have antiquated political arrangements. Toynbee believes that because local economic independence is impossible for many nations, the multinational firm could become the dominant economic and political form of organization, superseding the traditional nation-state.

McMillan's (1973) explanation is more complex. He suggests that the multinational corporation is a consequence of corporate choices made to implement product-market strategy: as corporations begin to produce a complex range of products, these are to be sold in different markets through multiple channels of distribution. McMillan's explanation, which, as will be seen later, is solidly within contemporary organizational theory, suggests that multinational corporations are in essence inevitable. Even in a no-growth economic situation, the desire to cut costs or maintain the share of the market would lead to international expansion. Egelhoff (1982) follows much the same line of reasoning, but adds in factors such as product-market diversity, product change, and size of operations.

Each of the foregoing explains part of the international growth of organizations. Each also explains why organizations in general seek to expand their influence over the environment as a means of protecting their flanks and expanding their operations. These explanations all view the organization as acting in a rational manner, which as we will see is a highly questionable assumption. Interestingly, these analyses have all dealt with organizations that produce goods. Relatively little attention has been paid to multinational service organizations, such as international banking, which appear to be of crucial importance. International hotel operations, while of less importance, are also very evident.

Multinational firms have several kinds of impacts on their host countries and governments. Clegg and Dunkerly (1980) claim:

> It must be recognized that multinational organizations are different from the kind of organization traditionally studied by organizational theorists. Their size and complexity and their capacity for capital investment in countries of their choice makes them able to control their environment in hitherto unknown ways. The fact of being independent of national governments in many instances enables them to pursue their goals in a ruthless and unaccountable manner. (pp. 390–91)

Clegg and Dunkerly go on to note instances in which the Ford Motor Company influenced many governments to pass laws or to provide investment capital in order to attract Ford installations. The most dramatic instance of multinational influence came in Chile in 1970, when the Marxist Allende government was in power. In addition to the United States's CIA, multinational firms such as ITT and Ford played a significant part in the downfall of that government.

Clegg and Dunkerly also note several other consequences of multinational corporations. Considerations of what is best for a national economy are secondary to consideration of what is best for the corporation as a whole. Although the multinational is frequently welcomed in areas of high unemployment, their presence can create a situation of extremely high dependence on the firm. Once the local economy is dependent on such a firm, the firm itself has a great deal of power. The multinational is also often able to avoid paying taxes at the rate paid by domestic corporations through reporting profits in countries with lower tax rates and other forms of financial shifts. When a multinational moves some of its production operations overseas, of course, domestic employment is adversely affected.

There is an aura of inevitability in most discussions of multinational firms. This aura is generally warranted, but there are conditions which could drastically affect the operations of multinational firms. National revolutions or elections can turn the host country to the point that all industries are nationalized or all foreign investments confiscated. The case of Iran and the United States is a graphic illustration here. Not all multinational ventures are successful. Nonetheless, the multinational corporation appears to be an increasing part of the international scene and will continue to influence international events.

WHY STUDY ORGANIZATIONS?

This chapter ends with the very question with which it began. The complete answer to the question will not be known until we have covered all of the subject matter. From the review of the impact of organizations on our lives, our initial answer is essentially depressing. From the standpoint of empirical research on organizations, it would appear that Child (1976) is correct in his conclusion that organizations will continue to grow, bureaucratize, and centralize. In other words, more of the same.

At the same time, there are organizational theorists who see organizations as the only way by which desirable ends such as peace, prosperity, and social justice can be achieved. Etzioni (1968) uses organizations as the basis for his call for an "active" society. Based on his analysis of French society, Crozier (1973) sees the modern organization, if it can be democratic, as the means by which the now less rigid populace can make choices by which creativity and innovation can be captured.

In a very real sense, we are now living in an "organizational state" (Laumann and Knoke, 1987) in which the major actors in national policy events are organizations and interorganizational networks. Economists Cohen and Zysman (1988) suggest that manufacturing in the United States has fallen behind that in other nations because American organizations have not been able to adopt or adapt production innovations which have been developed in other nations. I would argue that this is a consequence of organizational characteristics. This is a very different approach from that taken by writers such as Hayes and Abernathy (1980) who believe that it is management that is to blame for a decline in American technological competitiveness. In the pages that follow, I will argue that studying organizations will lead to some useful conclusions regarding why organizations are in their present condition.

One of the major contributions that organizational theory can make will be to point out the limitations on what is feasible for organizations themselves and for the wider social system. We will also point out that organizations contain some inherent contradictions which limit the impact that individual actors can have.

Jackall (1988) has noted that business is a "social and moral terrain." The same point is true for all organizations. Moral and ethical issues are confronted whenever decisions are made. In a book prepared under the auspices of the Business Roundtable, an organization made up of the chief executive officers of many of the largest and most powerful American business firms, Steckmest (1982; also see Burke, 1986)) urges corporate social responsibility. The argument of his book is that corporations need to "develop executives and functions (e. g., government relations and consumer affairs staffs) to monitor effectively, and interact responsibly in, an increasingly complex sociopolitical environment" (Yeager, 1982, p. 748). Again, the notion of corporations has to be expanded to all organizations, including those that are part of government itself.

Lammers (1981) believes that organizational theory has much to contribute to "clients" of many types, ranging from politicians and journalists in the public-at-large to workers and managers within organizations to opponents of organizations who operate inside and outside of the organizations themselves. The true relevance of organizational theory lies in Brown's (1978, p. 378) conclusion: "The more we are able to create worlds that are morally cogent and politically viable, the more we are able, as workers and as citizens, to manage or resist" (p. 378).

SUMMARY AND CONCLUSIONS

The purpose of this chapter has been a simple one—to indicate the importance of organizations at every level of human life. Thus, the individual, classes of individuals, the community, the society, and the international order were examined in terms of the manner in which organizations have outcomes for them. Organizational analysis is dull until the crucial and central role of organizations is understood. If organizations are understood, then individuals have a tool by which they can deal with the reality that they face.

The astute reader has no doubt noticed that the subject matter of this book—organizations— has not been defined or delineated. It is to this that we now turn.

2

On the Nature
and Types
of Organizations

This chapter has three purposes. First, organizations will be defined. The intent is to indicate that we are dealing with a single subject matter—all organizations have characteristics that permit them to be considered as one type of social phenomenon. We will differentiate organizations from other social forms and from individuals. This is the second purpose of the chapter—to indicate that organizations have a reality of their own. The final purpose is seemingly contradictory to the first two. Here we will differentiate among organizations. Common sense tells us that large and powerful national or multinational organizations are different from small local organizations. The attempt here will be to present ways in which organizations might be typed or classified.

DEFINITIONS FROM THE PAST

Discussions of definitions can be quite deadly. This one may be deadly, also, but it is necessary. Although some writers (for example, March and Simon, 1958, p. 1) argue that definitions of organizations do not serve much purpose, a more reasonable approach would appear to be that definitions provide a basis for understanding the phenomena to be studied. Here we will consider the definitions developed by some classical writers in the field and then offer our own approach to the subject.

Weber Like any other field of study, and like organizations themselves, organizational analysis has a tradition. The tradition centers heavily on Max

Weber, who is known for his analyses of bureaucracy and authority, topics which will be considered later, but he also concerned himself with the more general definitions of organizations. Weber first distinguishes the "corporate group" from other forms of social organization (Weber, 1947). The corporate group involves: "a social relationship which is either closed or limits the admission of outsiders by rules, ...so far as its order is enforced by the action of specific individuals whose regular function this is, of a chief or 'head' and usually also an administrative staff" (pp. 145–46).

This aspect of the definition contains a number of elements requiring further discussion, since they are basic to most other such definitions. In the first place, organizations involve social relationships. That is, individuals interact within the organization. However, as the reference to closed or limited boundaries suggests, these individuals are not simply in random contact. The organization (corporate group) includes some parts of the population and excludes others. The organization itself thus has a boundary. A major component of this definition, the idea of order, further differentiates organizations from other social entities. Interaction patterns do not simply arise; a structuring of interaction is imposed by the organization itself. This part of the definition also suggests that organizations contain a hierarchy of authority and a division of labor in carrying out their functions. Order is enforced with specific personnel designated to perform this function.

To the idea of the corporate group, Weber adds some additional criteria for organizations. In organizations, interaction is "associative" rather than "communal" (pp. 136–39). This differentiates the organization from other social entities, such as the family, which share the other, aforementioned characteristics of the corporate group. Weber also notes that organizations carry out continuous purposive activities of a specified kind (pp. 151–52). Thus, organizations transcend the lives of their members and have goals, as the phrase "purposive activities" suggests. Organizations are designed to do something. This idea of Weber's has been retained by most organizational analysts.

Weber's definition has served as the basis for many others. His focus is basically on legitimate interaction patterns among organizational members as they pursue goals and engage in activities.

Barnard   A different focus has been taken by Chester Barnard and his followers. While in agreement with Weber on many points, Barnard stresses a different basis for organizations. His definition of an organization is "a system of consciously coordinated activities or forces of two or more persons" (Barnard, 1938, p. 73). Activity is accomplished through conscious, deliberate, and purposeful coordination. Organizations require communications, a willingness on the part of members to contribute, and a common purpose among them. Barnard stresses the role of the individual. It is they who must communicate, be motivated, and make decisions. While Weber emphasizes the system, Barnard is concerned with members of the system. The relevance and implications of these contrasting approaches will be taken up later.

Marx   Although Marx did not develop a formal definition of organizations, his analyses of the social order contain many implications about organizations. According to Heydebrand (1977), the key notion is praxis or human practical activity. Praxis is historically situated and may refer to both individual and collective activity. It is the collective that is relevant here. Heydebrand summarizes the Marxian approach to organizations as follows:

> In very general terms, the Marxian notion of praxis includes the following basic processes which can take the form of collective organizing activity: Producing the means of subsistence (i. e., work and material production), producing language and the means of communication and interaction (i. e., symbolic production, consciousness as a process), engaging in creative and innovative activity (material and symbolic, including artistic activity), reproducing human existence through biological, social, and ideological reproduction processes, and developing and expressing needs, including the creation of "new needs." (pp. 84–85)

Another key component of the Marxian perspective is *outcomes*, which, of course, are of major interest here. Heydebrand notes that there are two types of outcomes. The first is products, artifacts, or constructs, while the second is the activities themselves. A form of outcome of organizations is the organizing process itself—the ways in which work is carried out, the procedures used, the power arrangements, and the like.

Organizations and Social Organization

Organizations are major components of the broader notion of "social organization," which complicates the task of defining our subject matter. *Social organization* refers to the "network of social relations and the shared orientations...often referred to as the social structure and culture, respectively" (Blau and Scott, 1962, p. 4). Social organization is the broader set of relationships and processes of which organizations are a part. Organizations thus affect, and are reciprocally affected by, social organization (Coleman, 1974).

There have been efforts made to develop adjectives which describe our subject matter, such as "large-scale organizations," "formal organizations," or "complex organizations" (see Blau and Scott, 1962), but none of these efforts have been especially successful. We will keep the matter simple and refer only to organizations.

The analysis of organizations as a distinct subject matter in sociology emerged in a full-blown manner in the 1960s. In that decade, Etzioni (1964) and Scott (1964) made important definitional statements. Etzioni's is:

> Organizations are social units (or human groupings) deliberately constructed and reconstructed *to seek specific goals* (emphasis added).

> Corporations, armies, schools, hospitals, churches, and prisons are included; tribes, classes, ethnic groups, and families are excluded. (p. 3)

Scott adds some elements to the definition:

> ...organizations are defined as collectivities...that have been established for the pursuit of relatively specific *objectives* on a more or less continuous basis. It should

be clear...however, that organizations have distinctive features other than goal specificity and continuity. These include relatively fixed boundaries, a normative order, authority ranks, a communication system, and an incentive system which enables various types of participants to work together in the pursuit of common *goals* (emphases added). (p. 488)

The issue of goals or objectives is one which has interested and divided organizational analysts for some time. We will examine the importance of goals at several points in our analysis. For our definitional task here, there are several points that are important. First, many things go on in organizations that are *not* goal related. When people are on coffee breaks and talking about the past weekend, goals are not involved. When a business firm uses its private jet aircraft to fly a single executive around the country at a much higher cost than even first-class commercial air fare and with much higher risk, goals are not involved. When I am daydreaming about skiing, goals are not involved.

Second, goals can be considered as reifications or "having an existence and behavior independent of the behavior of its members" (Simon, 1964, p. 2). Simon, who won a Nobel Prize in economics for his work on organizations does not believe that goals should be considered apart from individual actors, even though he does refer to goals as constraints on "organizational decision making" (1964, p. 7). In the present analysis I will consider goals in the reified manner—they exist apart from individual organizational members.

The final aspect of goals that is important here is that we are using the term *goals* in the true plural sense. Organizations have multiple goals. For the most part, these multiple goals are also contradictory. Thus, issues such as short-term versus long-term profit, quality versus quantity, teaching versus research, and so on, are part of the very fabric of organizations.

Scott (1964) included the idea of organizational boundaries in his definition, and they have become an important component of his more fully developed conceptualization of organizations (1987b). In some situations, the issue of boundaries is very clear. For example, I put on the uniform of the National Ski Patrol System, Inc., when I go skiing. I am a member of that organization, and we wear uniforms to make us visible to the skiing public. Only ski patrol members may wear them—the boundary is clear. The boundary issue becomes cloudy when another example is considered. The local political party has a small paid staff to answer mail, phones, and so on. The membership swells, however, at election time, with the headquarters filled with activities and people. Both the ski patrol and the political party are voluntary organizations, but this does not account for ambiguity in the conceptualization of boundaries. As another example, the computer firm that supplies the mainframe computer for my university has personnel permanently assigned to the university. These personnel become more a part of the university than the computer firm. They also have better parking than I do.

The idea of boundaries suggests that there is something outside the organization—its environment. As we will see, contemporary organizational theory has a strong focus on the environment. Organizations have both physical and social environments. The physical environment, which is often overlooked by organizational analysts, cannot be ignored. The State University of New York at Albany is usually blanketed by a lot of snow in the winter, and snow removal costs are not an incidental part of its budget. This is not a major budget consideration at the University of California at Los Angeles. The social environment has been the major focus of research and theory, since it contains competitors, regulators, and other sources of pressure and opportunities for organizations. The environment is also the source of inputs for the organizations and is the recipient of organizational outcomes (Thompson, 1967; Katz and Kahn, 1978).

With these considerations in mind, the definition of organizations to be used here can now be presented: *An organization is a collectivity with a relatively identifiable boundary, a normative order, ranks of authority, communications systems, and membership coordinating systems; this collectivity exists on a relatively continuous basis in an environment and engages in activities that are usually related to a set of goals; the activities have outcomes for organizational members, the organization itself, and for society.*

This is a cumbersome and perhaps unwieldy definition, but then so too is the subject matter.

Some Additional Definitional Issues

There are two additional points to be made in regard to the definitional issue. First, organizations are characterized by internal differentiation. Indeed, much of the research on organizational structure has been focused on such differentiation. Organizations are political entities, with various parties, both individuals and units, struggling for control. Writers such as Benson (1977) and Heydebrand (1977) have alerted us to the presence of contradictions within organizations. These writers focus on class interests in the contradiction process, but the class emphasis is not necessary for inclusion of the notion of contradiction. Organizations do contain oppositional forces. These forces vie for control. The nature of organizations is such that those in power tend to remain in power, but the fact that organizations contain internal oppositional forces is an important consideration. The definition just given should not blind us to the fact that organizations have internal differentiation and thus the seeds of possible dissension.

The second point is that it is frequently useful and necessary to consider parts or units of organizations as organizations in their own right. Hage (1980) notes that there are many "multi" organizations. These are organizations of such scope that it is wise to consider their component parts as separate organizations. Large government agencies, corporate conglomorates, and many multidivisional organizations have units that can and should be considered as separate organizations. For the purposes here, it is sufficient to note that an *autonomous* unit of a larger organization can be considered an organization in its own right (Warriner, 1980). If the unit can provide its own input and throughput and can distribute its outputs, it can be considered to be an organization. Thus, a new-car dealership that is totally dependent upon a single manufacturer for its input would not qualify as an organization on its own. A used-car dealership which relies totally on cars that it buys and sells would be an organization. This is a technical distinction, therefore, and one which actually interferes with some useful comparisons. The fact of the matter is, of course, that new-car dealers have other sources of inputs, such as service work and their own used-car business. The distinction does point out, however, the importance of clear boundary specifications.

The new-car dealership—used-car dealership distinction also highlights the importance of the way in which we go about classifying organizations. On one basis—selling cars—they are very similar, but on another—the degree of autonomy from a single supplier—they are not. The less autonomous might be more profitable, however, while the more autonomous might be less ethical. There are thus many dimensions along which organizations can be classified. Before considering classifications of organizations, however, an important but often overlooked question must be considered.

ARE ORGANIZATIONS REAL?

This question may seem inane. From the outset we have been considering the organizations that surround us and of which we are a part. We have examined some of the outcomes of organizations for individuals and society. A careful consideration of the question, however, reveals one of the basic dilemmas in sociology and in philosophy.

Most theorists have addressed this question one way or another. Simon (1964), for example, argues against reifying the concept of organization or treating it as something more than a system of interacting individuals. In his important treatise on exchange theory, Blau (1964) notes that individual behavior within organizations is based on direct or indirect exchanges among individuals, even when the exchanges are asymmetrical

Other analysts, such as Benson (1977), are even more individualistic, claiming that reality is a social construction in the minds of organizational actors. The position taken in the present analysis is that these individualistic approaches are incomplete in two ways.

Organizations and the Individual   In the first place, individuals in organizations frequently behave *without* engaging in direct or indirect exchange. There are many routine behaviors that are learned in an exchange situation but are then carried out without mental reference to the interaction process. The behavior becomes a type of learned stimulus-response mechanism, with the intervening interaction variable deleted as a consideration. Department store clerks are trained to input each transaction into the store's computer. Bank tellers routinely check the status of a customer's account. As computers make decisions about the status of our accounts, they essentially have taken over the routine activities that were previously carried out by individuals.

The organization trains, indoctrinates, and persuades its members to respond on the basis of the requirements of their position. Responses become quite regularized and routinized and do not involve the interaction frame of reference. In some situations even the emotions and feelings of the people involved can have an organizational basis. Hochschild's (1983) research on airline flight attendants demonstrates that at least some flight attendants learn to feel the friendly external demeanor that they portray. Their inner feelings, as well as their outward behavior, are based on organizational training.

The argument that behavior in organizations is organizationally, rather than individually or interactionally, based is not intended to mean that all behavior in organizations is so determined. There clearly are many times when individual discretion is called for, times when the individual is crucial for organizational survival. The point is that the organization can be the major determinant of individual actions in some situations and an important determinant in others. In discussing the factors that contribute to the kinds of role expectations one organizational member holds toward another (role expectations are of vital importance in any interaction situation), Kahn et al. (1964) note:

> To a considerable extent, the role expectations held by the members of a role set—the prescriptions and proscriptions associated with a particular position—are determined by the broader organizational context. The organizational structure, the functional specialization and division of labor, and the formal reward system dictate the major content of a given office. What the occupant of that office is supposed to do, with and for whom, is given by these and other properties of the organization itself. Although other human beings are doing the "supposing" and rewarding, *the structural properties of organization are sufficiently stable so that they can be treated as independent of the particular persons in the role set.* For such properties as size, number of echelons, and rate of growth, the justifiable abstraction of organizational properties from individual behavior is even more obvious (italics added). (p. 31)

Clegg and Dunkerly (1980) approach this issue from a power perspective. They suggest that the "capacity of management to impose its hegemony on the members of the organization" means that organizations assume a real existence for the people who are oriented to the organization. If an organization has power over the individual, then it is real (pp. 209–10).

The perspective taken here is that organizations are real to the extent that strictly organizational factors account for part of the behavior of individuals at all times in organizations. The exact proportion of the variation in individual behavior accounted for by organizational factors, as opposed to interactional or individual factors, cannot be exactly specified at the present time. The position taken here is that organizational factors can account for most if not all of the variation in behavior in some circumstances (this is the purpose of training and indoctrination programs in many kinds of organizations). In others, organizational factors interact with other behavioral determinants.

Organizations are realities for individuals in another crucial way. Kalleberg and Berg (1987) discuss firm internal labor markets (FILMs). These are the job structures in which people move in the course of their careers. The jobs exist prior to the individuals involved. White (1971) uses the idea of "vacancy chains" to describe the phenomena. As positions become vacant in an organization, a chain of vacancies is created as first one and then more vacancies are created. Kalleberg and Berg note that in large organizations, there are multiple chains in the various departments of the organization.

Organizations as Actors   The treatment of organizations as realities thus far has been concerned with the behavior of individuals. An even more basic issue is whether organizations have an existence of their own, above and beyond the behavior and performance of individuals within them. The question becomes, Do organizations act? The answer again is in the affirmative, and this is the second reason that viewing organizations just as interacting or reality constructing individuals is too narrow a conceptualization.

Some characteristics of the definitions just discussed provide indications of the existence of organizations. The fact that organizations persist over time and replace members suggests that they are not dependent upon particular individuals. Universities outlive the generations of students and faculty which pass through their gates. The General Motors Corporation has been in existence for a long time. The Roman Catholic Church is an even more striking example.

Organizations may indeed have a life cycle that includes decline and death (Kimberly and Miles and Associates, 1980), but the fact is that our dominant organizations persist across generations of members. Even when the life-cycle metaphor is used, it must be remembered that organizations can take actions which extend their lives, such as getting government loans, having favorable legislation passed, starting new advertising campaigns, or opening new markets.

When members enter an organization for the first time, they are confronted with a social structure that includes the interaction patterns among organizational members and these members' expectations toward them, and a set of organizational expectations for their own behavior. It does not matter who the individuals are; the organization has established a system of norms and expectations to be followed regardless of who its personnel happens to be, and it continues to exist regardless of personnel turnover. Individuals establish the norms and expectations, to be sure, but they persist long past the persons who established the policies in the first place.

Organizational factors influence decision making in organizations. Routine decisions can be preprogrammed, such as when computerized inventory records show that a particular item is apt to be in short supply and an order for additional such items is generated. More important decisions about future organizational directions and policies are also strongly affected by organizational factors. Decisions are strongly influenced by the power of the individuals making the decisions. Power, in turn, is the result of occupying an organizational position. Decisions are also based on tradition and precedent, as well as the organization's relationships with its environment. These organizationally based considerations have an impact on how individuals within the organizational hierarchy make decisions on behalf of the organization.

When we hear statements such as "It is company policy," "The White House today announced...," or "Z State University does not condone cheating," these are recognizable as being about organizations. Organizations have policies, make announcements, and may or may not condone cheating. They also manufacture goods, administer policies, and protect the citizenry. These are organizational actions and involve properties of organizations, not individuals. The actions are carried out by individuals—even in the case of computer-produced letters, which are programmed by individuals—but the genesis of the actions remains in the organization. The real heart of the matter is that organizations have outcomes of the sort that were considered in Chapter 1.

The argument being made here has certain philosophical assumptions that should be considered. Following Burrell and Morgan (1979, pp. 4–7), it can be noted that in terms of ontology, we are taking a realist as opposed to a nominalist position. The nominalist position is that reality is constructed through individual cognition, with the external world made up of artificial creations formed in people's minds. The realist position claims that the world external to individual cognition is a real world made up of hard, tangible, and relatively immutable structures. Warriner (1956) has taken the realist view toward groups, and we are taking it toward organizations. In essence, the realist view is that individuals, groups, and organizations can all be legitimately viewed as having a reality of their own. Some 90 years ago Simmel (1902; p. 193) wrote:

> The question now arises, however, whether traits of character in the total group are not derived from *definite* numbers of members, in which case, of course, the reactions between individuals constitute the real and observable event. The question merely assumes, however, that not the members in their individuality, but their assemblage in a picture of the whole, now constitutes the object of inquiry.

Our "picture of the whole" is the organization.

Epistemologically, the position taken here is a positivist one in that we seek to explain and predict what happens in the organizational world by searching for regularities and causal relationships among the elements related to organizations. Antipositivists suggest that the world is relativistic and can only be understood from the points of view of the actors in a particular situation.

Burrell and Morgan also suggest that assumptions about human nature must be considered in organizational analyses. They contrast the voluntarist position with the determinist perspective. Voluntarism sees humans as totally autonomous and free willed, while determinism sees people as totally controlled by the situation or environment in which they are located. The analysis here leans toward the determinist perspective without embracing it totally.

There is finally the methodological issue. On the one hand, there is the ideographic approach, which stresses detailed analyses of the meanings that social actors attach to situations and emphasizes that social actors' meanings should be stated in their own terms. The nomothetic approach emphasizes testing hypotheses with scientific rigor and the use of systematic research protocols. The nomothetic approach will be stressed in this analysis, with the realization that ideographic studies can provide useful insights and contribute to the development of rigorous tests of the insights.

Part of the difficulty that arises around the issue of organizational reality comes from the methodologies that have been employed. There is a long tradition of obtaining information about organizations from respondents in organizations. This is done through data collected from "key informants" or from samples of personnel in the organizations. Lazarsfeld and Menzel (1961; see also Barton, 1961) have suggested that it is possible to construct organizational properties from data gathered from individuals, through the use of averages, standard deviations, correlations coefficients, and other such figures. It is also possible to obtain data from individuals *about* the organization. Lincoln and Zeitz (1980) have demonstrated a technique by which data from individuals can be aggregated to the organizational level with strong explanatory power. It is also very possible to obtain data about organizations from members of other organizations, as research by Blau and Rabrenovic (1989) reveals. In their research they asked directors of nonprofit organizations in New York State to describe how frequently they interacted with other such agencies and whether or not there was any duplication of services. The directors apparently had no difficulty in identifying the other organizations and *simply treated them as real.* They were in their picture of the whole.

The final consideration in regard to organizational reality is that organizations have real outcomes. This point was made emphatically in Chapter 1 and need not be repeated here.

This rather lengthy expedition into the issue of organizational reality was conducted for the purpose of specifying the perspective that the analysis in this book takes. As Roberts, Hulin, and Rousseau (1978) conclude, social scientists vary in their interests, with some concerned with individual phenomena, some with group phenomena, and some with organizational phenomena. Each is a legitimate interest and can be an interesting picture. Pfeffer (1982) has shown that the structuralist versus individualist distinction pervades organizational theory. The present analysis is intentionally eclectic, with a strong structural lean.

TYPES OF ORGANIZATIONS

Our discussions of the different definitions of organizations and of the reality of organizations could lead to the conclusion that all organizations share common characteristics and are thus of one class or type. In one sense this is true. Just as there are defining characteristics that enable us to differentiate humans from other forms of life, we are also able to distinguish organizations from other forms of collectivities.

The importance of commonalities, of course, does not blind us to differences. The marvelous difference between men and women is a tremendously useful typology. This important difference is given a great deal of social meaning. Most of the typologies that we develop about people, such as age, attractiveness, or abilities, are based on socially developed meanings.

This same point is true in regard to typologies of organizations. Most of the distinctions that we commonly make between organizations, such as profit versus not-for-profit are social constructions. At times these social constructions are helpful; at other times they are not. Just as the distinction between men and women is very helpful in some circumstances, at other times it is harmful, such as when one is selecting a new faculty member or new students. In these latter cases distinctions based on gender are irrelevant. So too are the distinctions based on profit/not-for-profit when we examine an issue such as the relationship between organizational complexity and decision-making patterns.

Organizational analysts are well aware of the need for typologies. But at the same time they are convinced that the relatively simple, prima facie typologies probably add more confusion than clarity. Perrow (1967), for example, notes that

> types of organizations—in terms of their functions in society—will vary as much within each type as between types. Thus, some schools, hospitals, banks, and steel companies may have more in common, because of their routine character, than routine and nonroutine schools, routine and nonroutine hospitals, and so forth. To assume that you are holding constant the major variable by comparing several schools or several steel mills is unwarranted until one looks at the technologies employed by the various schools or steel mills. (p. 203)

While we might argue with Perrow and his emphasis on technology as the key variable, his point is very important. It is organizational characteristics that should serve as the classificatory basis. The great danger in most classificatory schemes is oversimplification; they are based on a single characteristic. Typologies thus derived "can be expanded indefinitely as some new factor is seized upon to indicate an additional class" (Katz and Kahn, 1966, p. 111). Such problems with typologies are not limited just to the study of organizations. Burns (1967) notes that "the history of sociology, from Montesquieu through Spencer, Marx, and up to Weber himself, is littered with the debris of ruined typologies that serve only as the battleground for that academic street-fighting that so often passes for theoretical discussion (p.119)."

Typologies that end in debris did not stop with Weber. As McKelvey (1982) has commented, "organizational science will remain wallowing in a swampy scientific tidal basin until significant progress in systematics is forthcoming" (p. 8). By systematics, McKelvey is referring to his own approach to classification, which will be considered shortly. Despite all these pleas and the recognized need, *we still do not have an adequate organizational typology.*

While some simple typologies can be used for limited analyses, such as comparing organizations in their turnover rates, growth rates, or rates of investment in research and development, classifications of this sort have only a limited usefulness. We end up knowing only one thing about organizations, not understanding them in their rich complexity.

The essence of any typological effort really lies in the determination of the critical variables for differentiating the phenomena under investigation. Since organizations are highly complex entities, classificatory schemes must represent this complexity. An adequate overall classification would have to take into account the array of external conditions, the total spectrum of actions and interactions within an organization, and the outcomes of organizational behaviors. A brief review of some of the efforts made to classify organizations will indicate the diversity of variables that have been considered, the relative fruitlessness of the schemes, and some possible future directions for typological efforts.

Some Typologies

For the purposes of the present analysis, we will use the terms *classification, typology, and taxonomy* interchangeably, although in a strict sense each term has a distinct meaning (Burns, 1967, p. 119; McKelvey, 1982). The most common form of typology is what Warriner (1980) has labeled the traditional, folk, or common sense typologies. Thus, organizations can be classified into profit or nonprofit categories. This is clearly an important distinction in some cases but not in others, as we will see.

Another form of common sense typology would be to classify organizations by their societal "sector," such as educational, agricultural, health and medical, and so on. Like the profit-nonprofit distinction, such classifications can obscure more than they illuminate. Warriner (1980) notes that such typologies contain dimensions that overlap in unpredictable ways. They are also unscientific in that the categories are not related to each other in any systematic way. The major problem with such common sense typologies is that they simply do not classify. The State University of New York, for example, contains two-year colleges, four-year colleges, graduate university centers, medical colleges and their attendant hospitals, specialized colleges in ceramics and forestry, plus an entirely noncampus-based administrative headquarters with no students. In addition, there is a semiautonomous research foundation that does not conduct research but rather seeks funds—an entrepreneurial role—and administers grants and contracts—an administrative role. In a similar manner, General Motors and U. S. Army maintain college degree–granting facilities. Are General Motors, the U. S. Army and the State University of New York the same type of organization? Of course not. The realization of this type of difficulty has led organizational analysts to try to develop other forms of classification. The first form to be discussed is the "intentional" (Warriner 1980) or "special" classification (McKelvey, 1978), which focuses on a limited aspect of the organization.

We will move from some relatively simple schemes to more elaborate formulations. Typical of the simple schemes is that of Parsons (1960, pp. 45–46), based on the type of function or goal served by the organization. In this analysis, Parsons is concerned with the linkages between organizations and the wider society. He distinguishes four types of organizations, according to what they contribute to the society.

The first type is the *production* organization, which makes things that are consumed by the society. The second type is that oriented toward *political* goals; it seeks to ensure that society attains its valued goals, and it generates and allocates power within the society. The third type is the *integrative* organization, whose purposes are settling conflicts, directing motivations toward the fulfillment of institutionalized expectations, and ensuring that the parts of society work together. The final form is the *pattern-maintenance* organization, which attempts to provide societal continuity through educational, cultural, and expressive activities.

While each of these activities is clearly important for society, this type of classificatory scheme does not really say much about the organizations involved. In the first place, some organizations can be placed in more than one category. A large corporation, such as IBM, is clearly a production organization. But it is also important in the allocation of power. It is also an important part of the research community. Through public relations, corporate contributions to foundations and colleges, and attempts at working with disadvantaged youths, the same corporation falls into the other categories. Its prime effort is production, but these subsidiary concerns make classificatory schemes such as Parsons's less than totally useful. Even more important, such a typology does not differentiate among the characteristics of organizations themselves. As Perrow noted, there can be as much—or more—organizational variation within such categories as between them.

Another approach to developing intentional typologies is exemplified by the works of Etzioni (1961) and Blau and Scott (1962). Both attempted to classify organizations on the basis of a single principle. Their prominence in the literature deserves continued attention.

Etzioni uses *compliance* as the basis for his system. Compliance is the manner in which lower participants in an organization respond to the authority system of the organization. Compliance is expressed through the nature of the lower participants' involvement in the organization. According to Etzioni, there are three bases of authority—coercion, remuneration, and normative. There are also three bases of compliance—alienative, instrumental or calculative, and moral. The resulting three-by-three classificatory scheme yields nine possible types of organizations, with most falling into "congruent" types. These are *coercive-alienative, remunerative-calculative, and normative-moral.* Incongruent types, such as coercive-utilitarian would tend to move toward congruency.

Etzioni's approach has been criticized from several standpoints. Burns (1967) notes that the reasons for congruence or incongruence are not well explained. Hall et al. (1967) found that it was difficult to place some organizations into Etzioni's categories. Public schools, for example, can yield alienative, calculative, and moral compliance on the part of various students. In addition, they found that the typology did not relate well to important structural characteristics such as complexity or formalization (see Weldon, 1972, and Hall et al. 1972, for additional discussion of this). Clegg and Dunkerly (1980, pp. 142–54) further criticize the Etzioni scheme on the grounds of its logical inconsistency and its inattention to organizational environments.

Lest this discussion lead to the conclusion that Etzioni's work makes little or no contribution, it should be noted that Etzioni (1975) followed up his original work by compiling the results of some 60 studies which used his typology. He found that the compliance patterns which were predicted by the typology generally were found. The compliance typology thus does appear to differentiate organizations in terms of the compliance patterns of its members, but it is not an inclusive typology. If one wants to study compliance patterns, it is useful, but it is not for other purposes.

Blau and Scott's basis of classification is the question of *who benefits* or *cui bono.* The prime organizational beneficiary serves as the basis for their fourfold classification. The types are *mutual benefit* organizations in which the members themselves are the prime beneficiary, *businesses* with owners as the beneficiaries, *service* organizations with clients as the beneficiaries, and *commonweal* organizations in which the public-at-large benefits.

Burns (1967) suggests that it is difficult to isolate a single explicit, stable, and coherent group served by an organization. The beneficiaries themselves have factions, disagree, and engage in power struggles. Clegg and Dunkerly

(1980) point out that this approach also does not deal with the critical issue of who actually controls the organization or of who does *not* benefit from its activities. Hall et al. (1967) found difficulty in placing organizations, such as schools, into a single category, as was the case with the Etzioni approach. It must be recognized, of course, that Blau and Scott's concern with who benefits is the indirect forerunner of the concern in this volume with organizational outcomes— who benefits and who is harmed.

As a final example of this form of building intentional typologies, we will turn to the work of Mintzberg (1979). This is a multifaceted approach, based largely on the ways in which organizations are structured to meet various contingencies which they face. The first type is the *simple structure*, as exemplified by the brand-new government department, an automobile dealership with a flamboyant owner, a small college headed by an aggressive president, or a new government headed by an autocrat. Supervision is direct. The organizations are small and exist in dynamic environments. Their technologies are not sophisticated.

The second type is the *machine bureaucracy*, such as a postal system, a steel manufacturing firm, an airline, or a custodial prison. These share the characteristics of standardized work, large size, stable environments, and control by some external body.

The third type is the *professional bureaucracy* such as a university, law firm, social welfare agency, craft production firm, or medical center. Work is standardized through professional or craft training, and the environment is stable, but does not contain external controls on the organization. The key factor here is the skills and knowledge of the operating workers who are professionals or highly skilled craft workers.

The fourth type is the *divisionalized form*, as exemplified by the large corporation, multicampus university, or socialist economy. Each division has its own structure, which may take one of the other forms already listed in this typology.

Finally, there is the *adhocracy*. This complex form is exemplified by space agencies, new artistic organizations, and research and development laboratories at the frontiers of science. Their environment is dynamic and unknown, and their structure can change rapidly as events demand adjustment.

Mintzberg has a complex scheme from which these types of organizations are developed. The important point here is the fact that the groupings shatter common sense notions of how and why organizations differ. Mintzberg is suggesting that we look at organizational characteristics themselves as the basis for our classification schemes. This is exactly what those who advocate empirical taxonomies propose.

Organizational Taxonomy

A very different approach to the classification issue has been taken by those who have advocated and tried to develop organizational taxonomies (Haas, Hall, and Johnson, 1966; Pugh, Hickson, and Hinings, 1969; McKelvey, 1975, 1978, 1982; Pinder and Moore, 1979; Warriner, 1980; Carper and Snizek, 1980; Miller and Friesen, 1984). Taxonomy refers to the theory and practice of classification (McKelvey, 1982; p. 462).

The Haas, Hall, and Johnson effort was designed to be a taxonomy of organizations, similar to that used in zoology to differentiate vertebrata at phyla level (amphibia, mammalia, aves, and reptilia), at the class level, and so on. Using data from 75 organizations and some 100 different organizational variables, this study was able to generate some nine major classes of organizations. Unfortunately, the bases for differentiation among the classes were seemingly trivial as organizational properties. The reason for the rather unusable findings may have been the type of measurement used or it may have been the fact that certain key variables were not included in the analysis. In any event, this initial effort at developing a classification scheme from empirically based characteristics did not produce usable classifications.

The Pugh, Hickson, and Hinings classification effort is an attempt to type organizations according to important structural characteristics. It is also empirically based and uses the following structural dimensions: (1) the structuring of activities, or the degree of standardization of routines, formalization of procedures, specialization of roles, and stipulation of specific behavior by the organization; (2) the concentration of authority, or the centralization of authority at the upper levels of the hierarchy and in controlling units outside the organization; and (3) the line control of work flow, or the degree to which control is exercised by line personnel as opposed to control through impersonal procedures. Using a sample of 52 English organizations and the three bases of classification, Pugh, Hickson, and Hinings developed a taxonomy which had seven basic types.

Miller and Friesen (1984) used 81 published case studies to derive their taxonomy. This effort was limited to business firms and is thus not an organizational taxonomy in the true sense.

McKelvey (1975) has criticized the Haas et al. and the Pugh et al. efforts on several grounds and his criticisms point to the difficulties and complexities in taxonomic efforts. He notes that

1. Broad populations of organizations should be included, and if this is not possible, a significant cultural unit such as a nation-state should be used.

2. A probability sample of organizations should be employed.

3. The organizational attributes should be inclusive as possible.

4. Given the large array of possible organizational attributes that could be used, a probability sampling of these attributes should be used.

5. The observers (measures) or organizational characteristics should be as inclusive as possible.

6. Where necessary, use a stratified probability sampling plan for selecting observers (measures).

McKelvey has four additional criticisms of a technical-statistical analytical nature that will not concern us here, but McKelvey's work in general makes a seminal contribution.

Advocates of the taxonomic approach (Warriner, 1979, 1980; McKelvey, 1978, 1982; Pinder and Moore, 1979; Carper and Snizek, 1980; Warriner, Hall, and McKelvey, 1981) argue that a sound taxonomy is the only way in which theoretical advances in organizational analysis can be made. The argument is that unless there is an adequate taxonomy or classification system, both theorists and practitioners have little guide for action. Practitioners have no way of knowing if what works in one organization will work in another, since they have no basis for knowing if the organizations are of the same type. The theorist cannot theorize in the absence of an adequate system.

McKelvey's (1982) work is a major step in the taxonomic direction. Basing his approach on *systematics* or the science or study of diversity, McKelvey has developed a complex and comprehensive scheme by which an ultimate organizational classification might be possible. The details of McKelvey's suggestions are beyond the scope of the present analysis, but include the kinds of issues which have been discussed in this section. McKelvey bases his approach from an evolutionary, population-based perspective.

For the purpose here, two points from McKelvey's work are most relevant. First, is the emphasis on *populations* of organizations. This is equivalent to species of biological creatures. In simple terms, populations of organizations are organizations of the same type. Fast-food restaurants or computer chip manufacturers could be thought of as populations of organizations. The process of identifying distinct populations, of course, is what the taxonomic effort is all about. The second important point is McKelvey's notion of *dominant competence*. This refers to the technical and managerial knowledge and skills that enable an organization to survive. McKelvey believes that dominant competencies are probably the key basis on which organizations can be differentiated. A concrete example here would be that small liberal arts colleges can be differentiated from large research universities on the bases of the competencies needed by the administrators in the two different populations of organizations of higher education. What works in one setting would not work in the other.

On What Variables Should We Classify?

There is a set of variables which appears to be important in any classificatory or taxonomic effort. At the common sense level is the *size* variable. As we will see, this is more complex than it seems at face value. It would be foolish to develop any typology that does not include size. Granovetter (1984) has reminded us of the importance of small organizations in the overall organizational world. The size variable is important in relation to all the other factors to be considered.

A more complex variable is the *publicness* of the organization (Bozeman, 1987). This interesting variable refers to "the degree to which the organization is affected by political authority" (Bozeman, 1987, p. xi). In his analysis, Bozeman makes the interesting point that "an organization is public to the extent that it exercises or is constrained by political authority... and it is private to the extent that it exercises or is constrained by economic authority" (p. 84). The key point here is that publicness is a variable, as is privateness. Public wars on drugs or AIDS are differentially constrained by economic authority. Private venture in banking or airlines are differentially constrained by publicness.

This last variable brings us back to the issue of *profit versus nonprofit* organizations. There are public and private nonprofit organizations. The public organizations are government agencies, while the private nonprofit organizations would be represented by organizations such as the Red Cross. The profit-nonprofit distinction is critically important for economists. For example, Weisbrod (1989) notes:

> The nonprofit sector of the U. S. economy is large and growing in comparison with the rest of the economy. The principal source of its theoretical justification is also the source of its principal liability—the nondistribution constraint. This legal restriction on distributing profit to anyone who has control over the organization has the adverse effects of reducing managerial incentives to minimize costs, seek out new markets, and innovate. It also has the favorable effect of reducing incentives to engage in anti-social activity, including taking advantage of consumers' information handicaps. These handicaps can be substantial in some industries—particularly when either collective-type goods are involved, such as scientific research or aid to the poor, or goods characterized by severely underinformed consumers, such as purchasers of nursing home and day care center services. (p. 545)

Weisbrod goes on to suggest that neither the profit nor nonprofit form is best under all conditions. Instead, he suggests that a mixture of forms is economically optimal. For our purposes, I would suggest that profit-nonprofit is a variable that must be included in our typological considerations.

Another variable that is interesting to consider in a typology is the extent to which an organization is *democratic*. Rothschild and Whitt (1986) argue that democratic organizations, in which "control rests ultimately and overwhelmingly with the members" (p. 2) can be found in all sectors of the organizational world. Thus employee-owned business firms and cooperative day care centers would share space on the democratic end of the continuum.

There is a final element that must be included in any comprehensive taxonomic or classification effort. This is the degree of *market power* or *environmental dominance* that an organization possesses. The proponents of the taxonomic approach seldom consider this issue, but it appears to be of critical importance in understanding organizations. Baron and Bielby (1984) argue that enterprises (organizations) can be distinguished along two interrelated dimensions. One of the dimensions is the market power and environmental dominance factor. The other factor contains variables that are typically included in any taxonomic efforts, such as size, structure, and technology. While Baron and Bielby's research was concerned with the distribution of work in labor markets, their findings are of clear relevance for typological considerations.

After all this discussion, I do not propose a typology or taxonomy, since I believe that a meaningful effort in this area requires empirical verification. In the last few paragraphs I have suggested a set of variables that appears to be of crucial importance. They are a set of overlapping and intertwining dimensions along which organizations might be classified. They are also complex, but so is our subject matter.

THE VOLUNTARY ORGANIZATION

Most of the discussion and examples used thus far have focused on organizations with paid members or employees. Another set of organizations confuses typological and general theoretical concerns: these are *voluntary organizations.* According to Knoke and Prensky (1984):

> Voluntary associations are formally organized named groups, most of whose participants do not derive their livelihoods from the organizations' activities, although a few positions may receive pay as staff or leaders. A substantial proportion of associations consist of organizations or persons with economic interests, such as trade associations, professional societies, and labor unions, while many others promote the noneconomic concerns of their members. Association boundaries are often fuzzy and porous (Aldrich, 1971), since many involve episodic supporters and passively interested constituents who can be mobilized under exceptional circumstances to provide financial or political sustenance. (pp. 3–4)

The issue is more complex than Knoke and Prensky portray. The Roman Catholic Church has long been viewed as one of the more complex and comprehensive bureaucratic organizations in the world, with thousands of paid employees. Local parishes, on the other hand, are exactly like the voluntary organizations just described. Professional associations, such as the American Medical Association or the American Nurses' Association have extensive professional staffs. On the other hand, of course, there are organizations that are strictly voluntary, such as the Greater Loudonville Association or the Willard Mountain Ski Patrol (in both of which I am a member). The Greater Loudonville Association is an association of homeowners concerned primarily with community beautification. This can be contrasted with the Love Canal Homeowners Association, which was concerned with matters of life and death (Levine, 1982).

Knoke and Prensky believe that traditional organizational theory has limited usefulness for voluntary organizations. They base their conclusion on the basis of analyses of incentive systems and participant commitment, formal structures, leadership and authority, environmental conditions, and organizational effectiveness issues. Table 2–1 summarizes their conclusions.

From a taxonomic perspective, voluntary organizations probably form several separate classes of organizations. At the same time, to make matters more complicated, there are forms of work organizations that share the characteristics of the voluntary associations that Knoke and Prensky describe. Many new, small business firms and some employee-owned firms are very collectivist (Rothschild-Whitt, 1979; Rothschild and Whitt, 1986) in their membership orientations, leadership patterns, and so on. For the analysis here, voluntary organizations will be treated as a separate category, with most of the focus on

TABLE 2–1   A Comparison of Business Firms and Voluntary Organizations

DIMENSION	INCENTIVE SYSTEMS AND PARTICIPANT COMMITMENT	FORMAL STRUCTURES	LEADERSHIP AND AUTHORITY	ENVIRONMENTAL CONDITIONS	EFFECTIVENESS
Firms	Utilitarian-centered incentives systems Resources from markets	Complex division of labor, vertical and horizontal differentiation	Hierarchical authority patterns Centralized decision making Professionalized leadership	Specialized structures favored in stable environments Occupy central positions of power and prestige in interorganizational networks	Goals of profits, growth Quantifiable performance indicators
Associations	Normative, affective-centered incentive systems Dependent on members and constituents for bulk of resources	Simple division of labor and formal internal structure	Collegial, confederated authority patterns Democratic ideology and decision making Amateur leadership	General structures favored in turbulent environments Occupy peripheral, dependent positions in networks	Goal of aggregating and expressing member interests Ambiguous and diffuse measures of goal attainment

Source: David Knoke and David Prensky, 1984, "What Relevance Do Organizational Theories Have for Voluntary Associations?" *Social Science Quarterly,* 65 (March), 14.

organizations with employees, fairly clear boundaries, and the other characteristics given in the earlier definition.

SUMMARY AND CONCLUSIONS

This chapter may have raised more questions than it resolved. After developing an inclusive definition, we then considered the thorny and unresolved issues of the reality of organizations and their classification. The position to be taken in this book is that organizations are real and that they do act. The position was also taken that an empirically based taxonomy would be the best basis for classifying organizations and some suggestions were made about the dimensions on which a taxonomic effort might be begun.

By raising these issues and taking a stand on them, it has been my intent to help in the understanding of organizations. Now that the definitional, reality, and classification issues have been raised and confronted, we can turn to the actual analysis of organizations by beginning to examine organizational structure.

3
Organizational Structure: Forms and Outcomes

The idea of structure is really quite simple. It is the way in which the parts are arranged. Our automobiles have structures and so do the buildings in which we work, study, and live. The building analogy is a useful, but not perfect, way to move into the analysis of *organizational* structure.

Buildings have doors through which we enter. Organizations have "ports of entry" as well. Hallways govern our movements. Organizations have rules and procedures that serve this purpose for their members. Some buildings are small and simple, like my garage; others are complex and multilayered with intricate linkages to other buildings. Organizations vary in their degree of complexity. In some buildings the heating and air conditioning are centrally controlled; in others each room is essentially autonomous and its heating destiny can be controlled by the occupants. Organizations vary in the degree to which people and units are given autonomy.

This chapter will describe the nature of structure. In the next chapter we will consider the reasons why structural forms take the shape that they do. At the outset, it should be noted that the reason why the building analogy is not perfect is the fact that organizational structures are continually emergent as they are influenced by successive waves of members, interactions among the members, and incessant environmental pressures. At the same time, the emergent nature of structure should not blind us to the fact that structure has a strong inertial tendency.

What is structure? A formal definition will be given at a later point. Here, some examples will be presented to begin to indicate the nature of the topic. The examples will be drawn from my own university, the State University of New

York (SUNY). Readers in other kinds of settings or who have had their educational experiences in similar or different settings can make comparisons with the examples based on their own experience.

SUNY is quite *complex*. It has units scattered throughout the State of New York and an office in Washington, DC. It has myriad divisions and departments, both by academic specialty and by administrative division. It has a tall hierarchy, with a chancellor, vice chancellors, assistant vice chancellors, and other ranks at the central office and presidents, vice presidents, associate and assistant vice presidents, deans, associate and assistant deans, faculty members of various ranks, and clerical and service personnel arranged along an array of civil service rankings. By almost any standard, it is a very complex organization. Very complex organizations face very complex coordination and control problems and SUNY is no different. One way in which coordination and control can be accomplished is through effective communications among units. This can be facilitated by the use of computerized record keeping and information transfer, which is part of what SUNY does. This is not necessarily successful, of course, and the system can be plagued with missing or absent information.

SUNY is *formalized* to varying degrees. In some areas rules and procedures are spelled out in minute detail, while in other areas low formalization exists. High formalization at SUNY-Albany is evident when each department (both academic and administrative) is required to prepare an annual update on its "three-year plan." This is a formal document which is reviewed by at least three levels before it reaches the president. The format of the plans is specified in advance, as is the review procedure. At the low end of the formalization continuum is the classroom. Individual faculty are almost totally free to select their texts and their methods of classroom presentation. Only in truly extreme cases would the organization intervene into the classroom. For students, the registration process is highly formalized, with specific dates and times to register, steps to be taken in the process, and forms to be completed. Again, the classroom is at the opposite extreme, except in the case of laboratories, with no rules on attendance, method of taking notes, or studying for exams.

Another aspect of structure, *centralization*, varies in a manner similar to formalization in that there is both high and low centralization. Low centralization is evidenced by the fact that academic departments are almost totally free to select potential faculty members for hiring on the basis of their own judgment. There is a minimal amount of power utilized at the campus or central administrative levels. The potential for the exercise of power is there, but it is seldom invoked. High centralization occurs when decision-making power is retained at or near the top of the organization. When new academic programs are developed, and particularly when these involve scarce resources, the central administration is heavily involved in the decision-making process. As a general rule, it appears that the higher the quality of the higher educational organization, the lower the level of centralization (Blau, 1973), but that is not the issue here. The important conclusion is that complexity, formalization, and centralization can vary within a single organization. They are multidimensional phenomena.

Almost all the research to be considered in the next two chapters is comparative in the sense that data are collected from more than one organization (Heydebrand, 1973). Some of the research is comparative in the sense that there is an attempt to compare organizations in different settings or societies. Comparative research is emphasized in the belief that it permits generalizations beyond a single research setting. As the discussion of typologies suggests, of course, in the absence of a sound typology such generalizations are risky. Most analysts try to make their findings as widely usable as possible, but the problem of crossing "types" should continue to be recognized. Indeed, as will be evident in the discussion, some of the major research projects have included such a limited range of organizations that it does make generalization difficult.

There is an additional problem in the studies to be considered, and this involves measurement (Price and Mueller, 1986). Data can come from organizational documents and records, key organizational informants, samples of members from the whole organization, or published data sets. (See Pennings, 1973; Azumi and McMillan, 1974; Dewar, Whetten, and Boje, 1980; and Lincoln and Zeitz, 1980, for more detailed discussions of some of the methodological issues.) The problem has been that measures of different types, which are designed to measure the same phenomena, such as formalization, do not correlate well together. It may be that the multidimensionality of the concept leads to the situation in which formalization measures are weakly or negatively correlated (Pennings, 1973), or it may be that some measures are simply not measures of what they are purported to be. These problems of typologies and measurement cannot be resolved here. The problems were raised simply to indicate that the analyses to be considered are themselves in process as researchers have sought to develop a cumulative and integrated set of findings.

COMPLEXITY

The term *complex organizations* describes the subject matter of this entire book—and indeed is the title of several important works. In this section we will look carefully at the concept of complexity, noting what it is and what are its sources and its consequences. From this examination it should become clear that the complexity of an organization has major effects on the behavior of its members, on other structural conditions, on processes within the organization, and on relationships between the organization and its environment.

Complexity is one of the first things that hits a person entering any organizational form: division of labor, job titles, multiple divisions, and hierarchical levels are usually immediately evident. Any familiarity with large corporations (and many small ones), the government, the military, or a school system verifies this. Organizations that seem very simple at first glance may exhibit interesting forms of complexity. Local voluntary organizations, such as the Rotary Club, labor union locals, and garden clubs usually have committees for programs, publicity, membership, community service, education, finance, and other matters, all with their attendant structure. These kinds of organizations must make provisions for the control and coordination of activities just as their more complex counterparts must.

The issue is itself made more complex by the fact that individual parts of an organization can vary in their degree of complexity. In a study of the regional office of a major oil company, for example, it was found that there were six divisions, as shown on the organization chart, Figure 3–1. The heads of the divisions had equal rank in the organization, and each was thought to be equally important to the overall success of the organization. When the divisions themselves were examined, it was found that they varied not only in size—from 3 to 100 members—but also in complexity. The largest division, distribution, had five separate hierarchical levels with three important subdivisions, each of which was further specialized by tasks performed by specific work groups. The smallest division, which performed legal services associated with land acquisition and other problems of service station development, was composed of a lawyer and two secretaries.

Intraorganizational variations in complexity can also be seen in manufacturing firms with research and development departments. These departments are likely to be characterized by a hierarchy shallower than that of other divisions of the organization. While there may be several levels above them, the research and development workers will be rather loosely supervised, with a wide span of control. In manufacturing departments, the span of control for each supervisor is shorter and the whole unit will look more like a pyramid. (See Figure 3–2.)

These examples indicate the obvious—complexity is not a simple issue. The concept contains several components, which do not necessarily vary together. At the same time, the concept itself conveys a meaning in organizational

FIGURE 3–1   Regional Office Organization

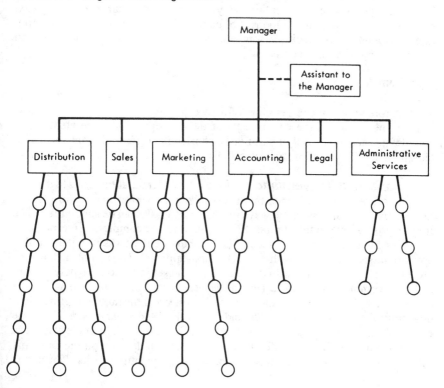

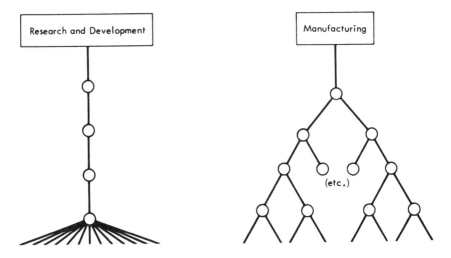

FIGURE 3–2   The Shape of Two Departments in the Same Organization

literature: complex organizations contain many subparts requiring coordination and control, and the more complex an organization is, the more serious these issues become. Since organizations vary widely in their degree of complexity, regardless of the specific component of complexity used, and since wide variations are found within specific organizations, the issue is important for the overall understanding of organizations.

Complexity as a Variable

Before we can make sense out of the various research studies on complexity, we must examine the components of the concept. The three elements of complexity most commonly identified are horizontal differentiation; vertical or hierarchical differentiation; and spatial dispersion.

Horizontal Differentiation   Horizontal differentiation refers to the subdivision of the tasks performed by the organization. Unfortunately for conceptual clarity, there are two basic ways in which such tasks can be subdivided. The first way is to give highly trained specialists a rather comprehensive range of activities to perform, and the second is to subdivide the tasks minutely so that nonspecialists can perform them. The first approach is exemplified by the professionals or craftpersons in the organizational setting who are solely responsible for complete operations. (For a discussion of craft-organized work, see Stinchcombe, 1959; for a comprehensive discussion of the nature of professionally controlled work, see Ritzer and Walczak, 1986.) They are given the responsibility and the authority to carry out the task to its completion. The second form of horizontal differentiation is most plainly seen on the assembly line, where each worker performs only one or a few repetitive tasks. The nature of the task itself is important here, since it is the routine and uniform task that is most amenable to the second type of differentiation; nonroutine and quite varied tasks are more commonly subdivided according to the first type.

Several writers have developed specific definitions for these forms of horizontal complexity. Hage (1965), in his "axiomatic" theory, defines complexity as the "specialization in an organization...measured by the number of occupational specialties and the length of training required by each. The greater the number of occupations and the longer the period of training required, the more complex the organization" (p. 294). Hage's assumption is that the more training people have, the more they are differentiated from other people who might have similar amounts of training but in different specialities. This definition is almost identical in its implications to that of Price (1968), who states: "Complexity may be defined as the degree of knowledge required to produce the output of a system. The degree of complexity of an organization can be measured by the degree of education of its members. The higher the education, the higher the complexity" (p. 26).

In some later research, Hage and Aiken (1967a) develop this approach further:

> We interpret complexity to mean at least three things: the number of occupational specialities, the professional activity, and the professional training. Organizations vary in the number of occupational specialties that they utilize in achieving their goals. This variable was measured by asking respondents to report their major duties; each respondent was then classified according to the type of occupational specialty, e.g., psychiatrist, rehabilitation, counselor, teacher, nurse, social worker, and so on. The variable, degree of professional activity, reflects the number of professional associations in which the respondents were involved, the number of meetings attended, and the number of offices held or number of papers given at professional meetings. The amount of professional training was based on the amount of college training as well as other professional training. (pp. 79–80)

Hage and Aiken's research was carried out in health and welfare organizations, where the emphasis on professional backgrounds was very appropriate. While this emphasis is not universally applicable in all types of organizations, the point regarding extent of training and depth of experience would hold across organizations.

This form of horizontal differentiation introduces additional complications for the organization, in that a high level of specialization requires coordination of the specialists. In many cases, personnel specifically designated as coordinating personnel have to be assigned to ensure that the various efforts do not work at cross-purposes and that the overall organizational tasks are accomplished.

A different approach to horizontal differentiation can be seen in the work of Blau and Schoenherr (1971). Their definition is the "number of different positions and different subunits in the organization," and their emphasis is on the formal structure as defined by the organization (p. 16). An organization is more complex if it has more such positions and subunits. Organizations spread out horizontally as work is subdivided for task accomplishment. This definition is similar to the indicators of complexity used by Hall, Haas, and Johnson (1967).

They used the number of divisions within an organization and the number of specialities within the divisions as complexity indicators. Pugh, Hickson, Hinings, and Turner (1968) approach the issue in a closely related way, although they use the term "specialization" in their discussion of this phenomenon. They also introduce the concept of "configuration" as an overall indicator of the "shape" of the organization. This latter concept contains the vertical as well as the horizontal factor of work subdivision by task.

These two approaches to horizontal differentiation appear to have very similar roots, since both are concerned with the division of labor within the organization. The critical difference between these forms of horizontal differentiation appears to be the scope of the ultimate tasks of organization (Dewar and Hage, 1978). Organizations that attempt to carry out a wide variety of activities and that have clients or customers who require a variety of services would divide the labor into work performed by specialists. The more minute division of labor would occur when the organization's tasks are not so diffuse and when the organization has grown in size, since such a division of labor provides an economy of scale. These two forms of complexity are not alternative ways to organize for the same task.

Vertical Differentiation   Vertical or hierarchical differentiation is a less complicated matter than is horizontal differentiation. Research into this vertical dimension has used straightforward indicators of the depth of the hierarchy. Meyer (1968a) uses the "proliferation of supervisory levels" as his measure of the depth of an organization. Pugh, Hickson, Hinings, and Turner (1968) suggest that the vertical dimension can be measured by a "count of the number of job positions between the chief executive and the employees working on the output" (p. 78). Hall, Haas, and Johnson (1967) used the "number of levels in the deepest single division" and the "mean number of levels for the organization as a whole" (total number of levels in all divisions/number of divisions) as their indicators (p. 906).

These direct indicators of vertical differentiation involve an important assumption that should be made explicit: authority is distributed in accordance with the level in the hierarchy; that is, the higher the level, the greater the authority. Although in the vast majority of cases this would be a valid assumption, there are situations in which proliferation of levels can represent phenomena other than the distribution of authority. For example, in organizations that utilize professional personnel, arrangements may not have been made to allow advancement within the same job title. Physicists may be hired as physicists, but if the organization's policies do not allow much of a salary range for that job title, some physicists may be "promoted" to a higher position without an actual change in their work or increase in authority—this is known as the "dual ladder."

Both horizontal and vertical differentiation present organizations with problems of control, communication, and coordination. Subunits along either axis (this would include both aspects of horizontal differentiation) are nuclei that are differentiated from adjacent units and the total organization according to horizontal or vertical factors. The greater the differentiation, the greater the potentiality for difficulties in control, coordination, and communications.

Spatial Dispersion   The final element in complexity— spatial dispersion—can actually be a form of horizontal or vertical differentiation. That is, activities and personnel can be dispersed in space, according to either horizontal or vertical functions, by the separation of power centers or tasks. An example of the former case are field offices of sales or welfare organizations, in which the tasks performed by the various field offices are essentially identical (low complexity on the horizontal axis) and the power in the organization is differentiated between the central office and the field offices. An example of the latter case are local plants of a manufacturing concern, each of which is specialized by product and technology.

Spatial dispersion becomes a separate element in the complexity concept when it is realized that an organization can perform the same functions with the same division of labor and hierarchical arrangements in multiple locations. A business firm, for example, can have a complex set of sales procedures requiring highly specialized sales personnel in the field. These sales personnel can be dispersed from a central office or through regional or state or local offices, with essentially the same hierarchical arrangements. Complexity is thus increased with the development of spatially dispersed activities, even if the horizontal and vertical differentiation remains the same across the spatially separated units.

The spatial-dispersion concept is relatively simple to operationalize. In a study of labor union locals, Raphael (1967) notes:

> The spatial dispersion of members refers to the number of spatially separated places in which the members of a local union are employed. This...is a continuous quantitative variable. At one extreme of the continuum, organizations have memberships concentrated in one-plant settings. At the opposite end of the continuum, the members are so extremely dispersed spatially that they even rotate continuously among numerous shops, jobs, and employers within a geographical space of at least several square miles. (p. 770)

Hall, Haas, and Johnson (1967) used the following indicators in their study: (1) the degree to which physical facilities are spatially dispersed, (2) the location (distance from the organizational headquarters) of the spatially dispersed facilities, (3) the degree to which personnel are spatially dispersed, and (4) the location of spatially dispersed personnel (p. 906). These indicators are highly correlated.

Variance of Complexity Elements

The discussion thus far has suggested that the three major elements of complexity vary, often independently of each other. Before further discussing such independent variance, it should be stressed that these elements can obviously vary together. Organizations with little horizontal, vertical, or spatial complexity can easily be identified—the small business firm with a single product or service and a single location comes most readily to mind. The same phenomenon can occur, however, in large organizations. Crozier's (1964) analysis of two separate government organizations in France graphically demonstrates this. This first organization, a clerical agency, was characterized by a very simple division of labor: while tasks were highly routine and repetitious, there was little differentiation among them. Also, considering the size of the organization, there was a very shallow hierarchy. The organization was not complex on the horizontal and vertical axes.

The third axis of spatial dispersion is added when the French tobacco company (the "industrial monopoly") in Crozier's analysis is considered. Thirty spatially dispersed plants comprise the system. The plants are fairly large, with 350 to 400 employees, on the average, but there are only six categories of workers in each plant. Production workers, who are paid equal wages throughout the system, comprise the bulk of the labor force, and there is little differentiation among their tasks. Maintenance workers are more specialized, with electricians, boilermakers, and metal workers in this group. The third group is the shop foremen, who hold supervisory positions in both plant and white-collar office operations. Even here, the tasks performed are quite similar. Administrative jobs, such as personnel, purchasing, or accounting, are few in number and minimally professionalized. There is one technical engineer per plant. The top position is that of the plant director, who usually has an assistant.

This relatively large dispersed organization is structurally very simple. The simplicity does not mean that it does not face severe problems—Crozier documents these in great detail—but that the problems are based on external and internal conditions that are not related to its structure. The imposition of civil service personnel regulations, the power of the maintenance personnel—who can actually control the output of the plants by the speed at which they maintain the equipment—and certain characteristics of the French society combine to make these organizations much less efficient and effective than they might be. It seems clear that increased complexity on the vertical and horizontal axes would do little to improve the performance of these plants. These noncomplex organizations are massive systems designed to perform simple and unchanging tasks. It can be hypothesized that if the tasks and technology were altered to develop a more effective system, the organizations would become more complex.

In direct contrast to the simple organizations just described, the diversified industrial or government organization serves as an example of the organization that is complex on all three axes. Huge industrial concerns, such as Standard Oil of New Jersey or Du Pont, are characterized by extreme complexity. The same would be true for operations of national, state, and some local governments, as well as such diverse organizations as the Roman Catholic Church, the New York City school system, and the University of California.

These extreme cases serve as a reminder that organizations can be highly or minimally complex in all facets of complexity. Other commonsense examples suggest that such is not the necessary pattern. A college, for example, usually has a low degree of vertical differentiation and usually no spatial dispersion, but a high degree of horizontal differentiation. Most manufacturing plants would have a greater division of labor along the horizontal axis than those studied by Crozier, although the hierarchical levels may be the same. The offensive unit of a football team is highly specialized but essentially has only two ranks. High vertical differentiation with little horizontal differentiation is exemplified by the army battalion.

An assumption throughout this discussion is that most organizations are complex in one of the various configurations discussed. Another assumption, verifiable from a variety of forms of evidence, is that *there is a strong tendency for organizations to become more complex as their own activities and the environment around them become more complex.* Organizations that survive tend to grow in size and size and complexity are related. Increased complexity leads to greater problems of coordination and control, and we now turn to this outcome of complexity for organizations.

Coordination and Control

In their landmark study, *Organization and Environment,* Lawrence and Lorsch (1967) examined the sources and consequences of complexity (they used the term "differentiation" for complexity). Lawrence and Lorsch note that structural differentiation includes differences in attitude and behavior on the part of members of the differentiated departments. These include orientations toward the particular goals of the department, differing emphases on interpersonal skills, varied time perspectives, and the type and extent of formalization of the structure. Departments, therefore, vary not only in the specific tasks they perform, but also in the underlying behavior and outlooks of their members.

The data for the analysis of differentiation come from firms in three industries in the United States. The first set of industries was comprised of firms making and selling plastics in the form of powder, pellets, and sheets.

> Their products went to industrial customers of all sizes, from the large automobile, appliance, furniture, paint, textile, and paper companies to the smaller firms making toys, containers, and household items. The organizations studied emphasized specialty plastics tailored to specific uses rather than standardized commodity plastics. They all built their product-development work on the science of polymer chemistry. Production was continuous, with relatively few workers needed to monitor the automatic and semiautomatic processing equipment. (p. 24)

These organizations were in a highly competitive market situation. According to the executives interviewed, the major competitive issue was the development of new and revised products and processes. The life cycle of any product was likely to be short, since competitors were all engaged in intensive research and could make even a very successful product quickly obsolete. The executives noted that "the most hazardous aspect of the industrial environment revolved around the relevant scientific knowledge" (p. 25). These organizations were in a changing and "turbulent" environment, with both input—in the form of scientific knowledge—and the consumption of output—in the form of customer satisfaction from purchasing the product—highly uncertain. On the other hand, the production process itself was characterized by its certainty. Once the original technical specifications for a particular product were developed, the production process could proceed quite automatically, since the mix between such production variables as pressure, temperature, and chemical composition could be easily measured, and monitoring was a part of the production process itself.

The six organizations studied within the plastics industry each had four basic functional departments—sales, production, applied research, and fundamental research—that differed in their own structures. The production departments were the most formalized, the fundamental research units the least. Sales department personnel were the most concerned with interpersonal relationships, and production departments were the least, with the two research units falling in between. The interesting dimension of the time perspective taken by the personnel shows the departments falling into a predictable pattern—from shortest to longest time perspective, with sales, production, applied research, and fundamental research fitting the time perspective framework in that order. The members of the various departments were also differentiated in terms of personal goals, with sale personnel concerned with customer problems and the marketplace; production personnel with cost reduction and efficiency; and research personnel concerned with scientific matters, as well as the more immediate practical issues of process improvement and modification. The scientific personnel were not as concerned with purely scientific matters as the authors had anticipated, but they did have clearly different goals from those of the members of other departments.

These differences in task, behavior, and attitude are directly related to the kind of environment that various departments must work with in their short- and long-run activities. *A high degree of differentiation (complexity) is therefore related to a highly complex and differentiated environment* (Burns and Stalker, 1961). In this case the complexity refers to the competitive situation in which the organizations find themselves (this degree of competition is not limited to profit-making organizations) and to the rapidly changing and complicated technological world in which they must survive.

To provide contrasts for the plastics firms, Lawrence and Lorsch studied two other industries; the major factor in their selection was the rate of environmental change. The second industry chosen was the standardized container industry. The rate of sales increase in this industry was at about the level of the rate of population growth and the growth of the gross national product, so the organizations in the industry were approximately keeping even with the environment in these respects. More important for the purposes of their study, no significant new products had been introduced in two decades. The major competitive factors were "operational issues of maintaining customer service through prompt delivery and consistent product quality while minimizing operating costs" (p. 86). While these are not easy or simple tasks to perform, they are stable, and the problems and prospects for the future are much more certain than in the plastics field.

The third set of organizations studied was in the packaged foods industry. In terms of environmental conditions, these organizations were intermediate between the plastics and container firms. While they engaged heavily in innovations, the rate of new-product introduction and the growth of sales were less than in the plastics industry, but more than in the container field.

When the differentiation within the organizations in these three industries was examined, the findings were as predicted—the plastics firms were the most differentiated, followed by the food firms, and then by the container firms. Lawrence and Lorsch did not stop their analysis with differentiation, however.

They extended their analysis around the concept of *integration*, which they define as "The quality of the state of collaboration that exists among departments that are required to achieve unity of effort by the demands of the environment" (p. 47). The authors were also concerned with the *effectiveness* of the organizations. Here they used rather standard and appropriate market and economic measures, such as profit. Organizations are more effective when they meet environmental pressures and when they allow their members to achieve their individual goals.

The results of the analysis of integration and effectiveness are in some ways surprising. In the plastics industry, the most effective organizations were those with the greatest degree of differentiation, and these also faced the most severe integration problems. Their effectiveness in the face of high differentiation was explained by their successful conflict resolution. It is not the idea of successful conflict resolution that is surprising; it is the fact that the effective organizations were characterized by a high degree of conflict in the first place—that they were not totally harmonious, with all personnel working as members of one happy team. From the data discussed earlier, it is apparent that the differentiation in terms of departmental and individual attitudes and behavior would lead inevitably to conflict. In these organizations, such conflict contributes to effectiveness.

Conflict per se, of course, would be detrimental to the organization if it were not resolved. So another important contribution of this research is its analysis of conflict resolution. The authors do not suggest that there is one best form of such resolution. Rather, they provide evidence that conflict-resolution processes vary according to the specific conflict situations in a particular form of organization. In the case of the highly differentiated plastics organizations, integration is achieved by departments or individuals who are in a position, and have the knowledge available, to work with the departments involved in conflict situations. In this case, the position is relatively low in the managerial hierarchy rather than at the top. This lower position is necessary because of the specific knowledge required to deal with the departments and issues involved. The highly differentiated and effective organization thus anticipates conflict and establishes integrating (conflict-resolving) departments and individuals whose primary purpose is to work with the departments in (inherent) conflict. Another important consideration is that the integrating departments or individuals are equidistant between the conflicting departments in terms of their time, goal, interpersonal, and structural orientations. This middle position leads to effective resolution, not through simple compromise, but rather through direct confrontations between the conflicting parties. Conflict resolution in this setting thus becomes a process whereby the parties thrash out their differences in the open with the assistance of integrators who understand both their positions.

In the container corporations, with their lesser degree of differentiation, conflicts also arose, but not to the extent found in the plastics firms, owing to less differentiation. In the container industry, conflicts were resolved at the top of the organization, because those at the top had greater knowledge, made possible by the stable environment and the lack of differentiation between organizational segments. With less differentiation, knowledge was not as specialized, and a top executive could have a good grasp of what was going on in the major divisions. Lawrence and Lorsch suggest that in this case, and in others like it, decentralization of influence would be harmful. The food-processing firms generally fell between the plastics and the container firms in the extent of their differentiation and in the integration problems faced.

A major conclusion from this analysis is that *effectiveness is not achieved by following one organizational model.* While our concern at this point is with neither effectiveness nor organizational models, this conclusion is vitally important for understanding organizations. In other words, *there is no one best way to organize for the purpose of achieving the highly varied goals of organizations within highly varied environments.* This is a *contingency* approach to organizational structure, which says that under some conditions, one form of structure is more effective or efficient, while under other conditions, alternative forms would be more effective or efficient. The contingency model remains a dominant force in organizational theory.

Argote's (1982) research in a very different setting—hospital emergency units—reached a very similar sort of conclusion. She found that in situations of low uncertainty, programmed coordination contributed to greater effectiveness, while in situations of high uncertainty, nonprogrammed modes of coordination were more effective. The structural arrangements are contingent upon the situation being faced.

This conclusion is further strengthened from a consideration of Blau and Schoenherr's (1971) findings, which were based on research into government finance and public personnel agencies. They also find that increased complexity engenders problems of communication and coordination. Personnel in the managerial hierarchy spend more time in dealing with these problems than in direct supervision in a highly complex organization. There is also pressure in complex organizations to add personnel to handle the increased control and coordination activities, increasing the proportion of the total personnel devoted to such activities. This is known as administrative intensity.

This last finding introduces an interesting paradox into the analysis of organizations. While large organizations can experience savings through economies of large size, the complexity that is related to large size creates cross-pressures to add managerial personnel for control, coordination, and conflict reduction. Decisions physically to disperse, add divisions, or add hierarchical levels may be made in the interests of economy. At the same time, the economies realized may be counterbalanced by the added burdens of keeping the organization together. There is yet another paradox which McKinley (1987) identifies. While there is a positive relationship between technical and structural complexity and administrative intensity when an organization is growing, the relationship weakens when organizations are in a period of decline.

Complex organizations are thus complex in more ways than just their structure. The processes within such organizations are also complex. The techniques that are effective and efficient within a simple structure just may not be effective or efficient in a more complex case.

Some Additional Correlates of Complexity

Complexity is related to additional characteristics of organizations. Hage and Aiken's (1967b) analysis of program change in the 16 welfare organizations they studied illustrates this point well. Program change in these agencies involves the adoption of new services and techniques—implicitly to increase the quality of the services rendered. When this study was being conducted, a great number of new social programs were being introduced.

Hage and Aiken found that both vertical and horizontal differentiation are related to higher rates of program change. This finding suggests that when such forms of differentiation are present, much information will be flowing in the system—information that will contain conflicting ideas and proposals. Organizations that are complex in this way face the problem of integrating the diverse occupations and ideas deriving from the different organizational members. Later studies confirm that such conflict is present and must be dealt with by the organization. The proper method of handling such conflict is not by suppression; we have already seen that this would represent the exact opposite of the effective utilization of highly trained personnel. We will see later that such conflicts actually work to the organization's advantage.

Hage and Aiken's work on program change implies that organizational change is related to organizational characteristics. This implication is supported in later research by Baldridge and Burnham (1975). Their research compared the effects of structural characteristics (such as size and complexity), together with environmental conditions (changing or heterogeneous), with individual characteristics (age, attitudes, and education) in terms of their impact on organizational innovation. They found that the organizational characteristics were more strongly related to innovation in organizations. This does not negate the role of the individual, but suggests that factors such as complexity are crucial in understanding how and why processes such as innovation occur.

Aiken and Hage (1968) continued their investigation of these 16 agencies three years later, following up some of the leads from the previous research. The dependent variable in this study was organizational interdependence, as indicated by the number of joint programs in which the agencies participate. The findings from this analysis are not surprising in light of the earlier findings and discussion. *"Organizations with many joint programs are more complex organizations, that is they are more highly professionalized and have more diverse occupational structure"* (p. 920). The interpretation given to these findings is that a decision to engage in joint programs leads to the importation of new specialties into the organization, since joint programs are likely to be highly specialized and the personnel in the agency would not have the skills necessary for participation.

These findings have interesting implications for organizations and for the society of which they are a part. Aiken and Hage note that there is a tendency for organizations to become more complex because of internal and external pressures. The implication of these findings is that joint programs and other interorganizational relationships will continue to develop, probably at an increasing rate. In the long run this would lead to a society in which the web of interrelationships between organizations would become extremely intricate and the total society more organizationally "dense." This, in turn, implies a condition in which both individuals and the society as a whole are dependent upon fewer and more complex organizations. The nature of these organizations and their orientation toward the good of the few or of the many present the society with the dilemma of the source of control of the organizations. If this trend is realized, decisions regarding organizational futures become decisions about society.

The short-run implications of these findings would seem to be that the more complex an organization is, the more complex it will become, since the development of new programs and interorganizational relationships both lead to additional complexity. The Aiken–Hage approach to complexity has been organized around the utilization of professionals to accomplish and advance the tasks of the organizations studied. Since not all organizational members are professionalized, and since horizontal differentiation involves more than this variable, our focus will now shift to alternative modes of differentiation and their relationships with other variables.

There is another important interplay between organizational complexity and social issues. Organizations provide the *internal labor markets* by which people are distributed in the social stratification or attainment systems. Promotion and salary ladders, distributions of personnel by gender or race, clusters of skills, and the general structure of opportunities are all determined by organizations, and all have a major influence on society (Baron et al., 1986, 1988; Bills, 1987; Pfeffer and Davis-Blake, 1987; Stewman, 1986).

In an analysis of a very different situation, Vaughan (1983) concludes that corporate *crimes* are related to complexity. In her formulation, organizations may become so diversified and complex that top management may not be able to control subunits. The same argument is frequently made in regard to intercollegiate athletics and the illegal recruitment and other problems with college athletes.

In yet another direction, complexity has been found to be related to the chances of an individual's being laid off by an employer. Cornfield (1983) analyzed the layoff process in a single business firm. He found that the position of an employee in the division of labor, along with external market conditions and technological developments, influenced job elimination. Direct production workers are most likely to be laid off. Cornfield concludes that structure is independent of seniority, race, and education in determining who is and who is not to be laid off.

Complexity is a basic structural characteristic. It is linked to the fate of the organization and the fates of individuals within organizations. There appears to be strong evidence that particular degrees of vertical, horizontal, or spatial complexity are related to organizational survival and continuity in particular situations. If an organization chooses an inappropriate form or is unable, for whatever reason—economic, personnel, tradition, leadership—to adopt its structure to changed situations, it will likely soon be in trouble.

FORMALIZATION

We have already alluded to formalization several times. In this section the exact nature of this important aspect of organizational structure will be explicitly defined. The antecedents and outcomes of formalization will also be spelled out. In addition, the reactions of individuals to the degree of formalization will be analyzed. In many ways, formalization is the key structural variable for the individual because a person's behavior is vitally affected by the degree of such formalization. The amount of individual discretion is inversely related to the amount of preprogramming of behavior by the organization.

Formalization is not a neutral concept. Indeed, the degree to which an organization is formalized is an indication of the perspectives of its decision makers in regard to organizational members. If the members are thought to be capable of exercising excellent judgment and self-control, formalization will be low; if they are viewed as incapable of making their own decisions and requiring a large number of rules to guide their behavior, formalization will be high. Formalization involves organizational control over the individual (Clegg and Dunkerley, 1980) and thus has an ethical and political meaning in addition to being a structural component.

The introduction of the individual does not mean a shift away from the organizational level of analysis. Formalization has important consequences for the organization and its subunits in terms of such processes as communications and innovation.

The rules and procedures designed to handle contingencies faced by the organization are part of what is called formalization. The extent of rules and procedures varies. The simple matter of what time a person gets to work can differ widely among and within organizations in regard to the degree to which this act is formally specified. At the high end of the formalization continuum are organizations that specify that people must be at their desk or workstation at 8 A.M. or they will be "docked" a half-hour's pay. At the other end of the continuum are situations in which there are no rules about being in the office or shop at the particular time, just as long as the work gets done. This is typified by many academic institutions.

Maximal Formalization   Rules, therefore, can vary from highly stringent to extremely lax. These variations exist on the whole range of behaviors covered by organizational rules. The same kinds of variations exist in terms of *procedures.* Simple examples of highly formalized procedures are an assembly line, where a piece of material is always passed in the same direction, with the same work being performed on it, or, an office setting, where letters requesting a certain type of information are always processed in the same way, with the same type of information returned to the requester. The extreme examples of this, of course, are the computer-prepared responses to inquiries about such things as under-or overpayments of credit-card bills. This is one example of a highly formalized procedure in which the organization has been able to preprogram its responses to a wide variety of contingencies. Much of the frustration that people feel when they receive a computer printout rather than a personal letter is due to their feeling that their request was apparently just like everyone else's—that they are not unusual cases and therefore can be treated in a highly formalized way. The real frustration comes, of course, when it is in fact an unusual case and the computer procedures are inappropriate to the request. Despite the personal exasperation that this can develop, the fact remains that a large proportion of the communications that come into an organization can be handled by such formalized procedures.

Minimal Formalization   At the other end of the formalization-of-procedures continuum would be cases that are unique and for which no procedures have been developed. In these cases, members of the organization must use their own discretion in deciding what to do. At the extreme would come the cases that Perrow (1967) has said call for intuition, and even perhaps inspiration, in solving—unique situations with no preprogrammed answers. Nonformalized organizations are those that deal constantly with new situations for which precedents do not exist—such as, for example, organizations engaging in frontier areas of scientific research of which the forthcoming results are not known. Organizations dealing with human problems, such a mental health clinics, would be in a similar situation. Lipsky (1982) has noted that teachers, social workers, police officers, judges, lawyers, and prison guards have a great deal of working discretion as they carry out their work in "street level bureaucracies." While much of this work cannot be programmed or formalized in advance, much of it is also routinized.

Measures of Formalization   At this point it should be noted that it usually doesn't matter whether the procedures or rules are formalized in writing. Unwritten norms and standards can frequently be just as binding as written ones. Nevertheless, most research utilizes the written system as the basis for assessment and analysis.

Hage (1965) makes essentially the same point when he states:

> Organizations learn from past experiences and employ rules as a repository of that experience. Some organizations carefully codify each job, describing the specific details, and then ensure conformity to the job prescription. Other organizations have loosely defined jobs and do not carefully control work behavior. Formalization, or standardization, is measured by the proportion of codified jobs and the range of variation that is tolerated within the rules defining the jobs. The higher the proportion of codified jobs and the less the range of variation allowed, the more formalized the organization. (p. 295)

In their later research, Hage and Aiken (1967a) follow essentially the same definition of formalization:

> Formalization represents the use of rules in an organization. Job codification is a measure of how many rules define what the occupants of positions are to do, while rule observation is a measure of whether or not the rules are employed. In other words, the variable of job codification represents the degree to which the job descriptions are specified, and the variable, rule observation, refers to the degree to which job occupants are supervised in conforming to the standards established by job codification. Job codification represents the degree of work standardization while rule observation is a measure of the latitude of behavior that is tolerated from standards. (p. 79)

These variables are operationalized by asking the members of organizations to respond to a series of questions bearing directly on these issues. Measures of their perceptions of their own organization are thus used to determine the extent to which the organizations are formalized.

A similar definition perspective is found in the work of Pugh, Hickson, Hinings, and Turner (1968). They define formalization as "the extent to which rules, procedures, instructions, and communications are written" (p. 75). They also include "standardization" (the extent to which "there are rules or definitions that purport to cover all circumstances and that apply invariable") as one of their basic dimensions of organizational structure (p. 74). These variables are operationalized by using official records and documents from the organization to determine such matters as the number of procedures of various kinds and the proportion of employees who have handbooks describing their tasks. An analysis of the data from the English firms studied reveals that standardization and formalization combine with specialization when the component scales are factor analyzed. The authors call this the "structuring of activities" (p. 84). They note that this brings the issue of role specificity to the forefront as an important organizational consideration. In highly formalized, standardized, and specialized situations, the behavior of role occupants is highly specified, leaving them few options that they can exercise in carrying out their jobs.

The similarities between these definitions point up the general consensus about the meaning of formalization. Even when quite different measures of this variable are used in research, the same meaning is utilized, an all too rare occurrence in organizational analysis. Unfortunately, research (Pennings, 1973; Dewar, Whetten, and Boje, 1980) has indicated that these different measures are themselves only weakly related. Thus while there is conceptual closure in regard to formalization, measurement problems are yet to be fully resolved.

Formalization and Other Organizational Properties

Centralization of Power   Power is an important component of all organizations. In fact, Gilb (1981) sees organizational structure itself as a form of private government. The distribution of power in organizations is usually conceptualized as the degree of centralization, which is the topic of the next major section of this chapter. Here we consider the relationships between formalization and centralization.

In their study of social welfare agencies, Hage and Aiken (1967a) found that formalization was rather weakly associated with a centralized decision-making system. Organizations in which the decisions were made by only a few people at the top relied on rules and close supervision as a means of ensuring consistent performance by the workers. These organizations were also characterized by a less professionalized staff. Thus, the presence of a well-trained staff is related to a reduced need for extensive rules and policies.

This interpretation is supported in Blau's (1970) analysis of public personnel agencies. In organizations with highly formalized personnel procedures and rigid conformity to these procedures, Blau found a decentralization of authority. At first glance this is contradictory, since the evidence seems to say that formalization and decentralization are related. A closer examination reveals strong compatibility with the Hage and Aiken findings. In this case, adherence to merit-based personnel procedures ensures the presence of highly qualified personnel at the local (decentralized) level. These people are then entrusted with more power than are personnel with fewer qualifications. Formalization in one area of operations is thus associated with flexibility in another.

On this point Blau states:

> Rigidity in some respects may breed flexibility in others. Not all aspects of bureaucratization are concomitant. The bureaucratic elaboration of formalized personnel procedures and rigid conformity with these personnel standards do not necessarily occur together, and neither aspect of bureaucratization of procedures gives rise to a more rigid authority structure, at least not in employment security agencies. Indeed, both strict conformity with civil service standards and the elaboration of these formalized standards have the opposite effect of fostering decentralization, which permits greater flexibility. (p. 160)

This rather simple set of findings reinforces a notion expressed earlier—complex organizations are complex. Formalization in one area brings pressures to bear to decrease formalization in another area. Organizations are thus constantly in conflict, not only between individuals or subunits, but also between and within the processes and structures that make up the organization. Formalization is not just a matter of internal adjustment.

It is important to note that the research of Hage and Aiken and of Blau deals with relatively professionalized work forces. One of the hallmarks of professionalization is the ability and willingness to make decisions based upon professional training and experience. It is not surprising to find lower levels of formalization in such situations. When the work force under consideration does not or is assumed not to have this decision-making capacity, the implications of the Blau findings have to be reexamined. In that case, formalized personnel procedures would probably be associated with a more centralized decision-making system, with the formalization level probably more consistent in all phases of the operation. It must be noted that the organization retains control over the individual in both cases. By selecting highly qualified or indoctrinated individuals, it assures itself that the individuals will act according to organizational demands (Blau and Schoenherr, 1971, pp. 347–67).

Program Change   Further research by Hage and Aiken (1967b) into the rate of program change in the agencies reveals that formalization is also related to the number of new programs added in the organizations. In this case, formalization is negatively associated with the adoption of new programs. The reduction of individual initiative in the more formalized setting is suggested as the major reason for this relationship. In organizations that establish highly specific routines for the members to follow, there is likely to be little time, support, or reward for involvement in new ideas and new programs.

Technology   In their continuing research in these 16 agencies, Hage and Aiken follow the suggestions of Perrow (1967) and Litwak (1961) in regard to the nature of the technology which the organizations used on their clients (we will consider technology in greater detail in the next chapter. They divide the organizations into "routine" and "nonroutine" categories of technology. Even though these are all social agencies, there is a marked difference in the degree of routineness.

> The highest on routineness is a family agency in which the case-workers use a standard client interview that takes less than fifteen minutes. The purpose of the interview is to ascertain the eligibility of clients for county, federal, or state medical aid. An interviewee said: "...somewhat routine—even though each patient is individual, the type of thing you do with them is the same...." The organization at the other extreme is an elite psychiatric family agency in which each member is an experienced therapist and allowed to work with no supervision at all. (Hage and Aiken, 1969, p. 369)

The relationship between routinization and formalization is in the expected direction. *"Organizations with routine work are more likely to have greater formalization of organizational roles"* (Hage and Aiken, 1969, p. 371; italics in original). Since these organizations tend to be on the nonroutine end of an overall continuum of routineness, the findings are even more striking: had organizations more toward the routine end of the continuum been included, the differences observed would probably have been greater.

Hage and Aiken's research, one of the most thorough and systematic programs of research available in the literature, is based on data from a limited number of organizations of relatively similar characteristics. The limitations inherent in using this type of data base are difficult to avoid, given the intrinsic difficulties in organizational research. But despite these limitations, their findings are generally consistent with those of Pugh's research team, known as the Aston Group, which proceeded independently and with very different measures.

It will be remembered that the Pugh research was carried out on a sample of English work organizations. These researchers were interested in obtaining indicators of the organizations and the contexts in which they operated. Their major indicator of technology was work flow integration.

> Among organizations scoring high, with very integrated, automated, and rather rigid technologies, were an automobile factory, a food manufacturer, and a swimming baths department. Among those scoring low, with diverse, nonautomated, flexible technologies, were retail stores, an education department, and a building firm. (Pugh, Hickson, Hinings, and Turner, 1969, p. 103)

While they contain more diversity than those in the Aiken and Hage study, these organizations are clustered toward the routine end of the routine-nonroutine continuum. As would be expected from the previous discussion, technology emerges as an important predictor of the degree to which activities are structured in these organizations.

Another study which examined the technology-formalization linkage found strong evidence in favor of the high routinization–high formalization conclusion. Dornbusch and Scott (1975) studied an electronics assembly line, a physics research team, a university faculty, a major teaching hospital, a football team, schools, a student newspaper, and a Roman Catholic archdiocese. Their evidence, from this diverse set of organizations, is consistent with the technological argument that has been presented.

Lest it appear that the relationship between technology and formalization is settled because of the weight of the evidence presented, it should be noted that Glisson (1978) essentially reverses the causal ordering. He finds that procedural specifications (formalization) determine the degree of routinization in service delivery. In the case of the Glisson study, a decision made in regard to how to structure the organization led to the utilization of a particular service delivery technology. While the high correlation between routinization and formalization remains, the reason for the correlation is reversed in this case.

Tradition   One additional component should be added to these considerations. Organizations emerge in different historical eras (Meyer and Brown, 1977), face varying contingencies, and develop different traditions. These differences, in turn, influence how factors such as technology affect the degree of formalization. For example, if for some reason—such as the belief system of an important early top executive—an organization became highly formalized in its codification of job descriptions in writing, it would probably continue to be more formalized over time than other factors would predict. Organizations develop characteristics that are embedded in the formal and informal systems of the organization. This point is well recognized by scholars who study organizational culture (see Frost et al., 1985).

By its very nature, formalization is central to the life of and in organizations. The specification of rules, procedures, penalties, and so on predetermines much of what goes on in an organization. Indeed, formalization is a major defining characteristic of organizations, since behavior is not random and is directed by some degree of formalization toward a goal.

We have examined the relationships between formalization and other organizational properties. The focus will now shift to the individual in the organization. Like formalization, individuals, too, must be treated as variables, since they bring different abilities and habits and other behaviors with them into the organization. Formalization is designed to be a control mechanism over individuals (Clegg and Dunkerley, 1980). People react to rules and procedures in a variety of ways (Goffman, 1959). They "move" within the structure of rules (Burrell and Morgan, 1979). Silverman (1971) proposed an "action" frame of reference for organizational analysis. This approach emphasizes the meanings that people attach to their work environment and the individual meanings and actions that derive from the interpretations that people attach to their organizational roles. (See also Benson, 1977.) The emphasis on the analysis here is not on individual roles, but rather on the relationships among social phenomena. This is not to downplay more individualistic approaches, but rather to maintain the emphasis on organizational phenomena.

Formalization and Outcomes for Individuals

An extreme example of formalization can be found in Crozier's (1964) analysis of the two French organizations. He notes: "Impersonal rules delimit, in great detail, all the functions of every individual within the organization. They prescribe the behavior to be followed in all possible events. Equally impersonal rules determine who shall be chosen for each job and the career patterns that can be followed" (pp. 187–88). This extremely high degree of formalization, plus several other characteristics of the organizations, create a "vicious circle" in which the workers follow the rules for the sake of the rules themselves, since this is the basis on which they are evaluated. The rules become more important than the goals they were designed to help accomplish. The organization becomes very rigid and has difficulties dealing with customers and other aspects of the environment. Since the rules prescribe the kinds of decisions to be made, those in decision-making positions tend to create more rules when situations arise for which there are no precedents. Rules become security for the employee. There is no drive for greater autonomy, since that would be threatening. There is a strong desire to build safeguards through increased rigidity. The personnel in such a system become increasingly unable to operate on their own initiative and, in fact, seek to reduce the amount of freedom to which they are subject. To one who values individual freedom, this is a tragedy. It would be presumptuous to say that it is such for the individuals involved, even though the argument could be made that the long-run consequences for them and for the total social system may indeed be tragic from several moral and ethical perspectives. For the organization, the consequences are clear: it becomes maladaptive to changes of any sort.

These personal and organizational dysfunctions were recognized in Robert Merton's (1957) seminal discussion of the "bureaucratic personality." Merton notes that a trained incapacity can develop in the kind of situation under discussion. Actions and decisions based on past training and experience may be very inappropriate under different conditions. Merton suggests that the process whereby these conditions develop is part of the system itself.

> The bureaucrat's official life is planned for him in terms of a graded career, through the organization devices of promotion by seniority, pensions, incremental salaries, etc., all of which are designed to provide incentives for disciplined action and conformity to the official regulations. The official is tacitly expected to and largely does adapt his thoughts, feelings, and actions to the prospect of this career. But *these very devices* which increase the probability of conformance also lead to an over-concern with strict adherence to regulations which induces timidity, conservatism, and technicism. Displacement of sentiments from goals onto means is fostered by the tremendous symbolic significance of the means (rules) {italics in original}. (pp. 200–01)

Organizations are primarily concerned with the work behavior of their members. They also can extend their control into the other areas of life. Quinn (1977) has demonstrated the manner in which organizations attempt to control romance in organizations. While not claiming that organizations are a hotbed of romance, Quinn documents the obvious point that it does occur. When such romances develop, actions are taken to terminate the relationship, since it is typically seen as disruptive for the organization. Punitive actions, such as dismissals, are one course of action, a course which is much more likely to happen to the women involved rather than the men. Less drastic measures, such as transfers, reprimands, or simple efforts to persuade people to stop the romance were also found. The point is that even in areas of intimacy, organizations attempt to control behavior.

Reactions to Formalization

The rather dismal view of life in a highly formalized organization is extended by Thompson's (1961) description of "bureaupathic" and "bureautic" behavior. Thompson suggests that the kinds of behavior discussed by Merton are caused by feelings of insecurity. Bureaupathic behavior "starts with a need on the part of the person in an authority position to control those subordinate to himself." Superordinates themselves, except at the very top of the organization, are subordinate to someone else, and so this control can tend to be the too rigid adherence to rules that has been discussed, since this protects the individual from making possibly erroneous decisions and actions on his own.

Thompson suggests that the pressures lead to a "drift" toward the introduction of more and more rules to protect the incumbents of offices, exaggerated aloofness, resistance to change, and an overinsistence on the rights of office. These reactions are organizationally and personally damaging.

The second form of behavior—bureautic—is also personally and organizationally dysfunctional. This type of reaction involves striking out at the system, personalizing every encounter, and taking every rule as one designed to lead to one's own personal frustration.

> The bureautic employee is not likely to get into the hierarchy, and so may come to be regarded as a failure. Because of his inability to enter intelligently into abstract, complex, cooperative relationships, he tends to be pushed to one side, unless he has some unusual skill that the organization badly needs. He is often regarded as "queer." All of these facts add to his bitterness and increase his suspiciousness. He projects his failure onto the organization and the impersonal "others" who are his enemies. He feels he is surrounded by stupidity and maliciousness. He feels powerless and alienated from the system. (p. 176)

While some would argue with the psychological mechanisms that Thompson uses in his development of these reactions to the organization, the reactions themselves do exist. The emphasis in the last few paragraphs has been on negative reactions to formalization. If we refocus our analysis, we can try to understand how and why there are both positive and negative reactions to formalization.

Some insights on this issue can be found in the literature on professionals in organizations. There has been a strong interest in this topic since increasing numbers of professionals of all sorts are working in organizations, and many occupations are attempting to professionalize. Analyses of the relationships between professionals and their employing organizations formerly proceeded from the premise that there are built-in strains between professional and organizational principles and values (see, for example, Kornhauser, 1963; Blau and Scott, 1962). More recent research has challenged these assumptions. It is now viewed as quite possible that there can be situations in which professionals are able to carry out their work with a minimum amount of interference from the organization, while the organization is able to integrate the work of the professionals for its own benefit.

This approach is followed in Miller's (1967) analysis of the degree of alienation experienced by scientists and engineers employed in a large corporation in the aerospace industry. These professionals reported that they felt more alienation when their supervisor used directive, rather than participative or laissez-faire, supervisory practices, and less alienation in situations in which they themselves had some control over the decisions affecting their work. The same general pattern was found in regard to other incentives that the organization provided professionals. There was less alienation when the scientists and engineers had some part in deciding the nature of their own research efforts, when the company provided opportunities and a climate for the pursuit of their own professional careers, and when the company encouraged purely professional activities, such as the publication of papers or pursuit of additional training.

Miller also found that the length of professional training was associated with the extent of alienation felt. The more training a people have, the more they are likely to feel alienation under those conditions that produce it for the group of professionals as a whole. That is, for a Ph.D. scientist, the absence of encouragement of professional activities is more likely to produce alienation than it is for an M.A. scientist. Some differences were also found between the scientists and engineers, but this is not of importance in the present discussion.

Utilizing the idea of intraorganizational variations in structure, Miller also examined the extent of alienation felt by the professionals when the specific work location was controlled. Some of the professionals worked in a basic-research and development laboratory in the company, but most were employed in research and development in one of the major production units. As might be expected, the personnel in the basic-research laboratory experienced much less alienation than did those in the production-oriented unit.

The organizational structure in which these professionals worked was related to their degree of alienation from work. Professionals were chosen to be examined because they bring to the organization a set of externally (professionally) derived standards by which they can guide their own behavior. The presence of organizational guidelines (formalization) is thus a duplication and probably perceived as less valid than are the norms of the profession involved. For professionals, therefore, the greater the degree of formalization in the organization, the greater the likelihood of alienation from work.

This point is supported further when two additional research reports are considered. Part of the research of Aiken and Hage (1966) has been concerned with the degree of alienation felt by the professionals in the 16 social welfare agencies they examined. They too, were concerned with alienation from work, but they also looked at alienation from expressive relations. This was measured by responses to questions asking the degree of satisfaction felt about superiors and coworkers. The less satisfaction felt, the more the individual is alienated from expressive relations.

As would be expected from the direction of this discussion, the greater the degree of job codification of the organization, the more alienated were the workers in both areas of alienation. Alienation was much more strongly felt in terms of the job itself. "This means that there is great dissatisfaction with work in those organizations in which jobs are rigidly structured; rigidity may lead to strong feelings of work dissatisfaction but does not appear to have such a deleterious impact on social relations in the organization (p. 504). Strict enforcement of rules was strongly related to both forms of alienation; social relations are also disturbed when rules are strictly enforced. It was also found that both forms of alienation were high when authority in the organizations was centralized and the members had little opportunity to participate in decision making. Hage (1980) later reports similar findings from a longitudinal continuation of the original study and from a study in Japan. This relationship is thus not culture bound.

A different approach was taken in my analysis of the relationships between professionalization and bureaucratization (Hall, 1968). Bureaucratization is a broader concept than formalization, but it contains many of the same implications, as indicated in earlier discussions of the topic. I attempted to demonstrate that professionalization, like formalization, is a continuous variable, with some occupations being more professionalized than others. The study included physicians, nurses, accountants, teachers, lawyers, social workers, stockbrokers, librarians, engineers, personnel managers, and advertising account executives. After the occupations were ranked according to their attitudes toward several professional values, the average scores for each occupation were matched with the scores on bureaucratization measures for the organizational units in which these people worked. The results indicated that, in general, bureaucratization is inversely related to professionalization. This is consistent with the argument in this section. Examined more closely, these findings reveal some interesting patterns. There is a relatively weak inverse relationship between the hierarchy dimension of bureaucracy and the professional attitudes. The presence of a relatively rigid hierarchy may not adversely affect the work of professionals if the hierarchy is recognized as legitimate. This is similar to the findings of Blau (1968), who suggests that the presence of a hierarchy may facilitate communications from the professionals to the top of the organization. If the hierarchy of authority is legitimate and does facilitate communications, it apparently does not matter whether or not decisions are made in a prestructured way—and particularly if the work of the professionals can be carried out without extensive interference from the organization.

A weak relationship was found on the bureaucratic dimension involving the presence of rules. The kinds of rules the organizations developed in these cases apparently did not interfere with the work of the professional. There was a stronger negative relationship on the procedural-specifications dimension. As more procedures are specified by the organization, the burden on the professionals apparently was stronger. In this case, the professionals are likely to want to utilize procedures that they themselves develop on the job or through their professional training.

I then tried to view the professional-organizational relationship from the perspectives of both the organization and the professional:

> increased bureaucratization threatens professional autonomy. It is in these relationships that a potential source of conflict between the professional and the organization can be found. The strong drive for autonomy on the part of a

professional may come into direct conflict with organizationally based j
ments. At the same time, the organization may be threatened by strong p
desires on the part of at least some of its members. (Hall, 1968, pp. 10

Most of the studies that have been discussed have concluded that professionalization and formalization are incompatible. The more professionalized the work
force, the more likely that formalization will lead to conflict and alienation. A
major implication of these findings is that formalization and professionalization
are actually designed to do the same thing—organize and regularize the behavior
of the members of the organization. Formalization is a process in which the
organization sets the rules and procedures and the means of ensuring that they
are followed. Professionalization, on the other hand, is a nonorganizationally
based means of doing the same thing. From the organization's point of view,
either technique would be appropriate, as long as the work gets done.

It is exactly at this point that the organization faces a major internal
dilemma. If it allows too little freedom for its members, the members are likely
to feel oppressed, alienated, and "bureaucratic" and to engage in rule following
for its own sake. If, on the other hand, it allows more freedom, behavior is apt
to become erratic and organizationally irrelevant. A basic factor here appears to
be the kind of guidelines for behavior that the individuals themselves bring to
the organization. The more work standards they bring with them, the less the
need for organizationally based standards.

It is difficult, of course, for the organization to know what kind of standards
people bring with them. Even the use of a relatively common criterion, such as
membership in a recognized profession, is not a perfect predictor, since not all
members of a profession act in accordance with its standards and not all professional standards are good for all organizations. And when the organization
moves into other personnel areas, away from the professions or established crafts,
the availability of such external criteria may disappear. Because even well-de-
veloped external criteria, such as professionalization, may at times be organizationally irrelevant, the organization has to develop its own system of rules and
procedures to accomplish what it is attempting to do.

Before moving to additional implications of formalization for the individual and the organization, we must draw another conclusion from the analysis of
professionals in organizations. The emphasis in much of the research in this area
is on conflict between the professional and his employing organization. Evidence
from the Hall research suggests that such conflict is not inevitable and should
not be assumed without demonstration. This research found, for example, that
the legal departments of large organizations are not necessarily more bureaucratized than law firms of comparable size. The lawyer working in the trust
department of a bank may actually be working in an organizational environment
similar, and perhaps even identical, to the one he or she would find in a law firm.
This suggests that it is very possible to find organizational structures that are
compatible with the degree of professionalization of their members.

The finding that legal or other professional departments in organizations
may not be more bureaucratized or formalized than autonomous law firms raises
another issue. The legal department of a bank is clearly less formalized than the
division in charge of handling, sorting, and verifying checks. As is true of

complexity, degrees of formalization vary within the organization. This can be most easily seen between departments, but it also occurs between levels in the organization. In general, the higher the level, the less the formalization (Hall, 1962; Child, 1973).

Zeitz's (1983, 1984) research provides an appropriate way to conclude this section. He found that formal structuring of activities had positive effects on organizational members' levels of satisfaction and perceived organizational climate. At the same time, role constraints and rule enforcement had negative effects. Well-delineated rules apparently provide a meaningful framework in which to work. Organ and Greene (1981) also found that formalization reduced ambiguity for a sample of scientists and engineers. In both the Zeitz and Organ and Greene studies, the interactions between levels of formalization and organizational members' expectations were the key to the ways in which individuals reacted to their organizations.

CENTRALIZATION

Centralization refers to the distribution of power within organizations. Centralization is thus one of the best ways to summarize the whole notion of structure. Ranson, Hinings, and Greenwood (1980) deal with structure as constituted and constitutive. In the case of centralization, a given distribution of power is constitutive in that it generates other actions—people comply with organizational rules and decisions. Centralization is also constituted in that power distributions are subject to change, as groups and individuals gain or lose power over time. Power itself will be considered in detail in a later chapter. Here we will consider the nature and correlates of the structural aspect of power in organizations.

Centralization has been defined in several ways, with the emphasis always on the distribution of power. Hage (1980) defines centralization as "the level and variety of participation in strategic decisions by groups relative to the number of groups in the organization" (p. 65). The greater the level of participation by a greater number of groups in an organization, the less the centralization. Hage's approach emphasizes the fact that power is exercised in a variety of ways and in a variety of locations in an organization. For example, at my university—and at most good universities (see Blau, 1973)—the decision of *whom* to hire for a faculty position lies with the hiring department. The decision here is decentralized. The decision of whether a particular department will be able to hire someone is centralized, however. The central administration reviews faculty vacancies and determines whether or not there needs to be a redistribution of vacancies, with departments with declining enrollments and weaker programs likely to lose positions to departments with high enrollment demands and strong programs. This is a centralized decision.

Van de Ven and Ferry (1980) define centralization as "the locus of decision making authority within an organization. When most decisions are made hierarchically, an organizational unit is considered to be centralized; a decentralized unit generally implies that the major source of decision making has been delegated by line managers to subordinate personnel" (p. 399). Van de Ven and Ferry go on to note that the substance of the decisions is an important consideration. In a highly professionalized organization, for example, decisions in regard to areas of professional competence are left to the professionals involved. Areas that are considered to be outside the limits of professional competence are likely to be more centralized.

What Is Centralized or Decentralized?

Of the several aspects of centralization, the most obvious is the right to make decisions. This can be very specifically spelled out in terms of who or what has the right to make which kinds of decisions and when. If most decision making occurs at the top, the organization is centralized. The matter is not that simple, however, since the organization can have predetermined policies regarding even these decisions. Table 3–1 illustrates the intermixing of decision-making rights and organizational policies.

In the table it can be seen that in the "bureaucracy/centralized" cell (no. 12), operating personnel can make decisions, but they are limited by the policies of the organization. Because the extent to which situations are covered by policies can vary widely, however, centralization is not a simple matter of who makes decisions. If personnel at lower levels in the organization are making many decisions, but the decisions are "programmed" by organizational policies, a high degree of centralization remains.

TABLE 3–1   Forms of Centralization

Level for Referring Decisions Not Covered by POLICIES	POLICIES, PROCEDURES, AND RULES	
	FEW POLICIES/BROADLY DEFINED	MANY POLICIES/ NARROWLY DEFINED
TOP—Headquarters personnel	11 *Autocracy*/Highly Centralized. Few decisions are made by lower level personnel, and these are governed by broad policies. Most decisions must be referred to higher level management.	12 *Bureaucracy*/Centralized. Decisions are made by operating personnel within the framework of restrictive policies, procedures, and rules; problems not covered must be referred to higher levels for decisions or policy clarification.
BOTTOM—Operating personnel	21 *Collegial*/Highly Decentralized. Most decisions are made at lower levels without policy restrictions; other decisions made at lower levels within the framework of policies.	22 *Bureaucracy*/Decentralized. Most decisions are made at lower levels within the framework of the policies; personnel have discretion on problems *not* covered by policies.

Source: Arlyn L. Melcher, *Structure and Process of Organizations: A Systems Approach.* (Englewood Cliffs, NJ: Prentice-Hall, 1975), p. 150.

Another element of centralization is how activities are evaluated (Dornbusch and Scott, 1975, p. 82). The evaluation process involves the determination of whether work was done properly, well, or promptly. If evaluation is carried out by people at the top of the organization, there is centralization, regardless of the level at which decisions are made. A situation in which there is centralized evaluation would probably—but not necessarily always—also be one in which policies are centralized.

For the sake of clarity, it is important to distinguish centralization from *centrality*. The latter concept refers to a person's or a social role's position in work flow, communications, or friendship networks. Brass (1984) found that centrality was related to people being perceived as influential by both supervisors and nonsupervisors.

Centralization and Other Organizational Properties

Size   Research evidence in regard to the relationships between size and centralization is paradoxical. From their study of state employment security offices, Blau and Schoenherr (1971) conclude that "the large size of an agency produces conflicting pressures on top management, as it heightens the importance of managerial decisions, which discourages delegating them, and simultaneously expands the volume of managerial responsibilities, which exerts pressure to delegate some of them" (p. 130). The net result of increasing size is increased delegation or decentralization. The risk of delegation is lessened if personnel have expert qualifications. A centralized policy in regard to employee qualifications thus appears to contribute to delegated power.

One problem with this line of reasoning (a variation of the chicken-egg debate) should be noted: it is impossible to determine if increased size leads to pressures to delegate and thus to utilize experts, or if the hiring of experts leads to pressures to delegate, with size not really being a factor. The question cannot be answered with the kinds of data now available, but probably a combination of the two types of answers is most appropriate.

Blau's (1973) further research on colleges and universities revealed basically the same findings. Large universities were more decentralized than smaller ones. Academic institutions and government agencies show a major difference in the qualifications of their personnel. In the government agencies, qualified personnel were utilized to carry out the organization's policies; in the academic organizations, the highly qualified personnel were able to gain power for themselves and to exercise a great deal of power over educational policies.

In a study using the Aston data and their measures on a second set of data, Mansfield (1973) reaches conclusions essentially the same as those of the Blau research. Mansfield found that increasing size is related to the increasing use of rules. This leads to the decentralization of decision making but not to loss of control for the organization. In smaller organizations, specialists report directly to the top of the organization, while in larger ones, problems are handled at a decentralized level, but under the guidance of organizationally based rules. Kralewski et al. (1985) found that in large corporate medical practices, important decisions shifted from clinicians to administrators. In such medical practices, decisions have ramifications for the total organization.

Technology The technological factor has already been implied in the discussion. Some work is delegated, with the control remaining at the top of the organization by the use of rules governing the work. Other work is delegated to specialists who make their own decisions at lower levels in the organizations. Work that is delegated with controls is routine in terms of its technology (Child, 1973). In a bank, for example, each teller can handle thousands of dollars if the transactions are routine in the form of series of small cash deposits and withdrawals, but if an individual presents a check for $2,000 and asks for cash, it is a different matter. In this case, handling thousands of dollars is not delegated, but rather the decision moves back up the organization to the teller's supervisor.

Dornbusch and Scott (1975) contribute to the analysis of technology and centralization by noting that organizations deal with a variety of tasks that vary in their clarity, predictability, and efficacy. These are rather familiar distinctions in the literature on technology, with the possible exception of efficacy, which refers to "the means which have been developed for achieving desired outcomes" (p. 82). Dornbusch and Scott point out that the variety of tasks performed in an organization mean in essence that it has multiple technologies and thus must structure itself differently according to the task. This is in keeping with our earlier comments on intraorganizational structural variations. These variations are linked to these different tasks with their varied technologies.

Dornbusch and Scott utilize the concepts of "directive," guidance by rules, and "delegation," the actual decentralization of power to lower-level personnel. They conclude:

> Generally, in the interests of organizational effectiveness and efficiency, we would expect tasks which are high on clarity, predictability, and efficacy to be allocated by directive, tasks low on these three dimensions we would expect to be allocated by delegation. In its simplest terms, the argument is that, given high clarity as to the objectives to be obtained, high predictability of the resistance to be encountered, and established procedures for successfully handling this resistance, it is efficient to develop standardized, routine procedures which performers are directed to follow. High clarity contributes specific success criteria for use in designing sequences of activities. When the resistance confronted is predictable, it is possible to specify in advance the appropriate task activities to perform. When highly efficacious sequences of activities have been developed, performers will be expected to follow these set routines. (pp. 82–83)

These ideas were proven to be accurate by tests in a diverse set of organizations. It is thus critical to know what the task is before assuming a given degree of centralization will be found or before making a decision in regard to the appropriate degree of decentralization. The complex task will be delegated to a specialist, who uses his or her knowledge in handling the issue. As Blau's work suggests, organizations retain control through their hiring of specialists, but the control is not as tight as that which derives from organizational directives.

Dornbusch and Scott's findings receive corroboration from a variety of other studies. Hage and Aiken (1969), Comstock and Scott (1977), and Ouchi (1977) all report the same basic pattern. Ouchi notes that organizations can monitor peoples' behavior or their work outputs. He finds that a combination of large size and homogeneous tasks contributes to the utilization of output controls, such as monitoring the number of units produced, sales transacted, or cards punched.

Another aspect of technology adds some slight confusion to the discussion. Participative management, which means that subordinates are consulted in regard to decisions that affect them, was analyzed by Taylor (1971), who found that it was more likely to be successful in situations involving advanced technology. Advanced technology here refers specifically to that concentrated at the work flow level; thus, participative management is most effective in the more automated kinds of situations.

Hage and Aiken's (1967a) work has shown that participation in decision making—a different aspect of centralization—is related to the absence of rules, thus suggesting that centralization by rules and centralization by nonparticipative decision making tend to operate together. Hage and Aiken's work, it should be remembered, is based on reports from organizational members themselves rather than on official records such as the Aston and Blau researchers use. In this instance, the findings in regard to centralization appear to be equivalent. In routine situations, rules govern the actions of the organizational members, and there is likely to be little in the way of delegation of power through participation. In less routine situations, where there is task uncertainty, phenomena such as group meetings are likely to be held to attempt to come up with problem resolutions (Van de Ven, Delbecq, and Koenig, 1976).

The issue of routinization and uncertainty and their relationship to centralization is closely linked to the level of professionalization of the personnel in the organization. Lincoln and Zeitz (1980) report that individual professionals desire and achieve participation in decision making. They also find that the overall level of professionalization of an organization results in all employees experiencing an increase in influence.

There are two cautions that should be noted in regard to participation in decision making. First, the fact that there is participation by organizational members may *not* mean that power is actually delegated. If the final decision still rests in the hands of the superiors in the organization, little power is actually delegated and participation is advisory at best. Although participation *may* help in the implementation of a decision, there is no decentralization or delegation of power unless it contributes to the actual decision.

The other caution regards a phenomenon that is too seldom considered by sociologists and other organizational researchers—budgetary controls, such as internal audits. Although Hofstede (1972) and Ouchi and Maguire (1975) have dealt with this issue, it has tended not to be considered, which is a loss for organizational theory. Budgetary controls have the potential for retaining a great deal of control at the top of the organization. The studies which have been cited here have not included budgetary control mechanisms. It would certainly appear that budgetary matters could be centralized in ways different from the allocation of tasks or decision making on other issues.

Environmental Relations   The relationships among size, technology, and centralization have not been straightforward. The same pattern is found when studies of the relationships between organizations and their environments are considered. As we know from the Lawrence and Lorsch (1967) study, environments are critical for organizations.

A basic consideration is how much competition an organization faces in its environment. From their study of 30 business firms in India, Negandhi and Reimann (1972) suggest that competitive market conditions make decentralization more important for organizational success than do less competitive situations. This study was a successful replication of the Lawrence and Lorsch (1967) contingency theory previously discussed. Further analysis of their data indicated that the degree of dependence on other organizations was actually more strongly associated with decentralization than were the factors of size, technology, and market competitiveness (Negandhi and Reimann, 1973a). Negandhi and Reimann (1973a, b) indicate that the perceptions of the organizational decision makers are a critical mediating variable between the organization and the environment. It is they who make the strategic choices about the environment and about how the organization will respond to it. In this set of findings, the competitiveness of the environment affects the degree of decentralization.

A very different conclusion is reached in a study of 38 small manufacturing firms in the United States (Pfeffer and Leblebici, 1973). In this study it was found that a more competitive environment led to a greater demand for control and coordination. There was a greater frequency of reporting, more emphasis on written communications, and a greater specification of decision-making procedures—in short, a much greater degree of centralization. It was also found that in less competitive environments there were more changes in product design, productions processes, and number of products.

The contradictory findings seem to offer few conclusions about the effects of competition on centralization. A good part of the difficulty may lie in the fact that the more general characteristics of the organizational environments were not specified. For example, in an expanding economy in which the competing organizations are all gaining, decentralization may occur. If the economy is one of scarcity, in which one organization's gain is the others' loss, the tightening up and centralization that Pfeffer and Leblebici found would occur (Khandwalla, 1972).

Another aspect of organizational environments is their degree of stability. Whetten (1980) notes that research on this topic also reaches contradictory findings. Authors such as Burns and Stalker (1961) and Aldrich (1979) have argued that decentralization is more appropriate for conditions of turbulence or nonstability in the environment, while others (Hawley and Rogers, 1974; Yarmolinsky, 1975; Rubin, 1979) have argued in favor of centralization in such situations. Again, a resolution of the differences in these findings may be possible if it were possible to determine if the environment were expanding or contracting, as was suggested in the case of competition. In a situation of growth, decentralization might be the most appropriate response to turbulence, while centralization might be necessary in periods of contraction.

Closely related to centralization is the notion of "loose coupling" (Weick, 1976; Aldrich, 1979). This idea was developed to describe situations in which organizational units have low levels of interdependence. Whetten (1980) concludes that there is agreement that loosely coupled organizations tend to be more flexible and responsive to environmental pressures. The degree of coupling can be misleading, according to Gamoran and Dreeben (1986). They note that school organizations are commonly thought of as loosely coupled. In actuality, administrators can retain control through the allocation of resources such as curricular materials.

Loose coupling is not the same as decentralization, since the degree of coupling refers to the level of interdependence among units rather than to the distribution of power. In general, a loosely coupled organization would also be decentralized. An example of a loosely coupled organization is the business conglomerate. If the consumer products division is having a difficult time due to high interest rates, this would not affect the heavy machinery division whose market is growing. Such an organization would be loosely coupled. Each division may be more or less centralized in such a situation.

For some organizations the environment is a parent organization. Hsu, Marsh, and Mannari (1983) found that stronger centralized bureaucratic control was associated with the presence of parent organizations. Loose coupling was apparently not present in this situation.

Centralization is concerned with power. Since organizations are a major means by which power is exercised in society, an examination of the political systems in which organizations are located indicates that this aspect of organizational environments is important for centralization.

Centralization and Macropolitical Considerations

The overriding importance of organizations for the social order is underscored by considering some examples of their use for political purposes. Organizations can be shaped to be part of the process of political change and development. We have already seen how the Bolsheviks used their "organizational weapon" (Selznick, 1960). During the "Cultural Revolution," the Peoples' Republic of China used its organizations as a means of continuing political indoctrination and involvement. Yugoslavia developed a program of "self-management" in which the workers in an enterprise elected a workers' council that in turn elects that management of the enterprise. This is not participative management of the sort discussed earlier, but rather management by participation. Enterprises in the Israeli kibbutz system (composed of small organizations) have a socialist ideology that is promoted by a system of rotation of all people through all positions.

These ideological purposes are not always met. In Yugoslavia, participation is lower and alienation is higher than the ideology indicates or political leaders desire (see Rus, 1972). In Israel, nonkibbutz organizations are more like their Western counterparts than they are like the kibbutz. The uncertainties that have developed in the 1989–1990 period in socialist and communist systems should not obscure the crucial role which organizations have taken in those systems, as well as in capitalist systems.

A major study of differing patterns of centralization in ten nations has been conducted by Tannenbaum and his colleagues (1974, 1986). The original research was carried out in manufacturing plants in Austria, Italy, Israel, Yugoslavia, and the United States. Austria and Italy are basically capitalist, like the United States, and Israeli kibbutzim and the Yugoslav economy are socialist.

Israel and the United States contained the plants that were most successful—as defined by the standards used in the country in question, but included such universal factors as efficiency and morale. The kibbutz plants are highly decentralized, with the effects of hierarchy virtually eliminated. In the United States, hierarchy is present, but its effects are mitigated by several factors. There is a limited potential for upward worker mobility in the American plants, but it is greater than in the Italian plants. There is also greater participativeness in the American plants. Workers are consulted and treated more as equals, even though they are not equal in power, and the rewards are higher.

Nevertheless, in the American plants, there is no attempt to reduce inequality. This is a political stance, even though it may be unrecognized as such. The tendency toward participativeness in the American plants is viewed by some as manipulation. For example, the Tannenbaum researchers (1974) conclude:

> A position to which some of us subscribe, for example, argues that the approach to hierarchy described above supports techniques of "human relations" that maintain rather than eliminate substantial gradients of power and reward. It therefore covers over and diverts attention from the exploitation and injustice suffered by workers. Workers in the American plants, for example, do not *feel* as alienated as workers elsewhere but in fact they *are* powerless with respect to basic policy issues. Because of "human relations" a discrepancy exists between the subjective and objective experience of alienation. The Italian workers are more realistic and better adjusted in this sense. Jobs are frustrating to them, opportunities for self-fulfillment or for achievement are sparse, and workers feel dissatisfied and poorly motivated. Italian workers *know* they are without power and quite realistically, they *feel* alienated. This realism is a symptom of good adjustment, not bad, although in terms of our conventional measures the Italian worker looks poorly adjusted. American workers, on the other hand, appear well adjusted and they report high levels of opportunity and satisfaction. Some actually feel a sense of responsibility in their plant—at least more than do workers in other places. But this is only because the "human relations" approach is so effective in its manipulation. The approach no doubt works in mitigating some of the psychological effects of hierarchy, but it does so without making any basic changes in hierarchy and, in the view of some of us, it is therefore subject to question from a moral standpoint. (p. 220)

This Marxist approach gets at the very heart of the political issue involved in centralization. Management by participation, as in the case of Israel and Yugoslavia, is a direct attempt to alter traditional power arrangements within a society. The 1986 Tannenbaum study included Rumania, Bulgaria, and Hungary, along with West Germany and Ireland. On the face of it, the political efforts in the Warsaw Pact nations were unsuccessful.

The Chinese approach, which is not participative but rather was designed to strengthen the power of the regime, emphasizes political indoctrination and loyalty. It is highly centralized. The American approach, which increasingly features participation of some degree in decision making, does not attempt to redistribute power. It does, however, minimize the perceptible effects of power differences. Those of the Tannenbaum et al. researchers who judge this as immoral and misleading miss an important consideration. Even if it is agreed that workers are exploited to even a small degree, the end result remains in question: What is the more likely—a situation such as that in Italy, where the exploitation is definitely felt, or a situation such as that in the United States, where it is more moderately felt? It could be, for example, that at some time in the future, American workers, having experienced at least symbolic participation, would press very hard for actual participation. Those who had never experienced participation might not necessarily want to move in this direction. The final consideration, developed by the Dutch sociologist Lammers (1975), is that participative management involves taking part in decision making, while both management by participation and self-management involve workers taking over organizational management. The former is a functional form of decentralization that may lead to greater efficiency and effectiveness, while the latter two forms are structural decentralization that lead to power equalization.

True power equalization in organizations is extremely unlikely. The very nature of organizations requires some form of hierarchy, once organizations move beyond very small size, simple technologies, and low levels of complexity. As in the wider society, power differences are ubiquitous. The effects of such power differences can perhaps be minimized by making them less abrasive through participative schemes. As Child (1976) notes, however, demands for greater participation face situations of greater bureaucratization and centralization.

Centralization and Micropolitical Considerations

Organizations are part of the political system. They also contain their own internal political system, and this is an important consideration for centralization. Heydebrand (1977) has noted the contradiction between traditional control structures and new forms of organizing, as along the lines of professional organizations. As noted earlier, the presence of professionals increases the level of participation in the organization. The increased participation is not accomplished benignly. Instead, it is fought for and over, since those who had decision-making power are not likely to give it up easily to the professionals coming into the organization.

Some authors view the internal politics of an organization as a reflection of the external political system. For example, Marglin (1974) suggests that the technology employed in many factories is there not so much for technical efficiency, but rather as a means by which maximal control over labor can be achieved. Ongoing labor-management negotiations and battles over the prerogatives of management and workers can reflect wider political schisms. This is true particularly in Europe. Bacharach and Lawler (1980) have pointed out that power can be delegated to lower participants and that power can be taken by these same lower participants. Universities in the late 1960s and early 1970s exemplified the give and take of power as students gained in power and thus had the right to make decisions that previously had been made by faculty or administrators. This internal organizational power struggle was a reflection of the larger political context.

The exercise of power within organizations will be considered in a later chapter. In terms of centralization, it is critical to note that the micropolitics of

organizations (Pfeffer, 1978) involves the continuing power struggles
within organizations, whether among departments, hierarchical level
viduals. While the micropolitical approach emphasizes power struggle,
that power is distributed at one point in time (the pattern of centralizat ., will
have a crucial impact on the distribution of power at succeeding points in time.

The Outcomes of Centralization

The degree of centralization in organizations says a great deal about the
society in which they are found. A society in which the majority of organizations
are highly centralized is one in which the workers have little say about their work.
The same would probably be true in terms of their participation in the society.
The degree of centralization of organizations also is an indication of what the
organization assumes about its members: high centralization implies an assumption that the members need tight control, of whatever form; low centralization
suggests that the members can govern themselves. In both cases, it should be
remembered, the control is in behalf of the organization (Blau and Schoenherr,
1971). Professionals and other expert personnel in organizations do not work in
behalf of their professions. Their expertise is in behalf of the organization.

A major outcome of varying degrees of centralization is for the organization itself. High levels of centralization mean greater coordination, but less
flexibility; consistent organizationwide policies, but possibly inappropriate policies for local conditions; and the potential for rapid decision making during
emergencies, but overloaded communications channels during normal operations as communications flow up and down the hierarchy.

SUMMARY AND CONCLUSIONS

This chapter has considered the basic organizational characteristics of complexity, formalization, and centralization. These characteristics have outcomes for
the individuals who are in the organizations and who have contacts with it. They
also have outcomes for the organizations themselves and for the wider society
of which they are a part.

We have already begun an examination of the topic of the next chapter—the
explanation of structure. Issues such as size, technology, and relationships with
the environment have loomed large in analyses of structure. We will examine
these issues and also pay attention to some broader explanations that have been
recently introduced.

4
Organizational Structure: Explanations

In this chapter we will attempt to explain the forms of organizations that were described in the last chapter. Obviously, degrees of complexity, formalization, and centralization are neither random nor accidental. We have already developed the points that size, technology, and environment play roles in determining organizational forms. We will return to these factors here and then add in additional important considerations. Our conclusion will be that *organizational structures are a consequence of the simultaneous impact of multiple factors*

The idea of structure is basically simple, and we will return to our building analogy to illustrate this. Buildings have structures, in the form of beams, interior walls, passageways, roofs, and so on. The structure of a building is a major determinant of the movements and activities of the people within it. Buildings are supposed to have structures that fit the activities that go on within them. An office building is different from a factory. Factories where automobiles are made are different from those where computers are made. Architects design buildings to fit the needs of the activities that are to be carried out within them. They are designed to accommodate populations of various sizes—no architect would design a huge cathedral for a small congregation—and to withstand the environment in which they are located. Buildings in Minnesota are different from those in Arizona. While the size, the major activity or technology to be used, and the environment are all important in building design, so too is the element of choice—of style, color, and so on. Buildings also reflect the values and ideologies of the persons in control—corporate headquarters and state capitol buildings do not take the form they do by accident.

The analogy of organizational structures to those of buildings is not perfect, since organizations are not built by architects but by the people within them. These people are not necessarily in agreement about how the organization should be arranged. Like the design of buildings, of course, organizational structures can be copies of other organizations. They can also reflect the particular fads or fashions popular at the time of their construction. And, just as buildings can be renovated, organizations can be redesigned. As we now move into a consideration of definitions of organizational structure, we will see that our building analogy only works up to a point.

By organizational structure we mean "*the distributions, along various lines, of people among social positions that influence the role relations among these people*" (Blau 1974, p. 12, italics added). This simple definition requires amplification. One implication of the definition is the division of labor: people are given different tasks or jobs within organizations. Another implication is that organizations contain ranks, or a hierarchy: the positions that people fill have rules and regulations that specify, in varying degrees, how incumbents are to behave in these positions. This is exactly what we considered in the last chapter on complexity, formalization, and centralization.

Ranson, Hinings, and Greenwood (1980) have a slightly different perspective on organizational structure which forces us away from our building analogy. They conceive of structure as "*a complex medium of control which is continually produced and recreated in interaction and yet shapes that interaction: structures are constituted and constitutive*" (p. 3, italics added). This approach emphasizes that an organization's structure is not fixed for all time. Rather, it shapes what goes on in an organization and is shaped by what goes on in an organization. This point highlights the fact that organizations are by nature conservative. Their structure "constitutes" the interactions that take place within it. The structure does not yield total conformity, but it also prevents random behavior.

A very similar conceptualization of structure has been presented by Fombrun (1986). The juxtaposition of technological solutions, political exchanges, and social interpretation in and around organizations result in modes of structuring. Fombrun believes that there is a dialectical unfolding of relations among organizational actors. This results in consequences for organizational form. He suggests, as we have here, that this has consequences for society. *Structure is thus continually emergent.* At the same time it retains the properties of our building.

Organizational structure serves three basic functions. First and foremost, structures are intended to produce organizational outputs and to achieve organizational goals. Second, structures are designed to minimize or at least regulate the influence of individual variations on the organization. Structures are imposed to ensure that individuals conform to requirements of organizations and not vice versa. Third, structures are the settings in which power is exercised (structures also set or determine which positions have power in the first place), in which decisions are made (the flow of information which goes into a decision is largely determined by structure), and in which organizations' activities are carried out—structure is the arena for organizational actions.

In the discussion that follows, there is an unfortunate problem with much of the literature to be discussed: the overwhelming majority of studies of organizational structures wittingly or unwittingly make the assumption that there is *a* structure in an organization; but there is ample evidence that this is not the case (Litwak, 1961; Hall, 1962). There are structural differences between work units, departments, and divisions. There are also structural differences according to the level in the hierarchy. For example, a hospital admissions unit has explicit rules and procedures so that all persons who are admitted are treated the same way and so that employees are guided by a clear set of organizationally prescribed expectations. The physical rehabilitation unit of the same hospital has many fewer specific guidelines concerning what it is to do. Similarly, the behavior of lower-level workers, such as orderlies and kitchen workers, is prescribed to a much higher degree than is that of nurses and physicians. There is intraorganizational variation, both across organizational units and up and down the hierarchy.

Organizational structures take many forms. A brief review of some important earlier work in the area will demonstrate the manner in which variations occur. The seminal work on structure is Weber's (1947) description of the ideal type of bureaucracy. He states that a bureaucracy has a hierarchy of authority, limited authority, division of labor, technically competent participants, procedures for work, rules for incumbents, and differential rewards. If all these components are present to a high degree, it is the ideal-type bureaucracy. The important implication, of course, is that organizations in practice will vary from this ideal type as has been demonstrated (Hall, 1963). A bureaucratic organization is designed for efficiency and reliability (Hage, 1980; Perrow, 1979).

Burns and Stalker (1961) provided a major step forward by their development of a model of *multiple* organizational forms. They identified the "mechanical" form, which is very close to Weber's ideal type of bureaucracy, and the "organic" form, which is almost a logical opposite. Thus, instead of having hierarchical authority, organic organizations have a network structure of control; instead of task specialization, a continual adjustment and redefinition of tasks; instead of hierarchical supervision, a communication context involving information and advice; and so on. They see organizational form as being closely linked to the environment in which organizations are embedded, particularly in terms of the technology being employed by the organization, a point later emphasized by Lawrence and Lorsch (1967).

Hage (1965) moved the analysis of organizational forms a step farther. He first noted that structural characteristics, such as centralization, formalization, complexity, and stratification, vary in their presence from high to low. In a series of axiomatic hypotheses, he links these structural characteristics with each other and with a series of outcome variables, such as productivity, innovation, efficiency, and morale.

The present chapter is an attempt to explain the variations in organizational structures or forms. There is no single explanation for the forms of organizations. Rather, multiple explanations are needed to understand organizational structure. This is not a simple matter. Some factors operate together in a positively correlated manner, as when large size and routine technology combine to yield a highly formalized situation. In another situation, size and technology might operate in a negatively correlated fashion as when large size and nonroutine technology are present. These relationships could themselves be affected by differences in national cultures or by historical events.

There are two major categories of factors affecting structure. The first is the *context* in which organizations operate. Contextual factors include size, technology, the environment, and cultural conditions. Context here means the situation in which an organization is operating. This situation is simultaneously within and beyond an organization's control. For example, an organization can decide to expand its operations and in so doing expand its size. Once the size is expanded, it is part of the context of the organization, since the sheer factor of size has an influence on structure. The same process operates in terms of the technologies employed by an organization, the environments with which it deals, and the culture in which it is embedded. There is choice in regard to the context, but the context has its own influence.

The second category of explanations of structure is *design*. By design we mean the choices made in an organization about how the organization is to be structured. The major approaches here are *strategic choice* and *institutional* models of structure. Any consideration of design must consider the fact that not all actors within an organization will have the same judgment in regard to the design of structure. Organizational design is by definition a political issue.

CONTEXTUAL FACTORS

The Size Factor

At first glance, size appears to be a simple variable—the number of people in an organization. The size issue is much more complicated than that, however. The discussion of organizational boundaries suggested that it sometimes is problematic who is in or out of an organization. In a penetrating article, Kimberly (1976) demonstrated that size actually has four components.

The first component of size is the physical capacity of the organizations. Hospitals have a fixed number of beds. Production organizations have a relatively fixed capacity, such as the number of assembly lines and their speed, to transform raw materials. Universities have capacities in terms of classroom or dormitory space.

The second aspect of size is the personnel available to the organization. This is the most commonly used measure and conceptualization of size, being used in 80 percent of the studies reviewed by Kimberly. The basic problem with using this aspect is that the meaning of the number of personnel is ambiguous. For some religious organizations and universities, size in this form is actually a *goal* of the organization. Larger size can mean an increased budget. For other organizations, the goal is to keep the size of the organization at a minimum, to reduce costs.

The third aspect of size is organizational inputs or outputs. This can involve such factors as the number of clients or students served, or the number of inmates housed in a prison, as inputs and sales volume as an output. Kimberly suggests that this measure is limited in its usage to comparisons between organizations of a similar type.

The final aspect of size is the discretionary resources available to an organization, in the form of wealth or net assets. This is conceptually distinct from the other aspects of size.

Kimberly suggests that these aspects of size may be highly intercorrelated in some instances, and indeed they are, but that the conceptual distinctions among them are so great that they should be treated separately. He also notes that structural characteristics may be a consequence, covariant, or determinant of size, making the waters even more muddy and turbulent in regard to the utility of the size variable. Martin's (1979) research has verified Kimberly's conceptualization of the four aspects of size.

Much of the work relating size to organizational structure was conducted prior to Kimberly's analysis. We will review some of that literature now, with the realization that these studies are based almost exclusively on the number of personnel available. These studies do indicate the directions that have been taken in research on size, with some authors arguing that size is *the* determinant of structure and others arguing the opposite.

The major proponents of the importance of size as a determinant of structure have been Peter M. Blau and his associates (see Blau, Heydebrand, and Stauffer, 1966; Blau, 1968, 1970, 1973; Blau and Schoenherr, 1971; Meyer, 1968a, 1968b, 1971; also Blau, 1972; and Klatzky, 1970a). Their data were collected primarily from studies of government agencies, such as state employment services and municipal finance divisions, with supplementary data from universities and department stores. The data reveal some fascinating anomalies about organizations and also some important considerations about the role of organizations in contemporary society.

Blau's studies are concerned primarily with organizational size and differentiation. Differentiation is measured by the number of levels, departments, and job titles within an organization. This is the same as the concepts of vertical and horizontal complexity discussed here. The research findings indicate that increasing size is related to increasing differentiation. The rate of differentiation decreases, however, with increasing size. Administrative overhead is lower in larger organizations, and the span of control for supervisors is greater. Since administrative overhead is inversely related to size, and the span of control is directly, or positively, related to size, larger organizations are able to achieve an economy of scale. It is here that the first anomaly is demonstrated. Size is related to differentiation, and differentiation, bringing increased need for control and coordination, is related to increased requirements for administrative overhead. Size and differentiation thus work at cross-purposes. Blau concludes that the size factor is more critical and that economy of scale still results from large size. Mileti, Gillespie, and Haas (1977) extended these findings with a different set of data and concluded that these relationships may vary by type of organization.

The second major set of studies that find size to be the major determinant of organizational structure of those is that of the Aston group in England (see Pugh et al., 1963; Pugh et al., 1968; Hickson, Pugh, and Pheysey, 1969; Inkson, Pugh, and Hickson, 1970. These works represent the original Aston studies. More recent replications and extensions include Child and Mansfield, 1972; Donaldson and Warner, 1974; Hickson et al., 1974.) The major conclusion of these studies is that increased size is related to increased structuring of organizational activities and decreased concentrations of authority. Most of the data come from manufacturing organizations, but some are based on studies in government agencies and labor unions.

There is still other evidence in regard to the importance of size. Mahoney et al. (1972) report that managerial practices are related to the size of the unit being supervised. Flexibility in personnel assignments, the extent of delegation of authority, and an emphasis on results rather than procedures are related to larger unit sizes. At the same time, subunit size has been found to be negatively related to subunit performance (Gooding and Wagner, 1985). The size factor thus does not act in a unitary manner.

The evidence presented thus far has emphasized the strong, positive relationship between size and structure. Other researchers question this emphasis. For one thing, both Blau and the Aston group utilize the official documents approach to measurement of structure. In a study that used a subjective approach, Hall and Tittle (1966) found only a modest relationship between size and perceived degree of bureaucratization. In another study, utilizing an approach similar to that of Blau and the Aston group, Hall, Haas, and Johnson (1967b) came up with mixed findings in regard to size and structure. Using data from a set of 75 organizations of highly varied types, they concluded:

> In general, the findings of this study in regard to size are similar to those of previous research which utilized size as a major variable; this is, the relationships between size and other structural components are inconsistent.... There is a slight tendency for larger organizations to be both more complex and more formalized, but only on a few variables does this relationship prove to be strong. On others, there is little, if any established relationship.... (pp. 908–09)
>
> These findings suggest that size may be rather irrelevant as a factor in determining organizational structure. Blau et al. have indicated that structural differentiation is a consequence of expanding size. Our study suggests that it is relatively rare that the two factors are even associated and thus the temporal sequence or causality (expanding size produces greater differentiation) posited by Blau and colleagues is open to question. In these cases where size and complexity are associated, the sequence may well be the reverse. If a decision is made to enlarge the number of functions or activities carried out in an organization, it then becomes necessary to add more members to staff and new functional areas. (pp. 111–12)

These findings do not suggest that size is unimportant, but rather that factors other than size must be taken into account to understand structure. These additional factors will be discussed in the sections that follow.

Research on size has met with additional criticisms. Argyris (1972) has analyzed Blau's research and found it wanting in several regards. He first questions the reliance on official descriptions of organizational structures. Citing several studies that have found that organization charts are nonexistent or inaccurate, and that members of top management cannot always accurately describe their own organization, Argyris wonders if the approach that Blau has taken might not invalidate the results. He also suggests that size may be correlated with, but not generate or cause, differentiation.

Another major criticism of viewing size as the determinant of structure comes from Aldrich (1972a). (See also Hilton, 1972; Aldrich, 1972b; and Heise,

1972.) In a reanalysis of the Aston data, Aldrich suggests that size is actually a dependent variable: "the more highly structured firms, with their greater degree of specialization, formalization, and monitoring of role performance, simply need to employ a larger work force than less structured firms" (Aldrich, 1972a, p. 38). In Aldrich's reanalysis, technology emerges as the major determinant of structure.

Before turning to technology, two matters related to size should be noted. First, most organizations are small (Granovetter, 1984). Within small organizations, the effects of organizational design efforts are likely to have more direct consequences for the organization. Geeraerts (1984) found that the heads of small organizations who were professional managers were more likely to adopt bureaucratic practices than were heads of small organizations who were owner-managers. Geeraerts attributes this to the education and professional careers of the professional managers. He also suggests that this difference in orientation might contribute to the erratic findings of the relationship between size and structure.

The second matter is that small organizations are highly vulnerable. Most new organizations are small organizations. Research has consistently shown (see Starbuck and Nystrom, 1981) that young, new organizations have a low survival rate. Starbuck and Nystrom note that "nearly all small organizations disappear within a few years". (p. xiv). Interestingly, they provide data that support this conclusion for both governmental agencies and corporations. Apparently governmental organizations are not as protected as many people think. The corollary of this research, of course, is that large organizations are more likely to survive and are less vulnerable.

The Technology Factor

The concept of technology in organizational analysis involves much more than the machinery or equipment used in production. Interest in technology as a major component of organizational analysis was sparked by the work of Woodward (1958, 1965), Thompson (1967), and Perrow (1967). (See also Burns and Stalker, 1961; Blauner, 1964; Emery and Trist, 1965; Lawrence and Lorsch, 1967). Woodward's work is particularly interesting because she stumbled onto the importance of technology during the course of a research project in the United Kingdom. She found that several critical structural variables were directly linked to the nature of the technology of the industrial firms being studied. The organizations were categorized into three types: first, the small-batch or unit-production system, as exemplified by a shipbuilding or aircraft manufacturing firm; second, the large-batch or mass-production organization; third, the organization that utilizes continuous production, as do chemical or petroleum manufacturers.

Woodward's findings show that the nature of the technology vitally affected the management structures of the firms studied. The number of levels in the management hierarchy, the span of control of first-line supervisors, and the ratio of managers and supervisors to other personnel were all affected by the technology employed. Not only was structure affected, but the success or effectiveness of the organizations was related to the "fit" between technology and structure. The successful firms of each type were those that had the appropriately structured technical systems. Zwerman (1970) replicated Woodward's findings in the United States.

Thompson (1967) attempts to go beyond Woodward by developing a technology typology that encompasses all organizations. Again, a threefold system is derived. The first type is the long-linked technology, involving "serial interdependence in the sense that act Z can only be performed after successful completion of act Y, which in turn rests upon act X, and so on" (pp. 15–16). The most obvious example is the assembly line, but many office procedures would involve the same serial interdependency. The second form of technology is the mediating technology. This links "clients or customers who are or wish to be interdependent" (p. 16). Telephone companies, banks, employment agencies, and post offices are examples here. The final type is the intensive technology in which "a variety of techniques is drawn upon in order to achieve a change in some specific object; but the selection, combination, and order of application are determined by feedback from the object itself" (p. 17). This form of technology is found in work with humans, as in hospitals or universities, in construction work, and in research.

Thompson does not explicitly link these types of technology with organizational structure in the sense that it has been discussed here. It is these technologies, however, upon which all of the organization's actions are based as the organization attempts to maximize its goal attainment. Thus, "under norms of rationality, organizations group positions to minimize coordination costs..., localizing and making conditionally autonomous, first...reciprocally interdependent positions, then...sequentially interdependent ones, and finally,...grouping positions homogeneously to facilitate standardization" (p. 17). Such groupings are also linked through hierarchical arrangements.

Perrow's (1967) approach to technology is based on the "raw material" that the organization manipulates. This raw material

> may be a living being, human or otherwise, a symbol or an inanimate object. People are raw materials in people-changing or people-processing organizations; symbols are materials in banks, advertising agencies and some research organizations; the interactions of people are raw materials to be manipulated by administrators in organizations; boards of directors, committees and councils are usually involved with the changing or processing of symbols and human interactions, and so on. (p. 195)

The nature of the raw material affects how the organization is structured and operated. According to Perrow, the critical factors in the nature of the raw material, and hence the nature of the technology employed to work on it, are the number of "exceptional cases encountered in the work" and the nature of the "search process" that is utilized when exceptional cases are found (pp. 195–96). Few exceptional cases are found when the raw material is some object or objects that do not vary in their consistency or malleability over time. Many exceptions are found in the obvious cases of human beings and their interactions, or the less obvious cases of many craft specialities or frontier areas within the sciences. Search processes range from those that are logical and analytical to those that must rely upon intuition, inspiration, chance, guesswork, or some other such unstandardized procedure. Examples of the first form of search would be the engineering process in many industries and computer programming in most instances. The second form of search would involve such diverse activities as advertising campaigns, some biomedical research, or many activities of the aerospace industry. The examples in both cases have been chosen to suggest the manner in which both the nature of the exceptions and the search process can vary across traditional organizational types.

Both the variables discussed take the form of continua along which organizations vary. These continua interact.

> On the one hand, increased knowledge of the nature of the material may lead to the perception of more varieties of possible outcomes or products, which in turn increases the need for more intimate knowledge of the nature of the material. Or the organization, with increased knowledge of one type of material, may begin to work with a variety of related materials about which more needs to be known, as when a social service agency or employment agency relaxes its admission criteria as it gains confidence, but in the process sets off more search behavior, or when a manufacturing organization starts producing new but unrelated products. On the other hand, if increased knowledge of the material is gained but no expansion of the variety of output occurs, this permits easier analysis of the sources of problems that may arise in the transformation process. It may also allow one to prevent the rise of such problems by the design of the production process. (Perrow 1967, p. 197)

Perrow's framework has been tested several times with mixed results. In their study of welfare organizations, Hage and Aiken (1969) found good support for relating routineness of the work with structure. Lawrence and Lorsch's (1967) study of effectiveness in the plastics, food, and container industries utilized the basic technological approach. Comstock and Scott (1977) found that technology was more important than size in determining structure at both the work unit and organizational levels. Their study was conducted in hospitals. On the other hand, among a series of health departments, Mohr (1971) found only a weak relationship between technological manageability and the participation of subordinates in decision making. Further, the original Aston studies did not find a strong relationship between technology and organizational structure.

The mixed results in regard to technology appear to be based on several factors. In the first place, there has been uncertainty as to the level at which technology is operative in the organization. The Aston group sheds some light on the subject. Hickson, Pugh, and Pheysey (1969) break down the general concept of technology into three components: operations technology—the techniques used in the work flow activities of the organization; materials technology—the materials used in the work flow (a highly sophisticated technique can conceivably be applied to relatively simple materials); and knowledge—the varying complexities in the knowledge system used in the work flow. In their own research, these authors have been concerned with operations technology.

In the English organizations they studied, operations technology had a secondary effect in relationship to size. They conclude:

Structural variables will be associated with operations technology only where they are centered on the workflow. The smaller the organization, the more its structure will be pervaded by such technological effects; the larger the organization, the more these effects will be confined to variables such as job-counts of employees on activities linked with the workflow itself, and will not be detectable in variables of the more remote administrative and hierarchical structure (italics in original). (pp. 394–95)

These findings mean that operations technology will intervene before the effects of size in these work organizations. They also imply that the administrative element in large organizations will be relatively unaffected by the operations technology. It is here that the form of the knowledge technology, which was not examined, becomes important. Meyer (1968a) has found that the introduction of automated procedures into the administrative structures of state and local departments of finance results in more levels of hierarchy, a wider span of control for first-line supervisors, fewer employees under the direction of higher supervisors, and fewer responsibilities—with more communications responsibilities—for members who are nominally in supervisory positions. In these particular organizations, the introduction of automation would be found in relatively simple knowledge technologies.

If the converse of the Meyer findings is considered, a very different picture emerges. If administrative and organizational procedures are highly nonroutine and are laden with problems and new issues, a less complex, less formalized system would be expected. It is thus very possible, as has been previously suggested, that each of the various segments of an organization can have a structure quite different from those of other segments. The operations of some units of an organization could be highly formalized and complex, while other units take an entirely different form. Analyses of intraorganizational structural variations empirically verify that different units of the same organizations have different structural forms (Hall, 1962). Variations in knowledge technology would affect the administrative units of manufacturing organizations, just as operations technology affects the work flow in manufacturing. For organizations devoted wholly to administration, the knowledge technology would be of paramount importance.

Another basic problem with the studies on technology has been the kinds of organizations studied. The Aston group is most confident of its data when service and administrative units are removed from the sample. Child and Mansfield (1972) have noted that the type of industry and its technology are related—for example, the steel industry versus the computer industry—so that sampling differences between studies could increase or decrease the relationship between technology and structure.

The technology approach has also been criticized by Argyris (1972) on the ground that it is static, since change cannot be accounted for. Because organizations change, albeit slowly, there must be a reason for change. If technology is the sole source of structure, then technology must change before structure. If the technology is imported into the organization from outside, then someone or some set of individuals within the organization must decide to import the technological change. If the change is from within, again decisions have to be made. In addition, the technological approach does not include considerations of the role of individuals, separately or collectively, as they respond to or try to lead organizations.

The technology-structure issue has been approached in a diametrically different manner by Glisson (1978). He found that the structural attributes of division of labor and procedural specifications determined the degree of routinization and thus the nature of service delivery among a set of human service organizations. Glisson thus reverses the causal argument. The issue thus may be one of those chicken-versus-egg phenomena. Additional research, particularly longitudinal studies, are needed to begin to resolve this particular issue.

A good part of the literature on size and technology has been presented in an "either/or" fashion, with either technology or size being proposed as the key structural determinant. This was, in fact, a major debate in the early 1970s. Fortunately, researchers dropped the debate and began to examine size and technology together.

Van de Ven, Delbecq, and Koenig (1976) examined task uncertainty, task interdependence (technological variables), and work unit size as they related to coordination mechanisms within a large state employment security agency. They found that as tasks increased in uncertainty, mutual work adjustments through horizontal communications channels and group meetings were used instead of hierarchical and impersonal forms of control. As task interdependence increased, impersonal coordination decreased, while more personalized and interactive modes of coordination, in the form of meetings, increased. Increasing size, on the other hand, was related to an increased use of impersonal modes of coordination, such as policies and procedures and predetermined work plans. In a related study, Ouchi (1977) found that both size and homogeneous tasks were related to output controls on workers.

Blau and McKinley (1979) approached the issue somewhat differently. Their study of architectural firms revealed that structural complexity and task diversity were dependent upon size when there were uniform tasks, but the cognitive ideas and a professional orientation were more important with nonuniform tasks. Thus, size is important under one technological condition but not another.

The idea that size is important for certain structural variables while technology is important for other aspects of structure receives additional support from the research of Marsh and Mannari (1981). Using data from Japanese factories, they found that structural differentiation and formalization were more a function of size than technology. On the other hand, labor inputs, cybernetic complexity, costs and wages, differentiation of management from ownership, span of control of the chief executive, and union recognition varied more with technology than with size.

Dewar and Hage (1978) found that size and technology were both associated with complexity. They suggest that increases in size are related to the development of administrative specialities, while technological diversity is related to increased specialization among persons. Beyer and Trice (1979) reexamined the original Blau and Schoenherr (1971) study and suggest that the earlier findings, with their strong emphasis on size, were probably a result of the type of organizations studied—state employment agencies which had very routine technologies. Beyer and Trice's own data show that in nonroutine organizations, personnel specialization generates horizontal differentiation. They correctly suggest that a search for a single or primary cause of organizational complexity is doomed to failure. They also suggest that there should be a focus on the strategic choices that decision makers select, which may be an important step forward in the analysis of structure. We will consider this issue at a later point.

The final study to be considered in regard to the size-technology issue is that of Daft and Bradshaw (1980). In a study of universities, they found that a growth in administrative departments was related to large size, while growth in academic departments has more of a technological base. This is similar to the Dewar and Hage (1978) findings just discussed. Daft and Bradshaw go on to consider some additional explanations. They suggest that factors in an organization's environment, such as pressures from the community or government, contribute to differentiation among the academic departments. They also suggest that the decision-making process is critical and offer the interesting notion that there are two levels of decisions—the formal decision to add a department or program and an earlier decision by someone who senses a problem and becomes an "idea champion" who pushes for the formal decision. They are correct in this regard, of course, since the idea to make some kind of structural change has to begin somewhere. They do miss the fact that decisions in organizations are highly political (Pfeffer, 1978) and that many ideas that are developed never see the light of day in the sense that there is no formal action on them because they died in some committee. A final suggestion of Daft and Bradshaw's is that financial resources affect decisions about structural change. This is almost never considered by organizational analysts, economists aside, of course, but would appear to be of great importance.

The Environment Factor

In later chapters we will deal with organizational environments in detail; here the concern is simply to trace some of the implications of organizational environments for organizational structure. Of primary interest is the social environment of organizations, but the physical environment, such as climate or geography, can also be important, particularly for organizations that utilize or affect that physical environment.

Ranson, Hinings, and Greenwood (1980) suggest that environmental characteristics are constraints on organizations, affecting their scale of operations and their mode of technical production. They refer specifically to the socioeconomic infrastructure in which organizations are located. The demographic situation, including factors such as the racial and ethnic mixes present, constrains organizations as do the institutionalized values surrounding the organization. Thus, they suggest that as clergy revise their theology, the structural forms of religious organizations will be altered. Similarly, if teachers modify their pedagogical frames of reference, schools will change. The value changes are brought into the organization from outside. Organizational decision makers are faced with making the organizational structure congruent with the demands placed on it.

Meyer et al. (1987) report that the administrative complexity of school districts is related to the environmental complexity which the districts face. If schools receive federal funds, for example, the administration is most complex and fragmented, because of all the various reporting requirements.

Khandwalla (1972) analyzed the impacts of "friendly" versus "hostile" environments on organizations. By friendly, he means that the environment is supportive, providing funds and value support. A hostile environment is a situation in which the very underpinnings of the organization are being threatened. The grave doubts raised about the nuclear energy industry in the wake of the Three Mile Island accident in Pennsylvania, plus other assorted problems with the industry, made the environment hostile for organizations in that industry. Colleges and universities had friendly environments during the 1960s and early 1970s. Money poured in for new facilities and personnel and there was a general belief that education was the key to social and international problems. Obviously, this situation has moved from one of friendliness to one of neutrality, if not hostility.

Khandwalla suggested that in a friendly environment, organizations will be structurally differentiated. The environment will be monitored by differentiated personnel who are then integrated by a series of mechanisms, such as committees and *ad hoc* coordinating groups. If the environment turns hostile, the organization will "tighten up" by centralizing and standardizing its operations.

In a slightly different approach to the same issue, Pfeffer and Leblebici (1973) analyzed the effects of competition on structure. They found that in more competitive situations, there is a greater demand for control and coordination. Reports are more frequent and there are more written communications and a greater specification of decision procedures. When competition is less intense, there are more frequent changes in product design, production processes, and number of products. Less competition provides some "slack" so that the organization can afford to do more than its routine competitive activities.

Competition is an interesting phenomenon. It occurs in the public and private sectors. It also has ramifications above and beyond economic factors. DuBick (1978), for example, studied a set of newspaper companies. He found that in a competitive environment—for example, where there was more than a single newspaper in a city—the structure of the newspaper reflected the complexity of the community. If there was not competition, the newspaper did not mirror the community as closely. Thus, in the competitive situation, attention would be paid to all components of the community, such as minority group news. Without competition, these groups could be ignored.

A study of competition among hospitals shows an additional side of the noneconomic aspects of competition (Fennell, 1980). Fennell found that in competitive situations, hospital services increased. She attributes the increase in services to the competition rather than to service needs. Thus, competition here is counter to economic rationality, raising the costs of medical services as each hospital in a competitive situation adds more and more expensive equipment and services that are not actually needed.

Another approach to the analysis of environment on organizational structure is represented by those who have attempted to compare organizations in different social settings. Meyer and Brown (1977) made an historical analysis of government organizations in the United States. They found that the era of origin and subsequent environmental shifts were related to the degree of formalization, which is in turn related to multiple levels of hierarchy and the delegation of personnel decisions to lower levels in the organization. While the era of origin effects are pervasive, the environmental shifts force the organization to adjust continually to the context in which it is found.

Meyer and Brown studied organizations over time in one country. It is also possible to compare organizations across countries. Brown and Schneck (1979) compared Canadian and American firms. They were able to test the importance of foreign control on the structure of the organizations, with Canadian-owned firms in the United States and American-owned firms in Canada, as well as domestically owned firms in each country. They found the effects of foreign control to be problematic, with somewhat less innovation in the foreign-controlled firms, but with the rest of the relationships rather weak. Some earlier studies by the Aston group (McMillan et al., 1973; Hickson et al., 1974) reported the same basic findings in comparisons of organizations in the United Kingdom, Canada, and the United States.

Brown and Schneck (1979) did reach an important conclusion beyond the issue of foreign control. They suggest that government policy is very important for the organizations. National policies in areas such as health care or banking appear to have a direct impact on organizational structure, with clear differences here between Canada and the United States. The importance of national policies and resultant funding can be seen in Freeman's (1979) findings in regard to the structure of schools. Federal money typically goes to schools for specific programs, usually in terms of specific professional services. Freeman found that federally supported programs tended to be maintained even as the rest of the local school district shifted as a result of other environmental factors. Enrollment declines could lead to a reduction in the number of teachers, but not of federally funded or mandated program personnel, such as teachers of the educationally handicapped or personnel required for the completion of federal reports.

The nature of the environment is *perceived* by organizational decision makers and boundary spanners. The perception of the environment is then enacted in the organization through decision making. In an interesting examination of an aspect of this linkage, Leifer and Huber (1977) examined boundary-spanning behavior. They found that an organization's structure had a greater impact on the behavior of boundary spanners than did the nature of the environment that was perceived. The kind of boundary-spanning activity that concerned them was the frequency with which personnel dealt with groups and organizations outside of their own unit. They suggest that the activity of boundary spanning may affect structure, which in turn influences the perception of the environment. The environment is thus not something "out there" beyond the organization's boundaries. Rather, the environment is interpreted by individuals whose perceptions are, in turn, influenced by their position in the organizational structure. This, in turn, is reflected back into the organization and contributes to the "constituting of the organizational structure (Ranson, Hinings, and Greenwood, 1980).

The importance of the environment for organizations can be examined most clearly, perhaps, in cases of multinational organizations. The use of the multinational organization permits an examination of the effects of the country of origin versus the effects of the host country. Schollhammer (1971) suggested that the multinational firm is affected by its country of origin so that a Dutch-based firm would exhibit different characteristics from a Japanese-based firm in their American operations.

In an analysis of Japanese companies in the United States, Ouchi and Jaeger (1978) and Ouchi and Johnson (1978) found the following general differences between Japanese and American firms:

American	*Japanese*
Short-term employment	Lifetime employment
Individual decision making	Consensual decision making
Individual responsibility	Collective responsibility
Rapid evaluation and promotion	Slow evaluation and promotion
Explicit, formalized control	Implicit, informal control
Specialized career path	Nonspecialized career path
Segmented concern	Holistic concern

The last difference refers to the nature of supervisory practices, with the Japanese approach taking the whole person into account, including concern in regard to other family members. Ouchi and his associates present these differences in the form of an ideal type.

The Ouchi findings are that the Japanese firms with operations in the United States resembled the Japanese model more than the American model, suggesting that the country of origin is of critical importance. It is at this point that we must consider the extent and manner in which national cultural differences affect organizational structure.

The National Culture Factor

Lincoln, Olson, and Hanada (1978) approached the issue addressed by Ouchi somewhat differently. They found that the degree of presence of Japanese nationals or Japanese-Americans in a set of organizations located in the United States was related to the degree of specialization found, but not to centralization, formalization, and vertical differentiation. They suggest that their findings generally support those who say that the host country's characteristics are more important than are those of the country of origin. At the same time, they note that Meyer and Rowan (1977) have developed the notion of organizational structure as a myth, so that the companies involved adopt the structure which conforms to prevailing ideologies and norms. They also imply that there may be some sort of technological imperative involved—that there are only so many ways to structure the manufacturing of electronic goods or automobile production.

Birnbaum and Wong (1985) present findings that are in contrast with those of Lincoln, Olsen, and Hanada. In their study of multinational banks in Hong Kong, Birnbaum and Wong found support for a "culture-free" determination of structure. Centralization, vertical and horizontal differentiation, and formalization were not related to the cultures in which the multinational banks studied had operations. Marsh and Mannari (1980) also report that structural relationships found in the West tend to have the same form in Japan, rather than varying with culture. Conaty, Mahmoudi, and Miller (1983) found that organizations in prerevolutionary Iran were modeled after Western organizations.

These findings are, in turn, in contrast to the arguments presented by Maurice, Sorge, and Warner (1980). These researchers studied manufacturing plants in France, West Germany, and Great Britain. They suggest that the education, training, recruitment, and promotion processes lead to a situation in which the organizational processes of differentiation and integration are carried out by logics that are particular to a society and result in nationally different organizational shapes. My own students have informed me that organizations in the Peoples' Republic of China have generally the same structure as do those in the West, but that the issue is complicated by the fact that there is also an additional and parallel structure of Communist Party representatives for each level of the organizations.

There are thus contrasting findings and interpretations in regard to the importance of cultural differences for organizational structure. There are several possible explanations for these differences. Quite obviously different research methodologies were used in the various studies. Different conceptual frameworks were also in evidence. The most intriguing explanation for these differences is that of Birnbaum and Wong (1985). They suggest that cultural differences themselves might be the source of the different findings. In situations in which particular organizational forms are acceptable, as in the case of Western forms in prerevolutionary Iran, one would expect to find such forms. In postrevolutionary Iran, on the other hand, one would be surprised to find a preponderance of such Western forms.

Organizations are affected by the culture and environment in which they are located, just as they are affected by the size and technology factors. These factors are in interaction with one another, with no single factor dominating. Lincoln et al. (1986) suggest that national culture effects are additive in the sense that they are added to the variations in structure introduced by operations technology, size, and market constraints. These authors go on to note that there may be situations in which cultural factors could override technology.

While Lincoln et al. believe that the effects of culture are additive, Hamilton and Biggart (1988) argue that cultural effects and market factors explain organizational growth, but that authority patterns and legitimation strategies best explain organizational structure in their analysis of South Korean, Japanese, and Taiwanese organizations. Hall and Xu (forthcoming) disagree with Hamilton and Biggart in regard to Chinese and Japanese differences. Hall and Xu believe that differences in family and Confucian values in the two countries contribute to crucial differences in structure between the two countries.

The research we have been reviewing has two important characteristics. First, national culture is being moved to the forefront of explanations of organizational structure and organizations more generally. Second, the attention being paid to culture is being done with the realization that other factors affecting structure, such as size, technology, and other environmental conditions are not diminished in importance. They are retained in the explanatory equations.

As our attention now shifts to the ways in which organizational design affects structure, there is a final point in regard to our contextual factors. Organizational design strategies are themselves affected by the cultures in which the design efforts are made (Schreyögg, 1980; Schneider, 1989). American, British, Japanese, and Chinese organizations would all have their own techniques of formulating their strategies.

ORGANIZATIONAL DESIGN FACTORS

The notion of organizational design has a very rational ring to it. We simply design organizations to attain their goals. Fortunately or unfortunately, the matter is not that simple. Rationality itself is hard to accomplish, regardless of what is being planned. At the same time, events in organizations are not entirely random, since the very intent of structure is to provide some degree of certainty of action. In the sections that follow, alternative approaches to organizational design will be presented and evaluated.

The complicated nature of organizational design is well captured by Starbuck and Nystrom (1981):

> Concepts of design carried over from the physical sciences mislead because these concepts presume that humans inhabit a single, rather stable microcosm that is small enough to have uniform laws. This presumption of stability and uniformity implies that understanding greatly facilitates design and that designers should define problems clearly and thoroughly before trying to solve them. But the social sciences inhabit a rapidly changing and heterogeneous universe. To attain understanding is very difficult because distinct microcosms of the social universe follow different, evolving laws. The social sciences progress slowly, and most social problems change faster than scientists learn to understand them.
>
> However, being able to solve problems well may depend little on being able to understand the problems clearly and thoroughly, so organizational design may not be constrained by progress in descriptive organization theory. Evidently, people and organizations solve problems by processes that operate quite separately from the processes by which they characterize and perceive problems....This separation is probably beneficial, for people and organizations misperceive problems and they characterize problems in ways that grossly distort what they do perceive. When people and organizations generate solutions, the productive solution attempts combine multiple, simultaneous attacks on the components of problems. Solution attempts produce both predicted and unpredicted effects and both good and bad ones. Consequently, solution attempts become components of the problems they address. The initial problems, if they are solved, are ultimately solved through iterative sequences of solution attempts, and these sequences succeed because the people and organizations have observed and reacted to intermediate effects. Usu-

ally, of course, environmental changes render the initial problems and early solution attempts obsolete before the initial problems are actually solved.

The foregoing has prescriptive implications for organizational designers. They should assume that problems are misperceived, and they should be aware of organizations' characterizations of problems. Designs should mix simultaneous solution attempts. Perhaps most importantly, designers should pay careful attention to the consequences, predicted and unpredicted, of solution attempts, so that good effects can be reinforced and bad effects counteracted. Design improvements depend on monitoring actual effects and generating further solution attempts. A well designed organization is not a stable solution to achieve, but a developmental process to keep active. (pp. xix–xx)

Starbuck and Nystrom's comments suggest that organizational design is problematic and uncertain. Other observers are more sanguine and offer prescriptions such as Caplow's book (1983) *Managing Any Organization.* The very title smacks of rational organizational design. Peters and Waterman's (1982) long-running best-seller, *In Search of Excellence*, contains the kinds of prescriptions that are typical of the view that organizations can be the object of rational organizational design. They prescribe:

1. A bias for action—do it, try it, don't analyze the problem to death.
2. Stay close to the customer and understand the service or product needs.
3. Engage in entrepreneurship and promote autonomy within the organization.
4. Productivity is through people and not technology.
5. Have high values and demand excellence.
6. Stick to the knitting—do what you do best.
7. Keep the staff lean and simple.
8. Have simultaneous looseness and tightness—allow people to be autonomous, but at the same time be disciplined. (This summary is from Van de Ven, 1983, pp. 621–22.)

From the perspective of Starbuck and Nystrom and that taken here, these prescriptions are much too simplistic. They ignore the perceptual and judgmental difficulties that Starbuck and Nystrom stress and the weight of several bodies of literature. Organizational design does affect structure, but not in the simple, overly rational manner suggested by the authors of prescriptive solutions for organizations. In the sections that follow, we will consider alternative perspectives on organizational design, beginning with the idea that organizations make strategic choices in regard to how they are structured.

The Strategic Choice Factor

The idea of strategic choice is not a new one. Chandler (1962) emphasized the importance of strategic choices for business firms such as Sears, Roebuck and General Motors as they attempted to take advantage of perceived markets in their environment. The establishment of General Motors as a multidivisional form with Chevrolet, Pontiac, and the other automotive divisions was seen as a consequence of strategic choices.

Child (1972) advanced this argument by noting that the internal politics of organizations determine the structural forms, the manipulation of environmental features, and the choice of relevant performance standards that are selected by organizations. The internal politics are themselves dependent upon the existing power arrangements in the organization. Again, structure begets structure.

Strategic choices are made on the basis of "bounded rationality" (Simon, 1957). While the nature of rationality as a component of the decision-making process will be considered in detail in a later chapter, it is important here to note that the bounded rationality idea means that the strategic choices are not necessarily the optimal choices. Rather, they are those that appear to be optimal as a consequence of decisions made through the political process within organizations. Katz and Kahn (1966), in their consideration of organizations as systems, utilize the concept of "equifinality," or the presence of several means available to reach a given end. Organizations are faced with both equifinality of means to ends and the presence of multiple ends. This is why the notion of choice is important. An organization is faced with multiple environmental pressures and must choose one path among many options toward one of many objectives.

Approaching the issue from a somewhat different perspective, Miles, Snow, and Pfeffer (1974) noted that the size and technology approaches to structure have been found wanting. They suggest that organizations are faced with environments differing in their rates of change and degree of uncertainty. They also suggest that specific parts or organizations are affected by specific environmental elements. The legal department of an organization has different environmental interactions than does the public relations department.

Pfeffer (1978) and Pfeffer and Salancik (1978) have emphasized the political context of the decision-making process and its relationship to structure. Pfeffer (1978, p. 48) suggests, for example, that persons carrying out nonroutine tasks are likely to have power because of their expertise; those doing routine tasks do not have this power source. The persons with expertise can claim and receive more discretion, or decentralization on a broader basis, as something won from a position of power, rather than something delegated from above.

The power perspective is also taken by Ranson, Hinings, and Greenwood (1980). They note that the power holders in organizations decide what are issues and what are not issues. Thus the decision whether to make a strategic choice or not is based on power arrangements. The term that is most commonly used to describe power arrangements in organizations is the "dominant coalition" (Thompson, 1967). According to Pennings and Goodman (1977), the "dominant coalition comprises a direct and indirect 'representation' or cross-section of horizontal constituencies (that is, subunits) and vertical constituencies (such as employees, management, owners, or stockholders) with different and possibly competing expectations" (p. 152).

This approach does not see the dominant coalition as representative democracy. Rather, the dominant coalition is the outcome of the power held by the various parties in the coalition. Thus, some units are more powerful among the horizontal constituencies, and there is obvious power differentiation among the vertical constituencies. The dominant coalition, then, is comprised of the power center in the organization. This power center or coalition is that which makes the strategic choices in regard to the organization and its structure. In some cases, there is no dominant coalition, with a single individual dominating all others. Miller and Droge (1986) go so far as to suggest that personality characteristics of powerful chief executive officers may be a key determinant of structure in some instances. Most organizations are not dominated by a single individual.

Decision makers in the dominant coalition select those parts of the environment with which they will be concerned. This selection is done within a political framework in which membership in the dominant coalition can shift, as can the distribution of power within it. On the basis of selective perception of the environment, appropriate strategies can be selected for dealing with this environment. This decision making includes utilizing the appropriate technology for implementing the strategy. In the strategic choice perspective, technology is thus brought into the organization. The decisions also involve strategies for arranging roles and relationships to control and coordinate the technologies being employed. This is done to ensure continuity of the organization, its survival and growth (Chandler, 1962).

Strategic choices take place within *contexts*. For example, Palmer et al. (1987) examined the use of the multidivisional form, such as that employed by General Motors, among large business firms in the United States. They found that industrial diversity and geographical dispersion were strongly related to the presence of the multidivisional form, with organizational size having an indirect effect by contributing to diversity and dispersion. Conversely, the absence of diversity would limit the extent to which the multidivisional form is used. The industrial limits to choice is evident in the fact that the petroleum and agricultural industries were less diverse than other industries. Also, firms dominated by banks or by family members were less diverse and dispersed and had less multidivisional forms. The industrial context in which firms operated thus had a major impact on the form adopted.

The Marxian Twist   A sharply different perspective on organizational design has been taken by Marxist scholars. Goldman and Van Houten (1977, pp. 108–09) note:

> Recent research has shown the promise of a Marxist approach to bureaucracy. Marglin's (1973) analysis of hierarchy during the industrial revolution and Stone's (1973) discussion of the development of job ladders in the late nineteenth century steel industry show how changes in the division of labor stem as much from the desire to effect organizational control as from the need to apply continually advancing technology to production. Braverman (1974) and Edwards (1975), analyzing contemporary work organization, suggest that machinery and bureaucratic regulations in industry derive from managerial desires to effect substantial control over both labor market characteristics and the attitudes of workers. This research indicates that managerial thinking is attuned to the larger social, political, and economic setting, as well as to internal administration.
>
> Other Marxist or quasi-Marxist research informs the study of bureaucracy, albeit in a more indirect fashion. Studies of economic elites, focusing particularly on interinstitutional relationships and the interpenetration of economics and politics,

provide an alternative view of managerial behavior to that found in most literature on organizations.

Additional fuel for this fire was supplied by Clawson (1980) who traced the spread of Taylor's (1911) principles of "scientific management" through industry in the United States. According to Clawson, this had the result of more control by capital and less control by labor. Clawson's analysis focuses on the manner in which craft work was *deskilled* as factory work was more and more minutely subdivided into small, routine tasks. Clawson argues that this deskilling has continued into the present, with less and less control possible for workers in a wide variety of settings.

There are two major problems with this Marxist argument. First, the evidence in regard to the extent of the deskilling of labor is actually quite mixed. Form (1980), Spenner (1979, 1983), and Attewell (1987) have provided firm evidence that a great deal of work has not been deskilled. Indeed, there is evidence of skill enhancement for some kinds of work.

The second problem is that alluded to in the initial discussion of organizational design and strategic choice. Rationality is bounded and problematic. Just as a "perfect" solution to a design issue is unlikely, so too is the likelihood that managerial attempts at control will work perfectly. In addition, Edwards (1979) has shown that labor will strongly resist efforts at control.

Despite these problems, worker control must be considered a component of organizational design. Management *does* have interests that are different from those of the worker. The introduction of new machines and new forms of organization are at least in part attempts to control workers (Perrow, 1983; Sabel, 1982).

The worker control issue appears to be one among several that are faced by the dominant coalition in organizations as design attempts are made. Again, there appear to be industry effects on the forms of worker control and internal labor market strategies that are used (Baron et al., 1988; see also Bills, 1987). These authors argue strongly that there are multiple sources for organizations' personnel policies. Baron et al. (1988, p. 509) state that monocausal arguments are inadequate. I am in complete agreement.

The Institutional Factor   The final theoretical model to be considered is the institutional model. This model has become a major contributor to our understanding of organizational phenomena. It is another attempt to answer the question: Why do organizations take the forms that they do? Much of the research here has been carried out in not-for-profit organizations with rather indeterminate technologies. DiMaggio and Powell (1983) argue that "institutional isomorphism" is now the dominant reason why such organizations assume the forms that they have. According to DiMaggio and Powell, Weber's original (1952, 1968) analysis of the driving force behind the move toward rationalization and bureaucratization was based on a capitalist market economy, with bureaucratization an "iron cage" in which humanity was bound since the process of bureaucratization was irreversible.

DiMaggio and Powell believe that major social changes have altered this situation to such a large extent that an alternative explanation is needed. Their analysis is based on the assumption that organizations exist in "fields" of other, similar organizations. They define an organizational field as follows:

> By organizational field, we mean those organizations that, in the aggregate, constitute a recognized area of institutional life: key suppliers, resource and product consumers, regulatory agencies and other organizations that produce similar services and products. The virtue of this unit of analysis is that it directs our attention not simply to competing firms, as does the population approach of Hannan and Freeman (1977b), or to networks of organizations that actually interact, as does the interorganizational network approach of Laumann et al. (1978), but to the totality of relevant actors. (p. 148)

According to this perspective, organizations are increasingly homogeneous within fields. Thus, public universities acquire a sameness, as do department stores, airlines, professional football teams, motor vehicle bureaus, and so on. DiMaggio and Powell cite three reasons for this isomorphism among organizations in a field. First, there are *coercive* forces from the environment, such as government regulations and cultural expectations which can impose standardization on organizations. Government regulations, for example, force restaurants (it is hoped) to maintain minimum health standards. As Meyer and Rowan (1977) have suggested, organizations take forms that are institutionalized and legitimated by the state.

DiMaggio and Powell also note that organizations *mimic* or model each other. This occurs as organizations face uncertainty and look for answers to their uncertainty in the ways in which other organizations in their field have faced similar uncertainties. Rowan (1982) argues, for example, that public schools add and subtract administrative positions in order to come into isomorphism with prevailing norms, values, and technical lore in their institutional environment. DiMaggio and Powell argue that large organizations tend to use a rather small number of consulting firms which "like Johnny Appleseeds, spread a few organizational models throughout the land" (p. 152). A very concrete example, noted by DiMaggio and Powell, is the fact that Japan consciously modeled its courts, postal system, military, banking, and art education programs after Western models in the late nineteenth century. As DiMaggio and Powell note,

> American corporations are now returning the compliment by implementing (their perceptions of) Japanese models to cope with thorny productivity and personnel problems in their own firms. The rapid proliferation of quality circles and quality-of-work-life issues in American firms is, at least in part, an attempt to model Japanese and European successes. (p. 151)

Prokesh (1985) in a *New York Times* article reports that business firms are establishing formal intelligence departments to keep tabs on competitors from home and abroad. One sources is quoted as saying that "understanding your competitors' positions and how they might evolve is the essence of the strategic game." In DiMaggio and Powell's conceptualization, the field is more than simply competitors. The establishment of intelligence departments reflects the strong mimetic tendencies within organizations.

A third source of institutional isomorphism comes from *normative* pressures as the work force, and especially management, becomes more professionalized. Both professional training and the growth and elaboration of professional networks within organizational fields leads to a situation in which the managerial personnel in organizations in the same field are barely indistinguishable from one another. As people participate in trade and professional associations, their ideas tend to homogenize.

The institutional perspective thus views organizational design not as a rational process based on organizational goals, but rather one of both external and internal pressures which lead organizations in a field to resemble each other over time. In this perspective strategic choices are seen as coming from the institutional order in which an organization is embedded.

EXPLAINING ORGANIZATIONAL STRUCTURE

We have been considering a series of explanations of organizational structure. These have ranged from contextual factors such as size and technology to the design factors of strategic choice and institutional isomorphism. Which is the correct explanation? It should be obvious by now that neither an "all of the above" nor "none of the above" is the appropriate answer. The explanations of structure must be *considered in combination.*

This has become well recognized among sociologists. For example, Tolbert (1985) combined the environmental pressure and institutional perspectives in explaining aspects of the administrative structures of universities. Fligstein (1985) studied the spread of the multidivisional form among large corporations and found support for the strategic choice, member control, and institutional perspectives. Fligstein also suggests that in a different set of organizations, other explanations might be valid. Fligstein concludes (and I concur):

> ...each school of thought has tended to view its theory as a total causal explanation of organizational phenomena. This suggests that one of the central tasks in organizational theory is to reorient the field in such a way as to view competing theories as contributing to an understanding of organizational phenomena. (p. 377)

The healthy and informed eclecticism which Fligstein calls for has essentially become the norm in organizational analyses. Hamilton and Biggart's (1988) study of the importance of national culture for organizations in the Far East is another example of this multiple theory approach, as is Drazin and Van de Ven's (1985) analysis of the structures of a set of employment security units.

Organizations are structured in a context. Van Houten (1987) analyzed the various approaches to organizational design which were attempted in Sweden in the 1970s and 1980s. He concludes that these cannot be understood out of their historical context. Organizations are thus "complex structures-in-motion that are best conceptualized as historically constituted entities" (Clegg, 1981, p. 545). There are thus multiple explanations of structure. When these explanations are taken singly, in opposition to one another, and outside of their historical and cultural context, they have little to offer. When combined and in context, we are able to understand why organizations take the forms that they do.

As we turn to a consideration of organizational processes, it should be made clear that *organizational structures affect these processes and vice versa* (Miller, 1987). Structure affects the flow of information and the power arrangements in organizations. Decisions made in regard to attempted strategies affect structure. Unlike the building analogy at the outset of this chapter, structures are in motion.

SUMMARY AND CONCLUSIONS

We have considered the various explanations that have been developed to explain the forms that organizational structures take. Organizational structure is dynamic. Organizations change in size, adopt new technologies, face changing environments and cultures, adopt new strategies or find old ones, and adjust to other organizations in their field.

Implicit in the discussion has been the fact that the structure of an organization has important outcomes—for its members and the social system of which it is a part. It is within structure that the processes of power, conflict, leadership, decision making, communication, and change operate. We now turn to a consideration of these processes.

5

Power

Organizations and power are synonymous in many ways. After all, organizations are powerful tools of the powerful when we think of organizational outcomes. They are also power systems in terms of the ways in which people conform to organizational rules. They are political systems in terms of the allocation of resources. Power is distributed between the privileged and the underprivileged. In Mintzberg's (1983) terms, we can think of power "in and around" organizations.

In this chapter we will analyze the nature of power within organizations. A major focus will be on the way power relationships develop over time. In many ways, power is a most puzzling phenomenon. On the one hand, power is stable and self-perpetuating. Those in power have the resources to maintain themselves in power. On the other hand, as events in Eastern Europe and the Soviet Union in 1989–1990 demonstrated, entrenched power can be overthrown with startling quickness.

There are many ways in which power can be distributed in organizations. In Chapter 3, the discussion of centralization revealed that power can be concentrated in the hands of the few or be decentralized throughout the organization. Morgan (1986, p. 145) has provided a sixfold classification of power relationships in organizations that is useful here as an introduction.

First, organizations can be *autocracies*, with power held by an individual or small group with absolute control. Second, organizations can be *bureaucracies*, in which rules are written and power relationships are clearly specified. Third, they can be *technocracies*, where knowledge and expertise rule the system.

Fourth, there can be *codetermination*, where opposing parties in the organization share in the ruling system. Fifth, there is *representative democracy*, in which officers are elected and serve specific terms or for as long as they have worker support. This has been the system in Yugoslavia, which is now unraveling. Finally, there can be *direct democracy*, in which everyone participates and has the right to rule. This system has characterized many cooperatives as well as the kibbutzim in Israel. As Morgan points out, many organizations are mixed types, with elements of more than one form of rule. Bureaucracy is the dominant form and will be the primary focus here.

THE NATURE OF POWER IN ORGANIZATIONS

Power can usually be rather simply defined. Most of the many treatises dealing with the concept are in general agreement that it has to do with relationships between two or more actors in which the behavior of one is affected by the other. The political scientist Dahl (1957) defines power as follows: "*A* has power over *B* to the extent that *A* can get *B* to do something *B* would not otherwise do" (pp. 202–03). (For other general discussions of power, see Bierstedt, 1950; Blau, 1964; Kaplan, 1964; and Weber, 1947, pp. 152–93.) This simple definition is the essence of the power concept. It also implies an important point that is often neglected: the power variable is a relational one; power is meaningless unless it is exercised. A person or group cannot have power in isolation; it has to be in relationship to some other person or collectivity. One element missing in Dahl's definition is that power relationships involve much more than interpersonal power. In the case of organizations, it is vital to consider *interdepartmental* power relationships. We will also examine interorganizational relationships from the power standpoint at a later phase of the analysis. We have already considered the power of organizations in society. Power is thus a crucial process at every level of analysis.

Power Relationships

The relational aspect of power is specifically developed in Emerson's (1962) comments on the importance of dependency relationships in the total power constellation. He suggests that power resides "implicitly in the other's dependency"; in other words, that the parties in a power relationship are tied to each other by mutual dependency.

> Social relations commonly entail ties of mutual dependence between the parties. A depends upon B if he aspires to goals or gratifications whose achievement is facilitated by appropriate actions on B's part. By virtue of mutual dependency, it is more or less imperative to each party that he be able to control or influence the other's conduct. At the same time, these ties of mutual dependence imply that each party is in a position, to some degree, to grant or deny, facilitate or hinder, the other's gratification. Thus, it would appear that the power to control or influence the other resides in control over the things he values, which may range all the way from oil resources to ego-support, depending on the relation in question. (p. 32)

Dependency is particularly easy to see in organizations, which by their very nature require interdependence of personnel and subunits (see Bacharach and Lawler, 1980). The existence of power relationships is also generally easy to see. Wamsley notes (1970) that in highly bureaucratized organizations, "power or authority would tend to be hierarchic: each level would have just that amount of power necessary to carry out its responsibilities; ascendant levels in the hierarchy would have increasing power based on broader knowledge about the organization and/or greater task expertise" (p. 53). The design of these types of organizations rests largely on the power variable, with the intent of ensuring that each level in the organization has sufficient power. When an issue arises that is out of the purview of an office at a particular level, it is passed up the organization until it reaches the level where the decision can appropriately be made. Of course, few organizations approximate this ideal type, because the power arrangements are affected by informal patterns worked out over time and by personal differences in the exercise of the power available in an office. Nevertheless, in many organizations, power relationships are tightly prescribed and followed, and they are highly visible to all who enter the organization.

While in such settings power is very easily seen and experienced, in others it is more obscure. In some situations it is extremely hard to isolate. When a new or unanticipated situation arises, it may be difficult to determine exactly how and where power is to be exercised. In an analysis of a student-university administration confrontation during the 1960s, Bucher (1970) relates the following anecdote:

> According to the students' statements, the dean asserted that "nobody in the university has the authority to negotiate with the students...." "Obviously somebody in the university makes policy decisions," the statement said, "and until an official body comes forward, we consider the present situation a refusal to negotiate our demands." (p. 3)

In the situation described, neither the students nor the university administration in question could locate an office or individual who had the power to negotiate with students. The students' perception that this constituted a refusal to negotiate is only partially accurate. This type of matter had not arisen before, and there was undoubtedly no established way to handle such situations because the power relationship was yet to be determined. Wamsley (1970) notes that in such situations, power is "variable; situationally or issue specific; surrounded by checks and balances; an interdependent relationship, often employing negotiation and persuasion and often found in changing coalitions" (p. 53).

Power is as much a fact of university life as of corporate life, even if it takes a different form and is expressed in different ways. In campus situations such as student-administration confrontations, issues and relationships are being explored that had not really been part of the preexisting power system. Because more power is thus introduced into the system as arrangements are made to handle such incidents in the future, we see that there is not a fixed amount of power in the system for all time; the amount of power can contract or expand.

As suggested earlier, the subunits or departments in an organization also have varying amounts of power. Perrow (1970a), for example, in a study of industrial firms, found that the sales departments were overwhelmingly regarded as the most powerful units in the organizations involved. The members of the other departments regarded them that way and apparently behaved accordingly.

There have been several important studies that have examined the departmental origins of chief executives. This is done in the belief that the origins of the executives is an important clue for locating departmental power. Priest and Rothman (1985) find that lawyers (coming from legal departments) are disproportionately represented among corporate chief executives. They attribute this to the complex legal problems that modern organizations face. In an historical analysis of the 1919–1979 period, Fligstein (1987) reports that entrepreneurs or people who came up through manufacturing dominated corporate presidencies in the early decades of the century. The middle decades were dominated by sales and marketing. The last decades have been dominated by personnel from finance. The difference in the findings reported here (lawyers versus finance) is undoubtedly due to differences in samples of organizations studied. The important point here is that ignoring interdepartmental power relationships by looking only at interpersonal power obscures an important facet of organizational power.

Two additional aspects of power are important. First, power is an act; it is something that is used or exercised. Too frequently the act of power is ignored in analyses of power, which tend to focus on the results of a power act. These results can be of several forms, including compliance or conflict, but the exertion of power is what is of interest to us here. Biggart and Hamilton (1984) report that in order to sustain power, people must self-consciously exercise power to signify to others their awareness of their role obligations. The second point is that the recipient of power is crucial in determining if a power act has occurred. If recipients interpret an act as a power act, they will respond on that basis, whether or not the power wielder actually intended to utilize power.

Types of Power

The discussion thus far has treated power as a unitary concept, but there is a long history of distinguishing among *types* of power. Probably the best known and most widely used classification system is that of Weber (1947). Weber makes a basic distinction between power and *authority*. Power involves force or coercion and is only an important factor as an internal process in organizations in cases such as slave labor camps, some prisons, some schools, and so on. Authority, on the other hand, is a form of power that does not imply force. Rather, it involves a "suspension of judgment" on the part of its recipients. Directives or orders are followed because it is believed that they ought to be followed. Compliance is voluntary. This requires a common value system among organizational members, as Scott (1964) notes, and this condition is usually met.

It is useful at this point to distinguish between authority and influence (Bacharach and Lawler, 1980). Authority involves an acceptance of the power system as one enters the organization, while influence is a power situation in which the decision is made, consciously or unconsciously, at the particular moment the power appeal is sent from the power holder. When a persuader becomes institutionalized, in the sense of being always accepted and thus legitimated by the recipient, this becomes authority.

Weber (1947) further distinguishes between types of authority, developing his well-known typology of traditional, charismatic, and legal authority. *Legal* authority is the type of most power relationships in modern organizations; it is based on the belief in the right of those in higher offices to have power over subordinates. *Charismatic* authority stems from devotion to a particular power holder and is based on his or her personal characteristics. This type is certainly found in modern organizations, to which it can be either a threat or a benefit. If a person in an authority position can extend legal powers through the exercise of charismatic authority, there is more power over subordinates than that prescribed by the organization. If the performance of the subordinates is enhanced (assuming for the moment that their performance enhancement is also beneficial to the actors themselves), such an addition is beneficial. If, on the other hand, charismatic authority is present in persons outside the formal authority system, the system itself can be threatened.

The third form, *traditional* authority, is based on belief in the established traditional order and is best exemplified by operating monarchies. Vestiges of this form can be found in organizations in which the founder or a dominant figure is still present, when terms such as "the old man wants it that way" are verbalized and the wishes of the "old man" are followed. The Roman Catholic Church again serves as a good example here since traditional authority is clearly represented by the system of pope, cardinals, archbishops, and so on.

Dornbusch and Scott (1975) have added an important contribution to our understanding of authority. They found that control in organizations was based on the process of evaluation. The individual who evaluates one's work has authority. Control through evaluation is most effective when the individuals being evaluated believe the evaluations are important, central to their work, and capable of being influenced by their own efforts. If the evaluations are believed to be soundly based, they will be more controlled by the evaluation process. Dornbusch and Scott also note that authority is granted from above as well as from below. In a multilevel hierarchy, people in a position to evaluate others are legitimated from subordinates and also from their own superiors.

Power Bases and Sources

Organizational units and people in organizations get their power through their control of both power bases and power sources. Power bases refer to what power holders control that permits them to manipulate the behavior of others. Power bases include the ability to reward, or coerce, legitimacy, expertise, and serving as a referent for the power recipient (Etzioni, 1961; French and Raven, 1968). In addition, access to knowledge (Bacharach and Lawler, 1980) and family ties (Allen and Panian, 1982) have also been identified as power bases. In order to have power in a situation, the power base must be of value to the power recipient.

Bacharach and Lawler (1980) go on to make an additional distinction. They note that there are four sources of power in organizations. They use the term "sources" to refer to the manner in which parties come to control the power bases. The sources are (1) office or structural position; (2) personal characteristics, such as charisma; (3) expertise, which is treated as a source and a basis of power, since individuals bring expertise with them to the organization through such mechanisms as professional training, which is then converted into a power basis at a specific point in time; and (4) opportunity or the combination of factors which give parties the chance to utilize their power bases.

These sources of power are used in the power situations of authority and influence, which in turn utilize the bases of power that have been distinguished. Thus, an individual or unit in an organization has a power source, such as an official position in which power in the form of authority or influence is exercised. As the power is exercised, the power holder utilizes the power bases that are available. In this formulation, the bases cannot be used unless the power holder first of all has the appropriate power source. This is made all the more complicated by the fact that some exercises of power are issue specific, while others are more general (Enz, 1989). For example, the president of my university has general power, but defers to the expertise of the building and grounds superintendent in regard to the timing of snow removal.

HORIZONTAL POWER RELATIONSHIPS

It is easiest to conceptualize or visualize power along the vertical axis of organizations. The vertical dimension is only one part of power relationships in organizations. As we have already seen in the discussion of the differential power of departments, power is also exercised along the horizontal dimension. Interdepartmental, staff-line, and professional-organizational relationships are all familiar loci of the horizontal dimension.

The term "horizontal power relationships" seems to represent an inconceivable situation. If the parties in the relationship have exactly equal amounts of power, then as soon as one gains power at the expense of the other, a vertical element is introduced. But the concern here is with relationships among units and persons who have positions relative to each other that are basically lateral. In these lateral relationships, the power variable can become a major part of the total relationship. It is conceivable that power will not enter the relationship if the parties have no reason to attempt to influence each other's behavior. However, the power variable would almost inevitably enter such relationships when issues such as budgetary allocations, output quotas, priorities for personnel, and other such matters come into the picture.

Staff-Line Relationships

Horizontal or lateral power relationships have been carefully analyzed by Dalton (1959). Perhaps his best known contribution is the analysis of staff-line conflict. Dalton found that these personnel were in rather constant conflict in several areas. The staff personnel tend to be younger, have more formal education, be more concerned with proper dress and manners, and be more theoretically oriented than the line managers in the organizations studied. This is the basis for conflict, but it is also part of the power relationship. The power aspect, aside from its importance in actual conflict situations, comes in when the staff attempts to get some of its ideas implemented (expert power).

Power is also exerted in terms of the personal ambitions of the people involved. Dalton assumes that both sets of managers seek income, promotions, power in the organization, and so on. In the organizations studied, the line personnel held the power in controlling the promotion process; but at the same time, they feared that the staff might come up with ideas that would put the line's modes of operations under serious scrutiny as being outmoded or unimaginative. In this instance we have an example of two different forms of power as a part of one power relationship. The outcome is a series of conflicts between line and staff that, viewed from outside the organization, are costly to it. There is a fairly high turnover among staff personnel, who apparently feel that they are not getting anywhere in the organization. The staff resents the line, and vice versa.

In order to accomplish anything, the staff must secure some cooperation from the line. This requires giving in to the line by moderating proposals, overlooking practices that do not correspond to rigid technical standards, and in general playing a rather subservient role in dealing with the line. If this is not done, the staff's suggestions would probably go unheeded. This, in turn, would make their output zero for the time period, and their general relevance for the organization would then be questioned. This, of course, is not a unique situation.

The staff-line power interactions were studied in manufacturing organizations. The same forms of interaction would appear to characterize schools, where the teachers are the line and personnel such as curriculum specialists would be the staff. Unfortunately, there has been little additional research on staff-line relationships since Dalton's major study, although Jackall (1988) does touch on the topic briefly in his analysis of the moral development of managers in corporations. The issue is not dead.

Professional-Organizational Relationships

The analysis of staff-line relationships has largely disappeared from the literature. It has been replaced by a focus on the relationships between professionals and their employing organizations.

It is commonly noted in discussions of professionals in organizations that the "reward" power system for them is more complicated than for other organization members. Professionals typically desire the same kinds of rewards as other people, in terms of money and other extrinsic factors, but they are also likely to want recognition from fellow professionals as good lawyers, scientists, counselors, or whatever. In addition, evaluation of their work, which is difficult for someone not in that profession, is likely to be made by just such not-in-the-profession personnel. This is true in many cases even if the evaluator, in an administrative position, is a member of the same profession. For example, a research scientist in an organization is likely to be under the supervision of another scientist who has been promoted to research administration. The very fact that the latter is now working in administration prevents him or her from keeping up with developments in the scientific discipline; since they occur rapidly it is difficult even for the practicing scientist to keep abreast of what is occurring.

Since the organization must in some way control all its members, the issue becomes very difficult with respect to the professional. If it tries to exert legitimate control through the hierarchy, the professional is apt to resist it. If it turns over the control of the professional to other professionals, the organization not only loses control, but is uncertain as to whether the professionals involved are contributing to the organization exactly what the organization thinks they should. This dilemma is frequently resolved by allowing the professionals to control themselves, with a fellow professional (for example, the research administrator) held accountable for the work of that unit as a collectivity. This allows the professional to work in a situation of less direct scrutiny but provides the organization with a system of accountability.

The reward system in these situations is also frequently altered. Instead of promoting professionals by moving them higher in the administrative system, organizations are developing "dual ladders" for their promotion system, whereby professionals can advance either by being promoted in the traditional way or by staying in their professional unit and with their work, but at increasingly higher salaries. (For a criticism of this technique, see Argyris, 1969.) Additional rewards for professionals can come through publication and participation in the affairs of their profession. Organizations can also provide these kinds of incentives. As the professional becomes better known in the field, his or her own power increases. At the same time, the organization continues to have power by providing the reward system as a whole.

This discussion has involved ways in which the power issue may be resolved. But, obviously, in many cases the issues are not resolved, and professionals are in conflict with the rest of the organization. They may feel that the organization is intruding into their work through unnecessary rules and regulations or that their contributions are receiving insufficient attention and reward. The members of the organization in contact with the professionals, on the other hand, may view them as hopelessly impractical and out of touch with what is really important for the organization. These lateral power relationships will probably increase, because professionals and professionalizing occupations are becoming increasingly important to organizations of every variety.

Another form of lateral power relationship that would often involve professionals is in the area of expertise. Since there is no one universal organizational or societal truth system, experts can take differing views on what is good, rational, legal or effective for the organization. When the perspectives of accountants, lawyers, research scientists, management consultants, and executives are combined, it is extremely unlikely that a common viewpoint will emerge even after serious discussions. As the level of training and expertise increases in organizations, differences in perspective will be magnified, and the power of expertise may well become a greater source of conflict for organizations. Professionals in organizations will continue to seek more power (Hage, 1980).

Cliques and Coalitions

In his perceptive study of industrial organizations, Dalton (1959) found that cliques were an important component of the power system. Dalton showed that personal self-interest took the form of clique formation by individual members across organizational lines. Cliques were formed to defend the members in the face of real or imagined threats to their security by automation or reorganization. Aggressive cliques were formed to accomplish some purpose, such as to halt the expansion of a department perceived as usurping some of the power of clique members. Dalton's analysis shows that organizations are constantly filled with interpersonal power situations as events and conditions shift over time. These cliques need not, and in fact usually do not, follow the established organizational hierarchical or horizontal system.

Cliques can also be based on the sheer fact of differentiation within organizations. Mintzberg (1979) concludes that people in different parts of organizations deal with qualitatively different information. The sales representative, sales manager, and marketing vice president are in the same functional area, but deal with information with different time frames and referents. The sales representatives would be differentiated from other managerial personnel at the same level in the organization and would undoubtedly form cliques on this basis.

Some analyses of power in organizations have focused on *coalitions of individuals and groups* (Bacharach and Lawler 1980; Pfeffer 1981). Coalitions are formed as parties seek to advance their own interests. Coalitions seek to exert power over other coalitions and advance their own interests. Analyses of coalitions suggest that organizations are highly political, with shifting alliances and power arrangements. Pfeffer (1981, p. 37) suggests that factors such as age, position in the organization in terms of department, educational background, length of time in the organization, and personal values all may influence coalition formation. These factors also may lead the individual and groups into different coalitions, depending on the issue.

The analysis of cliques and coalitions can lead one to view organizations as a "bewildering mosaic of swiftly changing and conflicting cliques, which cut across departmental and traditional loyalties" (Mouzelis, 1967, p. 159). While this view is warranted as a check on an overstructured view of organizations, it is an overreaction. Cliques and coalitions would not form if there were not a common basis for interaction or if there were not already interaction among members. Rather than being random, clique and coalition formation obviously begins from the established organizational order and then becomes variations from that order. The fact that these cliques and coalitions can form vertically and horizontally and represent personal and subunit interests reflects the constant interplay of the power variables within the organization.

Uncertainty, Dependency, and Interdepartmental Power

Crozier's (1964) analysis of French organizations gives another view of power along the horizontal dimension. Departments in tobacco firms studied were in a constant power struggle, with maintenance men holding the most power because of their knowledge in repairing the equipment necessary to the production process. Production workers and their supervisors were essentially helpless unless the maintenance personnel performed their work. This, of course, gave the maintenance men a great deal of power in the organization. Crozier states:

> With machine stoppages, a general uncertainty about what will happen next develops in a world totally dominated by the value of security. It is not surprising, therefore, that the behavior of the maintenance man—the man who alone can handle the situation, and who by preventing these unpleasant consequences gives workers the necessary security—has a tremendous importance for production workers, and that they try to please him and he to influence them. (p. 109)

In analyzing this situation, Mouzelis notes:

> The strategy consists in the manipulation of rules as means of enhancing group prerogatives and independence from every direct and arbitrary interference from those higher up. But as rules can never regulate everything and eliminate all arbitrariness, areas of uncertainty always emerge which constitute the focal structural points around which collective conflicts become acute and instances of direct dominance and subordination re-emerge. In such cases the group which by its position in the occupational structure can control the unregulated area has a great strategic advantage which is naturally used in order to improve its power position and ensure a greater share of the organizational rewards. (p. 160)

This is a vivid example of the dependence relationship inherent in a power situation. If it were not for the essential expertise of the maintenance men in this situation, the production workers would not be so dependent. Although the Crozier study is perhaps an extreme case, it does illustrate how lateral relationships can become built around the power of the parties involved.

Additional insights into this kind of power relationship are provided by Perrow's (1970a) study which was directly concerned with the power of different departments in organizations. Using data from 12 industrial firms based on answers to the question, "Which group has the most power?" Perrow found that the firms were overwhelmingly dominated by their sales departments. This domination is shown in Figure 5–1. Although he does not have direct evidence, Perrow believes that this would be the case in most industrial firms in the United States. As noted earlier in this chapter, Fligstein (1987) has found that finance departments have replaced sales departments as the dominating force in business organizations. Figure 5–1 would thus show a drastic reconfiguration were it to be drawn today.

Perrow concludes that the most critical function in an organization tends to have the most power, linking his analysis to Crozier's. He notes that in the one firm that was production dominated, the production department was able to get control of the computer and inventory and purchasing. It was in a position to tell the sales department what could or could not be done under existing conditions. These same functions could be handled in the finance department, as was the case in another firm, with finance passing the information along to sales, thus giving sales power over production. *The combination of critical function and dependence gives sales its power position in these organizations.* We will now examine how these factors operate in a broader perspective on power.

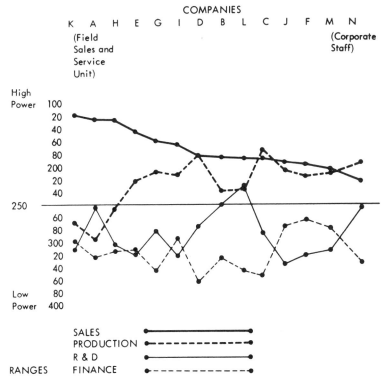

COMPANIES

Source: Charles Perrow, "Departmental Power and Perspective in Industrial Firms," in Mayer N. Zald, ed., *Power in Organizations* (Nashville, TN: Vanderbilt University Press, 1970), p. 64.

FIGURE 5–1   Overall Power of Departments in Industrial Firms (Means of Departmental Means)

A PERSPECTIVE ON POWER IN ORGANIZATIONS

The discussion thus far has been largely descriptive, dealing with various studies of the forms of vertical and horizontal power relationships. In this section, we will try to bring some of these considerations together in an overview of power in organizations.

Amount of Power

The first point to be made here is a quantitative one, concerning the amount of power in an organization. Lammers (1967) deals with this issue when he states: "To sum up, managers and managed in organizations at the same time come to influence each other more effectively and thereby generate joint power as the outcome of a better command by the organization over its technological, economic, and human resources in the service of certain objectives" (p. 204).

This joint influence is actually a condition of more power in the organization than was the case before mutual influence entered the picture.

If the French and Raven classification of power bases is utilized, it is obvious that the amount of power in an organization, as well as in a single interpersonal situation, is a variable as additional elements are brought into power relationships. The amount of power in an organization changes over time.

In summarizing a series of studies on the amount of power in organizations, Tannenbaum (1968) notes that the expansion of power

> may occur under either of two classes of conditions. The first is that of an external expansion of power into the organization's environment. The second concerns a number of internal conditions that subsume: (1) structural conditions expediting interaction and influence among members, and (2) motivational conditions implying increased interest by members in exercising control and a greater amenability by members to being controlled. These conditions may sometimes be related. For example, extending control by the organization into its environment may bring more decisions within the purview of the organization that are subject to the control of its members, thus increasing the possibility of a greater total amount of control. At the same time such increased opportunities to exercise control within the organization may increase the members' involvement in and identification with the organization and hence increase their interest in exercising control and their amenability to being controlled. Members, then, as possible control agents, engage in more frequent influence attempts, and as possible objects of control, provide new opportunities to one another to exercise control. Thus external developments may affect social and psychological processes within the organization conducive to a high level of internal control, just as conditions of a high level of involvement by members and of a high level of control within the organization may contribute to the strength of the organization and hence to its power in the environment. (pp. 14–15)

This view that the amount of power varies in organizations has to be approached with some caution. First, the amount does not vary dramatically from situation to situation. Factors leading to an increase or decrease would typically not be rapid or sudden in their impact—with the exception of something like a disaster, in which case the amount of power in the organization could change very dramatically. Generally, however, changes in the amount of power will be gradual. A second caution is that at any one point in time the amount of power in an organization is fixed—a zero-sum game. If one person or group gains in power, another loses. Power acts are carried out within a fixed-amount framework. It is the framework that is altered over time.

Factors Affecting the Distribution of Power

When the focus is shifted from the amount of power to the reasons why power is distributed as it is, several points stand out. The ability to cope with uncertainty has been found to make an important contribution to power differentials (Hickson, Pugh, and Pheysey, 1969). Coping with uncertainty means that an organizational unit is able to deal with some issue of concern to the organization. If the concern is financial, for example, the unit able to attract resources will gain in power (Salancik and Pfeffer, 1974). In the perspective of the Aston group, coping with uncertainty is coupled with both the centrality of the organizational unit to the total organization and its nonsubstitutability. Units that cope well with uncertainty and are irreplaceable and central to the work flow of the organization will have increased power.

An empirical examination of this theoretical approach revealed that this process did in fact operate, but with a minor modification (Hickson et al., 1974). The modification is the fact that some organizational units are delegated important tasks in the first place. They can increase their power by effective coping. In other instances, power can be developed in situations in which organizational units enter new and important areas of uncertainty, cope well, and develop more power. Hambrick (1981) found essentially the same pattern in an analysis of the amount of power held by executives. If executives coped with the dominant requirements imposed by the environment of their industry, they had high power. Asher and Shapiro (1988) adds the note that centrality to the flow of work in the organization is more important than centrality in the broader mission of the organization. Enz (1988) found that congruity in values among work unit members and top managers also contributed to unit power.

This approach implies that power is constantly shifting within organizations, as units or people gain or lose power according to how well they cope with uncertainty. While it is true that power is a component of any situation, the imagery of constantly shifting power is a mistake for two reasons. First, the importance of the established hierarchy and degree of centralization is ignored. While the coping with uncertainty approach is concerned with horizontal power relationships, the more vertical ones cannot just be ignored. Second, once an organizational unit gains power by its success in coping, it would try very hard to maintain its power. Earlier success gives a unit or a person an immediate advantage over other units or people because it already has more power. Indeed, Boeker (1989) found that the environment present at the time an organization is formed and the background of the founding entrepreneur influence the departmental areas which come to be regarded as more important. These historical influences carry over throughout the organization's history as "vestiges of early events." Lachman (1989) finds that an organizational units previous power position is the main predictor of its subsequent power.

We can see the importance of a unit's original power position in two studies of university budget allocation decisions. Pfeffer and Salancik (1974) found that the more powerful units received more resources—the rich get richer and the poor get poorer. Hills and Mahoney (1978) found this pattern to be particularly evident in times of financial adversity.

As Michels (1949) reminds us, power has a self-perpetuating aspect. Thus, those in power in an organization tend to remain in power. They have resources, and the power recipients do not. The very fact that legitimacy is such an important consideration in organizational power arrangements sets the stage for the perpetuation of existing power distributions.

Most of the discussion of power in organizations has been concerned with the manner in which an individual or unit is able to control the behavior of others in the organization. The emphasis has been on the idea that power is not a static phenomenon, even with the same personnel involved. But the issue becomes more complicated if problems of succession of personnel at all levels are considered. Studies by Gouldner (1954), Guest (1962), and Grusky (1961) have indicated that changes in the top management can have important repercussions for the total organization, particularly when the new leader tries to utilize a different power basis than did his or her predecessor. Turnover of personnel thus also contributes to the instability of power relationships.

The distribution of power in organizations has ramifications beyond those already discussed. The distribution of resources within an organization, including rewards, budget items, and personnel, is affected by the power system (Zald, 1970; Pondy, 1970). Since the allocation system is affected by the existing power system, it tends to perpetuate the existing system. Zald points out that the accounting and information systems within organizations are important agents of power; they determine the emphasis given to particular kinds of activities and the information that is available to various number of the organization. Zald also notes that the nature of the incentive system within the organization is an important power consideration, since it provides the basis, both in nature and extent, on which rewards are distributed.

As will be discussed in the next chapter, decision making is a critical organizational process. Power is obviously important in decision making as will be seen. Here we will simply note that power holders shape and decide what are issues and what are nonissues (Ranson, Hinings, and Greenwood 1980; Clegg and Dunkerley, 1980). If an organizational member believes that something is a burning issue, it will only become one in the organization if power holders also define it as such.

External Factors

The focus of this discussion has been primarily on factors internal to the organization. Zald points out that external considerations also play an important role in the power system of the organization. Here factors such as associations of similar organizations (trade associations or baseball leagues), relationships with suppliers and users of the organization's output, regulatory agencies, and other indirectly involved parties affect the amount and distribution of power within the organization. An example of this is provided by Peterson (1970), who notes that the National Labor Relations Board, after its establishment in the 1930s, facilitated the growth in power of labor unions. At the same time, the increasing complexity of labor laws and regulations led to the development of specialists in labor relations, and these personnel also gained in power in the organization, largely as a consequence of these external factors. External economic conditions also affect the power system in organizations as markets for labor and outputs shift, the source of "raw materials" is altered, and the nature of the organization's clientele varies.

In an analysis of United Fund agencies, Pfeffer and Long (1977) found that community organizations that themselves were successful in raising funds received greater allocations from the United Funds. These community organizations were less dependent upon the United Fund, while the United Fund had the fear that the community organizations might strike out on their own fund-raising efforts. The external world thus invades the power structure of these organizations. These analyses emphasize the importance of external relationships for the power distribution and exercise within organizations. External relationships also are important to the extent that they provide access to wealth and power for the organization (Aldrich, 1979). Power, like other organizational phenomena, does not occur in the vacuum of just the organization itself.

POWER IN VOLUNTARY ORGANIZATIONS

This analysis is meant to be applicable to all organizations. At the same time, a brief comment on voluntary organizations is necessary. Voluntary organizations have all the characteristics of other organizations in regard to the nature and importance of power as an internal process. They are somewhat different, however, because of the apparent need for membership participation in order for the organization to remain viable. Most analyses point to the cruciality of the democratic process for voluntary organizations, since this form of power determination tends to assure continued participation. Craig and Gross (1970) suggest that, in addition, voluntary organizations must remain permeable to new ideas and interests if democracy is to be maintained. This permeability assures continued participation by maintaining membership interest in issues that are new and around which power can cluster, thus preventing the tendency toward oligarchy. Maintaining membership involvement is crucial for such organizations.

POWER OF LOWER PARTICIPANTS

We have focused on vertical and horizontal components of power relationships in organizations. Before concluding this analysis, a final form of power relationship will be examined. This type is rare in organizations, but anyone who has had any contact with an organization has confronted it from time to time. The power of "lower participants" in organizations can be a source of both frustration and wonder; secretaries are capable of causing extreme frustration and embarrassment, among other things, for their bosses, and hospital attendants can in some cases make physicians dependent upon them (Scheff 1961).

Mechanic (1962) has identified some of the sources of power of lower participants. As we shall see, these are not too different from the general sources of power that have been discussed in the earlier sections. What is different is that these lower members of organizations are able to amass resources far beyond the wildest imagination if only their position is considered. The first source of power is expertise coupled with the difficulty of replacing the person in question. The maintenance men in Crozier's study had this form of power over the managers in the tobacco industry. Another example is a person in a clerical position who gains power by being the only one in an organization who knows how to perform a particular operation. This person thus becomes indispensable, with all work having to go through his or her hands. In some cases, patterns of personal likes and dislikes can "make or break" another person in the organization who ostensibly has a higher position; for example, requests for information can be conveniently "lost."

A second source of power is the amount of effort and interest e? the job. Mechanic notes the example of university departmental secretaи., can have "power to make decisions about the purchase and allocation of supplies, the allocation of their services, the scheduling of classes, and, at times, the disposition of student complaints. Such control may in some instances lead to sanctions against a professor by polite reluctance to furnish supplies, ignoring his or her preferences for the scheduling of classes, and giving others preference in the allocation of services" (p. 359). Removal of this power from secretaries itself involves the expenditure of time and effort. A departmental chair is unlikely to come down hard on a trusted secretary, whereas he or she might with younger or disfavored faculty.

Several other factors are associated with lower participants' power. One is the attractiveness of the individual involved; personal or physical attractiveness can lead to relationships that are outside the organization's (or individual's) intent. Physical location and position within an organization can make one person more critical than another; major information processors can have strong control over those who are dependent on them for accurate information. Coalitions among lower participants can also increase their power. Rules themselves can provide a source of power, in that strict adherence to a highly formalized rules system can hold up operations in the organization. A supervisor cannot really criticize subordinates if they point out that they are following the letter of the law.

SUMMARY AND CONCLUSIONS

This chapter has attempted to identify and trace the sources of power in organizations. Common sense suggests that these are important to the operations of any organization and that the lives and behavior of organizational members are vitally affected by their relative power positions. The discussion concluded that power is a reciprocal relational phenomenon between the parties involved and that each party is dependent on the other. The power relationships can be rigidly specified in advance or can develop as the relationship itself develops. This point reemphasizes the close connection between organizational structure and processes, since it is the structure that sets the original limits on the relationship.

Although power relationships are typically thought to be interpersonal, power differentials between organizational units are also important. Interunit power relationships usually take place along the lateral or horizontal axis in the organization. Vertical or hierarchical arrangements by definition involve a power component. Also on the vertical dimension, but not in an organizationally planned way, are the power bases developed by lower participants that allow them to exert power over those farther up the organizational hierarchy.

In addition to this directional aspect of power, we discussed the forms of power inside and outside organizations. There is agreement that power in organizations does not take just one form—legitimate authority—and that extraorganizational considerations are important in power relationships. The empirical research reviewed provided additional insights into these relationships.

From the outset it became apparent that most power relationships involve the use of more than one form of power. Because individuals and organizational units develop relationships over time, additional elements will almost surely be added to power arrangements.

The nature of the power system used in the organization has important consequences for the manner in which individuals attach themselves to the organization and for the more general issue of organizational effectiveness. If inappropriate power forms are used, the organization is likely to be less effective than it might otherwise be. Studies of power in organizations reiterate the dominant theme of this book—that organizational structure and processes are in constant and reciprocal interaction. Power relationships develop out of and then alter existing structural arrangements.

In a broader look at power, it was emphasized that power is not a fixed sum in organizations. The amount of power in the system can increase or decrease. Although a power system is often established by the organization, the considerations discussed above regarding multiple forms of power and the reciprocity involved in the power relationship make a general growth in power almost inevitable.

It was also pointed out in this section that the power variable is vital in determining internal resource allocations. This fact leads to the conclusion that power relationships in organizations tend to be stable, since the original allocation of resources will be an important determinant of future power relationships. The fact that external considerations affect the power distribution and relationships within an organization is a reaffirmation of the general approach that has been taken throughout. Organizational structure and processes are in interaction with the environment and organizational outputs affect the environment, which then in turn becomes a potentially altered form of input.

This chapter has intentionally omitted any serious mention of the outcomes of the exercise of power. The most dramatic outcome of power is conflict between the participating parties. In the next chapter we turn to conflict and the other, less dramatic consequences of the power act.

6

Conflict and Other Outcomes of Power

This will be a brief chapter, not because the topics to be considered are unimportant, but rather because there has been less quality conceptualization and research on the topics than on many of the other chapters or sections of this book. Nonetheless, if the exercise of power is important for understanding organizations, then it is imperative that we examine the outcomes of power.

OUTCOMES OF POWER RELATIONSHIPS

Compliance and Involvement

The most frequent consequence of a power act is *compliance*. This is frequently overlooked in analyses of power, since it is the resistance to a power act—conflict—that is more dramatic and exciting. The fact of the matter is that it is the less dramatic phenomenon of compliance that is much more frequent. And, despite the importance of conflict for organizations, compliance is really the core of organizations.

Etzioni (1961, 1975) made compliance the heart of his typology and conceptualization of organizations. It will be remembered from the discussion of typologies that Etzioni identified alienative, calculative, and moral involvement on the part of lower participants as they comply with the various forms of power used. Etzioni recognizes that in many cases there are mixed reasons for compliance. Thus, school children generally believe that their teachers are to be admired (normative power), but there is always the potential for punishment (coercive power). Etzioni's classification of power is similar to that developed in the last chapter, and his types of power are quite compatible with the power bases which have been discussed there.

The findings associated with the Etzioni scheme suggest that when organizations are able to develop moral involvement on the part of their members, their commitment to the organization is higher. This is particularly the case for voluntary organizations.

Wood (1975) examined churches as voluntary organizations. He was interested in the ways in which church leaders could pursue interests, such as civil rights and social justice, which church members did not necessarily embrace. He found that commitment or moral involvement contributed to members going along with church leaders' positions. In some churches, more formal commitment through submission to hierarchical authority also contributed to members' compliance with leaders' wishes. In some later research, Hougland, Shepard, and Wood (1979) and Hougland and Wood (1980) found that the amount of control exercised in church organizations was related to members' commitment to the organizations. Members who were committed to and satisfied with the organization reported that they also exerted more control in their organizations. Commitment thus increases moral involvement, but at the same time raises the level of control or power which the lower participants experience. There is an increase in the *amount* of power.

Compliance and involvement are interrelated phenomena. Voluntary organizations rely on moral involvement. Moral involvement is apparently increased when members are encouraged to participate and do participate. Participation thus contributes to compliance through the process of involvement.

In an earlier chapter we considered participation in relation to centralization. At this point we will examine the question of the extent to which participation in decision making affects the power of the individuals in power positions. There appears to be very little effect—although participation can sometimes increase the power of the power holder. Rosner et al. (1973) found that greater worker participation did not reduce the influence of the manager. Workers felt that they had more personal influence, trust, and responsibility, but the actual influence of the manager was unaffected. In a related study, Mulder and Wilke (1970) found that participation actually increases the power of the power holder. This occurs when neither the power holders nor recipients have expertise in the issue at hand. If the power recipients gain in expertise before the participation, their power relative to that of the power holder will increase.

Compliance, and even willing compliance, is common in organizations. People come to work on time, do what their bosses desire, and produce their goods or deliver their services. Organizational units generally also comply or obey. This is not the only response to power, however. As Blau (1964) has pointed out, the power recipient can *withdraw* from the situation or attempt to *circumvent* or go around the power holder. Withdrawal involves backing off from the power relationships. Circumvention would be exemplified by "going over the boss's head," which is a risky move, but certainly not infrequent. The power outcome of greatest interest, however, is conflict.

Interest in conflict in organizations has a strange and twisted history. Clark (1988) has issued a strong call for renewed interest in the subject. Indeed, many of the references in this chapter are nearly 30 years old, which suggests that conflict has not received ongoing serious interest. At the same time, Clark notes that Scott (1987a) claims that conflict is part of the mandatory rhetoric of Marxist analyses of organizations. Conflict is more than mandatory rhetoric, of course, since it is an inherent organizational process.

CONFLICT

Conflict arises whenever interests collide. The natural reaction to conflict in organizational contests is usually to view it as a dysfunctional force that can be attributed to some regrettable set of circumstances or causes. "It's a personality problem." "They're rivals who always meet head on." "Production people and marketing people never get along." "Everyone hates auditors and accountants." Conflict is regarded as an unfortunate state that in more favorable circumstances would disappear.

If our analysis ...is correct, however, then conflict is always present in organizations. Conflict may be personal, interpersonal, or between rival groups and coalitions. It may be built into organizational structures, roles, attitudes, and stereotypes, or arise over a scarcity of resources. It may be explicit or covert. Whatever the reason, or whatever the form it takes, its source rests in some perceived or real divergence of interests. (Morgan, 1986, p. 155)

Many of the major forms of conflict within organizations are already well known to anyone concerned with organizations or society in general. Labor-management conflict is a prominent part of our social heritage, as well as of organizational life. Writers such as Sabel (1982) view organizations in terms of the conflicts that are inherent between workers and management. In addition, divisions that exist along skill and ethnic lines can also be viewed as inherent sources of conflict.

Conflict in organizations involves more than simple interpersonal conflict. (Not that interpersonal conflict is necessarily simple, given the complexities of the human personality, but for our purposes it is only part of the picture.) The psychologist Sanford (1964) puts this point in an historical perspective when he states: "Twenty years ago, it seemed easy to account for organizational conflict by blaming the problem behavior of individuals. But the simple formula, 'trouble is due to 'trouble-makers,' is unfortunately inadequate in the light of our present knowledge of the social process" (p. 95). The inadequacy of the individualized approach to conflict is based on the fact that organizational considerations and the very nature of organizations themselves contribute to conflict situations.

Bases of Conflict

Another psychologist, Katz (1964), has identified three organizational bases of conflict. The first is "functional conflict induced by various subsystems within the organizations." This form of conflict involves the fact that

...every subsystem of an organization with its distinctive functions develops its own norms and values and is characterized by its own dynamics. People in the maintenance subsystem have the problem of maintaining the role system and preserving the character of the organization through selection of appropriate personnel, indoctrinating and training them, devising checks for ensuring standard role performance, and so on. These people face inward in the organization and are concerned with maintaining the status quo. People in the procurement and disposal subsystems, however, face outward on the world and develop a different psychological orientation. These differing orientations are one built-in source of conflict. Put in another way, the systems of maintenance, production, and adaptive development each develop their own distinctive norms and frames of reference which contain their own elements of potential conflict. (pp. 105–06)

Although the focus is on the psychological states of the members of the organizations, the point is important, since different subunits in organizations perform tasks that come into conflict because they are basically incompatible.

The second source of conflict is the fact that units may have *similar* functions. Conflict here can take the form of "hostile rivalry or good-natured competition" (p. 106). Such competition can be beneficial, but it can also be destructive. Conflicts may also develop when there is mutual task dependence (Aldrich, 1979). Aldrich also notes a conflict potential when there is asymmetric, or unbalanced, dependence among units in regard to a task. These first two sources of conflict stem from horizontal power relationships between people or organizational units.

Katz's final form of organizationally based conflict is "hierarchical conflict stemming from interest group struggles over the organizational rewards of status, prestige, and monetary reward" (p. 106). Since less than total satisfaction with the reward structure is common, and since subgroups develop their own communication systems and norms, it is normal that lower-level personnel "try to improve their lot by joining forces as an interest group against the more privileged members of the organization" (p. 106). Although one typically thinks of blue-collar workers and unions in this regard, the process would operate with white-collar workers and subgroups in the management hierarchy.

Robbins (1974) approaches the bases of conflict in a different manner. He suggests that conflict can result from imperfect communications. Communications can be distorted, semantic difficulties can exist, knowledge itself contains intrinsic ambiguities, and communications channels can be imperfectly used. Structural conditions also lead to conflict; large size, the heterogeneity of the staff, styles of supervision, and extent of participation, the reward system, and the form of power used are among such conditions. Robbins also notes that personal behavior variables are important in the areas of personality dimensions and interactions, role satisfactions, and individual goals. In addition, conflict can emerge from differences between occupational groups, such as different professions, or between groups with different power in the organizations, such as in labor-management conflict (see Dahrendorf, 1959; Hage and Aiken, 1970; Silverman, 1971; Hage, 1980). Furthermore, just as we cannot assume that the organization will always act rationally, there can be no assumption that individuals will not "depart from rational, reality-based behavior in their individual struggles against one another or in their participation in group struggles" (Katz, 1964, pp. 105–06)

These bases of conflict are an inherent element of organizations, and thus conflict itself must be viewed as inherent. At the same time, the fact that these antecedents or bases of conflict are present does not mean that conflict will take place. Before conflict can ensue, the parties involved must perceive that they are in a position to interfere with the other party (Kochan, Huber, and Cummings, 1975; Schmidt and Kochan, 1972). A decision must be made to engage in conflict. Whether the decision is based on rational calculation or fervid emotion, or is individual or collective, it does not occur automatically.

The Conflict Situation

We have been looking at the bases of conflict situations and the parties engaged in them. We will now examine the conflict situation itself and then turn to the outcomes of conflict. Boulding (1964) has provided a framework for a composite view of the total conflict situation. He suggests that there are four components in the process. First are the parties involved. Conflict must involve at least two parties—individuals, groups, or organizations. Hypothetically, therefore, there can be nine types of conflict—person-person, person-group, and so on. Boulding suggests that there is a tendency toward symmetry in these relationships, in that person-organizational or group-organizational conflict tends to move toward organizational-organizational conflict. This is based on the power differentials that are likely to exist between these different levels in the organization.

As the next component in his framework, Boulding identifies the "field of conflict," defined as "the whole set of relevant possible states of the social system. (Any state of the social system which either of the parties to a conflict considers relevant is, of course, a relevant state.)" (p. 138). What Boulding is referring to here are the alternative conditions toward which a conflict could move. If the parties in a conflict have a particular power relationship with one another, with one having more power than the other, the field of conflict involves a continuation of the present state, plus all the alternative conditions. These alternatives include both parties' gaining or losing power or one's gaining at the expense of the other. This concept is indicative of the process nature of conflict, in that the parties in the situation will seldom retain the same position in relation to one another after the conflict is resolved or continued. The field of conflict includes the directions of the movement as the process occurs.

The third component is the dynamics of the conflict situation. That is, each party in a conflict will adjust its own position to one that it feels is congruent with that of its opponent. If one of the parties becomes more militant, the other will probably do the same. This assumes of course that the power available to the two parties is at least moderately comparable. An interesting aspect of the dynamics of conflict is that conflict can "move around" in an organization (Smith, 1989). Parties in a conflict can "take it out on others" as they engage in their conflict.

The field of conflict can thus expand or contract as the dynamics of the conflict situation take place. The conflict can move around, allies can be sought or bought, and coalitions can be formed. A nonorganizational example of these dynamics can be found in international relations, where nations will intensify their own conflict efforts in anticipation of or reaction to their opponents' moves. This can escalate into all-out war and eventual total destruction, or can stabilize at some point along the way, with the conflict seldom being limited in its scope to the parties involved. The same phenomenon occurs in organizations, with the equivalent of all-out war in the case of labor-management conflicts that end in the dissolution of the company involved. The dynamic nature of conflict can also be seen in the fact that there is an increase and decrease in the intensity of a conflict during its course. While the field of conflict may remain the same, the energies devoted to it vary over time.

The final element in the Boulding model is the management, control, or resolution of conflict (p. 142). The terms used suggest that conflict situations are generally not discrete situations with a clear beginning and end. They obviously emerge out of preexisting situations and do not end forever with a strike settlement or lowering of the intensity of the conflict. Boulding notes that organizations attempt to prevent conflict from becoming "pathological" and thus destructive of the parties involved and the larger system. One form of conflict resolution is a unilateral move; according to Boulding, a good deal of conflict is resolved through the relatively simple mechanism of the "peaceableness" of one of the participants. While it relates primarily to interpersonal conflict, this idea can be utilized in the organizational setting. Peaceableness simply involves one of the parties' backing off or withdrawing from the conflict. The other party reacts to this in most cases by also backing off, even if it would prefer to continue, and the conflict is at least temporarily resolved. This kind of resolution is seen in labor-management disputes when one of the parties finally decides to concede on some points that were formerly "nonnegotiable."

Reliance upon peaceableness is potentially dangerous, however, because the parties just may not exhibit this kind of behavior. For the peaceable party itself, this strategy is hazardous if the opponent is operating pathologically or irrationally to any degree. For this reason, organizations develop mechanisms to resolve or control conflict. One technique here is to placate the parties involved by offering them both some form of "side payment" as an inducement to stop the conflict—for example, in professional-organizational conflict the professionals may be given concessions in the form of relaxing some organizational rules they feel to be excessively burdensome.

Conflicts in organizations can also be resolved through the offices of a third party. The third party might be a larger organization that simply orders the conflict behavior to cease under the threat of penalties (as when the government prohibits strikes and lockouts in a labor dispute that threatens the national interest) or might be a mediator. Since intraorganizational conflict takes place within a larger context, the organization can simply prohibit the conflicting behavior. This does not resolve the issues involved, but it reduces the intensity of the conflict behavior. Mediation can do the same, and can even lead to a complete resolution of the conflict by presenting new methods of solution that might not have occurred to the parties involved, or by presenting a solution that would not be acceptable unless it were presented by a third party.

The Outcomes of Conflict

The resolution of a conflict leads to a stage that Pondy (1967, 1969) calls the aftermath. This is a useful concept because conflict resolution does not lead to a condition of total settlement. If the basic issues are not resolved, the potentiality for future, and perhaps more serious, conflicts is part of the aftermath. If the conflict resolution leads to more open communications and cooperation among the participants, this, too, is part of the aftermath (see Coser, 1956, 1967). Since an organization does not operate in a vacuum, any successful conflict resolution in which the former combatants are now close allies is not guaranteed to last forever. Changes in the environment and altered conditions in the organization can lead to new conflict situations among the same parties or with others.

Conflict is not inherently good or bad for the participants, the organization, or the wider society. Power and conflict are major shapers of the state of an organization. A given organizational state sets the stage for the continuing power and conflict processes, thus continually reshaping the organization. In this way, conflict plays an important role in the development of variations between organizations. This may contribute to or detract from their survival (Aldrich, 1979).

Any analysis of conflict would be incomplete without noting that conflict can be viewed as a means by which organizational management can manipulate situations to its advantage (Rahim, 1986; 1989) In the introduction to his 1986 book Rahim notes:

> The thesis of this book is that the management of organizational conflict involves the diagnosis of and intervention in conflict to attain and maintain a moderate amount of conflict at various levels and to enable the organizational members to learn the various styles of behavior for effective handling of different conflict situations. (p. iv)

As with any management tool, the morality of using conflict in this manner is in the mind of the beholder and the activities of the managers and managed. There are also broader potential outcomes, as we shall shortly see.

THE SOCIAL OUTCOMES OF POWER

Any consideration of the outcomes of power and organizations would be incomplete without a deliberate focus on the power of organizations in society. In Chapter 1 there was an extensive discussion of the outcomes of organizations which will not be repeated, but there are two points of note here.

First, organizations are the means by which people are distributed in the social order (Baron, 1984; Hall, 1986). Since work is carried out in organizations, organizations determine the intrinsic and extrinsic rewards that people receive. For people not in the labor force, the organizational influence is still strong as they serve as the bases for retirement plans for older people and as the determinants of the place of education for younger people.

The second point is that organizational power in society is increasingly being viewed in terms of *interorganizational* power. Interorganizational relationships will be considered in a separate chapter. For our purposes here, it is sufficient to note that research has repeatedly shown that major corporations and particularly banks and other financial institutions have systematic interlocks with each other (Kerbo and Della Fave, 1983; Mintz and Schwartz, 1981; Useem, 1979). Whether or not this is for class interests, as Marxists strongly argue, or for rationality and expediency, there is strong cumulative evidence that interorganizational integration plays a powerful role in society. Using Canadian data, Ornstein (1984) argues that both class solidarity and organizational imperatives operate in the formation of interlocks. Pfeffer (1982) concludes that the evidence of class-based power is becoming quite strong. While the evidence regarding the presence of these interlocks is strong, there is less evidence of exactly how this power is wielded. It would be most useful to know how and where this power is used in a negative manner to stop some action or in a positive manner to initiate some action (Rus, 1980).

Organizational Conflict and Society

Organizational conflict is inevitable. Its consequences for organizations and their members is problematic. On the one hand, as Lawrence and Lorsch (1967) found, interdepartmental conflict can enhance organizational performance in some situations. It can also enhance individual performance as attention is focused and more energy is used. Writers such as Rahim see conflict management as a sound management tool.

Unfortunately, there is a darker side to all of this. As Clark (1988) notes:

> With unabashed commitment to the goals of negotiation, out-of-court settlements of enormous variety, and the powers of information, flexibility, and limited liability... risk and conflict management have become enablers of the transformation of many organizational actions from rule-guided competition to a more adventuresome conflict posture. The spirit of deregulation, the calls for improved organizational productivity, and the corporate drive to become "lean and mean," the frantic search for excellence and improved ratings all may be feeding the fires of organizational conflict at the expense of the rules of competition. (p. 154)

Like conflict, conflict management can thus get out of hand. Conflict becomes a tool by which the powerful can manipulate situations to the detriment of the less powerful, even without their awareness of being manipulated.

SUMMARY AND CONCLUSIONS

The discussion of conflict and the other outcomes of power was somewhat truncated because of their close relationships with power itself. Also, there has been a rather strange absence of research on conflict in the past several decades. Nonetheless, the identification of the various forms, stages, and consequences of conflict point up its endemic nature in organizations. Conflict is part of the normal state of an organization. The consequences of conflict are also normal in that they are both positive and negative for individuals and for organizations. Conflict management as a process was given skeptical attention.

In the next chapter we turn to leadership as an organizational process. Leadership will be viewed as a process that has varying impacts on organizations and their members.

7

Leadership

Is leadership important? Of course it is. Is it the key determinant of organizational success or failure? Of course it isn't. This seeming contradiction will be addressed, but not answered in this chapter.

Probably more has been written and spoken about leadership than about any other topic considered in this book. Whether the organization be the local school district, a labor union, an athletic team, or the nation, there seems to be a constant assumption that new leadership will turn it, the organization, around. In every election at every level of government, the call for leadership goes out. Anyone who follows sports is aware of the air of expectation surrounding the appointment of a new coach or manager. A new school superintendent or university president is selected by a blue-ribbon committee with extensive inputs from all of the parties likely to be involved. Even as these pages are being written I am a member of the search committee for a new president of my university. There is an air of excitement and uneasy expectation in the process. All the committee members are aware of the importance of the outcome.

The plate-shifting changes in Eastern Europe, South Africa, and Central America in 1989–90 are frequently viewed from the perspective of leadership. Interestingly, from the point of view of this analysis, the changes are attributed not only to leadership, but also to sweeping historical events. These sweeping historical events are labeled environmental changes in this analysis.

Elections in labor unions and other voluntary organizations always contain the assumption that continuation of the old or the election of the new leaders will make an important difference in the continuing operation of the organization. In short, leadership would seem to be the crucial thing to understand about organizations.

The perspective presented in this chapter is quite different. In the research and theory to be examined, it will be found that leadership is heavily constrained by many of the factors discussed in previous chapters—organizational structure, power coalitions, and environmental conditions. It will also be argued that, for most organizations in most circumstances, changing leadership is little more than a cosmetic treatment.

WHAT IS LEADERSHIP?

Why is leadership the subject of such belief and sentiment? Why is it romanticized (Meindl et al., 1985)? Leadership seems to be an extremely easy solution to whatever problems are ailing an organization. Looking to new leadership can mask such issues as inappropriate structural arrangements, power distributions that block effective actions, lack of resources, archaic procedures, and other, more basic organizational problems.

With all this, one might wonder, then, why study leadership, and why have there been so many studies in the past? The fact is that in certain situations, leadership is important, even critical. The situations, however, are much more limited and much more constrained than most treatises on leadership consider.

Despite this conclusion, leadership continues to fascinate. As Yukl (1989) notes:

> Leadership is a subject that has long excited interest among scholars and laypersons alike. The term connotes images of powerful, dynamic persons who command victorious armies, direct corporate empires from atop gleaming skyscrapers, or shape the course of nations. Much of our description of history is the story of military, political, religious, and social leaders. The exploits of brave and clever leaders are the essence of many legends and myths. The widespread fascination with leadership may be because it is such a mysterious process, as well as one that touches everyone's life. Why do certain leaders (Gandhi, Mohammed, Mao Tsetung) inspire such intense fervor and dedication? How did certain leaders (Julius Caesar, Charlemagne, Alexander the Great) build great empires? Why were certain leaders (Winston Churchill, Indira Gandhi, the shah of Iran) suddenly deposed, despite their apparent power and record of successful accomplishments? How did certain rather undistinguished persons (Adolph Hitler, Claudius, Caesar) rise to positions of great power? Why do some leaders have loyal followers who are willing to sacrifice their lives for their leader, and why are some other leaders so despised that their followers conspire to murder them (e.g., as occurred with the "fragging" of some military officers by enlisted men in Vietnam)? (p. 1)

What is leadership? Leadership is a special form of power, closely related to the "referent" form discussed in the earlier chapter, since it involves, in Etzioni's (1965) words, "the ability, based on the personal qualities of the leader, to elicit the followers' voluntary compliance in a broad range of matters. Leadership is distinguished from the concept of power in that it entails influence, that is, change of preferences, while power implies only that subjects' preferences are held in abeyance" (pp. 690–91).

For our purposes, Etzioni's general definition, if not the specific distinction made, is extremely useful. That followers do in fact alter their preferences to coincide with those of the leader is an important consideration. The followers want to go along with the wishes of the leader. Gouldner (1950) takes essentially the same position when he states that the leader is "any individual whose behavior stimulates patterning of the behavior in some group" (p. 17). The leader therefore is an influence on what the members of the group do and think. Katz and Kahn (1978) follow this line of reasoning when they note: "We consider the essence of organizational leadership to the influential increment over and above mechanical compliance with the routine directions of the organization" (p. 528). Thus, leadership is closely related to power, but involves more than simply the power allocated to a position in the organization or claimed by a member or members of organizations. Leadership is something that is *attributed* to people by their followers (Meindl et al., 1985).

Functions of Leadership

The differences between leadership and power are still insufficiently developed, however, since leadership can occur in any group at any level within the organization. Selznick (1957) provides the needed distinction when he notes that leadership involves critical decisions (p. 29). It is more than group maintenance. According to Selznick, the critical tasks of leadership fall into four categories. The first involves the *definition of the institutional (organizational) mission and role.* This is obviously vital in a rapidly changing world and must be viewed as a dynamic process. The second task is the "*institutional embodiment of purpose,*" which involves building the policy into the structure or deciding upon the means to achieve the ends desired. The third task is to *defend the organization's integrity.* Here values and public relations intermix: the leaders represent their organizations to the public and to their own members as they try to persuade them to follow their decisions. The final leadership task is the *ordering of internal conflict* (pp. 62–63).

Most analyses of leadership recognize the fact that leadership occurs at different levels in organizations. There is a critical omission in most leadership analyses, however. This is the fact that most studies of leadership have been concerned with lower-level leadership, such as that exerted by the first-line supervisor. Stogdill's (1974) major review of leadership studies does not consider the levels issue. It appears crucial to remember that what might contribute to leadership at one level might be totally inappropriate at another level. Leadership at the top level in the organization has the greatest impact on the organization, but involves behaviors and actions very different from those taken by leaders at the first line supervisor position.

One further set of distinctions should be made before we proceed with an analysis of leadership. Studies carried out in small-group laboratories have consistently found that leadership is actually a differentiated process, with *task* or *instrumental* activities rather clearly separated from *socioemotional* or *expres-*

sive activities. (See, for example, Bales, 1953; Bales and Slater, 1955.) Drawing on the work of Bales and his associates, Etzioni, (1965) develops a "dual leadership" approach to organizations, suggesting that in most cases leadership rests in the hands of more than one person and that the demands of the two forms may conflict. Organizational demands will determine which form will be successful, with socioemotional more effective in normative organizations and task in instrumental organizations. Etzioni concludes that, at least for first-line supervisors, attempts to improve socioemotional leadership qualities are doomed to failure, since these efforts will run headlong into the existing socioemotional leader, who has risen to the position in the interactions of the work group. This type of interpretation, of course, is counter to the ideas and ideals of "human relations" school of management, which stresses the utility of socioemotional interactions in the leadership process. There appears to be growing agreement that the use of human relations in leadership positions is no guarantee that any form of behavioral change by members of the organization will take place (Perrow, 1979, pp. 132–38).

It is critical to note again that leadership at the top of an organization is vastly different from leadership at the first-line supervisory level. The distinctions between task and socioemotional leadership are applicable at the first-line supervisory level. They are largely meaningless for top leadership, since the people at the top do not really engage in supervisory behavior.

Components of Leadership

Every organization has an individual or set of individuals at the top decision-making level who can exercise power simply by giving orders and making decisions. This is simple power of position and does not involve leadership as we will approach it here. Our view of leadership involves what a person does above and beyond the basic requirements of the position. *It is the persuasion of individuals and innovativeness in ideas and decision making that differentiates leadership from the sheer possession of power.* A mechanical reliance on organizational position would bring about a situation in which the characteristics of the individuals filling top positions would make no difference whatsoever. The organization would be totally constrained by precedent and its own structure.

The ideas expressed thus far have implied strongly that individual characteristics are crucial for the leadership role. Although this appears to be the case, extreme care must be taken to put it in the proper perspective. There is a very real danger in assuming that because individual characteristics are crucial for the leadership function, there is a set of *traits* that leaders possess. The literature regarding leadership took this approach at one time, with a major goal of the research being identification of the key leadership traits.

The trait approach didn't get very far, for two reasons. The basic one was that common leadership traits could not be identified. No set of characteristics is possessed by leaders and not by followers. This realization led to the second contributing factor in the downfall of the trait approach. Attention increasingly turned to the *situation* in which leadership was exhibited (Gouldner, 1950).

The situational approach takes the position that the set of conditions of the moment—the situation—defines by whom and in what manner leadership will be exercised. In one situation, one individual will emerge as the leader; in another situation, another individual. This approach has largely dominated the sociological approach to leadership, especially in small-group studies, but in recent years it has come under fire for its inattention to the characteristics of those who rise into leadership positions. The emergent position is that while different situations demand different forms of leadership and thus generally different individuals, particular skills and behaviors will be called for in each different situation. This is a blending of the trait and situational approaches to avoid the serious pitfalls of each (see Yukl, 1981; 1989, for an extended discussion of these points).

This combination approach is used by Hollander and Julian (1969). They reject the trait and situational approaches per se, noting that both tell us something about leadership, but not the whole story. To the ideas that have already been stated, they add the important element of interaction between leader and followers. The leader influences followers in the interaction process, and their reactions, of course, have an impact on the leader's own behavior.

From the perspective taken here, organizational leadership is a combination of factors. The most obvious is the position in the organization. This gives the leader the power base and leads followers to the expectations that there is a legitimate right to that position and that the leader will in fact engage in the leadership process by shaping their own thoughts and actions and performing the leadership functions for the organization as a whole. These expectations can be seen even in periods of dissidence within the organization, when there is leadership succession and the followers express the hope that the new person will provide what the old one did not.

In addition to the position held, the leadership role demands that the individual behave in such a way that the expectations of the followers are fulfilled. Here the interrelationships between the characteristics of the individual and the position filled become crucial. Rather than suggesting that there is one set of leadership "traits," the evidence indicates that the particular characteristics giving rise to leadership behavior vary with the situation.

A very useful synthesis of the factors involved in leadership is provided by Yukl (1981). Figure 7–1 indicates how leader traits and skills affect behaviors and power. These, in turn, interact with external or exogenous situational variables and intervening variables and contribute to end-result variables, such as group performance and organizational goal attainment.

The advantage of the Yukl framework is that it identifies the factors that contribute to leadership *and* those that could block leadership efforts. For example, it is quite possible that subordinate individuals might not have the necessary skills (intervening variable) or the technology available (exogenous situational variable) might be insufficient for the tasks at hand so that leadership efforts are thwarted. Another advantage of Yukl's framework is that it can deal with leadership at various levels within the organization. The framework also calls attention to end-result or outcome variables to which we now turn.

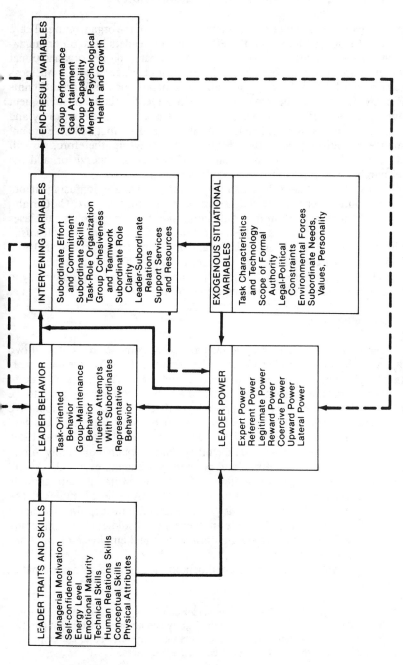

Source: Gary A. Yukl, *Leadership in Organizations* (Englewood Cliffs, NJ: Prentice Hall, 1981.), p. 270.

Figure 7–1 Leadership Variables

THE OUTCOMES OF LEADERSHIP FOR ORGANIZATIONS

In this section the focus will be on leadership at the *top* of the organization. There is little direct evidence regarding the effect that top leaders have on organizations, simply because there has been very little research on top organizational leadership. Organizational researchers have not gotten access to top business and government leaders. Some organizational scholars such as Warren Bennis and Richard Cyert have become university presidents, but their subsequent writings have not reflected these experiences. There have been books by and about business leaders, such as Lee Iacocca and Donald Trump, but these are not informative for our purposes. In order to study leadership, therefore, we will have to extrapolate from the large number of studies of supervision and the smaller number of studies of top leadership succession.

Studies of supervisory leadership in organizations are confusing, if not downright chaotic, even to those who are well versed in the literature (Cartwright, 1965, p. 3). A major factor in the confusion, aside from the ideological biases evident in some investigations, is the large number of dependent variables used in leadership analyses. If variations in the amount or style of leadership are taken as the independent variable, then a whole series of variables has been treated as the dependent ones. These run the gamut from hard measures of productivity to the more elusive factors of morale and satisfaction.

Leadership Styles

Research regarding supervisory leadership has come to focus around two contrasting styles or approaches to the leadership role. These are the authoritarian (task) and supportive (socioemotional) approaches. The biases alluded to earlier are evident and understandable when these two terms are brought into the discussion (who would want to support authoritarianism?). The supportive leader is "characterized by...employee oriented, democratic behavior, uses general supervision, and is considerate of this subordinates" (Filley and House, 1969, p. 399). The authoritarian leader, on the other hand, is much more likely to rely on the power of his or her position and be more punishment centered. A very evident problem for the discussion here is that the authoritarian form actually may not be leadership in the way we have defined it. A series of studies at The Ohio State University used the terms "initiating and consideration" to make essentially the same distinctions, while another series of studies at the University of Michigan used the terms "production orientation and employee orientation" with little difference in meaning.

The supportive leader utilizes socioemotional appeals to subordinates. This involves:

> *Consideration for Subordinates.* The leader considers the needs and preferences of his subordinates, whom he treats with dignity and kindness, and is not punitive in his dealings with them. Such a leader is frequently referred to as "employee-centered" as opposed to "work-centered" or "task-centered."
>
> *Consultative Decision Making.* The leader asks his subordinates for their opinions before he makes decisions. Such a leader is consultative, participative, or

democratic (as opposed to unilateral, autocratic, or arbitrary) in his decision making.

General Supervision. The leader supervises in a general rather than a close manner, delegates authority to his subordinates, and permits them freedom to exercise discretion in their work rather than imposing tight controls and close (frequently overbearing) supervision. (pp. 399–400)

In their review of the research in the leadership area, Filley and House find that supportive leadership, as opposed to autocratic leadership, is quite consistently related to several indicators of subordinate satisfaction and productivity:

1. There is less intragroup stress and more cooperation.
2. Turnover and grievance rates are lower.
3. The leader himself is viewed as more desirable.
4. There is frequently greater productivity.

The evidence here is confounded, unfortunately, by the possibility that the workers themselves may contribute to their greater satisfaction and productivity by their own attitudes and behavior, independent of that of the leader. They might just be high-producing, positively oriented employees who "do not require close, autocratic supervision, and therefore it is possible for the supervisor of such employees to be more human-relations oriented" (p. 462). Despite this possibility, the weight of the evidence is that supportive leadership does lead to more positive attitudinal responses, particularly on the part of subordinates. This pattern seems to hold even in organizations which are thought to favor more authoritarian leadership styles. In a study of police units, Jermier and Berkes (1979) found that satisfaction and commitment to the organization were related to more supportive leadership.

The productivity issue is not as clear as the attitudinal one. While some evidence does suggest that greater productivity is associated with supportive supervision, other studies report no difference, or that there is actually more output when autocratic styles are used (Dubin, 1965). Even more confusion is brought into the picture when Lawler and Porter's (1967) conclusions are brought into the picture. They suggest that the causal ordering between satisfaction and productivity might be reversed. It is typically thought that satisfaction leads to productivity, but Lawler and Porter suggest that productivity might lead to satisfaction. For the analysis of leadership, increasing satisfaction to increase productivity might be totally futile.

An obvious question here is: What does the organization want? If satisfied employees are desired, then the supportive approach has clearly been shown to be more effective. Short-run output gains, on the other hand, may be more easily achieved under an autocratic system. There is also evidence to suggest that when workers expect to be supervised in an autocratic style, supportive supervision can be counterproductive and satisfaction threatening.

In summarizing these leadership studies, Filley and House conclude that supportive leadership behavior is most effective when:

1. Decisions are not routine in nature.
2. The information required for effective decision making cannot be standardized or centralized.
3. Decisions need not be made rapidly, allowing time to involve subordinates in a participative decision-making process.

(and when subordinates)

4. Feel a strong need for independence.
5. Regard their participation in decision making as legitimate.
6. See themselves as able to contribute to the decision-making process.
7. Are confident of their ability to work without the reassurance of close supervision. (pp. 404–05)

This particular kind of organization is similar to some that have already been described in the section on organizational structure: the less formalized organizations that must rely on the inputs of their own members if they are to be effective. Their technology is such that there is a constant search for new ideas and solutions to problems. The obvious corollary of the findings as to the kind of organization in which supportive leadership styles are likely to be effective is that in the opposite kind of organization, such forms of leadership are least likely to be effective. That is, in organizations in which decisions are routine, information is standardized, and so on, effective leadership is more likely to take the task-oriented form, because inputs from the individual members of the organization are not so important and there is not the same need for time spent in the decision-making process. In addition, there may be organizational members who either are threatened by the decision-making process or have no wish to participate in it, and for whom the provision of ready-made answers in the form of formal procedures or decisions made for them is a satisfying or at least nonthreatening situation.

These interpretations are strongly buttressed by the findings emerging from Fiedler and his colleagues' (1967, 1972, 1982, 1987) continuing studies of the leadership process. Fiedler finds that in stable, structured situations, a more strict, autocratic form of leadership is most likely to be successful, while in a situation of change, external threat, and ambiguity, the more lenient, participative form of supervision would work better. Of course, in many organizations conditions will change in one direction or another, suggesting that an effective leader in one situation may not be such in another. Thus, another contingency approach is evident.

Factors Affecting Leadership Outcomes

As indicated earlier, most of the studies just cited have been performed with personnel from relatively lower echelons in the organization. Regardless of the level within the organization, it is clear that the situation being faced, and the personnel being led are important determinants as to which form of leadership is likely to be most effective. It can be argued that it would be good, from an individual or societal perspective, if all personnel were self-motivating and desirous of participating in decision making, and that the organization as a whole would be healthier if it were constantly innovating and engaging in continual interactions with its environment; but the facts suggest that neither condition necessarily exists in practice. This then leads to the conclusion that a revamping of leadership styles in organizations is no panacea to be applied to all organizations and all members therein.

The important aspect of the research for our purposes is the demonstrated fact that leadership at this level *does* make a difference in terms of objective performance indicators and the attitudes of the personnel involved. The question is not one of style but of impact. If production can be increased or the acceptance of a new mode of organization quickened, leadership is an important process. The extrapolation from this conclusion to top leadership is relatively easy, if unsupported by existing research. The range of behavior affected by first- or second-line supervisors is actually quite small. If the jump is made to the range of behavior that can be affected by those at the top of the organization, the potential for a real impact of leadership can be readily seen. Even in terms of performance and attitudes, the high-level subordinates of top administrators can be affected, and their performance, in turn, has an impact right down the organization.

All these conclusions must be tempered by the realization that organizations face limits on what leaders can do. The limits can be technological—there are only so many ways to run a hospital or computer manufacturer—or environmental—rising oil costs cannot be eliminated by leadership alone. The nature of the limits on leadership and the leadership process itself can be further understood by evidence from studies of changes in personnel at the top of the organization.

Leadership Succession

Probably the best known case study of managerial succession is Gouldner's *Patterns of Industrial Bureaucracy* (1954), an analysis of a gypsum plant and mine that underwent a major and dramatic change in top personnel. The former manager had engaged in loose, almost indulgent practices in regard to rule observance and other standards. The parent organization, concerned about the production record of the plant, replaced the old manager with a new manager who had the specific mandate of increasing production. The new manager knew he would be judged by his record of production, so his alternatives were to continue the established pattern—a procedure that probably would not have worked in any event, since he did not have the personal ties of his predecessor— or to enforce the already-existing rules of conduct and performance. He chose the latter course, and as a result the total system became "punishment centered." This led to a severe increase in internal tension and stress.

This example is in direct contrast to another classic case described by Guest (1962). Guest's study was made from observations in a large automobile factory. He states:

Both studies (his and Gouldner's) examine the process by which organizational tensions are exacerbated or reduced following the succession of a new leader at the top of the hierarchy. Succession in Gouldner's case resulted in a sharp increase in tension and stress and, by inference, a lowering of overall performance. The succession of a new manager had the opposite results in the present case. Plant Y, as we chose to call it, was one of six identical plants of a large corporation. At one period in time the plant was poorest in virtually all indexes of performance—direct and indirect labor costs, quality of output, absenteeism and turnover, ability to meet schedule changes, labor grievances and in several other measures. Interpersonal relationships were marked by sharp antagonisms within and between all levels.

Three years later, following the succession of a new manager, and with no changes in the formal organizational structure, in the product, in the personnel, or in its basic technology, not only was there a substantial reduction of interpersonal conflict, but Plant Y became the outstanding performer among all of the plants. (p. 48)

The dramatic differences between these two cases might lead one to some sort of "great person" theory of leadership, with Gouldner's successor a nongreat person and Guest's the opposite. Guest correctly rejects this approach and instead attributes the differences to the actions each manager took when confronted with an existing social structure. A major aspect of this social structure was the expectations of higher management in the organizations involved. While both new managers were expected to improve the situation, the new manager at the gypsum plant felt that he was expected to get rid of the personnel who were not performing properly by enforcing rules to the letter of the law—dismissing men, for example, for offenses that had previously been largely ignored. He felt that he was—and probably actually was—under severe pressure to turn the organization around in a short period of time.

There were some other important differences in the organizations. The tradition in the gypsum plant was that the new top manager came from "inside," and in this case he did not. In addition, the former manager had been active in the community surrounding the plant. The successor thus came into a situation in which there were negative feelings from the outset. The former manager also had a cadre of subordinates tied to him through personal loyalty. The successor had little recourse but to use the more formal bureaucratic mechanisms of control. At the automobile factory, on the other hand, the total social setting was different. The factory was in a large metropolitan area in which the previous managers had not become involved. The history of top management succession was one of relatively rapid turnover (three to five years), with the new manager coming from outside the plant itself. Thus, unlike the gypsum plant personnel, the auto plant personnel were used to the kind of succession they experienced.

Another, more subtle difference that Gouldner describes is the fact that in the gypsum plant, the indulgency pattern and the developed social structure among the personnel were such that there was no orientation toward cutting costs and improving productivity. The previous system was a comfortable one in which rewards, both intrinsic and extrinsic, came without an orientation toward efficiency and productivity.

The predecessor at the auto plant had attempted to use his formal powers to increase productivity. Like his successor, he was under great pressure to improve the operation, but he chose to attempt this by close and punitive supervision. The successor decided to move in a different path by using more informal contacts with his subordinates and bringing them into the decision-making process and by relegating "rule enforcement to a second level of importance." Also, this manager worked through the existing organizational hierarchy, whereas the new manager at the gypsum plant, after some failures with the established subordinates, brought in some of his own supporting staff, thus setting up a formal hierarchy that was in a sense superimposed on the existing social structure.

Guest moves beyond his data and draws a conclusion from the comparison between his and Gouldner's cases. He suggests that the success of the auto plant manager was due in large part to gaining the consent of the governed, or democratization of the leadership process. Gouldner, in a comment regarding Guest's research, notes that the total situations in which the successions occurred were different. The gypsum plant event occurred during a period of recession, with labor relatively plentiful, but with the pressures for improvement probably more intense. The implication here is that when the total situation is viewed, it is incorrect to conclude that one or another approach to the leadership process is always the correct one, even though in both of these cases the autocratic approach was less successful.

From the evidence presented in these two studies, it should be clear that top management has the potential for really drastic impacts on the organization, although it cannot yet be stated what proportion of the variance of organizational performance can be accounted for by this leadership role. Indeed, it would appear that this would vary according to the situation, since the range of alternatives even formally allowed would vary widely. Nevertheless, leadership can be seen as having a major impact on what happens to and within the organization.

Some further indications of the factors associated with leadership's potential for major impact emerge from studies of managerial succession and organizational size. There have been several attempts to specify the relationship between organizational size and the rate of succession. Grusky (1961) examined the largest and smallest deciles of the 500 largest companies in the United States (in terms of sales volume), and Kriesberg (1962) looked at state and local mental health agencies and public health departments. Both came to the conclusion that size and rate of succession are related. That is, the larger the organization, the higher the rate of succession. Gordon and Becker (1964), noting some contradictions between these findings and some others, reexamined the Grusky data and supplemented it with additional information from a sample of the next 500 largest business organizations. They found an inverse relationship between size and rate of succession, with the smaller companies having a slightly higher turnover rate among top management. In commenting on this finding, Kriesberg (1964) notes that the rate of succession is undoubtedly affected by more than the size factor, with the typical career lines within the organization a major consideration. If the organization builds in the expectation of rapid executive turnover, they will obviously increase the rate. An additional important factor noted by Kriesberg is the likelihood of interindustry differences. An industry-by-industry analysis would be more definitive than a simple lumping together of all organizations. In keeping with the general theme of this analysis, an adequate typology of organizations should allow some prediction of the kinds of organizations in which succession rates will be high. Without such a typology, the technology factor, implied by Kriesberg, would appear to be important.

There is one point in regard to organizational size that is clear and important: other things being equal, the *larger* the organization, the *less* the impact of succession would be. Large organizations are apt to be more complex and formalized, and thus more resistant to change. It would therefore be likely that top leadership would be unable to "turn the organization around" in either direction in a short period of time, unless it were a totally autocratic system.

An indication of the extent of the difference that leadership can make on the organization can be found in some rather offbeat research regarding baseball, football, and other sports. Baseball managers stand in an unusual organizational position. In relation to the total baseball organization, their role is similar to that of the foreman; but in relation to the playing team only, their role is similar to that of the top executive. Baseball teams are convenient units for analysis since they "ideally, were identical in official goals, size, and authority structure" (Grusky, 1963, p. 21). Grusky was concerned with the relationship between managerial succession and organizational effectiveness. Here, again, baseball teams are ideal because effectiveness is reflected directly in the won-lost statistics; how you play the game is not a crucial variable in professional sports.

The findings from the analysis were that the teams with the poorest records had the highest rates of succession. In interpreting these findings, Grusky rejects the commonsense notion built around succession as the dependent variable—that low effectiveness leads to a vote of confidence from the owner, then a firing. Instead, he develops a more complicated analysis:

> If a team is ineffective, clientele support and profitability decline. Accordingly, strong external pressures for managerial change are set in motion and, concomitantly, the magnitude of managerial role strain increases. A managerial change may be viewed in some quarters as attractive in that it can function to demonstrate publicly that the owners are taking concrete action to remedy an undesirable situation. The public nature of team performance and the close identification of community pride with team behavior combine to establish a strong basis for clientele control over the functioning of the team. These external influences tend to increase the felt discrepancy between managerial responsibility and actual authority. Since the rewards of popularity are controlled externally, individual rather than team performance may be encouraged. Similarly, the availability of objective performance standards decreases managerial control and thereby contributes to role strain. The greater the managerial role strain, the higher the rates of succession. Moreover, the higher the rates of succession, the stronger the expectations of replacement when team performance declines. Frequent managerial change can produce important dysfunctional consequences within the team by affecting style of supervision and disturbing the informal network of interpersonal relationships. The resulting low primary-group stability produces low morale and may thereby contribute to team ineffectiveness. Declining clientele support may encourage a greater decline in team morale and performance. The consequent continued drop in profitability induces pressures for further managerial changes. Such changes, in turn, produce additional disruptive effects on the organization, and the vicious circle continues. (p. 30)

This rather complicated explanation is challenged by Gamson and Scotch (1964). Based on a different approach to baseball teams' won-lost records, Gamson and Scotch advance a "ritual scapegoating no-way casualty theory." This theory essentially suggests that the manager doesn't make any difference:

> In the long run, the policies of the general manager and other front-office personnel are far more important. While judicious trades are helpful (here the field manager may be consulted but does not have the main responsibility), the production of talent through a well-organized scouting and farm system is the most important long-run determinant. The field manager, who is concerned with day-to-day tactical decisions, has minimal responsibility for such management functions. (p. 70)

Gamson and Scotch note that the players are a critical factor, suggesting that at one point in baseball history, regardless of who was manager, "the Yankees would have done as well and the Mets would have (or more accurately, could have) done no worse. When the team is doing poorly, the firing of the field manager is ritual scapegoating. "It is a convenient, anxiety-reducing act which the participants of the ceremony regard as a way of improving performance, even though (as some participants may themselves admit in less stressful moments) real improvements can come only through long-range organizational decisions" (pp. 70–71). Gamson and Scotch add that there does seem to be at least a short-run improvement in team performance in cases where the manager is changed in midseason. They suggest that this might be attributable to the ritual itself.

Grusky (1964), in a reply to the Gamson—Scotch criticism, further analyzes the data regarding midseason changes. Adding the variable of whether the new manager came from inside or outside the organization, he finds that the inside manager is more successful. He takes this as partial evidence that his more complicated theory is more reasonable, since the inside manager is likely to be aware of the interpersonal arrangements and the performance of his predecessor and thus more likely not to make the same mistakes again.

Sports teams provide a unique opportunity for analyzing leadership effects. Eitzen and Yetman (1972) studied college basketball teams and Allen, Panian, and Lotz (1979) reexamined major league baseball teams. These studies conclude that succession doesn't really change things—poor performance in the past leads to poor performance after succession. Brown (1982) continued this line of research with a study of coach succession in the National Football League. The findings in regard to the football teams are consistent with those of the other sports teams. Brown concludes that succession is cosmetic, which is consistent with the ritual scapegoating approach. The head coach is fired and replaced by a successor with little opportunity to change policies, procedures, or personnel in the short run.

This may seem at first glance a lot of words spilled over a relatively minor matter in the larger scheme of things, but the points that these authors are addressing are very relevant for the present analysis. While Gamson and Scotch follow the line of reasoning taken here, that those of the very top of the organization have a greater impact than do those farther down the hierarchy,

Grusky and Brown's argument that external and internal pressures for success affect performance is directly in line with the evidence presented by Gouldner and Guest. The kinds of personnel available are modified by the social system of which they are a part. It is within this framework that leadership behavior takes place. Although the important question of just how much leadership behavior actually contributes to the organization is left unanswered, the sports studies do suggest that both positive and negative results ensue with managerial succession. Few cases of neutral effects are found in the analyses. Impressionistic evidence that the conclusions of these sports studies are relevant for other organizations can be seen in Bauer's (1981) analysis of the firings occurring among top executives in the United States. In this journalistic account, many of the factors identified in the sports studies are also reported.

Additional research findings on rates of executive succession should be noted. In an analysis of a business firm and a military installation, Grusky (1970) came to the conclusion that rapid rates of succession are associated with limitations on executive control. In the military, which is characterized by a high degree of formalization, thereby limiting the discretion of any one individual, there is an intentional high turnover among all ranks. Pfeffer and Moore (1980) examined the length of tenure of academic department heads or chairs. They found that an important consideration was the "paradigm development" of the various disciplines. This refers to the extent to which there is agreement on and use of a common theoretical basis. With higher paradigm development, the tenure of the head was longer. Larger size operated against long tenure. The effects of both size and paradigm development were found to be more pronounced in periods of environmental scarcity. This is in line with Meyer's (1975) conclusion that the situation in which leadership is imbedded needs study. In periods of uncertainty, both in terms of the environment and the nature of the organization itself (low-paradigm-development departments) there is likely to be a greater rate of succession. In this sense, executive succession is the easy answer to organizational problems. Like most easy answers, it appears not to make as much difference as people might hope.

Our implication here is that in organizations with relatively loose structures and where the leadership is expected to have a great deal to do with what goes on in the organization, leadership behavior will have a large impact. Since most organizations are in fact relatively highly structured, either in terms of the formal system or the more informal interpersonal system, there are finite limits on what the leader can accomplish. Succession in the U. S. presidency, which is accompanied by pomp, circumstance, and lavish ceremonies, tends not to make as much difference as the partisan supporters of the new incumbent would hope. Indeed, there is evidence that the total system serves to frustrate the implementation of new policies. The suggestion has been made, for example, that each new administration of the U. S. government be allowed to replace civil servants with their own appointees (assuming that the appointees can qualify by civil service criteria), so that program implementation can be achieved.

The argument thus far has been that organizational structure conditions affect how much impact leadership can have. There are several other important considerations. As noted, Grusky believes that whether the successor is an insider or outsider (to the organization) makes a difference, suggesting that, for baseball teams at least, the insider is more successful. In terms of overall change in the organization, however, it appears that the person brought in from the outside will be more able to institute greater changes. Helmich and Brown (1972) suggest that the outsider is able to replace subordinates with selected lieutenants of his or her own choice. The constellation of immediate personnel around the outsider can be changed more easily than the insider's could be. The decision to move to an insider or outsider is not always available, of course. Political considerations within an organization, its financial situation, and a dearth of outsiders may force an organization to go with insiders, thus limiting the amount of change possible. (In many cases, of course, change is not necessary or seen as desirable, so that the question of insider versus outsider is not a critical one.)

Reinganum (1985) found that the overall context was the critical factor in the successions he studied. He was concerned with the relationship between executive succession and stock price changes related to the succession. He found significant positive effects of succession, in terms of stock price increases, but only for external appointments in small firms—again the size factor is operative. These stock price increases were found when the departure of the former officeholder was announced along with the appointment of the successor. The size factor was also found important in a study of the rates of death among newspaper organizations, following the succession of the newspapers' founders (Carroll, 1984). These newspaper organizations would be small organizations which are vulnerable to high death rates to begin with and the succession of the publisher makes the situation even more risky.

Several recent studies highlight the political nature of the succession process. Allen and Panian (1982) studied the effects of the locus of control in organizations and succession. Direct family control of firms occurred when the chief executive was a member of the family controlling the organization. Indirect family control is a situation in which the chief executive is not a family member. Managerial control of firms occurs when management dominates the board of directors. On the basis of data regarding 242 large industrial firms in the United States, Allen and Panian conclude:

> To begin with, there was a direct relationship between managerial power and corporate performance, on the one hand, and managerial tenure and longevity, on the other. Chief executives of more profitable firms and those who were members of controlling families usually had longer tenures and were usually older at the time of their succession than the chief executive officers of less profitable firms and those who were not members of controlling families. Similarly, there was an inverse relationship between managerial power and the probability of managerial succession during periods of poor corporate performance. Chief executive officers who were members of controlling families were somewhat less likely to experience succession during unprofitable or only marginally profitable years than chief executives who were not members of controlling families. (pp. 545–46)

These results were contingent on the extent of stock ownership of the controlling family. It obviously helps to have ties into the controlling family, even more so when this control is extensive. What is interesting about this piece of research is that family ties made top leadership succession less sensitive to performance variation than was the case when a chief executive officer did not have these family ties.

Smith and White (1987) found that chief executive officers tend to be succeeded by individuals with the same career specialization, such as finance, sales, or legal. This selection process is based on previous strategies and power coalitions within the organization. They note that this process can involve poor strategy following poor strategy, so that this process is not necessarily beneficial. It is based around the notion of strategic contingencies developed in the chapter on power.

The political process can be seen in an additional light. Salancik and Mindl (1984) report that managers of unstable firms strategically manipulate causal attributions to manage the impression of the degree to which they are in control of the situation, even though they may not have any real control over organizational outcomes. They go so far as to claim responsibility for positive and negative outcomes, indicating their awareness and attempts at controlling the situation. These strategies are designed to maintain their positions.

Any person coming into a top leadership position is, in a very real sense, a captive of the organization. Galbraith (1974), for example, has noted that, for many substantive decisions involving pricing, investment, merchandising, and new products, the chief executive of an organization is actually the "victim" or "captive" of the organization. He notes, however, that the chief executive does have powers of appointment to critical positions and can initiate studies that later bring about major changes.

Another set of constraints on what the top leadership of an organization can or cannot do consists of the external *environment* of the organization. This is dramatically seen in an analysis of 167 major U.S. corporations by Lieberson and O'Connor (1972). They were concerned with the sales, earnings, and profit margins of these corporations over a 20-year period. Their ingenious research considered the issue of executive succession and its impact on these performance criteria. The effects of succession were also lagged over 1-, 2-, and 3-year periods to permit the maximum impact of leadership change to demonstrate itself. They also considered the economic behavior of the industry (for example, steel versus air transportation), the position of the corporation within the industry, and the state of the economy as a whole. Their findings are startling to those who really believe in leadership: "All three performance variables are affected by forces beyond a leader's immediate control" (p. 124).

For sales and net earnings, the general economic conditions, the industry, and the corporation's position within it were more important than leadership. Leadership was important for profit margins, but still heavily constrained by the environmental conditions. These findings were replicated (with slight modification) by Weiner (1977) and Salancik and Pfeffer (1977). Salancik and Pfeffer looked at the impact of change in mayors on city budgets.

Lieberson and O'Connor's findings have created a great deal of controversy, since they fly in the face of much conventional wisdom and in the face of scholars who believe in leadership. Thomas (1988) has reexamined the evidence of the sort that Lieberson and O'Connor used and comes up with an interesting interpretation. He notes that changes in the order in which variables are entered into the regression equation regarding performance can essentially reverse the findings. Rather than reversing Lieberson and O'Connor's findings, which Thomas believes would be implausible, Thomas suggests that leadership has little impact at the aggregate level, but a substantial impact at the level of the individual firm. Cases of effective leadership would cancel out cases of ineffective leadership.

Lieberson and O'Connor do not claim that leadership is unimportant; nor is the claim made here. Leadership is clearly important in changing organizational directions, developing new activities, considering mergers or acquisitions, and setting long-run policies and objectives. At the same time, from all the evidence that has been presented, it must be realized that the organizational and environmental constraints drastically limit the likelihood of major change on the basis of leadership alone. The implications of such findings are crucial for organizational analysis and for understanding a total society. In established organizations or nations, the impact of leadership is heavily constrained, and leadership change (whether to a new organizational or national leader) may not make too much of a difference. For the new organization or nation, leadership is obviously more important. Leadership is also crucially important in times of organizational crisis.

The impact of leadership is thus variable. It can range from "transformational" (Bass, 1985) in which both behaviors and emotions of followers are altered and the entire organization is changed to situations in which the person in the leadership role can do nothing about the events happening to the organization.

This discussion of leadership has ignored an important consideration— the motivations of the leaders. More than two generations ago, Berle and Means (1932) had argued that corporate executives have become technical managers, separated from the concerns of capitalist owners. More recently, Zeitlin (1974) and others have argued that corporate leadership is the modern capitalist class with phenomenal power and wealth in their organizations and in society as a whole (see also Allen, 1976; Zeitlin, 1976). From this perspective, organizational decisions are made on the basis of continued acquisition of power and wealth. James and Soref (1981) report that corporate presidents, whether they are owners or managers, are fired on the basis of poor profit performance, thus disconfirming the Berle and Means hypothesis on the separation of ownership and management. We have already noted that such changes in top leadership may be little more than cosmetic. For the analysis of organizations, however, it may not matter if the top leaders are interested in their own power or wealth, if they are really controlled by owners, or if they are simply technocratic managers, since their organizational roles and impacts would not differ. The question of the organization's outcomes for society remains a major one, however, since what is good for the organization may not be good for society. This is true whether the organizations are corporations, schools systems, or churches.

LEADERSHIP IN THE VOLUNTARY ORGANIZATION

The discussion thus far has concerned the work organization, in which the leader is appointed on the basis of criteria set up in advance. The situation is somewhat different in the voluntary organization, in which the leader is elected to office. It has long been noted that in voluntary organizations there is a tendency toward oligarchy, in that the group in power wants to stay there and will endeavor to ensure its continuation in office (Michels, 1949). In looking at union leadership, Tannenbaum (1968) notes that leaders have higher incomes than the rank and file they represent. In fact, they are more likely to live like their adversaries in management than like their own union members.

> In addition to its clear financial superiority, the leader's job places him in a world of variety, excitement, and broadened horizons which is qualitatively richer and psychologically more stimulating than his old job in the plant. There are also many tensions and frustrations in the leadership role, and long hours are often required. But these are part of the deep involvement which leaders have in their work. By and large, a return to the worker role would represent an intolerable loss to most leaders. (p. 752)

This personal desire to stay in the leadership position is coupled with several other factors that can lead to oligarchy. The leaders may be able to develop a monopoly on the kinds of skills required for leadership, such as verbal ability, persuasive techniques, and so on. They obtain political power within the organization through patronage and other favors. Given their position, it is relatively easy to groom their successors. Since the nature of unions involves a time cycle in regard to contract negotiations, the leaders can provide the membership with continual reminders of what they have achieved and what they are going to try to achieve the next time. The skills developed in this phase of the union's operation are unlikely to be part of the rank and file's repertoire.

The tendency toward oligarchy is apparently found in most voluntary organizations where there is a wide gap between members and leaders in the rewards (intrinsic and extrinsic) received. Where the gap is not so great, there is a great tendency toward democracy. Lipset, Trow, and Coleman's (1956) analysis of the International Typographical Union demonstrates this point. This union is one in which the members enjoy relatively high pay and a strong sense of community with their fellow members and leaders alike, and it is quite democratic.

Voluntary organizations can also be differentiated from work organizations on the basis of the strong likelihood of a form of "dual leadership." Analyses of political parties have indicated the existence of both public and associational leadership. The public leaders are those who run for and hold public office, while the associational leaders operate behind the scenes. An exception would be the British parliamentary system, where the two forms of leadership tend to coincide. While unofficial power arrangements certainly exist in work organizations, they appear to be more fully developed in the voluntary organization, since the latter is characterized by much looser structural arrangements. And this looser structuring would appear to be related to another important consideration: in voluntary organizations, the leader is more likely to have a strong impact than in more structured organizations, because there are more possibilities for variation in the voluntary setting.

SUMMARY AND CONCLUSIONS

In this chapter, the attempt was made to place a human factor, leadership behavior, within the larger framework of analysis. We began with the empirical conclusion that leadership behavior affects followers. To this was added the idea that since our concern was with top organizational leadership, the impact on the followers and the organization should therefore be greater. Since there is not as much information about this form of individual input into the organization as is desirable, the topic had to be approached somewhat indirectly.

It was first noted that the current conceptualization of leadership involves a combination of factors. *The position in the organization itself, the specific situations confronted, the characteristics of the individuals involved, and the nature of the relationships with subordinates all affect leadership behavior and the impact of that behavior.* Since all these except the position itself are variable, it is exceedingly difficult to develop single standards or prescriptions for leadership. From the many studies of leadership effectiveness at lower levels in the organization, the conclusion was reached that there is no one style of leadership that is successful at all times. The total situation must be viewed if leadership is to be understood.

The important question of whether or not leadership makes any kind of difference in the organization was of necessity also approached indirectly. Since it has been found that leadership behavior affects both behavior and attitudes at lower levels in the organizations, the extrapolation was made that it is important at the top. The studies of top management succession led to the same conclusion, tempered by the many other factors that also determine what happens to the organization. It is unfortunate that we do not know exactly in what ways and under what conditions such impacts occur. From the perspective of the total analysis, it is clear that top leadership is important for the organization as a whole. But we cannot specify how much more or less important, or under what conditions, it is of importance when compared with some of the other factors considered, such as the existing organizational structure, informally derived power relationships, pressures from the environment, relations with other organizations, and so on. We can state, however, that it *is* important and hope that future research will begin to assess the relative strengths of these factors under various conditions. We do know that one thing that leadership involves is decision making and it is to that topic that we now turn.

8

Decision Making

This chapter is a result of decision making. In previous editions of this book, the topic of decision making was incorporated into the chapter on leadership. The decision to have a separate chapter on decision making was the consequence of discussions with students and colleagues. There is no way in which I would claim that the decision is rational. I have no idea what the outcome of the decision will be or even if there will be any outcome at all. At the same time, the decision is not a wild shot in the dark. There is a strong literature on decision making. I have participated and continue to participate in decision making at all levels in various organizations.

Just as leadership takes place throughout organizations, so too does decision making. And, in the interest of symmetry, just as the focus in the last chapter was primarily on leadership at the top of the organization, the focus here will be primarily on decision making at the top of the organization.

STRATEGIC DECISIONS

These decisions at the top of organizations are usually labeled as *strategic decisions* (Hickson, 1987; Heller et al., 1988). They are the big, high-risk decisions that are made. They can involve entering new markets, developing new services or products, starting new programs, closing existing programs or facilities, or more generally breaking new ground in terms of personnel, priorities, programs, and initiatives.

From the outset it must be made clear that *no assumptions of rationality are being made*. For example, Staw and Ross (1989) point out that people and organizations can become committed to losing courses of action, which they call escalation situations. Escalation situations occur when organizational projects have little salvage value, when decision makers want to justify their own past behavior, when people in a project are bound to each other, and when organizational inertia and internal politics combine to prevent a project from being shut down. This point is well recognized, of course. Many organizations will set up subsidiary organizations to try out new projects, with clearly defined "sundowns" or dates by which judgments will be made about a project's success or failure. Nonetheless, escalation situations do take place with amazing regularity.

Several writers have developed some vivid imagery to try to portray the complexity and intricacy of strategic decision making. Weick (1976), for example, claims that it is an "unconventional soccer match," with players coming and going as they like, the field sloping and round, and goals scattered about apparently at random. Hickson (1987) likens it to an American football game:

> It is seen as a game of powerful groups in which some teams are much bigger and have "thicker protective padding and harder helmets" (Hickson et al., 1986). Boundaries are elastic, the field is bumpy, and the number of teams in play fluctuates. They disagree as to where the ends of the field are, but eventually "one team or coalition of teams pushes through holding the ball to where it says the end is" (Hickson et al., 1986). This is a game in which the heavier or better protected players have a greater chance of shaping what is going on and where it is going to. The shape of the ball itself can be changed. (p. 166)

The players are the participants in the decision making. Scores are made by the powerful who define the rules (rationality) of the game. The components of the decision-making process can be seen graphically in Figure 8–1, which differentiates between high-risk or strategic decisions and decisions with less risk involved.

Hage's (1980) figure contains most of the elements that will be considered here. For example, in the high-risk decision example, note that the terms "coalitions" and "intensity" and "extensity" of conflict are used. This is consistent with the idea that the exercise of power is an important component of decision making. Notice, also, that "information search" and "discussion" are important components. This involves the communication process, which is itself problematic. The fact that there is information search and discussion is also a component of the issue of rationality. The search process and discussions do not yield clear answers on many issues. In fact, the more important the strategic decisions, the higher the levels of uncertainty.

Variables and Constraints

A useful approach to the kinds of decisions that have strategic importance for the organization is provided by Thompson (1967). Thompson notes that "decision issues always involve two major dimensions: (1) beliefs about cause/effect relationships and (2) preferences regarding possible outcomes"

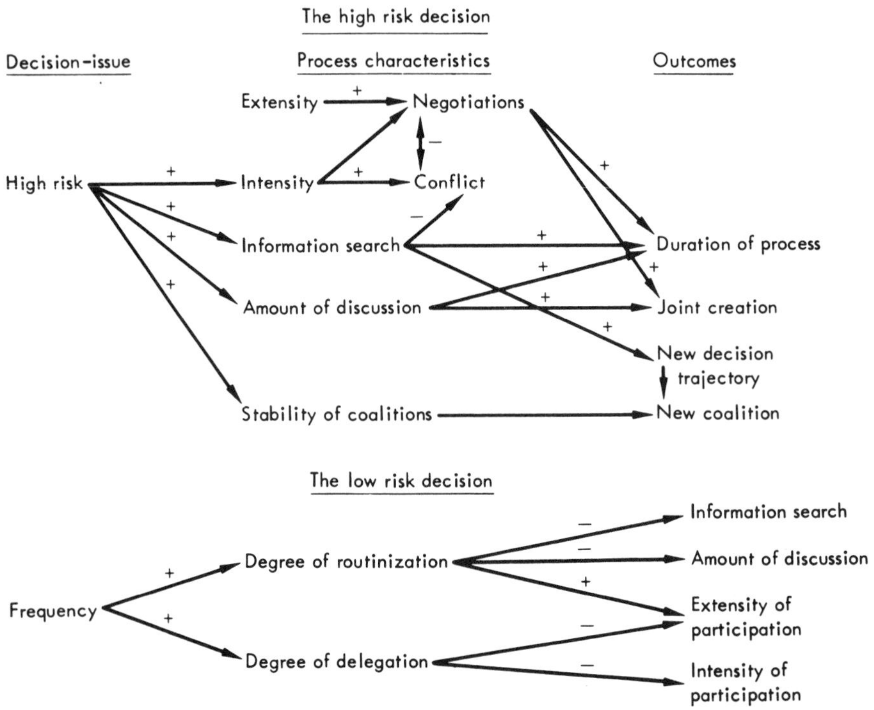

Source: Jerald Hage, *Theories of Organizations* (New York: John Wiley, 1980), p. 121.

FIGURE 8–1   Decision Characteristics and Decision Trajectory

(p. 134). These basic variables in the decision-making process can operate at the conscious or the unconscious level. As an aid in understanding the process, Thompson suggests that each variable can be (artificially) dichotomized as indicated in Figure 8–2.

Source: James D. Thompson, Organizations in Action (New York: McGraw-Hill, 1967), p. 134.

FIGURE 8–2   Decision processes

In the cell with certainty on both variables, a "computational" strategy can be used. In this case the decision is obvious and can be performed by a computer with great simplicity. An example here would be simple inventorying, in which, when the supply of a particular item reaches a particular level, it is automatically reordered. Obviously, this is in no way a strategic situation and will not be of concern to us here. The other cells present more problems and are thus more crucial for the organization.

> When outcome preferences are clear, but cause/effect relationships are uncertain, we will refer to the judgmental strategy for decision making. Where the situation is reversed and there is certainly regarding cause/effect but uncertainty regarding outcome preferences, the issues can be regarded as calling for a compromise strategy for decision making. Finally, where there is uncertainty on both dimensions, we will speak of the inspirational strategy for decision making, if indeed any decision is forthcoming. (pp. 134–35)

One obvious critical factor in this framework is information. The amount and kind of information determine the certainty in the decision-making process. The implication is that the more certain that knowledge, the easier and better the decision making. Unfortunately, information does not flow automatically into an organization. Whatever is happening inside or outside an organization is subject to the perceptions and interpretations of the decision makers (Duncan, 1972). Miles, Snow, and Pfeffer (1974) suggest that decision makers can take four stances in their perceptions. They can be "domain defenders," who attempt to allow little change to occur; "reluctant reactors," who simply react to pressures; "anxious analyzers," who perceive change but wait for competing organizations to develop responses and then adapt to them; or "enthusiastic prospectors," who perceive opportunities for change and want to create change and to experiment. These different perceptual bases are developed through the individual decision maker's experiences in the organization. Thus, the same external or internal conditions can be viewed differently, depending upon who is doing the perceiving. Jackson and Dutton (1988) found that decision makers are more likely to discern threats than opportunities. Decision makers are thus not automatons or computers who respond to all messages in equal ways.

Information is part of the communications process within organizations. As will be seen in the next chapter, the communications process itself is almost guaranteed to withhold, expand, or distort information. In addition, organizations scan different environments in different fashions. For example, although they usually use as much information as they can from outside the organization, they apparently cease to do this when they develop bases in other countries as multinational corporations have (Keegan, 1974). In these cases, the information-scanning process turns inside the organization, with the potential that much will be missed on the outside.

Although information is a critical component of decision making, equally important are beliefs about cause and effect. In some areas of knowledge, certainty about cause and effect is quite well developed, while in others the knowledge is probabilistic at best. Since all organizations are social units interacting with society, any involvement of humans in either the cause or the effect part of the equation introduces an element of uncertainty. Complete knowledge is undoubtedly rare in the kinds of decisions with which we are concerned. In discussing the effects of the incompleteness of knowledge and information, Thompson notes that in organizations working at the frontiers of new knowledge—such as those in the aerospace industry and in medical research—the presence of imperfections and gaps in knowledge lead to the use of the judgmental strategy, even though all the variables that are known to be relevant are controlled as far as possible. Knowledge about cause and effect is further weakened when some elements of the process are beyond the organization's control. Welfare programs, for example, are affected by the people being served and the wider community that supports or rejects the total program. Still another situation in which the cause-and-effect relationship becomes unclear is when the organization is in competition with another organization over which it cannot exercise control. In this case the judgmental strategy is also used, since the organization cannot decide for sure exactly what will happen as a result of its own efforts.

In addition to changes in the nature of the cause-and-effect knowledge system that occur as new knowledge becomes available—as in the case of new medical discoveries that alter the approach of hospitals to their patients—another important component of the system must be specified. The nature of cause and effect is actually really certain in only a few cases. Cause-and-effect "knowledge" is vitally affected by the belief or truth system that is prevalent in the organization. The importance of this can be seen clearly in the case of welfare systems that have two major alternative truth systems, which can lead to different interpretations of the same knowledge inputs. The organizations can believe, on the one hand, that those on some form of welfare assistance are in that condition through their own fault or, on the other hand, that the condition exists because of societal imperfections. While there would seldom be a complete acceptance of either extreme position, the dominant truth system would serve as the mechanism by which information coming into the system is interpreted on a cause-and-effect basis, leading to different kinds of decisions being made. Similar examples can be noted concerning the strategies adopted in regard to supervisory practices, international relations, and most other organizational decisions. From the cause-effect standpoint, then, while information is a key factor, interpretation of it remains a variable that, while usually constant in most organizations, still affects the outcomes of the decisions that are made. The adoption of a different truth system could lead to entirely different decisions, based on the same information.

The outcome-preference side of the Thompson paradigm contains even more ambiguities for the organization than the cause-effect side. The choice among outcome preferences, or *goals*, is a major issue in which power is exercised and over which conflicts occur. As Pinfield (1986) reports, there can be *structured* decision making when there is agreement on goals and *anarchic* decision making when there is no agreement. In cases of structured decision making, problems can arise because the participants and environments can change. At the same time, a focus on anarchy overlooks the regularities inherent in organizations due to the ongoing structure. The imagery here is intended to lead to the conclusion that *decision making is a process in which both rationality and power are problematic.*

Rationality

There is a limited amount of rationality available in the decision-making process. As Simon (1957) has so ably pointed out, decisions are made on the basis of "bounded rationality." The reasons for the limits on rationality are linked to the inability of the system as a whole to provide maximum or even adequate information for decision making and to the inability of the decision maker to handle intellectually handle even the inadequate information that is available. Leaving the issue of information aside for the moment, it is clear that the more important a decision is for the organization, the greater the number of factors contributing to the condition of the organization at the moment that the decision has to be made and the more far reaching the consequences of the decision. The intellectual ability to handle these multitudinous factors is just not available among current and past organizational leaders to the degree that they and those affected by the decisions would desire. This approach, by the way, contributed to Simon's Nobel Prize in Economics.

This line of reasoning is extended by Cohen, March, and Olsen (1972) in their "garbage can" model of decision making, in which it essentially is argued that organizations have a repertoire of responses to problems (located in the garbage can). If a proposed solution to a problem appears to be satisfactory or be appropriate, it is applied to the problem. Interestingly, this model also suggests that the garbage can also contains the problem. What this means is that organizational decision makers do not perceive that something is occurring about which a decision has to be made until the problem matches one with which they have already had some experience. According to Masuch and LaPotin (1989) human decision making is a symbol driven search activity. The garbage can approach stresses that we look for the familiar symbols that we have used in the past.

The garbage can imagery has elements of both truth and cuteness. Too quick acceptance of the imagery can miss an important consideration in decision making. Garbage cans of organizations, as well as those of individuals do not contain random responses, problems, or other debris. Instead, garbage cans reveal a great deal about the life-styles and interests of organizations and individuals. Thus, organizations turn to previous decisions that have been discarded or put aside. This means that little in the way of new decisions will enter the decision-making situation. According to Starbuck (1983) decisions are made by managers in small increments that make sense to them. The actions that are generated are made to make the managers look good. Indeed, Anderson's (1983) analysis of decision making during the Cuban missile crisis led him to conclude that decisions were made to avoid failure rather than to achieve success.

In another examination of rationality in decision making, Alexander (1979) concluded that the choices which determine outcomes in organizational context are made informally and intuitively, before the evaluation of the consequences of the decisions are made. The suggestion here is that top decision makers make their decisions and then develop the rational-sounding reasons for the decisions after the fact. As to rationality, then, we can conclude that there are severe limitations on the extent to which it can be found in organizations. Even though writers such as Grandoci (1984) continue to claim that decision makers can classify the degrees of uncertainty and conflicts of interest that characterize a conflict situation, eliminate strategies that are not feasible in that situation, and select a feasible strategy, most contemporary research on decision making is not that sanguine. Nutt's (1984) conclusions are typical of the approach to decision making that now dominates the literature. In this picture of decision making, decisions are solution centered. This restricts innovation and limits the number of alternatives considered. It can also perpetuate the use of questionable tactics. The solution-centeredness is based on immediate problems faced rather than on longer-run objectives.

There clearly are limits to rationality. At the same time, decisions are not just entirely random. As Levitt and Nuss (1989) note, there is a "lid on the garbage can." Decision making and access to decision making are constrained by forces in organizations' institutional environments, according to these authors. I would add organizational structural constraints to the environmental constraints.

Participants in decision making are confronted with uncertainty. The level of uncertainty varies—in some cases choices would appear to be almost random, while in others there is a more programmable sequence. To make matters all the more complex, just as there is variance in rationality possible, there is also variance in the power to participate in decision making.

Power and Decision Making

Since our primary focus is on strategic decision making, it should be obvious that ideologies and values commonly enter the decision making process (Beyer, 1981). Hage (1980) and Bacharach and Lawler (1980) emphasize the fact that decisions are made by coalitions of interest groups. Interest group interests may or may not coincide with the best interests of the organization. They certainly will not coincide with the interest of those groups not in power. Milgrom and Roberts (1988) conclude that those in power have an economic incentive to manipulate information to influence decisions in their favor.

Hills and Mahoney (1978) found that in times of adversity, decisions were shaped by power considerations rather than by more bureaucratic considerations, such as work load. In periods of affluence, the more bureaucratic approach was used. This is similar to the findings of Pfeffer, Salancik, and Leblebici (1978), who found that social influence and social familiarity were used more in decision making during periods of adversity.

Most strategic decisions are centered at the top of organizations, since that is where the power lies. At the same time, there are instances in which subordinates are brought into the process. As we have seen previously, participation by subordinates has mixed consequences for the organization and the participants. The same is true of decision making. Alutto and Belasco (1972) indicate that greater participation can be dysfunctional if the participants already feel satisfied or even saturated with their role in decision making. If they feel deprived, bringing them into the decision-making process will increase their involvement in the acceptance of the decision that is made. A useful insight on participation in decision making is provided by Heller (1973): if a decision is important for the organization, a nonparticipative style is likely to be used; if the decisions are important for the subordinates in terms of their own work, a more participative approach would be taken. If the organizational decision makers believe that the subordinates have something to contribute to the decision or its implementation, then participation is more likely. Again, this is done on the basis of limited or bounded rationality.

THE DECISION-MAKING PROCESS

Hickson (1987) has suggested that decision making ought to be approached from a *dual rationality* standpoint in that both problems and politics are involved. Participants in decision making must be concerned with the problems faced and the political process of developing support for the decisions that are made.

The entire decision-making process can be viewed as a dialectical process (Alexander 1974). The "thesis" is the condition in which the organization grows over time in a relatively stable environment (and with relatively stable personnel). The organization attempts to limit its risks, and decisions are made in a discrete sequence. Unanticipated, sudden changes in the environment (or the participants) provide the impetus for the "antithesis," in which the previous operations no longer work. Older modes of decision making are inappropriate. New decision-making modes, however rational, are established, forming the new "synthesis." This, in turn, becomes standardized and the sequence is repeated. Again, this is solution centered.

There is an additional and not so incidental component of the decision making process. This is the "nondecision" (Bacharach and Baratz 1962). This refers to situations in which (1) a decision has already been made, but the decision-making process is followed as thought it were not, (2) issues are not allowed to surface as matters for decision ("I wouldn't bring that up if I were you" Hickson, 1987, p. 175), or (3) there are issues that are believed to be unthinkable in the values of the powerful groups in the organization. Added to this is the fact that there can be decisions made to take no actions at all in regard to some contingency. Thus, while decision making can usually be thought of in an active mode, there are instances in which there are no actions.

Good and Bad Decisions

"Well, it seemed like a good idea at the time." This phrase, which we have all used in our personal lives also characterizes organizational decisions. The quality of decisions can only be judged over time. Even the time frame is problematic. The 40-plus years of Russian rule in Eastern Europe appeared to be successful decision making on their part. The Ford Motor Company produced both the Mustang and the Edsel. Junk bonds appeared to be good investment strategy in the 1980s for many pension funds. The list of what now appear to be good and bad decisions could be expanded for pages. For the purposes here, it is sufficient to conclude that what appear to be successful dually rational decisions at time 1 will eventually be problematic in terms of either aspect or both at time 2. Problems and politics both change.

SUMMARY AND CONCLUSIONS

Decision making is crucial and problematic. The importance of information and the nature of the belief systems of those involved has been stressed. The complexity of the conditions under which decisions are made and the difficulties in predicting outcomes were also discussed. Like the rest of organizational life, decision making takes place in a situation characterized by many cross- and conflicting pressures, so that a movement in one direction is likely to trigger countermovements in others. At the same time, it is critical for the organization as new contingencies are continually faced. Problems and politics are in continual flux.

Since information is central to decision making, and since communications allow information to flow, we will now examine this process in organizations.

9

Communication

Organizations are information processing systems. One of the vivid metaphors or images that Morgan (1986) uses is the organization as a *brain*. This imagery captures the idea that organizations capture and filter information, process it in terms of what it has already learned, interpret it, change it, and finally act on it. There are also memory lapses. If one takes the imagery even further, there would be mind altering stimulants and depressants—organizational highs and lows.

Communication is commonly viewed as "a panacea for whatever ails and organization" (Price and Mueller, 1986, p. 84). At the same time, research on communication in organizations is woefully inadequate. Price and Mueller, (1986) note that measurement of communication is a neglected topic. My own literature review of sociological sources for this revision of this book revealed *no* new relevant references in the major journals over the past five years. Research on communication is not reaching the major organizational and sociological journals. Nonetheless, the topic is important and necessary.

The communications process in organizations contains elements that are strongly organizational and strongly individual. At the individual level, consider the simple example of classroom examinations. If there were not individual differences in cognition and interpretation, everyone would give the same answer to an essay question. This obviously does not take place, as every student and faculty member knows. The organizational input into the communication process comes from the structured communication channels and the positions that people occupy. For example, the year I spent as acting vice president for research and dean of graduate studies at my university led me to interpret information from that position. Information of a particular sort had a different meaning than when I returned to the position of professor of sociology. *The interpretation of communication by individuals is strongly influenced by their organizational positions.* In this chapter, the factors that affect the sending, receiving, perception, and interpretation of communications will be examined.

THE IMPORTANCE OF COMMUNICATION

Organizational structures, with their varying sizes, technological sophistication, and degrees of complexity and formalization, are designed to be or evolve into information handling systems. The very establishment of an organizational structure is a sign that communications are supposed to follow a particular path. The fact that the officially designated structure is not the operative one indicates only that communications do not always follow the neatly prescribed lines. Power, leadership, and decision making rely upon the communication process, either explicitly or implicitly, since these other processes would be meaningless in the absence of information.

Organizational analysts have ascribed varying degrees of importance to the communication process. Barnard (1938), for example, states: "In an exhaustive theory of organization, communication would occupy a central place, because the structure, extensiveness, and scope of the organization are almost entirely determined by communication techniques" (p. 91). This approach essentially places communications at the heart of the organization. Katz and Kahn (1978) state: "Communications—the exchange of information and the transmission of meaning—is the very essence of a social system or an organization" (p. 428). Other theorists, on the other hand, pay scant attention to the topic (for example, see Aldrich, 1979; Clegg and Dunkerley, 1980). Instead of declaring that communication is at the heart or the periphery of organizational analysis, a more reasonable view is that communication varies in importance according to where one is looking in an organization and what kind of organization is being studied.

Katz and Kahn (1978) note this varying importance of communication when they say:

> When one walks from a factory to the adjoining head-house or office, the contrast is conspicuous. One goes from noise to quiet, from heavy electrical cables and steam pipes to slim telephone lines, from a machine-dominated to a people-dominated environment. One goes, in short, from a sector of the organization in which energic exchange is primary and information exchange secondary, to a sector where the priorities are reversed. The closer one gets to the organizational center of control and decision making, the more pronounced is the emphasis on information exchange. (p. 428)

The crucial role of communications for the organizational center of control and decision making can be seen vividly in studies of managers and their work. Kanter (1977) found that the managers she studied spent an overwhelming proportion of their time in communications. These communications usually involved face-to-face interactions with subordinates, superiors, peers, and customers. There were also meetings of one kind or another. Mail and phone messages had to be answered. In short, the business of the managers was communications. Klauss and Bass (1982) estimate that some *80 percent* of the time of managers is spent on interpersonal communications. As one moves away from the top of organizations, the proportion of time devoted to communications decreases. It should be noted, of course, that the work of clerical personnel is overwhelmingly concerned with information processing.

These intraorganizational differences are important. Equally important are *inter*organizational differences. Wilensky (1967) suggests that four factors determine the importance of communications or intelligence for the organization:

(1) the degree of conflict or competition with the external environment—typically related to the extent of involvement with the dependence on government; (2) the degree of dependence on internal support and unity; (3) the degree to which internal operations and external environment are believed to be rationalized, that is, characterized by predictable uniformities and therefore subject to planned influence; and affecting all of these, (4) the size and structure of the organization, its heterogeneity of membership and diversity of goals, its centrality of authority. (p. 10)

Communication is most important, therefore, in organizations and organizational segments that must deal with uncertainty, that are complex, and that have a technology that does not permit easy routinization. Both external and internal characteristics affect the centrality of communication. The more an organization is people and idea oriented, the more important communication becomes. Even in a highly mechanized system, of course, communications underlie the development and use of machines. Workers are instructed on usage, orders are delivered, and so on. At the same time, the routineness of such operations leads to a lack of variability in the communication process. Once procedures are set, few additional communications are required. While communications occur rather continuously in such settings, their organizational importance is more limited unless they lead to severe distortions in the operations.

Daft and Macintosh (1981) have examined information processing in different work units by using Perrow's (1967) technology framework. In this framework tasks vary along two dimensions. The first dimension involved the extent to which tasks or problems are varied; the second dimension is concerned with the degree to which tasks or problems are analyzable. As they expected, Daft and Macintosh found that when there were situations in which there were a large variety of problems being considered, a large amount of information processing was present. Contrary to their expectations, when there was uncertainty in regard to the determination of cause and effect (analyzability), there was *less* information processing. They attribute this finding to the difficulty in developing organizational coding systems to cope with this uncertainty. Based on their research, Daft and Macintosh suggest that an information processing scheme like that depicted in Figure 9–1 might be operative across organizational units.

The process of communication is by definition a relational one; one party is the sender and the other the receiver at a particular point in time. The relational

Unanalyzable	Craft Technology
	Information Processing:
	    Amount = Low
	    Equivocality = High
	
	Small amounts of qualitative information – past work experience and observation, occasional face-to-face and group exchanges.
		Nonroutine Technology
		Information Processing:
		    Amount = Moderate
		    Equivocality = High
		
		Moderate to large amounts of primarily qualitative information – frequent face-to-face and group exchanges, unscheduled meetings, also trial and error experience.

Analyzable	Routine Technology
	Information Processing:
	    Amount = Moderate
	    Equivocality = Low
	
	Moderate amounts of clear, often quantitative information – written reports, rules and procedures, schedules, some statistical data reports.
		Engineering Technology
		Information Processing:
		    Amount = High
		    Equivocality = Low
		
		Large amounts of primarily quantitative information – Large computer data bases, written and technical materials, frequent statistical reports.

(Vertical axis label: Analyzability; Horizontal axis: Low — Variety — High)

Source: Richard L. Daft and Norman Macintosh, "A Tentative Exploration into the Amount and Equivocality of Information Processing in Organizational Work Units." Administrative Science Quarterly, 27, (June 1981), 221.

FIGURE 9–1   Information Processing in Organizations

aspect of communication obviously affects the process. The social relations occurring in the communication process involve the sender and receiver and their reciprocal effects on each other as they are communicating. If a sender is intimidated by a receiver during the process of sending a message, the message itself and the interpretation of it will be affected. Intimidation is just one of myriad factors that have the potential for disrupting the simple sender-receiver relationship. Status differences, different perceptual models, sex appeal, and so on can enter the picture and lead to distortions of what is being sent and received.

These sources of distortion and their consequences will occupy a good deal of attention in the subsequent discussion. Ignorance of the potentiality for distortion has been responsible for the failure of many organizational attempts to improve operations simply by utilizing *more* communications. Katz and Kahn (1978, p. 430) point out that, once the importance of communications was recognized, many organizations jumped on a communications bandwagon, believing that if sufficient communications were available to all members of the organization, everyone would know and understand what was going on and most organizational problems would disappear. Unfortunately, organizational life is not that simple, and mere reliance on more communications cannot bring about major, positive changes in an organization.

Before we turn to a more comprehensive examination of communications problems and their consequences in organizations, a simple view of optimal communications should be presented. The view is simple because it is complementary to the earlier discussion of rationality and decision making.

Communication in organizations should provide accurate information with the appropriate emotional overtones to all members who need the communication content. This assumes that neither too much nor too little information is in the system and that it is clear from the outset who can utilize what is available. It should be evident that this is an impossible condition to achieve in a complex organization. Indeed, Feldman and March (1981) claim that organizations gather more information than they use, but also continue to ask for more. They attribute this to decision makers' needs for legitimacy.

In the sections that follow, the factors contributing to the impossibility of perfect communications systems will be examined, from those that are apparently inherent (through learning) in any social grouping to those that are peculiarly organizational. The focus will be primarily on communication within organizations. Communication with the environment of organizations will be considered at a later point.

INDIVIDUAL FACTORS

Since communication involves something being sent to a receiver, what the receiver does with or to the communicated message is perhaps the most vital part of the whole system. Therefore, the perceptual process becomes a key element in our understanding of communications in organizations.

The perceptual process is subject to many factors that can lead to important differences in the way any two people perceive the same person or message. Zalkind and Costello (1962) have summarized much of the literature on perception in the organizational setting and note that even physical objects can be perceived differently. Perceivers may respond to cues they are not aware of, be influenced by emotional factors, use irrelevant cues, weigh evidence in an unbalanced way, or fail to identify all the factors on which their judgments are based. People's personal needs, values, and interests enter the perceptual process. Most communications take place in interaction with others, and how one person perceives the "other" in the interaction process vitally affects how a person will perceive the communication, since other people are more emotion inducing than physical objects. For example, research has shown that a person's interactions, and thus perceptions, are even affected by the *expectations* of what the other person will look like.

These factors are common to all perceptual situations. For the analysis of perceptions in organizations, they must be taken as basic conditions in the communication process. So it is obvious that perfect perception, that is, perception uniform across all information recipients, is *impossible* in any social situation. The addition of organizational factors makes the whole situation just that much more complex.

Communications in organizations are basically transactions between individuals. Even when written or broadcast form is used, the communicator is identified as an individual. The impression that the communication receiver has of the communicator is thus crucial in terms of how the communication is interpreted. Impressions in these instances are not created de novo; the receiver utilizes his or her own learned response set to the individual and the situation. The individual's motives and values enter the situation. In addition, the setting or surroundings of the act of communication affect the impression. A neat, orderly, and luxuriously furnished office contributes to a reaction different from the one given by an office that looks like a leftover locker room. Since the perceptual process itself requires putting ideas and people into categories, the interaction between communicators is also subject to "instant categorization"; that is, you cannot understand another people unless they are placed in some relevant part of your learned perceptual repertoire. Zalkind and Costello point out that this is often done on the basis of a very limited amount of evidence—or even wrong evidence, as when the receiver notes cues that are wrong or irrelevant to the situation in question (p. 221).

The role that the individual plays in the organization affects how communications are perceived or sent (Wager, 1972; Roberts, Hulin, and Rousseau, 1978). In almost all organizations, people can be superordinates in one situation and subordinates in another. The assistant superintendent of a school system is superordinate to a set of principals but subordinate to the superintendent and the school board. Communications behavior differs according to one's position in a role set. If the individual is in a role in which he or she is or has been, or feels, discriminated against, communications are affected. Athanassaides (1974) found that women who had suffered discrimination in their roles had a lower feeling of autonomy than others in the same role. This, in turn, was related to distortions in the information which they communicated upward in the organization.

All these factors are further complicated by the well-known phenomenon of stereotyping. This predisposition to judge can occur before any interaction at all has taken place. It can involve labels such as "labor," "management," "minority group," or any other such group membership. The characteristics of the individuals involved are thus assumed to be like those of the group of which they are a member—and in probably the vast majority of cases, the characteristics attributed to the group as a whole are also great distortions of the actual world. In the sense being used here, stereotyping involves the imposition of negative characteristics on the members of the communication system. The reverse situation—attributing socially approved characteristics—can also occur, of course, with an equally strong potential for damage to the communication process.

Other factors that enter the communication process in somewhat the same manner are the use of the "halo effect," or the use of only one or a few indicators to generalize about a total situation; "projection," or a person's assuming that the other members of a communications system have the same characteristics as the person's own; and "perceptual defense," or altering inconsistent information to put it in line with the conceptual framework already developed. All the factors that have been mentioned here are taken note of in the general literature on perception and must be assumed to be present in *any* communications system. They are not peculiar to organizations. The literature has also indicated that the characteristics of the perceived person affect what is perceived. Zalkind and Costello cite four conclusions from research regarding the perceiver:

1. Knowing oneself makes it easier to see others accurately.
2. One's own characteristics affect the characteristics that are likely to be seen in others.
3. The person who is self-accepting is more likely to be able to see favorable aspects of other people.
4. Accuracy in perceiving others is not a single skill. (pp. 227–29)

These findings are linked back to the more general considerations—tendencies to stereotype, project, and so on. It is when the characteristics of the perceived are brought into the discussion that organizational conditions become important. Factors such as status differences and departmental memberships affect how a person is perceived. The person may be labeled a sales manager (accurately or not) by a production worker, and the entire communications system is affected until additional information is permitted into the system. The situation in which the communication takes place also has a major impact on what is perceived. This is particularly vital in organizations, since in most cases the situation is easily labeled and identified by the physical location.

ORGANIZATIONAL FACTORS

The rather general conclusions from the literature on perception are directly relevant for the understanding of communications in an organization. All the factors discussed are part of the general characteristics of communications. Organizations develop their own *cultures*, with language, rituals, and styles of communications (Frost et al., 1985; Morgan, 1986; and Ott, 1989). In Kanter's (1977) study of a large corporation, she found that the company systematically hired white males as managers on the assumption that this social homogeneity would contribute to clearer communications. It is clear that organizations attempt to socialize their personnel so that communications problems are minimized (Pascale, 1985). *Despite the presence of a common culture and socialization efforts, however, organizations contain the seeds of communication problems when their vertical and horizontal components are considered.*

Vertical Communication

Patterns of vertical communication have received a good deal of attention, primarily because they are seen as vital in organizational operations. From the lengthy discussions of organizational structure, power, and leadership it should be evident that the vertical element is a crucial organizational fact of life. Since communication is also crucial, the vertical element intersects in a most important way. Vertical communications in organizations involve both downward and upward flows.

Downward Communication   Katz and Kahn (1978, pp. 440–43) identify five elements of downward communication. The first is the simple and common job instruction, in which a subordinate is told what to do through direct orders, training sessions, job descriptions, or other such mechanisms. The intent of such instructions is to ensure reliable and consistent job performance. The more complex and uncertain the task, the *more* generalized such instructions. As a rule, the more highly trained the subordinates, the *less* specific such instructions are, because it is assumed that they will bring with them an internalized knowledge of how to do the job, along with other job-related knowledge and attitudes.

The *second* element is more subtle and less often stressed. It involves the rationale for the task and its relationships to the rest of the organization. It is here that different philosophies of life affect how much this sort of information is communicated. If the philosophy is to keep the organizational members dumb and happy, little such information will be communicated. The organization may feel either that the subordinates are unable to comprehend the information or that they would misuse it by introducing variations into their performance based on their own best judgment of how the task should be accomplished. Even apart from the philosophy-of-life issue, this is a delicate matter. All organizations, even those most interested in the human qualities of their members, have hidden agendas of some sort at some point in time. If the total rationale for all actions were known to all members, the potential for chaos would be high, since not all members would be able to understand and accept the information at the cognitive or emotional levels. This danger of too much communication is matched by opposite danger of the too little, which also has strong potential for organizational malfunctioning. If the members are given too little information, and do not and cannot know how their work is related to any larger whole, there is a strong possibility of alienation from the work and the organization. Obviously, the selection of the best path between these extremes is important in the establishment of communications.

The *third* element of downward communications is information regarding procedures and practices within the organization. This is similar to the first element, in that it is relatively straightforward and noncontroversial. Here again, whether or not this is linked to the second element is problematic.

Feedback to individuals regarding their performance is the *fourth* part of the downward communication system. This is almost by definition a sticky issue, particularly when the feedback has a negative tone to it. If the superior has attempted at all to utilize socioemotional ties to his or her subordinates, the issue becomes even more difficult. And it becomes almost impossible when the work roles are so thoroughly set in advance by the organization that the worker had no discretion on the job at all. In these cases, only a totally conscious deviation would result in feedback. In the absence of deviation, there will probably be no feedback other than the paycheck and other routine rewards. Where discretion is part of the picture, the problem of assessment deepens, because feedback is more difficult to accomplish if there are no clear criteria on which to base it. Despite these evident problems, feedback is a consistent part of downward communications.

The *final* element of downward communication involves attempts to indoctrinate subordinates into accepting and believing in the organization's (or subunit's) goals. The intent here, of course, is to get the personnel emotionally involved in their work and add this to the motivational system.

In relation to the first-line supervisor-worker relationship, these elements seem simple; they become more complex when the focus is shifted to the managerial level. While the same elements are present, the kinds of information and range of ideas covered are likely to be much greater in the last example. Parsons (1960, pp. 63–69) provides a way of understanding these differences, when he categorizes organizations by institutional, managerial, and technical levels. The *institutional* level is concerned with relating the organization to its external world by ensuring that the organization continues to receive support from its constituency and other organizations in contact. Common examples here are boards of directors or trustees whose primary function is often to maintain this sort of support. The college or university president, for example, has had a predominantly institutional role in recent history. Fund-raising and legislative relationships occupy a great deal of public university presidents' time.

The *managerial* level deals with the internal administration of the organization. Once strategic decisions are made, they must be administered, and the managerial level is concerned with how the organization will carry out these decisions. The *technical* level is involved with the translation of this information into specific job descriptions and direction.

The existence of these three levels requires that communications be translated or interpreted as they cross levels. While it might be assumed that all levels speak the same language and indeed that each may understand completely what the others are doing, the fact remains that the tasks are different and the content and intent of communications are also different at different organizational levels.

Upward Communication   Contrary to the law of gravity, communications in organizations must also go up, even when nothing is going down. According to Katz and Kahn (1978):

> Communication up the line takes many forms. It can be reduced, however, to what people say (1) about themselves, their performance, and their problems, (2) about others and their problems, (3) about organizational practices and policies, and (4) about what needs to be done and how it can be done. (p. 446)

The content of these messages can obviously range from the most personal gripe to the most high-minded suggestion for the improvement of the organization and the world; and they can have positive or negative consequences for the subordinate, from a promotion or bonus to dismissal. Whistleblowers are constantly in fear of dismissal. The most obvious problems in upward communication is again the fact of *hierarchy*.

People are unlikely to pass information up if it will be harmful to themselves or their peers. Thus, the amount and kind of information that is likely to be passed upward is affected by hierarchy. Anyone who has been in any kind of organization knows that discussions with the boss, department head, president, supervisor, or other superior are, at least initially, filled with something approaching terror, regardless of the source of the superior's power in the organization.

Another facet of upward communications is important: whereas communications downward become more detailed and specific, those going up the hierarchy must become condensed and summarized. Indeed, a major function of those in the middle of a hierarchy is the filtering and editing of information. Only crucial pieces of information are supposed to reach the top. This can be seen in clear relief at the national level, where the president of the United States receives highly condensed accounts of the huge number of issues of national and international concern. Regardless of the party in power, the filtering and editing process is vital in the hierarchy, since the basis on which things are "edited out" can have enormous repercussions by the time the information reaches the top. Here as well as in downward communications, the perceptual limitations we noted earlier are in operation, so there is a very real potential for distorted communications and, more important, for decisions different from those that would have been made if a different editing process were in force (Wilensky, 1967).

Dysfunctions of Hierarchy and Some Positive Outcomes   The very presence of hierarchies in organizations introduces still more complications into the communications than those already discussed. The form of interaction itself is apparently affected by level in the hierarchy. Brinkerhoff (1972) found that at higher levels in organizations, communications tend to take the form of staff conferences, while at the first-line supervisor level the communications are more often in the form of spontaneous communicative contacts. Even when new contingencies were faced by the higher levels, the spontaneous form did not occur. This does not mean that the spontaneous form is necessarily more appropriate, but rather that there is an apparent use of established protocol even in the face of new situations.

Information content is also related to hierarchy. O'Reilly and Roberts (1974) found that favorable information is passed upward, while unfavorable information, as well as more complete, more important information, tends to be passed laterally, rather than up or down the hierarchy. They also suggest that trust between superior and subordinate lessens the impact of hierarchy.

Blau and Scott (1962, pp. 121–24) have pointed out several specific dysfunctions of hierarchy for the communications process. In the first place, such differences inhibit communications. Citing experimental and field evidence, Blau and Scott note the common tendency for people at the same status level to interact more with one another than with those at different levels. At the same time, there is a tendency for those in lower-status positions to look up to and direct friendship overtures toward those in higher-status positions. This increases the flow of socioemotional communications upward, but at the same time leaves those at the bottom of the hierarchy in the position of receiving little of this type of input. This situation is further complicated by the fact that those in higher-status positions also direct such communications upward rather than reciprocating to their subordinates, thus reducing the amount of satisfaction derived for all parties.

A second dysfunctional consequence is the fact that approval is sought from superiors rather than peers in such situations. Nonperformance criteria enter the communications system, in that respect from peers, which can be earned on the basis of performance, can become secondary to approval-gaining devices that may not be central to the tasks at hand. The plethora of terms ranging from "apple polishing" to more profane expressions is indicative of this.

The third dysfunction identified by Blau and Scott has to do with the error-correcting function of normal social interaction. Interaction among peers tends to sort out errors and at least enter a common denominator through the interaction process. This is much less likely to happen in upward communication. Subordinates are unlikely to tell a superior that they think an order or an explanation is wrong, for fear of their own position. Criticism of one's superior is not the most popular of communications in organizations.

These problems associated with upward communication in organizations are compounded by the previously discussed factors affecting individual perception. Since rank in an organization is a structural fact, it carries with it a strong tendency for stereotyping. The very terms "management," "worker," "student," "general," and so on, are indicative of the value loadings associated with rank. As will be seen shortly, these status differences do have their positive side; but the negative connotations attached to many of the stereotypes, and the likelihood that communications will be distorted because of real or assumed differences between statuses, builds in difficulties for organizational communications.

In keeping with the earlier discussion in which it was noted that complex organizations contain characteristics that work in opposition to each other, there are also beneficial aspects to hierarchical patterns for the communication process. The studies by Blau and his associates (1966, 1968), cited earlier, are a case in point. It will be recalled that, in organizations with highly trained or professionalized personnel, these studies found that a tall or deep hierarchy was associated with effectiveness. The explanation was that the hierarchy provided a continuous source of error detection and correction. The presence of experts in an organization also increases the extent of horizontal communications (Hage, Aiken, and Marrett 1971). These can take the form of scheduled or unscheduled committee meetings or more spontaneous interactions. Communications are a vital source of coordination when organizations are staffed with a diverse set of personnel offering different forms of expertise (Brewer, 1971). If a tall hierarchy is found in an organization with a low level of differentiation in terms of expertise, it is apparently due to the need for extensive downward communications. There is an additional aspect of hierarchy that should be noted. Unless one assumes that people always rise to a level just above that of their competence (Peter and Hull, 1969), the superiors may in fact be superior. That is, they may actually have more ability than their subordinates. If this is recognized and legitimated by the subordinates, some of the hierarchical problems are again minimized.

The most obvious contribution of a hierarchy is coordination (Hage, 1980). If one accepts the common model of communications spreading out in more detail as they move down the hierarchy, then the role of the hierarchy becomes clear. It is up to the superior to decide who gets what kind of communications and when. The superior becomes the distribution and filtering center. Given the vast amount of information that is potentially available for the total organization, this role is crucial.

HORIZONTAL COMMUNICATION

Communications in organizations go in more directions than up and down. Horizontal or lateral communication is a regular and important facet of organizational life. The focus of most analyses of communication has been on the vertical axis, primarily because this was the focus of the classic writers in the field (Simpson, 1969). The horizontal component has received less attention, even though a greater proportion of the communication in an organization appears to be of this type. Simpson's study of a textile factory indicates that the lower the level in the hierarchy, the greater the proportion of horizontal communication. This is not surprising; if for no other reason than, in most organizations, there are simply more people at each descending level. This fact and the already-noted tendency for communication to be affected by hierarchical differences make it natural for people to communicate with those at about the same level in the organization. And those at the same level are more apt to share common characteristics, making horizontal communication even more likely.

It is important to distinguish between communication *within* an organizational subunit and those *between* subunits. Within unit communication is "critical for effective system functioning" (Katz and Kahn, 1978, p. 444). In most cases, it is impossible for an organization to work out in advance every conceivable facet of every task assigned throughout the organization. At some point there will have to be coordination and discussion among a set of peers as the work proceeds. The interplay between individuals is vital in the coordination process, since the supervisor and the organization cannot anticipate every possible contingency. Communication within subunits contains much richer content than organizational task coordination materials. Katz and Kahn state:

> The mutual understanding of colleagues is one reason for the power of the peer group. Experimental findings are clear and convincing about the importance of socio-emotional support for people in both organized and unorganized groups. Psychological forces always push people toward communication with peers: people in the same boat share the same problems. *Hence, if there are no problems of task coordination left to a group of peers, the content of their communication can take forms which are irrelevant to or destructive of organizational functioning.* (italics in original). (p. 445)

The implication here is clear. It is probably beneficial to leave some task-oriented communications to work groups at every level of the organization so that the potentially counterproductive communications do not arise to fill the void. This implication must be modified, however, by a reference back to the general model that is being followed here. It will be remembered that organizational, interpersonal, and individual factors are all part of the way people behave in organizations. If the organizational arrangements are such that horizontal communications are next to impossible, then there is little likelihood of any communication. Work in extremely noisy circumstances or in isolated work locales would preclude much interaction. (These situations, of course, contain their own problems for the individual and the organization.) On the other side of the coin, too much coordination and communications responsibility left to those who, through lack of training or ability, are unable to come to a reasonable joint decision about some matter would also be individually and organizationally disruptive.

While it is relatively easy, in abstract terms, to describe the optimal mix between vertical and horizontal communications in the sense that they are being described here, another element of communication among peers should be noted. Since the communications among peers tend to be based on common understandings, and since continued communications build up the solidarity of the group, work groups develop a collective response to the world around them. This collective response is likely to be accompanied by a collective perception of communications passed to or through the work group. This collective perception can be a collective distortion. It is clear that work groups (as well as other interest groups) can perceive communications in a totally different light from what was intended. A relatively simple communique, such as a memo about possible reorganization, can be interpreted to mean that an entire work force will be eliminated. Work groups can develop complete sets of meanings which are entirely apart from what was intended. Collective distortion of communication is very possible.

Interaction among peers is only one form of horizontal communication. The other major form, obviously vital for the overall coordination of the operations, occurs *between* members of organizational subunits. While the former has been the subject of some attention, the research concerning the latter has been minimal (for an exception, see Hage, 1980). The principal reason seems to be that such communications are not supposed to occur. In almost every conceivable form of organization, they are supposed to go through the hierarchy until they reach the "appropriate" office, at the point where the hierarchies of the two units involved come together. That is, the communications are designed to flow through the office that is above the two departments or units involved, so that the hierarchy is familiar with the intent and content of the communications. In a simple example, problems between production and sales are supposed to be resolved through either the office or the individual in charge of both activities.

Obviously, such a procedure occurs in only a minority of such lateral communications. There is a great deal more face-to-face and memo-to-memo communication throughout the ranks of the subunits involved. A major reason for this form of deviation is that it would totally clog the communication system if all information regarding subunit interaction had to flow all the way up one of the subunits and then all the way back down another. The clogging of the system would result in either painfully slow communications or none at all.

Therefore, the parties involved generally communicate directly with each other. This saves time and can often mean a very reasonable solution worked out at a lower level with good cooperation. It may also mean that those further up the hierarchy are unaware of what has happened, however, and this can be harmful in the long run. A solution to this problem is to record and pass along the information about what has been done; but this may be neglected, and even if it is not neglected, it may not be noticed.

While the emphasis in this discussion has been on coordination between subunits, it should be clear that much of the communication of this sort is actually based on conflict. The earlier discussions of the relationships between professionals and their employing organizations can be brought in at this point. When professionals or experts make up divisions of an organization, their areas of expertise are likely to lead them to different conclusions about the same matter (Hage, 1974, pp. 101–24). For example, in a petroleum company it is quite conceivable that the geological, engineering, legal, and public relations divisions could all come to different conclusions about the desirability of starting new oil-well drilling in various locations. Each would be correct in its own area of expertise, and the coordination of top officials would obviously be required when a final decision had to be made. During the period of planning or development, however, communications between these divisions would probably be characterized as nonproductive, since the specialists involved would be talking their own language, one that is unfamiliar to those not in the same profession. From the evidence at hand, each division would also be correct in its assessments of the situation and would view the other divisions as not understanding the "true" meanings of the situation.

This type of communications problem is not limited to professionalized divisions.   Communications between subunits inevitably contain elements of conflict. The conflict will be greater if the units involved invest values in their understanding and conceptualizations. Horizontal communications across organizational lines thus contain both the seeds and the flower of conflict. Such conflict, by definition, will contribute to distortion of communications in one form or another. At the same time, passing each message up the line to eliminate such distortion through coordination at the top has the dangers of diluting the message in attempts to avoid conflict and of taking so much time that the message can become meaningless. Here again, the endemic complexities of an organization preclude a totally rational operation.

Communications Networks   Before turning to a more systematic examination of the consequences of all these communications problems in organizations, a final bit of evidence should be noted regarding the manner in which communications evolve. The communication process can be studied in laboratory situations; among organizational characteristics, it is perhaps the most amenable to such experimentation. There has been a long history (Bavelas, 1950; Leavitt, 1951) of attempting to isolate the communications system that is most efficient under a variety of circumstances. These laboratory studies are applicable to both the vertical and horizontal aspects of communications, since the manner in which the communications tasks are coordinated is the major focus. Three primary communications networks between members of work groups have been studied. The "wheel" pattern is one in which persons at the periphery of the wheel all send their communications to the hub. This is an imposed hierarchy, since those at the periphery cannot send messages to each other; it is the task of the hub to do the coordinating. The "circle" pattern permits each member of the group to talk to those on either side, with no priorities. The "all-channel" system allows everyone to communicate with everyone else.

Using success in arriving at a correct solution as the criterion of efficiency, repeated investigations have found the wheel pattern to be superior. The other patterns can become equally efficient if they develop a hierarchy, but this of course takes time, and meanwhile efficiency is reduced. Katz and Kahn (1978, pp. 437–38) and Blau and Scott (1962, pp. 126–27) note that the more complex the task, the more time is required for the communications network to become structured. The importance of these findings for our purposes is that whether the communications are vertical or horizontal, hierarchical patterns emerge. In the vertical situation, the hierarchy is already there, although the formal hierarchy can be modified through the power considerations of expertise or personal attraction. In the horizontal situation, a hierarchy will emerge. Communication takes place on the basis of organizational structure; it also contributes to the development of structuring.

Now let us examine in more detail the consequence of the communications patterns we have discussed.

COMMUNICATION PROBLEMS

From all that has been said, it should be clear that communications in organizations are not perfect. The basic consequence of existing communications systems is that messages are transformed or altered as they pass through the system. The fact that they are transformed means that the ultimate recipient of the message receives something different from what was originally sent, thus destroying the intent of the communication process.

Omission

Guetzkow (1965, p. 551) suggests that there are two major forms of transformation—omission and distortion. Omission involves the "deletion of aspects of messages," and it occurs because the recipients may not be able to grasp the entire content of the message and only receives or passes on what they are able to grasp. Communications overload, to be discussed in more detail later, can also lead to the omission of materials as some messages are not handled because of the overload. Omission may be intentional, as when certain classes of information are deleted from the information passed through particular segments of the organization. Omission is most evident in upward communications, since more messages are generated by the large number of people and units lower in the hierarchy. As the communications are filtered on the way up, the omissions occur. As was indicated earlier, when omissions are intentional, it is vital to know the criteria for decisions to omit some kinds of information and not others. It should be noted that omission can occur simply as a removal of details, with the heart of the message still transmitted upward. This is the ideal, of course, but is not usually achieved, since part of the content of the message is usually omitted also.

Distortion

Distortion refers to altered meanings of messages as they pass through the organization. From the earlier discussion of perceptions, it is clear that people are selective, intentionally or unintentionally, about what they receive as messages. Guetzkow states that:

> because different persons man different points of initiation and reception of messages, there is much assimilation of meanings to the context within which transmission occurs. Frames of reference at a multitude of nodes differ because of variety in personal and occupational background, as well as because of difference in viewpoint induced by the communicator's position in the organization. (p. 555)

Distortion is as likely to occur in horizontal communications as in vertical, given the differences between organizational units in objectives and values. Selective omission and distortion, or "coding" in Katz and Kahn's terms, are not unique properties of organizations. They occur in all communications systems, from the family to the total society. They are crucial for organizations, however, since organizations depend upon accurate communications as a basis for decision making.

Overload

A communications problem that is perhaps more characteristic of organizations than other social entities is communications overload. *Overload leads to omission and contributes to distortion.* It also leads to other coping and adjustment mechanisms on the part of the organization. Katz and Kahn (1978, pp. 449–55) note that there are adaptive and maladaptive adjustments to the overload situation. Omission and distortion are maladaptive. They are also normal.

Another device used when overload occurs is queuing. This technique lines up the messages by time of receipt or by some other such criterion. Queuing can have positive or negative consequences. If the wrong priority system is used, less important messages may be acted upon before those that are really crucial reach the recipient. At the same time, queuing does allow recipients to act on messages as they come in without putting them in a state of inaction because of total overload. An example of this is an anecdote from a disaster following a major earthquake. Organizations dealing with the earthquake were besieged with messages. Those to which the victims could come and plead for help on a face-to-face basis, crowding into an office and all talking at once, quickly brought the organizations involved to a halt. The overload was so great that the communications could not be filtered in any way. Another organization received its messages by telephone, a device providing an arbitrary queuing mechanism based on an operating phone and the luck of finding an open line. This organization was able to keep functioning, because the messages came in one at a time. In such a queuing situation, of course, there are no real criteria concerning which messages get through and which do not, other than time phasing and luck in getting a phone line.

A useful modification of queuing is the filtering process previously mentioned, which involves setting priorities for messages. The critical factor here is the nature of the priorities.

All the communications problems discussed derive from the fact that communications in organizations require interpretation. If there is a case of extreme overload, the interpretive process becomes inundated with so much material that it becomes inoperative. Queuing and filtering are techniques designed to sort messages into priorities. Any priority system established in advance means that an interpretation of messages has already been made, with some deemed more important than others. Thus, interpretation occurs regardless of whether or not priorities are set in advance or simply as messages are received.

Organizations generate and receive a vast amount of material. If we think of an organization in the shape of a pyramid, we see a huge mass at the base of the pyramid. This is analogous to the information entering an organization's communication system. As information moves up and through the organization, it is filtered and condensed. It arrives at the top in the form of an "executive summary." The amount of information, like the pyramid, keeps getting smaller as it rises in the organization. Here the pyramid analogy must be abandoned, since the determination or which information moves on up is subject to the types of human and organizationally based interpretations we have been considering.

COMMUNICATION FROM OUTSIDE THE ORGANIZATION

The focus thus far has been on internal organizational communication. The communication complications and problems that have been identified are made even more severe when we realize that so much of what is really important for an organization comes into it from its environment–competitors, creditors, customers, regulators, taxers, constituents, and so on. In addition, there are the more general environmental messages that are sent into an organization, such as changes in prime interest rates, demographic shifts, or petroleum price increases. We will deal with the environment in detail in Chapters 11 and 12. The point here is that communication with the environment greatly compounds the communication problems that have already been identified.

Possible Solutions

With all the problems, potential and real, in the communication process, it is obvious that a "perfect" communications system is unlikely. But although perfection, like rationality, will not be achieved, organizations do have mechanisms by which they attempt to keep the communications system as clear as they can. Downs (1967) suggests several devices that are available to reduce the distortions and other complications in the communication process. Redundancy, or the duplication of reports for verification, while adding to the flow of paper and other communications media in an organization, allows more people to see or hear a particular piece of information and respond to it. This is a correction device. Several means are suggested to bring redundancy about, including the use of information sources external to the situation—such as reports that are generated outside the organization itself—thus ensuring that reporting units and individuals coordinate their communications. This coordination can lead to collusion and thus more distortion, but it can be controlled through other monitoring devices.

Downs also suggests that communications recipients should be aware of the biases of the message senders and develop their own counterbiases as a protection device—a process that, of course, can be carried too far and be overdone, but that is the "grain of salt" that is part of all communications. There is no guarantee, of course, that the recipient knows what the sender's biases are. Another method Downs advises is that in vertical communications the superior should often bypass intermediate subordinates and go directly to the source of the communications. While this can help eliminate some distortion, it can also lower morale in those bypassed.

Hage (1974, p. 241) has suggested that adding communications or coordination and control specialists is another possible answer to communications problems. These would facilitate feedback in the communications process and also enhance the socialization of organization members. Hage also suggests that communications with the external environment are crucial and that the "boundary-spanning" role is crucial to the overall communications viability of the organization.

A common solution to at least some aspects of communication problems is the ubiquitous *meeting*. Kanter (1977) has described the extensive formal and informal meetings that are a part of the communication system of the organization which she studied. Meetings have the potential for yielding common meanings among participants, particularly when the intent of the meetings is to achieve consensus. While meetings are quite valuable, it is obvious that time spent in meetings is time not spent on other activities. When I have a day filled with meetings, I have a day when I will not get any research, writing, or preparation for classes accomplished.

Another way in which communication problems can be reduced is through matrixlike systems. Blau and Alba (1982) studied a psychiatric hospital in which committees or teams were composed of personnel from the various occupational specialties in the hospital and from the established departments in the hospital. The teams were designed to deal with various issues and programs of the hospital and hospital personnel served on multiple teams. In addition, traditional rankings were eliminated. For example, a team could have a nurse as the team leader, with psychiatrist team members. Blau and Alba report that these overlapping circles of weak ties inhibited segmentation and sustained participation because participants were rewarded for participating. Their data indicate that there was extensive interunit communications. There are limitations to this approach, of course. Its applicability in other forms of organizations is uncertain, and the approach requires the commitment of all the participants up through the head of the organization.

Some organizations have turned to "project groups" as a means of solving communication problems. These groups, or task forces as they are sometimes called, are typically composed of personnel from a variety of organizational units. Their purpose typically is to develop a new product or service for the organization. They may be isolated from the rest of the organization with the hope that this will enable them to think and work together. Katz (1982) analysis of research and development project groups composed of scie engineers, found that such groups became increasingly isolated from 1 mation sources within and outside their own organizations. Over time, their productivity decreased, with the communication process increasingly focused inward. Such project groups or task forces are probably better off with a short time span of existence and a sunset clause specifying a termination date.

The nature, problems, and suggested solutions of communications all point to the centrality of this process for much of what happens in an organization. But it is evident that the communications system is vitally affected by other structural and process factors. Communications do not exist outside the total organizational framework. They cannot be over- or underemphasized. More and more accurate communications do not lead inevitably to greater effectiveness for the organization. The key to the communication process in organizations is to ensure that the correct people get the correct information (in amount and quality) at the correct time. All these factors can be anticipated somewhat in advance. If organizations, their members, and their environments were all in a steady state, the communications tasks would be easier. Since obviously they are not, the communication process must be viewed as a dynamic one, with new actors, new media, and new definitions constantly entering the scene.

The media of communication in organizations have received little attention in our analysis here. Breakthroughs in the forms of information and word processing, photocopying, faxing, electronic message sending and receiving, and so on continue to be developed. Communication technology itself is not the panacea for organizational communication problems. The problems are rooted in the nature of organizations, their participants, and their interactions with their environments.

SUMMARY AND CONCLUSIONS

The communications process in organizations is a complicated one—complicated by the fact that we as individuals have our idiosyncracies, biases, and abilities and complicated by organizational characteristics such as hierarchy or specialization. Nonetheless, communications within organizations are central for the other processes of power, leadership, and decision making. Communications are shaped by organizational structure and continue to reshape structure.

The "perfect" communications system is yet to be devised and probably will never be. Technological changes in various forms have contributed to the processing of information, but the issues and problems considered in this chapter are not erased by advanced technology; in fact, in some instances they are exacerbated.

Less than perfect communications systems and the search for improvements contribute to both changes and innovations in organizations. Change and innovation are related to more than communications, however, and it is to this topic that we now turn.

10

Change

The analyses of power, leadership, decision making, and communication have stressed the dynamic aspect of organizations. In this chapter, we will analyze the ways in which organizations change and the reasons why change does and does not take place. At times, change is virtually forced on an unwilling organization, while at other times, change is openly embraced and sought. Change can be beneficial or detrimental to organizations. Change can bring growth or decline or an alteration in form. The analysis of change has become a dominant focus in organizational research and theorizing. Several alternative and competing views of change will be considered in the analysis that follows.

THE NATURE OF ORGANIZATIONAL CHANGE

Organizational change has been approached from a variety of perspectives. Kimberly, Miles, and Associates (1980) have examined the "life cycle" of organizations. The use of this biological metaphor, which they note is imperfect, sensitizes us to the fact that organizations do not go along in the same state for eternity. Kimberly and Miles note: "Organizations are born, grow, and decline. Sometimes they reawaken, and sometimes they disappear" (p. ix).

This fact, of course, is well recognized in the private sector, as investors try to determine which organizations are in a growth phase and which are in the decline phase. While organizational analysts are now turning to an analysis of phenomena such as the organizational life cycle, we have not yet developed the tools by which we can diagnose exactly where an organization is in the cycle at a particular point in time. If we could, of course, we should probably stop being academic organizational analysts and become full-time stock market investors. That consideration aside, growth and decline are important components of organizational change.

There is important aspect of organizational change *not* contained in life-cycle analyses, in my opinion. Organizations can change in form irrespective of the life cycle. Hage (1980) defines organizational change as "the alteration and transformation of the form so as to survive better in the environment" (p. 262). This is a good definition of organizational change, with a major exception. The exception is that Hage does not consider *organizational goals* in this formulation of change. As will be argued in detail at a later point, analyses of organizations that do not include goals are shortsighted, since organizations engage in many activities and make many decisions that are not related to survival in the environment, but are related to goals.

Organizational survival, or the avoidance of death, is, of course, the ultimate test of an organization, but at any point in time, unless death is really imminent, what goes on in an organization is based on both environmental pressures and goals. Changes are made to make more profit or to secure more members. These have both an environmental and goal relationship.

The distinction between environmentally and goal-based change is at the heart of the major theoretical arguments currently being waged in organizational theory. On the one hand, authors such as McKelvey (1982) argue forcefully that the overwhelming majority of changes in organizations are due to external (allogenic) forces as opposed to internal (autogenic) forces. Other theorists, particularly those concerned with organizational design issues, emphasize internal or goal directed forces. Included in this latter camp would be theorists as diverse as Thompson (1967), who analyzed how managers would act under conditions of rationality, and Benson (1977), who argued for a Marxian dialectical view of organizations. In the discussion that follows we will be alert to this debate, but will probably not totally resolve it. The discussion will begin with a consideration of the change potential within organizations.

The Potential for Change

Some analysts view organizations as being in constant flux. Child and Kieser (1981) state:

> Organizations are constantly changing. Movements in external conditions such as competition, innovation, public demand, and governmental policy require that new strategies, methods of working, and outputs be devised for an organization merely to continue at its present level of operations. Internal factors also promote change in that managers and other members of an organization may seek not just its maintenance but also its growth, in order to secure improved benefits and satisfactions for themselves. (p. 28)

While we may agree or disagree in regard to the attribution of managerial motivation, Child and Kieser's conclusion is that organizations are constantly in motion. An alternative and highly individualized approach to the potential for change is taken by Hedberg (1981) who notes that individuals are constantly learning and unlearning from their actions. The organization is viewed as the stage on which this learning takes place and thus the organization is seen as learning and unlearning.

The individual can also be taken as the point of departure for the diametrically opposed position that organizations have limited potential for change. For example, Staw (1982) argues that individuals get locked into courses of action. They can have their commitment to courses of action escalate when they have already invested previous effort in their behavior. They defend their turf and their previous behaviors by continuing to act in the same manner. At the organizational level, Staw notes that standard operating procedures are difficult to change and that powerful coalitions do exist which will block change if it is not to their interests. Programs can be in motion which have the backing of key figures in the organization ("It's the president's baby"). In Staw's view, there are thus individual and collective or organizational counterforces to change.

Organizational personnel are seen as a potential source of inertia by Hannan and Freeman (1984) from an additional standpoint. They note that when personnel are selected on the basis of reliability and accountability, organizational structures become reproducable. This refers to the fact that the same organizational forms will continue to remain in place because there is no differentiation among the personnel. This tendency toward inertia because of commonalities in personnel is more likely in larger, older, and more complex organizations.

Pfeffer (1983) also considers the personnel composition or *organizational demography* to be an important consideration in organizational change. In Pfeffer's view organizational demography is affected by both organizational policies in regard to issues such as compensation and promotion and by environmental factors such as the rate of growth of the industry in which an organization operates. Organizational demographic characteristics in turn affect the patterns of change since it will impact on succession and power differences among age cohorts.

One of the premier analysts of organizational change has been Herbert Kaufman (1971), who states:

> In short, I am not saying that organizational change is invariably good or bad, progressive or conservative, beneficial or injurious. It may run either way in any given instance. But it is always confronted by strong forces holding it in check and sharply circumscribing the capacity of organizations to react to new conditions— sometimes with grave results. (p. 8)

Kaufman then goes on to describe the factors within organizations that resist change. These include the "collective benefits of stability" or familiarity with existing patterns, "calculated opposition to change" by groups within the organization who may have altruistic or selfish motivations, and a simple "inability to change" (pp. 8–23). The last point refers to the fact that organizations develop "mental blinders" that preclude change capability. These occur as personnel are selected and trained to do what was done in the past in the manner in which it was done in the past. Some people attribute the difficulties of American automobile manufacturers to just this point. People have been hired and trained into executive positions from just one mold. Change is resisted because it is uncomfortable and threatening.

Katz and Kahn (1978) approach resistance to change from a slightly different perspective. They suggest that there are six factors that contribute to change resistance:

1. Organizations are "overdetermined." This means that there are multiple mechanisms to ensure stability. Personnel selection, training, and the reward system are designed to lead to stability.

2. Organizations commit the error of assuming local determinism, or believing that a change in one location won't have organizationwide impacts. In addition, a change in local operations can be nullified by the larger organization.

3. There is individual and group inertia. The force of habit is very hard to overcome.

4. Organizational change can threaten occupational groups within organizations. Some specialities can foresee that they will no longer be needed if certain changes are implemented.

5. Organizational change can threaten the established power system. Management, for example, might foresee some of its power going to other groups.

6. Organizational change can threaten those who profit from the present allocation of rewards and resources. This can occur horizontally, between organizational units, as well as on the vertical axis. (pp. 414–15)

The basic point is that organizations by their very nature are conservative. Even organizations that try to have a radical impact on society demonstrate this conservatism. The history of the Christian religion or the Communist party is one of conservatism, with deviants subject to inquisitions, purges, or Siberia.

There are additional factors which contribute to resistance to change. Kaufman (1971, pp. 23–39) calls these "systemic obstacles" to change. These are obstacles within the overall system in which organizations operate. They include such factors as "sunk costs" or investments in the status quo; the accumulation of official constraints on behavior, such as laws and regulations; unofficial and unplanned constraints on behavior in the form of informal customs; and interorganizational agreements, such as labor-management contracts.

Another systemic obstacle to change involves resources. Organizations may not have the financial or personnel capabilities to engage in change efforts even if the need is identified. *Despite all these obstacles, of course, organizations do change.* The dialectical pressures for and against change are not counter balanced.

THE CHANGE PROCESS

There are multiple explanations for change in organizations, Kaufman (1971) concludes that change takes place through *personnel turnover*. Despite careful selection and training, successive generations of organizational personnel are not clones of one another.

At other times change is literally forced on an organization from the environment. Affirmative action personnel practices have drastically altered many organizations, as have pollution control regulations. Meyer and Rowan (1977) have argued that organizations are sometimes driven to incorporate policies and practices which are a part of the prevailing ethos in the society in which they are embedded. The environment has institutionalized concepts of how organizations should operate and this leads organizations to incorporate the institutionalized practices. In an extension of this line of reasoning, Tolbert and Zucker (1983) analyzed the adoption of civil service reforms in city governments for the time period of 1880–1935. They found that the speed of the adoption of a policy or programs is importantly determined by the extent to which the change is institutionalized by law, which leads to quicker adaptation, or by legitimation, which is a more gradual process.

While there may be a legal mandate to make a change, it does not simply just happen. Biggart (1977) has documented the enormous power struggles which took place within the U.S. Postal Service in 1970–1971. She concludes: "The reorganization of the U.S. Postal Service unleashed incredible forces both in and out of the organization; the forces were aimed at protecting or consolidating the power of interest groups" (p. 423). This conclusion is in line with Hage's (1980) emphasis on the importance of interest groups within organizations. These interest groups can be based on occupational specialities or hierarchical position.

Organizational Change Cycles

This section will closely follow the idea of organizational life cycles, which was noted earlier. The life-cycle approach of birth, transformation, and death has informed a great deal of organizational theory, but the biological analogy is potentially confusing. The human species, for example, has a largely predictable life span, while organizations do not. Human life expectancy can be threatened or extended by our own actions or inactions. This is also true for organizations, but they have the potential for lasting long after the life span of individuals—indeed, this is one of the major characteristics of organizations. Hypothetically organizations could last indefinitely. There is only one method of human conception, but organizations can be created by entrepreneurs and by legislatures. Organizations can also be created by other organizations, as when subsidiaries are founded by a parent organization. Subsidiaries are often used to try out a new product or service. We will thus utilize the life-cycle terminology, without completely accepting the analogy.

Births and Foundings   According to Delacroix and Carroll (1983) an organizational birth is the "creation of an operating entity that acquires inputs from suppliers and provides outputs to a given public (customers, clients, patients, etc.)" (p. 276). Births also take place through legislative actions as government organizations are born. Building on Stinchcombe's (1965) seminal work, research has documented the fact that environmental conditions, such as the characteristics of metropolitan areas for industrial firms (Pennings, 1982), the existing density of organizations for women's medical societies (Marrett, 1980), and political turbulence for newspapers (Delacroix and Carroll), have been closely related to the birth frequencies for the organizations studied. It is interesting to note that the term "founding" has now replaced "birth" in the literature, apparently as a reaction to the biological analogy. In a later study, Carroll and Huo (1986) suggest that political turbulence serves as part of the institutional environment or value system in which newspapers are embedded. This institutional environment affects both organizational foundings and failures. Preexisting organizations in an environment provide important resources for similar new organizations—the preexisting organizations serve as sources of legitimation and domain definition (Wiewel and Hunter, 1985). This line of reasoning is taken a few steps farther by Hannan and Freeman (1987). In a study of American labor unions, they found that the founding rate varies with the number of other recent union foundings in a curvilinear manner. A surge of recent foundings leads to imitation and more foundings and then a competition for scarce resources. The irony is that a big surge in foundings exhausts resources.

The social environments of organizations thus affect their rates of birth. They also have long-lasting effects into their futures. It must be reiterated that this point is also true for organizations created by an arm of government. For example, the Morrill Act of 1862, which established landgrant colleges, has had a continuing effect on those particular colleges and on higher education in general.

There is one more important step in understanding organizational foundings. Kimberly (1979) found that the environment at the time of founding *and* characteristics of the founder had important implications for the structure of a medical school. Bringing the founder back into the equation is necessary for a complete understanding of the process. Founders must adopt strategies that are appropriate for the environment that is faced (Romanelli, 1989).

✓ **Transformations**   Once born, organizations change. The most likely change is death, since new organizations have exceptionally high death rates (Carroll and Delacroix, 1982; Freeman et al., 1983; Starbuck and Nystrom, 1981). New organizations are usually small organizations and suffer a liability of newness (Freeman et al., 1983). Starbuck and Nystrom (1981) report that this high mortality rate is also found among government organizations. Population ecology theorists ascribe this high death rate among new organizations to their inability to find or carve a niche in their environment (McKelvey, 1982; McKelvey and Aldrich, 1983).

Ecological theory also has a great deal to say about subsequent transformations that take place among the organizations to survive. A basic premise of ecological theory is that organizations *adapt* to their environment (Hannan and Freeman, 1977b; Aldrich, 1979; McKelvey, 1982; McKelvey and Aldrich, 1983; Kasarda and Bidwell, 1984; Bidwell and Kasarda, 1985).

The ecological perspective has a second basic premise. This is that organizations and organizational forms are *selected* by the environment for survival. Again, the analogy is to biological systems, with a heavy emphasis on evolution and "natural selection." In the discussion that follows, I will utilize McKelvey and Aldrich's (1983) summary of the ecological framework.

McKelvey and Aldrich present four principles that operate in the ecological process. These principles determine which organizations will survive and which will not. The first principle is that of *variation*. Any sort of change is a variation. Variations can be purposeful or blind.

> Purposeful variations occur as an intentional response, when environmental pressures cause selection of adaptations. Blind variations are those that occur independent of environmental or selection pressures; they are not the result of an intentional response to adaptation pressures but rather occur by accident or chance. (p. 114)

Organizational analysts are essentially split on the extent to which variations are blind or purposeful. Any consideration of purposefulness would have to consider the problems of decision making that were specified in the previous chapter. Despite the problems surrounding decision making, I believe that the evidence favors at least a moderate degree of purposefulness, as will be documented in a later section.

The second principle is *natural selection*. Variations differ in the degree to which they enable organizations to acquire resources from the environment. Useless or harmful variations are likely to bring in fewer resources and thus reduce the chances of survival. With the passage of time, organizations that survive are likely to have beneficial variations. Resource acquisition involves much more that financial resources, although these are of crucial importance. Other resources would include personnel, power, political support, and legitimation.

The third principle is that of *retention and diffusion*. In McKelvey's (1982) terms, this involves the passing of competencies (knowledge and skills) on to succeeding members of organizations over generations. The competencies are those which have enabled organizations to survive in the first place. The competencies are diffused to other organizations as skilled and knowledgeable people change jobs and work for new and different organizations. Competencies are retained by the information flows within organizations and would involve formal and informal training. In a study of the microcomputer, cement, and airline industries, Tushman and Anderson (1986) found that technological breakthroughs can enhance or destroy organizational competencies. Knowledge and skills can become highly valuable or obsolete on the basis of technological change.

The final principle is the *struggle for existence*. This involves competing with other organizations for scarce resources. As McKelvey and Aldrich note, there are periods in which resources are unusually rich for some organizations. They cite the example of solar energy companies prior to the Reagan administration. These organizations had tax credit and government subsidies to the extent that almost any organization could enter the field and survive. With the Reagan administration cutbacks, there was a greatly increased mortality rate among these firms.

Another concept from the ecological perspective is the niche in which organizations survive (Bidwell and Kasarda, 1985, pp. 52–65, have a useful discussion of this concept). Organizations enter niches in the environment. The niche contains the resources for the organization. The niche is likely to contain other organizations fighting for the same resources. The organization that survives is that which is able to make the adaptations which enable it overcome or at least coexist with its competitors. These *adaptations* are organizational change.

The ecological perspective on change is a powerful explanation of the change process. Few would argue that resource acquisition within a competitive environment is not crucial for all organizations. The key aspect of this approach, for our purposes, involves variation. I have already argued that variation is more purposeful than some ecological theorists believe. Child and Kieser (1981) believe that organizations can take steps to safeguard or enhance an organization's position in its environment. These steps include (p. 32):

> (a) securing the benefits of growth, (b) enhancing competitive power or public approval through efficiency and rationalization or through the incorporation of technological progress, (c) establishing a secure domain in the environment through the negotiation of agreement as to the legitimate field of activity for the organization to occupy or through the finding of ecological niches—areas of activity that are relatively protected and that suit an organization's specific competences, and (d) the creation of the capacity to respond flexibly to external change through the improvement of management techniques.

Child and Kieser's suggestions contain an element that weakens the ecological argument. This is the point that an organization can develop agreements with other organizations that lessen competition. While antitrust legislation diminishes the ability to establish monopolies, organizations do reach agreements to minimize survival-threatening competition. The presence of trade associations, which are designed to cope with forces and demands that firms within an industry face, is an example of this (Staber and Aldrich, 1983). Another example would be intercollegiate athletic conferences, such as the Big Ten or the Ivy League. Long-term contracts are another device for reducing environmental effects. Singh et al. (1986) found that voluntary social service organizations could enhance their likelihood of surviving by obtaining legitimation from the environment. They interpreted this finding as support for both the population ecology and institutional perspectives.

In addition to agreements with other organizations, organizations have *constituents* who work for organizational survival. In their interesting book titled *Permanently Failing Organizations*, Meyer and Zucker (1989) document how workers, customers, and communities can fight to keep an organization going in the face of evidence that it is about to die. Examples here include employees buying out a failing firm, church members fighting an archdiocese and keeping a parish church open, and community fights to prevent plant closings.

There is yet another component of organizational transformation that a totally ecological perspective misses. This is the movement into new areas of activity. Kimberly and Quinn (1984) capture this idea well in their comments on transitions:

A transition is a major change in organizational strategy, structure, or process. Transitions can be precipitated by a variety of factors, such as declines in performance, perceptions of new opportunities, changes in legislation, or the development of new technologies. They may take a variety of forms, such as increasing formalization of structure, redefining principal operating units, broadening or narrowing market definitions, or engineering a shift in culture. (p. 1)

According to Kimberly and Quinn, transitions can take the form of restructuring the organization, repositioning the organization in its marketplace or environment, and revitalizing an organization that is slipping. While our interest is not in management, as is Kimberly and Quinn's, their point that organizations can take actions that are not necessarily related to environmental pressures is vital for our considerations. This involves a form of *entrepreneurism* within the organization. Entrepreneurism involves the process of unprogrammed recombinations of preexisting elements of reality (Peterson, 1981, p. 65). It is also possible to conceive of programmed recombinations. Peterson correctly notes that such entrepreneurship can take place outside of business firms. Government agencies and universities can be quite entrepreneurial, for example, in their contracting arrangements. These new forms can again develop in the absence of environmental pressures.

These last few paragraphs have been arguing against a totally environmentally based perspective on change. This not to downplay the importance of the environment, but rather to emphasize that the environment is only one source of change. Two leading population ecologists (Carroll and Hannan, 1989) have recognized this point by noting that environments differ in their degree of *density*. In highly dense and competitive situations, environmental pressures are greatest. In less dense situations, there is less competition and more emphasis on achieving legitimation from sources in the environment. This finding parallels that of Singh et al. (1986), which plotted the manner in which voluntary social service organizations obtained legitimation from their environments and enhanced their survival opportunities. As a finale element of the transformation process, March (1981) has pointed out that organizational change frequently happens by *accident*. Things just happen. In summary, then, transformations occur because of environmental forces, by accident, and by rationality.

Deaths   The idea of organizational death or mortality has become one of the hottest topics in the organizational literature. Carroll and Delacroix (1982) approach organizational death in the following manner (p. 170):

What is an organizational death? The question may seem trivial because all agree on the unproblematic case: an organizational death occurs when an organization fails, closes down its operations, and disbands its constituent elements. But what about mergers? When two organizations combine, at least one ceases to exist and this must be considered a death. If the merger involves a dominant partner that has absorbed the resources of the other partner, then the subordinate organization dies and the dominant organization experiences a change in structure. If, however, neither merger partner assumes a dominant position, it is difficult to assign a death to one organization and a structural alteration to the other. Instead, it is useful to consider the resulting organization as new and the two merger partners as dead.

Organizational death is the final and ultimate outcome of organizational *decline*, a process which itself has received a great deal of attention (Whetten, 1980). Cameron et al., (1987) define organizational decline as "a condition in which a substantial, absolute decrease in an organization's resource base occurs over a specified period of time" (p. 224). Weitzel and Jonsson (1989) suggest that there are five stages in the decline process. These are illustrated in Figure 10–1.

In this portrayal of the decline process, the first stage of decline occurs when the organization is blind to the signs of decline. The second stage occurs when the organization recognizes the need for change, but takes no action. In the third stage, actions are taken, but they are inappropriate. The fourth stage is the point of crisis, and the final stage is dissolution.

Another highly graphic depiction of the decline process has been presented by Hambrick and D'Aveni (1988). They picture decline into failure as a downward spiral, as seen in Figure 10–2.

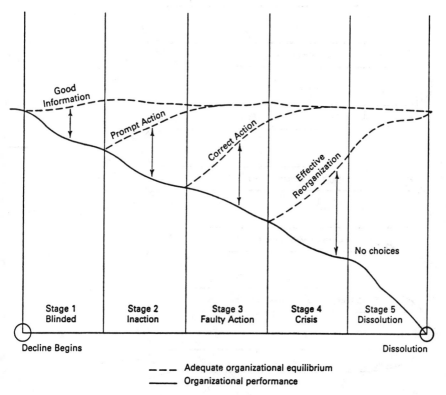

Source: Reprinted from William Weitzel and Ellen Jonsson, "Decline in Organizations: A Literature Intergration and Extension." *Administrative Science Quarterly*, 34, no. 1 (March 1989), 102. by permission of *Administrative Science Quarterly*. © 1989.

FIGURE 10–1 Widening performance gap as decline deepens.

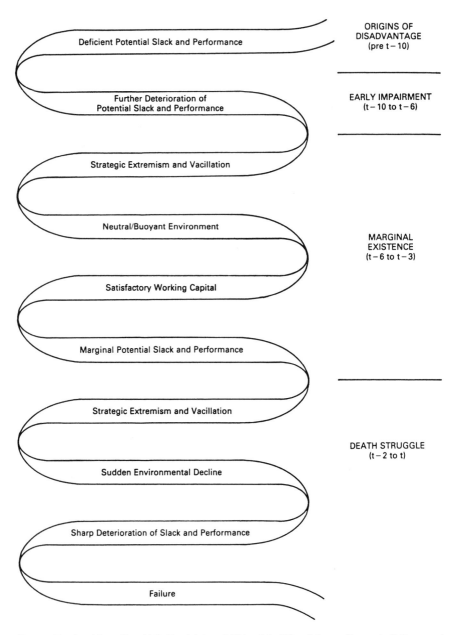

FIGURE 10–2   Organizational decline as a downward spiral.

Here the decline process is seen as weaknesses in organizational slack and performance, followed by extreme and vacillating strategies that lead to even further problems. Lest these last two studies be taken as proof that all organizations are in a decline phase, it should be noted that Hambrick and D'Aveni's study matched 57 firms that went bankrupt with another 57 firms that survived.

Organizational deaths are usually seen as the outcome of the decline process. Carroll and Delacroix (1982) point out that this is only partially accurate. Many merger partners are actually highly successful, since who would want to merge with a failing organization? The many hostile corporate takeovers of recent years indicate the attractiveness of some organizations to others for the sake of merger. Death is thus not necessarily the outcome of failure, but it is the end of the organizational change cycle.

The process of death itself is not a simple matter. Harris and Sutton (1986) examined a set of dying organizations in both the private and public sectors—public sector organizations do have death rates that match private sector rates (Starbuck and Nystrom, 1981)—and found that there were repeated social occasions, such as parties and picnics, that accompanied the deaths. The organizations included academic units, stores, manufacturing firms, and a hospital. Some were free-standing, independent organizations, while others were part of larger organizations. In all cases, organizational deaths were traumatic for the people involved.

Sutton's (1987) further analysis of the same cases revealed that death is not a simple matter in many ways. For some organizations, debts were not paid, thus affecting other organizations. In other instances, the personnel from the dead organizations reconnected after the deaths in new organizations. Organizational death is painful and complicated.

In this discussion of organizational change cycles, and now with a consideration of organizational deaths, we should not lose sight of the fact that many large and powerful organizations persist. The Roman Catholic Church is the obviously the best example here. Organizational longevity has not received as much attention as decline and death, but would be well worthy of study.

Organizational change must be viewed within a broad context which includes the environment, which itself consists of other organizations as well as economic, political, and social patterns and changes, and the change efforts of organizations themselves.

Innovation in Organizations

We will now narrow our focus and consider innovations in organizations. The focus is narrower here because an innovation may only have an impact on a small part of an organization. An innovations is a departure from existing practices or technologies and represents a significant departure from the state of the art at the time it appears (Kimberly, 1981). (See Downs and Mohr, 1976, for an extensive discussion of the nature of innovation.) Most analyses of innovation have focused on the technological side of the coin, with studies of the patterns by which hospitals adapt new medical techniques or examinations of the patterns of utilization of computers. Other forms of innovation involve organizational or administrative practices. In a study of administrative practices and technological innovations in libraries, Damanpour and Evan (1984) found that technological innovations were adapted at a faster rate than were innovations involving administrative practices. At the same time, adaptation of an administrative innovation tended to trigger the adoption of technological innovations more readily that the reverse.

Innovations can vary in their degree of radicalness (Hage, 1980, p. 191). A radical innovation is a significant departure from previous practices. Innovations can develop within an organization or be imported from outside. Innovations can also be things that are totally new and never tried before, or they can be only new to a particular organization.

Innovations within an organization are not random; innovation occurs in relation to the past and present conditions of the organization. Zaltman, Duncan, and Holbek (1973) suggest that there are three forms of innovation, or change, that can take place in organizations. The first is the *programmed* innovation that is planned through product or service research and development. *Nonprogrammed* innovations occur when there is "slack" in the organization in the form of more resources available than are presently needed. These are then used for innovative purposes. They are nonprogrammed because the organization cannot really anticipate when such extra resources will be available. Innovation is *distressed* when it is forced on the organization, such as when a crisis is perceived and new actions are taken. Innovations can develop within the organization or be imposed upon it by forces in the environment.

The characteristics of the innovation itself are of critical importance in determining whether or not it will be adapted. Zaltman, Duncan, and Holbek (1973) note that the following characteristics of an innovation make them more or less attractive and thus more or less likely to be utilized by an organization:

1. *Cost.* Cost factors involve two elements, the economic and the social. Economic costs include the initial cost of adapting an innovation or new program and the continuing costs of keeping it in operation. Social costs involve changed status arrangements within the organization as individuals and groups gain or lose power because of the new developments. Either type of cost is likely to be viewed as exorbitant by opponents and minimized by proponents of a proposed change.

2. *Return on Investment.* It is obvious that innovations will be selected which will yield high returns on investments. The situation is much more difficult, when an innovation or technological policy is in the nonbusiness sector.

3. *Efficiency.* The more efficient innovation will be selected over a less efficient status quo situation or alternative innovation.

4. *Risk and Uncertainty.* The less the risk and uncertainty, the greater the likelihood of adapting an innovation.

5. *Communicability.* The clarity of the results is associated with likelihood of innovation.

6. *Compatibility.* The more compatible the innovation is with the existing system, the more likely it is to be adapted. This, of course, implies that organizations are likely to be conservative in their innovations or technological policies, since what is compatible is unlikely to be radical.

7. *Complexity.* More complex innovations are less likely to be adapted. Again, this is a strain toward conservativism.

8. *Scientific Status.* If an innovation is perceived to have sound scientific status, it is more likely to be adapted.

9. *Perceived Relative Advantage.* The greater the advantage, the more likely that adaption will occur.

10. *Point of Origin.* Innovations are more likely to be adopted if they originate within the organization. This is based at least partially on the perceived credibility of the source of the innovation.

11. *Terminality.* This involves the timing of the innovation. In some cases, an innovation is only worthwhile if it is adopted at a particular time or in a particular sequence in the organization's operations.

12. *Status Quo Ante.* This factor refers to the question of whether or not the decision to innovate is reversible. Can there be a return to the previous state of the organization, or is the decision irreversible? Related to this is the question of whether or not the innovation or technological policy is divisible. Can a little bit at a time be tried, or does a total package have to be adopted?

13. *Commitment.* This involves behaviors and attitudes toward the innovation. Participation in the decision to innovate tends to raise the commitment of organizational members toward the innovation. A higher level of commitment is associated with more successful innovation.

14. *Interpersonal Relations.* If an innovation or technological policy is likely to be disruptive to interpersonal relationships, it is less likely to be adopted.

15. *Publicness Versus Privateness.* If an innovation is likely to affect a large part of the public, it will typically involve a larger decision-making body than an innovation that is limited to a private party. The larger decision-making body will tend to impede adoption.

16. *Gatekeepers.* This refers to the issue of whether or not an innovation must pass through several steps of approval or only one or two. The greater the number of gatekeepers, the more likely that an innovation will be turned down.

17. *Susceptibility to Successive Modification.* If an innovation itself can be modified as conditions or the technology itself changes, it stands more chance of adoption. This is related to the idea of reversibility, since the organization is not "locked" into a path that might begin to move away from the original objective.

18. *Gateway Capacity.* The adoption of one innovation or the development of a technological policy is likely to lead to the capacity to involve the organization in additional such actions.

19. *Gateway Innovations.* This refers to the fact that some innovations, even small changes in an organization's structure, can have the effect of paving the way for additional innovations. (pp. 33–45)

What these characteristics suggest, of course, is that innovations that are less radical are the ones that are most likely to be adopted. Innovations just do not arrive at an organization's doorstep with adaption automatic. Instead, innovation characteristics interact with organizational characteristics, with both innovation characteristics and organizational conditions embedded in an environmental situation.

Organizational Characteristics   The characteristics of the innovation interact with the characteristics of the innovating organization. Hage and Aiken (1970) have found that the following organizational characteristics are related to high levels of innovation:

1. High complexity in the professional training of organizational members.
2. High decentralization of power.
3. Low formalization.
4. Low stratification in the differential distribution of rewards (if high stratification is present, those with high rewards are likely to resist change).
5. A low emphasis on volume (as opposed to quality) of production.
6. A low emphasis on efficiency in the cost of production or service.
7. A high level of job satisfaction on the part of organizational members. (pp. 30–61)

Hage (1980, pp. 205–06) continues this line of reasoning. He argues that more radical innovations will occur when there is a high concentration of cosmopolitan professionals or specialists. Hage also concludes that the values of the dominant coalition are critical. If these values are prochange, then innovation is more likely.

Moch (1976) and Moch and Morse (1977) supplement the directions taken by Hage and Aiken. They find that adaption of innovations is related to organizational size, specialization, differentiation, and decentralization. They also consider the role of values, but focus on the values of lower-level decision makers, whose perspectives and interests must be compatible with the innovation.

There is some controversy regarding the relative importance of organizational characteristics versus the attitudes of organizational members. Baldridge and Burnham (1975), for example, have argued that organizational characteristics are more important to the innovation process than the attitudes of the members of the organization. Hage and Dewar (1973) argue the opposite, that the values of the elites in organizations are more important than structural characteristics. This is another example of the chicken-egg situation, since the interaction of elite values and organizational characteristics is undoubtedly what leads to high or low rates of change. For example, a highly specialized organization headed by a dominant coalition that favors change is much more likely to change than is a nonspecialized organization headed by a coalition that values stability. Other combinations of organizational characteristics and elite values would yield different rates of change.

The role of elite values can perhaps be seen more clearly if the process of change and innovation is viewed as a political process within the organization. In a study of the Teacher Corps, a federal program of the 1960s, Corwin (1973) found that the training programs were affected by the political economy of the colleges and universities involved. The economic conditions and the internal politics of the organizations involved affected how the innovation was adopted. Organizations are characterized by power struggles. The outcome of these struggles, together with organizational characteristics, determines whether or not a particular change will be made.

Another important element in the innovation process, ignored thus far, is the environment in which the innovation and the organization are found. In a study done during a period of growth, Daft and Becker (1978) found that innovation increases as incentives for innovation increase, the efficiency of organizational mechanisms for developing innovative alternatives increases, and the presence of organizational characteristics enabling innovation increases. This was a study of schools during a period of relative affluence, with schools being encouraged by federal policies and funds to try new programs. In essence, in this case, success in innovation led to more innovation.

Another study examined innovation in periods of adversity. Manns and March (1978) looked at university departments and found that under adversity, departments tended to increase the variety of course offerings, provide more attractive packaging, make courses more accessible, and increase course benefits, through such mechanisms as more credits and higher grades. A key finding of this study was that strong departments responded to adversity with fewer innovations than the weaker ones. The point here is that in adversity the less successful programs had to innovate more, while the stronger programs were insulated from adversity. The stronger programs had access to alternative sources of resources, such as federal grants.

The innovation process itself is not a simple matter. Zaltman, Duncan, and Holbek (1973) identified two stages in the innovation process—initiation and implementation. Hage (1980, pp. 209–10) expands the process to four stages—evaluation, initiation, implementation, and routinization. Regardless of the number of stages, there is agreement that successful innovation requires different organizational arrangements for each stage. Thus, decentralization might be most desirable in the initiation stage, while a more centralized approach might be more appropriate for the implementation stage.

As noted earlier, innovation can essentially be forced on an organization by other organizations. McNeil and Minihan (1977) document this in a study of hospitals and medical device manufacturers. Because of the growth of performance standards for hospitals, largely based on federal regulations, there is a growing dependence of hospitals on the medical device manufacturers. This dependence is due to the fact that the quality and reliability of the devices is in the hands of the manufacturers and not the hospitals. The adoption of devices, such as body scanners, are forced on hospitals, rather than the hospitals making adoption decisions on their own.

There is an additional environmental influence on innovation. Governmental policies can encourage or discourage innovation (Hall, 1981). It has been rather clearly demonstrated (Holden, 1980, pp. 751–54) that Japanese governmental policies—including tax, trade, tariff, and regulatory policies—are better coordinated and more conducive to innovation than are those of the United States. The result has been rapid and intense innovation by Japanese business firms.

We have now identified organizational characteristics, elite or dominant coalition values, and environmental conditions as critical factors in the adoption of innovations and in change itself. This has been largely a structural approach to change and innovation.

An alternative approach to these issues is provided by Weick (1979). He views organizations as constantly changing or "enacting" entities. He recognizes the importance of factors such as size and technology, but places much greater emphasis on individual perception and interpretation than has been the case in this analysis. In Weick's approach, constantly shifting constructions of reality within the organization mean that the organization is fluid as the environment is interpreted and enacted. I view organizations as much less fluid, with both structural factors and power arrangements playing key roles in the inhibition of change and innovation.

SUMMARY AND CONCLUSIONS

This chapter has examined the sources and processes of change within organizations. We found that while it is useful to focus in on environmental pressures as a source of change, it is impossible to ignore internal sources of organizational change. Organizations have varying potential for change. Both individual and organizational characteristics inhibit and encourage change. Organizational change cycles were considered. In this we borrowed heavily from the ecological approach to organizations, since, despite its limitations, it offers strong insights into the change process.

The chapter has also analyzed innovation from the perspective that there are organizational characteristics that resist and facilitate the process. From the research findings in regard to innovation we concluded that organizational characteristics, the values of elites and environmental pressures all contribute to change and innovation. Thus far in the book we have been focusing on organizational characteristics, including the interplay between power, leadership, and decision making with elite or dominant coalition values. In the next section we will turn to a specific focus on the environment.

In regard to innovation and change, we can conclude that these are critical processes for organizations. They contribute to growth and survival and death. The purpose here is not to do a life-cycle analysis, but rather to demonstrate that these are not trivial processes for organizations. Again, if we could identify exactly what leads to growth or which changes or innovations are going to be successful, we would have the key to understanding and control of organizations. We do not have the key. We do have at least partial answers, however, which, it is hoped, have been identified in the analysis thus far. Bringing in the environment will add another element to our understanding.

11

Organizational
Environments

The critical importance of organizational environments has been emphasized throughout this analysis. In this chapter we will deal specifically with the nature and impact of organizational environments. By environment we mean "*all phenomena that are external to and potentially or actually influence the population under study*" (Hawley, 1968, p. 330, italics added). The population under study here, of course, is organizations.

In Chapter 1 we examined the outcomes of organizations on their environments; here the order is reversed. We will first examine the impact of environments on organizations. We will then turn to a more systematic analysis of how the environment affects the growth and development of organizations. We will next place the environment in usable categories so that it can be more easily understood. Finally, we will look at the manner in which the environment is perceived and reexamine some material on the impact of the environment on the organization.

SOME RESEARCH FINDINGS

In this section we will examine a set of selected empirical research findings. The studies have been chosen to illustrate the point that environmental factors have *theoretical* and *practical* outcomes for organizations.

Hospital costs have increased markedly and alarmingly in past decades. Part of the reason for the increased costs is increased service. Fennell (1980) found that hospitals expanded their services not because of needs within their patient population but rather because they believed that they would not be judged as fit themselves if they could not offer everything that other hospitals in their area provided. Fennell claims that hospitals are status, rather than market or price, oriented. For our purposes, the environment that is important to such hospitals is other hospitals and those people or groups in the community that are perceived to have budgetary and decision-making power about the hospitals. There are obviously other organizational actors in the hospital and health care cost equation. Insurance companies, medical societies, legislative bodies, and courts are all part of the picture.

In a study of school districts, Freeman (1979) found that "rational" decisions were not be made during a period of decline. When budgets and enrollments dropped, rational decisions hypothetically could have been made in regard to programs and personnel which might be terminated. Freeman found that this was not the case. Because of the demands of categorical programs from the federal government, some cuts could not be made in programs with little demand. Interest groups were able to maintain highly specialized programs through their abilities to convince federal program officers to maintain the programs. The cuts in the local school districts reflected external, environmental pressures rather than the decisions that the school organizations might have made themselves.

Turning to another kind of organization, Whetten (1978) found that the directors of work force agencies were subject to role conflicts based on environmental pressures. They had to cope with their own staffs, relevant community leaders, and regional and state administrators. In dealing with community leaders, they had to engage in behavior that made them visible to those leaders. Whetten notes that such behavior may or may not be related to organizational tasks.

Environmental effects are not just a part of the service type organizations which have been discussed. Pearson (1978) found that uranium mines did not make expenditures for remedial technology to combat injuries and disease until there was governmental (environmental) pressure. In addition to governmental pressures, the uranium mines were also subject to economic pressures such as lower demand, higher compensation claims, and an industry shift away from small mines. This particular study raises the interesting question of the role of government in the protection of workers, but for our purposes it offers yet another example of the ways in which organizational environments impinge upon operations.

Organizational responses to environmental pressures are neither automatic nor necessarily rational. McNeil and Miller (1980) have documented the manner in which U. S. automobile manufacturers did not respond organizationally to the pressure of foreign imports. The U. S. firms used a short-term accounting system, with a heavy emphasis on cost control. The emphasis was on immediate financial return on sales, service, and warranty work. According to McNeil and Miller, continued adherence to this particular sort of accounting system blinded the industry to the long-term ramifications of the coming era (p. 426). There is an irony here in that the short-term accounting system was itself a response to earlier crises of the 1920's.

Leblebici and Salancik (1981; 1982) have examined the volatility and uncertainty of environments. In their 1981 study of banks, they found that a volatile environment was associated with uncertainty in decision making. For example, loan officers in banks with volatile environments experienced greater uncertainty in regard to the probability of loan repayments than did loan officers in less volatile environments. When the banks faced highly diverse environments, they developed procedures to deal with this form of uncertainty. Using essentially the same framework in an analysis of the Chicago Board of Trade, they found (1982) that the working rules of this organizations shifted as it faced environmental uncertainty in the form of volatility of commodity prices.   A major outcome of such situations can be "design misfit" and lower organizational performance (Gresov, 1989).

There is an interesting concept that should be added here. This is the idea of the environmental "jolt" (Meyer, 1982). An environmental jolt is something that is simply unexpected. In the case of Meyer's study, the jolt was an unexpected strike by doctors that forced hospitals into a set of reactions to this unanticipated uncertainty. As would be predicted, organizations that had some slack resources or that were diversified fared better than those that did not have these resources.

We have noted that organizations can engage in illegal acts. Staw and Szwajkowski (1975) have found that activities such as unfair market practices and restraint of trade are related to environmental conditions. When resources in the environment are scarce, there is a greater tendency for illegal acts to occur. Later research by Staw et al. (1981) revealed that when organizations are faced with adversity (threat), they may become rigid. This involves a restriction of information processing and a constriction of control. This may well be a maladaptive response and contribute to organizational decline. Restrictions on information processing could also contribute to illegal acts as one part of the organization might not know what another part is doing.

These research findings provide a solid basis for concluding that the environments of organizations have a critical impact on the organizations themselves. In the last chapter we saw how the ecological approach to organizational change uses the environment as the major source of change within organizations. In the next section we will explore the importance of the environment for the development of organizations a little further.

The Environment and the Development of Organizations

Stinchcombe (1965) presented a seminal work on the interface between environments and the development of organizations. He notes (p. 143) that special-purpose organizations have taken over various social functions, such as economic production, policing, education, political action, military action, as so on, at different rates in different societies. These organizations have replaced or supplemented multipurpose groups such as the family or the community for these purposes.

If this is to occur, there must be an *awareness* of alternative ways of accomplishing these tasks. The alternative forms must be seen as *attractive* in terms of some kind of cost-benefit calculation, and the people involved must have sufficient *resources* in the form of wealth, power, legitimacy, and strength of numbers to get the new organization off the ground (Kimberly, 1975). These resources must be translated into *power* in order to overcome resistance from those interested in maintaining the older system.

These conditions have not been distributed randomly throughout history, but they have been present in sufficient degrees to allow new organizations and new organizational forms to emerge. Both new organizations and new organizational forms suffer the liability of newness that has been discussed. Stinchcombe notes that new organizations are more likely to survive than are new organizational forms.

Other Environmental Conditions   The conditions just discussed are actually intermediate variables between some more basic environmental characteristics and the rate of organizational development. One of these basic characteristics that is necessary for organizational development is the general *literacy* and specialized advanced schooling of the population. The presence of literacy raises the likelihood that each of the intermediate variables will be sufficiently present for organizational development to occur. Stinchcombe (1965) states that

> ....literacy and schooling raise practically every variable which encourages the formation of organizations and increases the staying power of new organizations. It enables more alternatives to be posed to more people. It facilitates learning new roles with no nearby role model. It encourages impersonal contact with customers. It allows money and resources to be distributed more easily to strangers and over distances. It provides records of transactions so that they can be enforced later, making the future more predictable. It increases the predictability of the future environment of an organization by increasing the available information and by making possible a uniform body of law over a large area. (pp. 150–51)

In addition to the key variable of education and literacy, several other factors are crucial for the conditions permitting organizational formation. *Urbanization* is a second factor identified by Stinchcombe in this regard. He notes that the rate of urbanization should be slow enough to allow the rural migrants to learn and develop routines of urban living. At the same time, the development of urban life is associated with greater heterogeneity of life-style, thus providing more alternative working and living arrangements. The urban scene is one of dealing with strangers, and this too assists organizational development, since ascriptive role relationships are likely to be minimized. Impersonal laws are necessary in urban areas just as they are in organizations. Urbanization, like education, increases the organizational capacity of populations, although not to the same degree, according to Stinchcombe.

Another important condition, and one that has long been identified, is the presence of a *money economy*. This sort of economy

> ...liberates resources so that they can be more easily recruited by new organizations, facilitates the formation of free markets so that customers can transfer loyalties, depersonalizes economic social relations, simplifies the calculation of the advantages of alternative ways of doing things, and allows more precise anticipation of the consequences of future conditions on the organization. (Stinchcombe, 1965, p. 152)

The *political* base of a society is also important. For the creation of a new organizations, political revolutions are held to be important because of their rearranging of vested interest groups and power systems. Resources are allocated on bases different from those in the past.

The final societal condition identified by Stinchcombe is the existing level of *organizational density*. The greater the density and the greater the range of organizational alternatives already available, the greater the likelihood that people will have had experience in organizations. This suggests that there is likely to be an exponential growth curve for organizations in a society—assuming, of course, that the other conditions are also present.

Stinchcombe's discussion is concerned with the conditions of the society that are important for the development of new organizations and new organizational forms. While the picture has been drawn in broad relief with historical data, the factors identified remain important for analyses at any particular point in time.

Technology and Organizational Form
Stinchcombe's article contains an additional set of ideas that is relevant for our purposes. He maintains that the technological conditions available at the time of the formation of an organization set the limits for the form the organization can take.

> Organizations which have purposes that can be efficiently reached with the socially possible organizational forms tend to be founded during the period in which they become possible. Then, both because they can function effectively with those organizational forms and because the forms tend to become institutionalized, the basic structure of the organization tends to remain relatively stable. (1965, p.153)

The emphasis on technology is consistent with the argument here, with the addition that if the newly introduced organizational form is compatible with the technology of the times, it tends to persist over time regardless of gradual changes in technology.

The emphasis in this section has been on the development of new organizations and new organizational forms. The implication is that the environment at the time of organizational formation is critical for the form that the organization takes and that this form persists over time. According to Meyer and Brown (1977), this is overly simplified. They demonstrate that the conditions surrounding the origins of an organization do persist in their impact on the organization, but that these conditions are constantly being confronted with ongoing environmental conditions. The organizational—environmental relationship is thus dynamic.

ENVIRONMENTAL DIMENSIONS

Thus far we have treated the environment in a rather undifferentiated manner. In this section we will consider two ways in which aspects of the environment can be categorized into useful dimensions. First, we will examine the environment in terms of its content, including technological and economic considerations. Then we will consider the environment from a more analytical perspective in terms of factors such as the stability or turbulence of the environment. We will then combine these sets of dimensions.

Technological Conditions

Technological conditions are a convenient starting point, since this topic and the research surrounding it have already been the subject of much attention and can set the stage for the less systematically researched topics that follow.

It will be remembered, following the works of Perrow, Lawrence and Lorsch, and others, that organizations operating in an uncertain and dynamic technological environment exhibit structures and internal processes different from those operating in a rather certain and unchanging technological situation. While we need not at this point review the direction of the relationships and the supporting evidence, it is important to recognize that the organization responds to this aspect of its environment. In fact, in the business firms Lawrence and Lorsch studied, special organizational divisions were established (research and development) to keep the organization current. In other organizations, departments such as industrial engineering, management analysis, and so on, are so designated.

Beyond their empirical evidence that technology is salient in the operation of organizations, these findings have implications vital to our understanding of organizational—environmental interactions. In the first place, technology and other environmental characteristics are something "out there." The organization does not exist in a vacuum. A technological development in any sphere of activity has the potential to get to the organizations related to it. New ideas come into circulation and become part of the environment as soon as they cease being the private property of any one individual or organization. Since the sciences have a norm of distributing knowledge, scientific developments become part of the public domain as a matter of course. A development that can be patented is a different matter, but if it is thought to be significant, other organizations will seek to buy it, copy it, or further extend the previous development. In any case, an organization must keep up with such developments in the technological spheres crucial to its continued success.

More subtle forms of the technological environment are found outside the hard sciences and engineering. In management and administration, new ideas are introduced through research, serendipity, or practice. In service-oriented organizations, such as schools, socialwork agencies, and hospitals, the same types of technological shifts can also be seen. An important mechanism appears to be the introduction of new personnel or clients who have had contact with alternative technologies and advocate their use in the organization in question.

Organizations do not respond to technological change through simple absorption. Instead, the organization's political process operates through the advocacy of change or stability. Organizations of every kind contain their own internal "radicals" and "reactionaries" in terms of their responses to technological and all other environmental conditions. Since the rate of technological and other environmental changes is not constant for all organizations, the degree to which they must develop response mechanisms varies. For all, however, technology remains an important consideration.

Legal Conditions

An environmental consideration often overlooked but which in reality is very critical is the *legal conditions* that are part of the organization's surroundings. At one extreme are organizations that operate outside the law and respond to the legal system by their attempts to evade the law at all costs and remain underground. At the other extreme would be local voluntary organizations that have no involvement whatsoever with safety, health, or other kinds of local, state, and national laws and regulations.

The overwhelming majority of organizations must live with federal, state, and local laws as constants in their environments. At the very least, they set many of the operating conditions of many organizations, ranging from specific prohibitions of certain kinds of behavior to regulations requiring reporting of income and staffing at periodic times of the year. The importance of laws is shown by the staffs of legal and other experts who form an integral part of many organizations and who are specifically charged with interpreting and protecting the organization's positions. The growing trend toward lawyers serving as chief executive officers is indicative of the critical nature of legal conditions for organizations (Priest and Rothman, 1985).

While the body of laws as a constant is an interesting analytical point, the dynamic aspect of the legal system points up the importance of laws for organizations. When a new law is passed or an interpretation modified, organizations must make some important changes if the law has relevance for them. Here again, relatively mundane matters such as tax and employment regulations are important. More striking are the cases of major shifts that affect organizations in the public and private sectors. For example, U. S. Supreme Court decisions regarding school desegregation have had tremendous impacts on the school organizations involved. Concern with the environment has resulted in laws and regulations concerning pollution that have affected many organizations as they utilize their resources in fighting or complying with the new statutes. It should be evident that legal conditions result from actions of legislative bodies, the judicial system, and the executive branches of government at all levels. As Champagne et al. (1981) note, it is thus imperative for organizations to select the appropriate legal strategy aimed at the appropriate arm of government. These authors also note that organizations are important actors in the development of laws through their lobbying efforts.

Political Conditions

Laws are not passed without pressure for their enactment. The *political conditions* that bring about new laws also have their effects on organizations. Strong political pressures to reduce or increase military and aerospace spending have led to crises or opportunities of one sort or another for organizations in those areas. Police departments have been buffeted back and forth between support for "law and order" and condemnation of "police brutality." School systems have drastically altered parts or all of their curricula in the face of threats from groups concerned with such topics as sex education or "left-wing" textbooks. Some organizations are directly affected by the political process because their hierarchy can be drastically changed by election results. All government units face this possibility after every election as top officials are changed at the discretion of a new administration.

Organizations in the private sector are less directly affected than public ones, but they must still be attuned to the political climate. Since lobbying for legislation that will be favorable in terms of tax advantages or international trade agreements is an accepted part of the legislative and administrative system of the United States, organizations must devote resources to the lobbying process. Jacobs (1987; 1988) has found that corporate tax rates are lower in states in which large corporations control a large proportion of the assets in the state. This does not happen by accident.

McCaffrey (1982) found that even once legislation is passed in the legal dimension, political pressures are still brought to bear in the implementation of regulations. McCaffrey studied the early history of the Occupational Safety and Health Administration (OSHA) in the United States and documents the strong political pressures that were placed on this organization. Anecdotal evidence suggests that this agency remains under intense political pressures.

The widespread illegal corporate contributions to domestic and foreign political parties and individuals is further evidence of the importance of the political factor for organizations. In a different arena "institutional advertising" is designed to generate public support through its portrayal of the advertising organization as a good corporate citizen.

Carroll and Delacroix's (Carroll and Delacroix, 1982; Delacroix and Carrol, 1983) research on the foundings (births) and mortality (deaths) of newspapers in Argentina and Ireland found that political turbulence was related to the founding of newspapers. At the same time, newspapers founded during periods of turbulence are outlived by newspapers born under stable conditions. Additional research on political conditions and organizations would undoubtedly reveal more such patterns.

Economic Conditions

An environmental condition that is more obvious, but again strangely neglected by most sociologists, is the state of the *economy* in which the organization is operating. To most business leaders, this is the crucial variable. In universities and in government work, experience also shows the importance of economic conditions when budgets are being prepared, defended, and appropriated. The sheer availability of financial resources is one of the crucial environmental conditions for the birth of organizations (Pennings, 1982). Changing economic conditions serve as important constraints on any organization. Burt (1988) reports that the market structure in the United States has been very stable over time. At the same time, of course, there are major swings through large and small recessions, depressions, inflationary periods, and so on.

Economic changes do not affect all parts of an organization equally. In periods of economic distress, an organization is likely to cut back or eliminate those programs it feels are least important to its overall goals, except, of course, for those instances in which external political pressures preclude such "rational" decisions (Freeman, 1979). Economic affluence permits government agencies to engage in a wider range of programs. Klatzky (1970b) found that state employment agencies in wealthier states provided unemployment insurance to a greater proportion of the unemployed than did the agencies in the poorer states. Since these agencies were paying out more, they also received a disproportionately larger share of federal funds than their less affluent peers in other states. The rich agencies get rich as the poor agencies get poorer. Of course, political changes can bring about changed economic conditions for these governmental organizations. It is impossible to disentangle political and economic factors in many cases.

Changing economic conditions are, in fact, excellent indicators of the priorities of organizations. That organizational programs vary according to the economic conditions that are confronted contributes to a paradox for most organizations. Since total rationality is not an assumption of this analysis, it can be safely assumed that an organization cannot be sure of exactly what contribution each of its parts makes to the whole. For example, research and development can be viewed as one of the luxuries that should go when an organization faces some hard times. But by concentrating on the production and distribution of what R & D has done in the past, the organization may miss the development of a new product that would be of great long-run benefit. Periods of economic difficulty do force organizations to evaluate their priorities and trim areas that are viewed as being least vital. As in the case of the communication process, the criteria by which the evaluations are accomplished are the key variables, and there is no assumption being made here that the decision process is rational.

Economic conditions surrounding organizations improve and decline with the organizations responding to the situation. In their responses in any situation, the important factor of competition is present. Economic competition can be most easily seen among business organizations, where success is measured in the competitive marketplace. While the competition is not "pure," it is still an evident part of the value system in a private-enterprise economy. Economic competition among organizations takes many forms. Burt (1983) examined the patterns of corporate philanthropy among a set of business firms. He concluded that corporate philanthropy was a co-optive relationship, akin to advertising. The reasoning behind this conclusion was that the proportion of net income that an organization gave to charity covaried with the extent to which the firms were dependent upon consumption by people who were able to do something about uncertainty in the demand for their product. A supermarket chain might thus engage in widely publicized charitable efforts in an effort to try to ensure continued patronage in a local market by appearing to be a good citizen.

Less evident than competition between business firms, but equally real, is economic competition among and within organizations outside the business sphere. From repeated experiences in government agencies at several levels, it is clear that competition is fierce during budget season (Wildavsky, 1964). Government agencies are all competing for part of the tax revenues, which constitute a finite "pot." Organizations that rely on contributions from members, such as churches, are also affected by the general economic conditions, since the contributors have more or less income available. An interesting research question is the extent to which the severity of economic competition varies among organizations in all sectors of society. It appears almost equal, regardless of the organization's major emphases.

Demographic Conditions

Demography is another frequently overlooked factor. The number of people served, and their age and sex distributions, make a great deal of difference to all organizations. As a general rule, an organization can predict its probable "market" for the future from information in census data, but population shifts are less predictable and make the organization more vulnerable. In a society where race, religion, and ethnicity are important considerations, shifts in these aspects of the demographic condition must also be considered.

The most striking examples of the importance of demographic change come from organizations located in the central cities of growing and declining metropolitan areas. Businesses, schools, and police departments have different clientele from what they once had, even though the organizations themselves might not reflect this. At least in the short run, it is the urban poor and minority group members who suffer the consequences. The organizations themselves, however, eventually undergo transitions (usually painful) as they begin to realize that their clientele has become different and that they themselves must change.

Pfeffer (1983) has shown that demographic distributions *within* an organization have important ramifications for a wide variety of organizationally important issues, such as performance, innovation and adaptability, turnover, and interorganizational linkages. For organizations that use an external labor market, demographic conditions in the environment would thus be reflected within the organization. Fast food restaurants experienced a shortage of younger workers in the late 1980s and turned to older workers for their counter staff.

Ecological Conditions

Related to the demographic scene is the general *ecological situation* surrounding an organization. The number of organizations with which it has contacts and relationships and the environment in which it is located are components of the organization's social ecological system. In an urban area, an organization is much more likely to have contacts with myriad other organizations than is one in a rural area. Since the density of other organizations around any particular organization varies widely, the potential for relationships also varies.

Shifting from social ecology to the physical environment, the relationships between organizations and ecological conditions become more evident because of the recent concerns about the total ecological system. It is increasingly clear that organizations have effects on the environment, as is abundantly demonstrated by the various organizations that pollute and the others that fight pollution.

A more subtle point is that the environment affects organizations. Factors such as climate and geography set limits on how they allocate resources. Transportation and communication costs rise if an organization is distant from its markets or clients. Even such mundane items as heating and cooling expenses must be considered limits on an organization. Organizations are physically located to take advantage of environmental conditions. This is most easily seen in the case of organizations using physical raw materials, such as ore or petroleum. More subtle is the fact that organizations such as national professional associations and trade associations tend to be located in just one location in the United States—Washington, D. C. This is the location where their action is. Although ecological factors are generally constants, since only in unusual circumstances are there significant changes, these conditions cannot be ignored in a total organizational analysis involving comparisons between organizations.

Cultural Conditions

The environmental conditions discussed thus far are fairly easily measured in terms of "hard" indicators of the degree to which they are present or absent. Other conditions in the external environment that are vitally important are more difficult to measure. The first of these is the *culture* surrounding an organization. In Chapter 4, the importance of national cultures for organizational structure was discussed in detail.

While the influence of the culture is now an accepted fact, it is not clear whether culture overrides other factors in determining how an organization is shaped and operates. There is evidence suggesting that organizations at an equivalent technological level—for example, at the same degree of automation of production—are quite similar in most respects, as was indicated in the chapters on structure. The basic problem is to sort out the influences of these various environmental factors as they impinge on the organization. Unfortunately, not enough is yet known for such fine distinctions to be made. The various factors discussed so far probably interrelate in their organization effects in a rather complex interaction pattern. For example, it appears that the more routine and standardized the technology, the less the impact of cultural factors. The production of children's toy automobiles is probably carried out in similar organizational forms in Hong Kong, London, Japan, Switzerland, or Tonka, Minnesota. When one moves to less routinized technological operations, such as local government, the administration of justice, or highway construction, the impact of culture is likely to be higher. Culture is important for organizational structuring. It also has an important impact on the ways in which organizations formulate their strategies for the future (Schneider, 1989).

In its impact on organizations, culture is not a constant, even in a single setting. Values and norms change as events occur that affect the population involved. If they involve conditions relevant to the organization, these shifts are significant for it. Newspaper editorials, letters to the editor, an other colorations of reports in the mass media indicate how values can change in regard to particular organizations or types of organizations. These value shifts may precede or accompany political shifts, which would have a more direct kind of impact. Changes in consumer tastes represent another way that cultural conditions can affect organizations. Examples of this are easily found; a dramatic one is that of the contrasting experiences with the Edsel and Mustang cars by the Ford Motor Company. Tobacco companies are faced with major shifts in values and scramble to reduce the damage (Dunbar and Wasilewski, 1985).

ANALYTICAL DIMENSIONS

Aldrich (1979, pp. 53–70) has developed a set of analytic dimensions of the environment. As we will see, it is possible to intertwine a variation of Aldrich's dimensions with those just outlined. Aldrich's list of dimensions follows.

Environment Capacity

The capacity of an environment refers to its "richness" or "leanness," or the level of resources available to an organization. According to Aldrich:

> Organizations have access to more resources in rich environments, but such environments also attract other organizations. Stockpiling and hoarding of resources is probably not as prevalent in rich as in lean environments. Lean environments also promote cut-throat competitive practices, and apart from rewarding organizations capable of stockpiling and hoarding, lean environments reward efficiency in the use of resources. Two alternatives are open to organizations in lean environments: move to a richer environment or develop a more efficient structure. The latter alternative can be accomplished by improving operating practices, merging with other organizations, becoming more aggressive vis-à-vis other organizations, or moving to a protected subenvironment through specialization. (p. 53)

Examples of such organization responses can be seen in many different cases. American Airlines moved its corporate headquarters from New York City to Dallas. Although the terms rich and lean environment were not used, the reasons given for the move essentially had that meaning, with the airline citing access to qualified personnel and more modern facilities as reasons for the move. At times, some of the responses which Aldrich suggests are not possible. Legal requirements, for example, may prevent merger because of the threat of monopoly. In such cases, as Pfeffer and Nowak (1976) point out, organizations may engage in joint ventures. Joint ventures involve the investment of resources from several organizations in a single large project, such as the Concorde airplane developed by France and England.

Environmental Homogeneity-Heterogeneity

This dimension refers to the degree of similarity or differentiation within the environment. According to Aldrich, a homogeneous environment is simpler for organizations, since standardized way of responding can be developed. Many organizations attempt to make their environment more homogeneous by limiting the kinds of clients served, markets entered, and so on. Social service organizations consistently attempt to make their environment homogeneous by referring clients that do not fit within their operations to other social service organizations. The result of this, of course, is that the most difficult clients get referred and referred and referred.

Environmental Stability-Instability

This refers to the extent of turnover of elements or parts of the environment. Stability, like homogeneity, permits standardization. Instability leads to unpredictability, which organizations resist. Any aspect of an organization's environment can be stable or unstable, be it economic, legal, or technological conditions.

Environmental Concentration-Dispersion

Concentration or dispersion in the environment involves the distribution of the elements in the environment. Are they located in one place or are they scattered across a large area? It is easier for an organization to operate with a more concentrated environment, as in the case of customers or clients.

Domain Consensus-Dissensus

Organizations claim a domain or market. This dimension refers to the degree to which these claims are recognized or disputed by other parties, such as government agencies. If the interested and relevant parties agree that a particular organization has the right and obligation to operate in a particular way in a particular area, there is domain consensus. This dimension is thus concerned with organizational "turf."

Organizations attempt to achieve domain consensus by securing protective legislation or regulations, such as import quotas, tariffs, or exclusive rights to a sales territory. In the public sector there are frequent consensus-dissensus issues in regard to federal, state, or local responsibilities for programs in transportation, education, or social welfare.

Environmental Turbulence

This is the most difficult of Aldrich's dimensions to understand, since the idea of turbulence seems a great deal like instability. Turbulence here means that there is a great deal of causal interconnection among the elements in the environment. In a turbulent environment there is a high rate of environmental interconnection. An economic shift has political and technological ramifications in a turbulent environment. The movement of business firms from the Northeast to the Sun Belt in the United States is an example of such turbulence. These moves have lowered the tax base in the Northeast, forcing raises in the tax rates to maintain essential and nonessential services, which in turn, leads to additional decisions to move. The effect of such moves spin off into other sectors, such as education, health, and social services.

On the basis of their research Dess and Beard (1984) believe that these six dimensions can be reduced to three dimensions. They propose that the dimensions of *munificence* (capacity), *complexity* (homogeneity-heterogeneity and concentration-dispersion), and *dynamism* (stability-instability and turbulence) capture the essence of Aldrich's distinctions. On this basis, we can now intertwine the content dimensions with the analytical dimensions as is demonstrated in Figure 11–1. Each of the content dimensions can be characterized by their munificence, complexity, and dynamism.

Before turning to an analysis of how the environment is perceived by the organization, one other distinction about the environment should be made. Jurkovich (1974) pointed out that a key issue is whether or not the environment itself is organized. This can be seen to be crucial in regard to consumers, where organized consumers can be much more threatening to an organization than nonorganized individuals. Rather obviously, most environmental pressures come from other organizations in the form of government agencies, competing organizations, cultural organizations, and the like. When we examine interorganizational relationships in the next chapter, the specific linkages between organizations and their counterparts will be analyzed in detail.

ANALYTICAL CATEGORIES

CONTENT CONDITIONS	MUNIFICENCE	COMPLEXITY	DYNAMISM
TECHNOLOGICAL			
LEGAL			
POLITICAL			
ECONOMIC			
DEMOGRAPHIC			
ECOLOGICAL			
CULTURAL			

FIGURE 11–1   Environmental Dimensions

Here it is sufficient to note that whether the environmental elements are organized or not is a consideration that should not be overlooked.

THE PERCEPTION OF THE ENVIRONMENT

We have been proceeding as though the environment is simply something "out there" beyond the organization, which anyone in the organization can readily spot and identify. It would be handy if this were the case, but it is not. The environment comes into the organization as information and, like all information, is subject to the communications and decision-making problems which have been identified. Environmental information is information to be processed.

People have different positions in organizations. Some people are identified as "gate keepers" (Nagi, 1974) or "boundary spanners" who are designated to admit certain information that is relevant to the organization. Their perceptions are influenced by their positions within the organization (Leifer and Huber, 1977). Of course, the very definition of where the organization stops and the environment begins is open to question. Starbuck (1976) has pointed out that different positions are at an organization's boundaries, depending on what the activity at the moment is. At times it can be the switchboard operator, while at other times it is the president or chief executive officer.

According to Starbuck (pp. 1078–80), an organization *selects* those aspects of the environment with which it is going to deal. The selection process is affected by the selection processes of other organizations with which it is in contact. At the same time, of course, interorganizational linkages are affected by environmental pressures (Provan, Beyer, and Kruytbosch, 1980). In this manner, organizations go about constructing or inventing their environments. Meyer (1975) finds that the scope of the domain or environment claimed or selected by organizations has an impact on its operations. Narrow domain claims are associated with stability and broad and inconsistent claims with loss of functions. Broad claims coupled with technological capacity and newness lead to domain expansion. Meyer concludes that domain claims actually seldom contract.

Organizational theory has stressed the importance of perceived uncertainty in the environment (Duncan, 1973; Leifer and Huber, 1977). It is equally important to stress the fact that much of the environment that is perceived is actually certain, rather than uncertain. Colleges and universities, for example, face a certain demographic profile of the number and distribution of potential students. Business firms face a rather certain environment of governmental regulations. The environment thus contains elements of certainty and uncertainty.

Just as the perceptions of individuals are shaped by their experiences, so, too, are organizations'. Starbuck maintains (1976, pp. 1080–81) that organizations are *more* realistic than individuals because of their constant comparisons with and sharing personnel among comparable organizations. Whether or not this is the case has not yet been demonstrated. It must be remembered that the perceivers of the environment are themselves individuals, with all of their (our) idiosyncrasies in perception.

THE IMPACT OF THE ENVIRONMENT ON THE ORGANIZATION

What do all these environmental factors, however selected and perceived, do to organizations? There are several answers. In the first place, organizations vary in their vulnerability to environmental pressures (Jacobs, 1974). The more dependent an organization is on its environment, the more vulnerable it is. An organization with strong financial resources is less vulnerable to economic fluctuations than is one with no reserves. In the 1970s and early 1980s, petroleum manufacturers were highly dependent and vulnerable to political shifts in their sources of raw materials and their markets. These firms attempted to manipulate their environment by stabilizing the political conditions. Cigarette companies are attempting to manage, regulate, and reduce the damage of the antismoking movement (Dunbar and Wasilewski, 1985). It is interesting to note here that the antismoking movement is the environment for tobacco companies and that this environment includes government agencies, citizen groups, airlines, and numerous other factions. Tobacco smoke is an alien part of my environment.

When an organization is vulnerable, it reacts to the environment. Several studies have shown that strong environmental pressures are related to increased formalization and a general "tightening" of the organization (see Freeman, 1973; Khandwalla, 1972; Boddewyn, 1974; and Pfeffer and Leblebici, 1973). It is odd that the environmental pressures do this, since in many ways the loosely coupled organization is more adaptive to the environment and is more likely to develop innovations that might be beneficial over the long run (Weick, 1976). Organizations that are vulnerable to the environment, of course, face a greater risk of failure if an innovation happens not to be successful.

Every organization is dependent on its environment to some degree. Each adapts internal strategies to deal with the perceived pressures (Snow and Hrebiniak, 1980). Contingency theory strongly suggests that there is no single best way to cope with environmental pressures. The specific stance that an organization takes derives from choices that are made within it. This decision-making process is a political one in the sense that different options are supported by different factions within the decision-making structure. The option finally selected is a consequence of the power of individuals and groups that support it. That environmental pressures often tighten the organization may be a consequence of the fact that this is the option that powerful segments of organizations have traditionally taken. It may not be the one most useful for the organization, of course.

Among the strategies that organizations develop for dealing with their environments, a critical one is to attempt to shape the environment itself. Hirsch (1975) has shown that the typical pharmaceutical manufacturing firm has been more successful than the typical firm in the phonograph record industry largely because the pharmaceutical firms have been able to control relevant aspects of their environments. The pharmaceutical firms could exert control over pricing and distribution, patent and copyright laws, and external opinion leaders. This control of the environment was a source of greater profitability. Organizations attempt to gain and maintain power over environmental conditions that are of strategic importance to them. In a situation of scarce resources, organizations may also resort to illegal acts such as price fixing or other activities to restrain trade. Thus, like the development of internal organizational power in which successful coping with strategic contingencies is linked to the development of power, so in its interactions with the environment the organization must be able to cope with and control external strategic and important contingencies.

Organizations compete with each other for technological, political, economic, legal, and other such advantage. This competition takes place in overlapping dimensions of the environment. A political advantage can contribute to economic advantage, and vice versa. For example, Roy (1981; see also Carstensen and Werking, 1983, and Roy, 1983) reports that the interests of the financial and industrial core industries became vested interests in the U.S. State Department in the 1886–1905 period, while other interests were not as well protected in foreign policy. In the same vein, Useem (1982) presents evidence that indicates that corporate elites in the United States and Great Britain have inclusive and diffusely structured economic and social relationships. These transcend individual firms and lead to interactions with government that promote policies favorable to these elites. Organizational environments are thus subject to actual, attempted, and perhaps even unintentional manipulation by the organizations within them.

SUMMARY AND CONCLUSIONS

Throughout our analysis we have identified environmental impacts on the structure and process of organizations. Pfeffer and Salancik (1978) suggest that organizations are *controlled* by environmental contingencies. Others, such as McNeil (1978) and Perrow (1979) suggest the opposite—that organizations control the environment. The truth of the matter undoubtedly lies somewhere between these extremes. Some organizations are controlled at some times; others control at some times. It is quite possible that an organization could move from one position to another, gaining or losing power in the environment. American automobile manufacturers appear to have lost significant power as regulation, competition, and apparent ineptitude have occurred. Regulation and competition are environmental controls; ineptitude is not. By the same token, some banks and other financial institutions, but not savings and loan associations, have retained their power and are not in a controlled situation. Part of the reason for this is the pattern of interorganizational linkages that they have been able to develop, as will be demonstrated in the next chapter.

In this chapter we have examined some of the impacts of the environment on organizations. We also noted the impact of the environment on the development of organizations and considered the various dimensions of the environment. The analysis has been on the general environment of organizations. In the next chapter we will consider the *specific* environment of organizations—other organizations.

12

Interorganizational Relationships

All organizations have relationships with other organizations. Some are relatively trivial, while others are of utmost importance for the parties involved. Some sets of relationships have strong societal outcomes, while others do not. Before moving to an analysis of interorganizational relationships (hereinafter, IOR), we will consider some of these variations.

Most organizations have vending machines of one sort or another. Coffee, candy, soda, and other snacks are available for employees at the drop of several coins. For the employing organization, the contract with the vending machine company is probably a rather trivial factor in their overall operations. For the vending machine company, a particular contract may be trivial or crucial, depending upon the scope of their operations and the size of a particular contract.

College and universities engage in many forms of interorganizational linkages. One of the more conspicuous ones is the National Collegiate Athletic Association. The NCAA has strong jurisdiction over inter-collegiate sports. Aldrich (1979, pp. 337–40) and Stern (1981) have documented the manner in which the NCAA rose to its position of power. Stern's work suggests that there is more close monitoring of successful teams than of less successful ones, as the University of Nevada at Las Vegas must recognize. IORs such as the NCAA are designed to regulate the power among the organizations involved.

Clients of social service organizations are vitally affected by IORs. A common practice is client referral. Theoretically, if one agency is unable to provide the needed services for a particular client, the individual is referred to an appropriate agency for service. What happens in practice is that clients that are easily treated or provided services are not referred, while the more difficult ones are referred, with the most difficult cases sometimes eventually "falling between the cracks" of the referring set of organizations.

At the societal level there has been a long-standing concern with the actual and potential power of the "military-industrial complex." This refers to interorganizational patterns linking the military with industry into a powerful set of organizations which can dominate other spheres of life. Linkages among powerful organizations through interlocking boards of directors have become the focus of intense scrutiny by political and organizational sociologists.

Cook (1977) concluded that organizational theorists began paying attention to IOR when they started looking beyond organizational boundaries into organizational environments and when urban sociologists began to recognize urban communities as networks of organizations, particularly in regard to the delivery of social services (Litwak and Hylton, 1962; Warren, 1967; Warren et al., 1974). There continues to be a strong interest in IOR and community structure (Galaskiewicz and Krohn, 1984; Mulford, 1984; Turk, 1973). While these community analyses are important, our focus here will be on interorganizational phenomena in their own right. In order to do so, we will first examine the variety of forms of IORs that can be identified. We will also identify various levels of analysis that can be utilized in the depiction of IORs.

IOR: FORMS AND LEVELS

There is a general agreement that IORs have three basic forms. These are illustrated in Figure 12–1. The dyad or pairwise relationship is the simplest form of IOR and has probably received the most attention in empirical research. The interorganizational set idea was derived from Merton's (1957) analysis of role sets. Evan (1966) and Caplow (1964) introduced the organizational set idea into the literature. The emphasis is on a focal agency (FA in Figure 12–1) and its dyadic relationships with other organizations. As Van de Ven and Ferry (1980) note, it is possible to trace the impact of changes in one dyadic relationship as they affect other pairwise relations within the set.

Aldrich (1979; see also Aldrich and Whetten, 1981) has introduced a variation on the organizational set. This is the action set, which is composed of "a group of organizations formed in a temporary alliance for a limited purpose" (p. 280). According to Aldrich, "action sets may have their own formalized agreements, internal division of labor, behavioral norms vis-à-vis other organizations, and clearly defined principles for the recruitment of new members" (p. 281).

Interorganizational networks are more inclusive. They consist "of all organizations linked by a specified type of relation, and (are) constructed by finding the ties between all organizations in a population" (Aldrich, 1979, p. 281). Van de Ven and Ferry (1980) define the network as "the total pattern of interrelationships among a cluster of organizations that are meshed together in a social system to attain collective and self-interest goals or to resolve specific problems in a target population" (p. 299). The Van de Ven and Ferry approach stresses the network in areas such as social or health service delivery within a community and would include all the organizations in that network of service

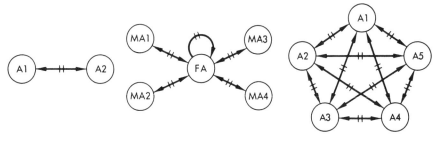

a. Pairwise or Dyadic   b. Interorganizational Set   c. Interorganizational Network
Interorganizational
Relationship

Source: Andrew H. Van de Ven and Diane L. Ferry, *Measuring and Assessing Organizations* (New York: John Wiley, 1980), p. 298.

FIGURE 12–1   Forms of interorganizational relationships

delivery. The Aldrich approach is different in that it does not concern itself with collective goals or target groups, but focuses instead on linkages, such as financial or other resource transactions. Personnel or client flows would be the linkages in the Aldrich scheme. In reality, an empirical analysis would probably find a close overlap between the two approaches, since organizations linked by resource flows in the health care area would also probably be those identified following the Van de Ven and Ferry framework.

Before turning to the issue of levels of analysis among these patterns of IORs, it should be noted that an analyst can focus on a variety of dimensions within these forms. Figures 12–2, 12–3, 12–4, and 12–5 demonstrate the complexity that exists when the organizational set concept is used.

The examples are drawn from research on the social-control system for problem youth which John Clark and I conducted. Figure 12–2 indicates the organizations in interaction with a focal organization, in this case the police. The frequency of the interaction is also indicated. Figure 12–3 indicates the degree of formalization of the relationship; Figure 12–4 indicates whether the relationship is cooperative or conflictual.

These figures include only a few variables and a few members of the organization set. The complexity of the relationships is indicated by the fact that frequent interactions do not necessarily mean highly formalized or cooperative relations. In addition, it can be seen in Figure 12–4 that cooperation and conflict can exist in the same relationship. The organizations cooperate on some issues but conflict on others.

Another meaning implicit in the idea of the organization set is indicated in Figure 12–5, where the major linkages for the police are seen to be with other law-enforcement agencies. While these relationships are based on contacts in regard to law-enforcement problems, they are also a major basis by which the focal police department determines how well it is doing. Organizations use other organizations of the same type both for comparison purposes and as a source of new ideas.

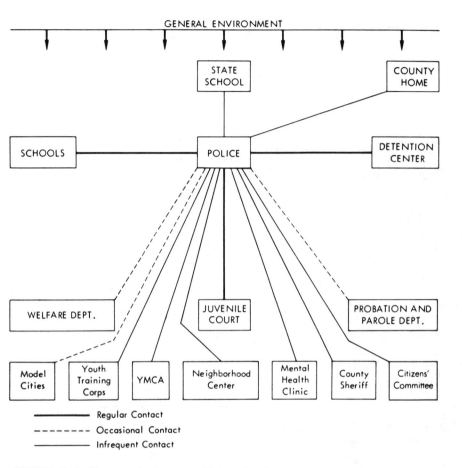

FIGURE 12–2   The organization set and interaction frequency

The analysis of IORs is complex. Not only does an organization like the police have relationships with the sets of organizations depicted in Figures 12–2 through 12–5, but they also have multiple other sets of relationships. Each organization must purchase goods and services. Many of these organizations have concerns other than problem youths. The welfare department, for example, is also involved in financial assistance programs with linkages to federal, state, and local organizations as well as citizen's groups.

There is yet another form of IOR. This is the joint venture (Pfeffer and Nowak, 1976). This form entails the creation of a new organizational entity by organizations joining in a partnership. The joint venture is a means by which illegal mergers can be avoided, but yet permits joint capital investment on the part of the organizations involved. Pfeffer and Nowak note that joint ventures may occur in profit and nonprofit sectors. Among profit-seeking organizations,

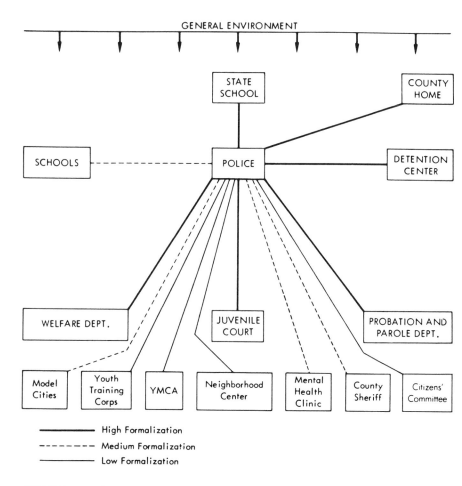

FIGURE 12–3 The organization set and formalization of relationships

oil and gas exploration efforts are a common form of joint venture, as the participating organizations, which have both competitive and symbiotic relationships among themselves, seek to reduce environmental uncertainty and reduce the risks for each participant. Joint ventures among nonprofit organizations are exemplified by alliances formed among private colleges. These alliances are a means by which they can achieve competitive advantages over independent colleges.

The joint venture is a good place to begin to analyze the issue of *level* of analysis. In the case of the joint venture, one could focus attention on the newly created entity *or* the participating organizations *or* both. This is the case of all forms of interorganizational interaction. In the case of the dyad, for example, the focus of interest can be on the organizations involved, on the relationship itself, or on the environment in which the dyadic relationship is based. One could

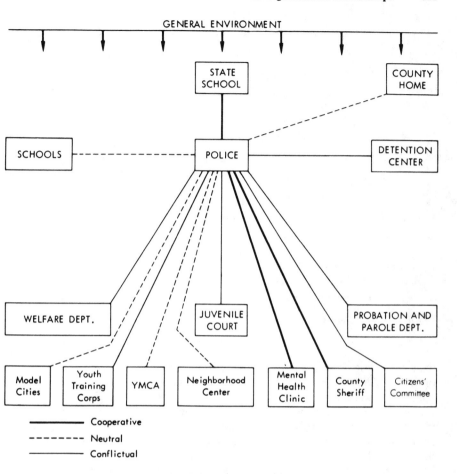

FIGURE 12–4 The organization set and conflict-cooperation

also focus on the individuals involved, such as boundary personnel, but that will not be our concern here. Schmidt and Kochan (1977), for example, focused on the motivations of the organizations to participate in interorganizational relationships. Hall et al. (1977) focused on the quality of relationships among the organizations that they studied.

When the analysis is focused on sets or networks, even more complexity is introduced, since the focus can be on the set or network, a focal organization within the constellation, other organizations, the relationships themselves, or the environment in which all this is occurring. Provan, Beyer, and Kruytbosch (1980) examined the linkages with environmental elements that modify power relationships within an organizational set. Klonglan et al. (1976) studied the relationship between organizational characteristics and IORs at different levels of government, such as the country or state levels. The focus here is on the

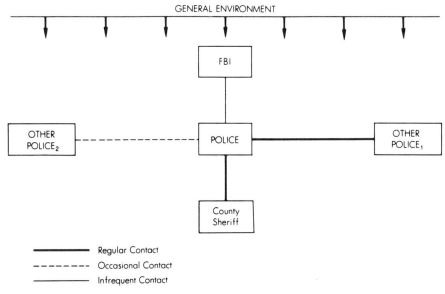

FIGURE 12–5   Another type of organization set

manner in which organizational characteristics are related to interorganizational patterns. Turning the analysis in another direction, Metcalf (1976) found that IORs serve organizations as they adapt for their own needs. IORs provide a means of adapting to, rather than merely responding to, environmental pressures. Interorganizational analysis is thus a complex and potentially confusing enterprise, since various studies have had different foci, with less clarity on the level of analysis than would be desirable.

A major difficulty in interorganizational analyses is the ordering among the units of investigation. Using a simplified set of distinctions among the environment, the organizations involved, and the qualities of the relationships, we can identify the following alternatives as shown in Figure 12–6.

Each alternative represents a possible assumption about causal ordering, with the situation made yet more complicated by the possibility of feedback loops for each alternative. Unfortunately, we do not have the answer regarding optimal ordering. The reason for this is that each component is interactive with the

FIGURE 12–6   Alternative Causal Orders

others. We probably have an extended example of the chicken-versus-egg argument here, with causal priority difficult to establish and probably not worth the effort, since each component does affect and is affected by the other.

Analyses of IORs have overwhelmingly been oriented to the delivery of human services such as health care, employment service, youth-serving organizations, welfare organizations, and the like. The reason for this has been the belief that interorganizational coordination would lead to improved service delivery and lower costs. Federal and state research support and programs reflected this emphasis and researchers in the area responded to these emphases. This has led to an underemphasis on interorganizational interactions in the private sector.

Private sector analyses are not completely absent, however. For example, Reve and Stern (1979) note that interorganizational analyses have missed marketing interactions in distribution networks, with their use of power and the pressures of conflict. Stearns et al. (1987) have documented the manner in which commercial television stations are linked to networks, wire services and newspapers. Galaskiewicz and Wasserman (1989) found that private business firms made charitable contributions to organizations whose executives were personally known to the business executives. The bulk of the research on IORs, nonetheless, has come from the human service delivery area.

A FRAMEWORK FOR IOR ANALYSIS

The focus of this chapter is on IORs themselves rather than on the participating organizations. The analysis is primarily inductive, based on research findings in the area. As Galaskiewicz (1985, p. 281) has noted, the body of accumulated knowledge is highly fragmented and the scholarship is uneven, but there is enough of a basis to serve as a guide to understanding. We will consider characteristics of the general environment that appear to be important, specific situational factors affecting relationships, the bases of the relationships, resource flows in relationships, actual transactions, and finally outcomes of the relationships. The framework is adapted from Morrissey, Hall, and Lindsey (1981).

General Environmental Characteristics

We earlier identified dimensions of organizational environments. These same dimensions are critical for IORs. Thus, technological, legal, political, economic, demographic, ecological, and cultural conditions have been identified. Hall et al. (1977) have identified legal mandates as an important basis for interaction. The cultural conditions in a community could support or repress IORs. Organizations in highly complex technological environments, such as nuclear waste management, are known to each other and can rank each others' performance (Shrum and Wuthnow, 1988).

Aldrich (1979) approached the environment along a different set of dimensions. As indicated in the last chapter, he identified environmental capacity, homogeneity-heterogeneity, stability-instability, concentration-dispersion, consensus-dissensus, and turbulence as the critical environmental dimensions.

Turbulence has been identified as an important factor because it refers to the increasing causal interconnection among the elements in the environment. This means that there is a greater rate of interconnection among the organizations in a system (Emery and Trist, 1965; Terreberry, 1968). As turbulence increases, we would expect a higher rate of IORs.

Environmental complexity would play a similar role, as the number of activities and situations in the environment rise with increasing complexity. Aldrich (1979) argues that organizations deal with complexity by specializing in a limited range of activities. This, in turn, leads to a loosely coupled system in which links among organizations are necessary for organizational survival. Aldrich's emphasis on survival suggests that organizations are not tightly bound to each other, but only to the extent that they need each other for survival. This is too limited a view of the importance of the environment, since other characteristics, such as legal or economic situations may lead to tighter binding than would simply be caused by complexity.

Homogeneity-heterogeneity would have an impact on the range of organizations that have interactions, with a heterogeneous environment having the capability for a wider range of interactions. Aldrich (1979) suggests that a heterogeneous environment leads to a proliferation of organizational programs, which may contribute to a higher level of interorganizational interaction.

Environmental capacity, in Aldrich's terms, is similar to the economic dimension, but also includes other resource bases. There are contradictory interpretations of the impact of environmental capacity. Galaskiewicz and Shatin (1981), on the one hand, report that poor neighborhoods draw fewer social service organizations and thus fewer interorganizational linkages. Aiken and Hage (1968), on the other hand, report that a shortage of resources draws organizations together. Turk (1973) found that the scale of municipal government was related to the development of interorganizational relationships. A rich environment may provide the organization with resources that permit it to engage in interorganizational relationships that it otherwise might not.

The stability-instability factor also appears to have mixed consequences. Galaskiewicz and Shatin report that stable clientele provide certainty for organizations and thus less need for interaction. Aldrich (1979) suggests that stability may permit the development of formalized or routinized relationships.

The concentration-dispersion dimension appears to be more straightforward. Aldrich (1979) reports that concentration of employment agencies contributes to interagency interactions. Similarly, the consensus-dissensus dimension also appears to have a one-directional relationship with interorganizational interactions, with domain consensus, which will be discussed in more detail later, contributing to interactions.

Quite obviously, more research is needed to determine the patterns of relationships between the environment, IORs, and the organizations involved. Such research is difficult to accomplish, since environmental qualities have to be measured over time as do IORs. The problem of causal ordering just referred to also presents severe analytical problems. Despite these problems, a full understanding of IORs is impossible without an adequate conceptualization and eventual measurement of these general environmental properties.

Situational Factors

There is agreement that the general environment is important as a setting for IORs. The specific situations in which IORs take place are also crucial. The situational factors that will be discussed represent preconditions or antecedents (Halpert, 1982) for interactions. There are five factors which appear to be important here.

(1) Awareness It has long been recognized that organizations operate in a "field" of other organizations (Warren, 1967). Less recognized is the fact that organizations vary in their awareness of the field around them. Awareness refers to both the recognition of other organizations and the recognition by organizational representatives that their organization is interdependent with other organizations in their field.

IORs do not occur automatically. A good part of interorganizational theory is predicated on the assumption that IORs will not occur unless there is awareness of potential or actual interdependence among the organizations involved (Levine and White, 1961; Litwak and Hylton, 1962; Levine, White, and Paul, 1963). Klonglan et al. (1976) have suggested that there is a form of hierarchy of awareness. First is a general awareness of the existence of other organizations and their activities. The next level involves mutual acquaintance among the directors of the organizations. The focus on directors is probably too narrow, since acquaintances among staff members would be of great importance in some instances. The next levels of awareness involve specific interactions and joint board membership among directors. We will deal with these latter issues separately, since they are a step beyond simple awareness.

Van de Ven and Ferry (1980) approach awareness from a different perspective. They suggest that there are two levels of awareness. At the more general level is the extent to which boundary spanners in organizations are knowledgeable about the goals, services, and resources present in other organizations. This awareness provides identification of alternative sources of services and resources. According to Van de Ven and Ferry, higher levels of awareness are likely to result in higher levels of interaction.

The second level of awareness involves interpersonal ties among organizational personnel (Boje and Whetten, 1981). These can involve old school ties, membership in common professional organizations, membership in common religious or fraternal organizations, simple friendships, or contacts that are based solely on work bases. Galaskiewicz and Shatin (1981) report that interpersonal ties are crucial for interorganizational relationships at periods of environmental turbulence. It is possible to develop sociometric measures of such acquaintanceships (Rogers, 1974). A higher level of interpersonal ties is seen to be linked to higher levels of interorganizational interaction. Overlooked in most analyses of such ties is their quality. Quite obviously, friendship will yield a different form of interorganizational relationship than will animosity. Interorganizational relationships are based on much more than the qualities of the individuals involved, but this factor should not be overlooked. As Halpert (1982) has noted, the interpretive schemes of the individuals involved in IORs are important preconditions for the relationships.

(2) Domain Consensus-Dissensus   The domain issue has already been discussed in terms of Aldrich's (1979) analysis of the dimensions of the general environment of organizations. The domain issue has particular salience in interorganizational relationships. Unfortunately, several meanings are embedded in the usage that the concept has received.

One meaning has a simple spatial referent. The domain is the geographical area served by an organization, such as the "service area" or "catchment area" used by neighborhood health centers or community mental health centers. In these spatial cases the issue of domain is usually settled in advance, with domain not really an issue except for potential clients who may reside on a border of two organizations' domains.

A more complex and important meaning of domain concerns the level of agreement about role or task differentiation among the organizations involved in IORs (Levine et al., 1963). The roles organizations play relative to one another, in terms of their programs and services and clients to be served, are critical issues for the organizations involved. Aldrich (1979) views domain consensus in this manner, in terms of the degree to which an organization's claim to a specific domain is disrupted or recognized by another organization. Molnar (1978) focused on whether or not organizational dyads served common clients, while Van de Ven and Ferry (1980) considered clients, services, and funding sources as indicators of organizations sharing similar domains.

Two issues are intertwined here. First is the issue of consensus or agreement on domain, while the second involves the commonness of the domain. It is quite possible that organizations could claim the same domain with consensus or dissensus.

Another aspect of the domain issue involves ideological considerations. Analysts such as Benson et al. (1973), Boje and Whetten (1981), Hall et al. (1977), Mulford (1980), and Schmidt and Kochan (1977) have grappled with this issue. Ideological issues can involve the compatibility of the goals of the organizations involved, conformity in terms of treatment ideologies in social service organizations, or compatibility in terms of understanding the nature of the issues faced. The ideological issue becomes important in practice. For example, police agencies typically have a different ideology toward problem youth than do social welfare agencies. These differences, which can be severe or mild, affect the qualities of interactions among the organizations.

Levine and White (1961) have argued that domain consensus must exist before exchange relationships among agencies are possible. Molnar (1978) suggests that organizations with intersecting domains tend to be more interdependent than those that do not share domains, with intersecting domains contributing to interorganizational relationships. Others, such as Schmidt and Kochan (1977) and Hall et al. (1977) have argued that interorganizational relationships do not depend on domain consensus. These authors do suggest that the level of consensus does affect the qualities of relationships but not their sheer existence. Cook (1977) has suggested that exchange relationships do not depend on such consensus. There is not consensus on domain consensus.

(3) Geographical Proximity   The distribution of organizations in space has received relatively little attention in the literature on organizations in general.

Geographical proximity refers to the spatial distance between organizations or their subunits. It has been noted that distance can facilitate or inhibit interactions (Broskowski, 1980). It is more difficult to establish or maintain relationships across distances, for both organizations and individuals. It can also be noted that the type of unit involved in an IOR interacts with the spatial issue. Modern communication techniques permit rapid information flows across space, but clients or staff members would be more difficult to transfer.

Reid (1969), Schermerhorn (1975), Boje and Whetten (1981), and Halpert (1982) have suggested that the decision to coordinate with another organization is easier if the organizations involved are physically close to one another. Proximity promotes familiarity of domains. In many communities several city or county agencies might be housed in the same building. This proximity would facilitate interactions in comparison with organizations that are spread throughout some geographical area.

(4) Localized Dependence Related to the issue of geographical proximity is the degree to which organizations are dependent upon a local area for their resources. Galaskiewicz (1979) and Maas (1979) have examined this factor. Their concern has been with the extent to which needed resources are obtained only from a local area versus a more widely dispersed resource base. If organizations with localized dependence are successful in commanding these localized resources, they are more powerful or central in the network of organizations in a community. If, on the other hand, there is high localized dependency with relatively weak access to resources, the organization is much more vulnerable to the power of other organizations.

(5) Size The final situational factor is the size of the actual or potential set or network of organizations. Most analyses have focused on the actual number of organizations in a network (Van de Ven and Ferry, 1980). Size is a situational factor in that at any given time there are a finite number of organizations available for interactions. In general, the number of organizations in a relationship is related to the complexity faced by any single organization. It is also likely that large numbers of relationships weaken the quality of the relationships (John, 1977; Caragonne, 1978; Agranoff and Pattahas, 1979). An increase in the number of organizations in a relationship affects dependencies, domains, and the potential rewards or resources for participating in the relationships. Again, the analogy with individuals is appropriate here. Many ties reduce the likelihood of each of the ties being strong, so that a greater proportion of linkages in a large network would be more superficial than in a smaller network. While weak ties among individuals have been shown to have great importance for their job seeking (Granovetter, 1973), there is no solid evidence regarding the impact of different forms of ties among organizations. It would appear that a large set or network would have the potential for dissipating resources and actions, but it could also lead to a situation in which there were many alternatives for an organization, in terms of resource acquisition, client flows, and the like.

Caplow (1964) has demonstrated the manner in which the number of relationships increases exponentially as group size increases. The same thing would occur among organizations. The number of organizations in a relationship or potentially available thus is an important situational factor for inter-organizational relationships.

Reasons for Interaction

IORs do not just happen. They occur in an environment and in a situational context. They also occur for reasons. Galaskiewicz (1985) has identified three basic reasons for IORs. The first is the procurement and allocation of resources such as facilities, materials, products, and revenues. These are crucial for organizational survival. The second reason is to form coalitions for political advocacy and advantage, while the third is to achieve legitimacy or public approval. The last reason can be seen in instances of interlocking boards of directors among cultural organizations and corporations. On the basis of a study in the Minneapolis-St. Paul area, Galaskiewicz found that:

> personnel from more influential companies tended to be recruited to more cultural boards and that companies tended to sit on the boards of more presti-gious cultural organizations. One interpretation of these findings is that cul-tural organizations were striving to enhance their own reputations by aligning with the more influential companies in the area; and corporations were striving to enhance their legitimacy by aligning themselves with more prestigious cultural organizations. (pp. 296–97)

Edström et al. (1984) suggest that there are two explanations for IORs. First is "outside-in" in which cooperation is based on the need to manage existing interdependencies in the environment. The second is "inside-out" in which cooperation is based on the need to acquire resources and establish new inter-dependencies. This formulation is based on cooperative programs and ventures.

We will identify *four* reasons or bases for contact here. They range from ad hoc situations to those which are mandated by law or regulation. The outcome from each basis is likely to be different for the organizations involved and for the relationship itself.

(1) Ad Hoc Bases   Relationships have an ad hoc basis when there is little or no previous patterning in the relationships among organizations. A specific need, problem, or issue may arise among two or more organizations. In the social service area, a client with an unusual problem may trigger one organization to call up another to get an opinion or to make a referral. Ad hoc bases are the least important for IORs, since they tend to be one-shot operations. If an ad hoc situation repeats itself or if more elements enter the relationships among the agencies involved, other bases for a continued relationship will develop.

(2) Exchange Bases   The exchange basis for IORs has been the domi-nant orientation toward such relationships since Levine and White's (1961) seminal paper. According to Levine and White, exchange is "any voluntary activity between two organizations which has consequences, actual or antici-pated, for the realization of their respective goals or objectives" (p. 120). Cook

(1977) has extended this formulation beyond the two-party implication of Levine and White. She examines exchange within networks of organizations and incorporates power differentials among organizations into her formulation. The exchange idea incorporates the notion that organizations must acquire resources and that exchange is the major mechanism by which this occurs (Thompson, 1967; Jacobs, 1974; Benson, 1975).

The exchange basis can be seen as a form of bargaining in which each organization seeks to maximize its advantage in acquiring resources from another organization (Schmidt and Kochan, 1977). Although the exchange formulation seems to imply that this is bargaining among equals, modern exchange theory, as exemplified by Cook's work, does not make that assumption. Power differences among organizations are taken into account. Schmidt and Kochan (1977) argue that even in a situation in which there is a great imbalance of power, the powerful organization which seeks to interact with a weaker organization can do so because of the power difference. The exchange is unequal, but the participants do engage in resource exchange. The exchange basis emphasizes the importance of resource acquisition for the organizations involved. It also contains an implication of rationality, as the organizations seek to maximize their gains in interaction. All the problems associated with decision making in organizations must be considered in exchange interactions, since decisions here cannot be assumed to be any more rational than decisions made in other spheres of organizational actions. Levinthal and Fichman (1988) found that business firms tend to continue relationships with their auditing firms over long periods of time. They conclude that history has its own consequences in that relationships appear to be maintained for their own sake.

Resource exchange has far-reaching consequences, according to Van de Ven and Walker (1984). They see the perceptions of resource dependence as an important spur for IORs. Resource dependence is a powerful direct determinant of IOR communications, resource transactions, and consensus. They also note that monetary transactions and client referrals involve different patterns of coordination.

Exchange is an important basis for interorganizational interactions. It becomes less of a factor, however, when the interactions between organizations become formalized. Formalization is likely if resource exchanges continue (Van de Ven and Walker, 1984).

(3) Formalized Agreements Marrett (1971) defines formalization as the degree to which the interdependency among organizations is given official sanction by the parties involved. This official sanction or recognition (Aldrich, 1979) is typically written down and may be legally or contractually binding (Van de Ven and Ferry, 1980). A formal agreement is based on exchange. Once the agreement is signed or otherwise authorized, it throws the relationship into a different light, since interactions are based on a specified pattern rather than ongoing through the exchange process at each interaction episode.

In our study of organizations concerned with problem youths, we (Hall et al. 1977) found that the presence of a formal agreement between organizations was related to the frequency and importance of interactions to a greater degree than to other bases of interaction. We also found that an organization did not need to evaluate other organizations when a formal agreement was in place. Apparently, the presence of a formal agreement is based on frequent and important interactions among organizations, with the agreement serving to simplify interactions, since each interaction does not have to be weighed in terms of its contributions to the organizations involved. The organizations have agreed to interact and the interactions take place.

Another basis for interaction has a very different source than agreements among the organizations involved. In many instances, interactions among organizations are mandated from outside the interacting parties.

(4) Mandatedness   This basis for IORs has received increasing attention in recent years. Mandatedness refers to the extent to which relationships are governed by laws or regulations. These laws or regulations are imposed on the relationship by legislative or administrative rulings. The organizational actors are brought together because of a legal-political mandate (Raelin, 1982). For example, laws regarding unemployment compensation may require a public employment agency to interact with a welfare department in order to determine client eligibility. Such interaction may or may not have occurred without a mandate present. Halpert (1982) points out that a mandated relationship may place an organization in a contradictory position. Compliance with the mandate may disrupt established procedures. At the same time, it may be necessary for the organization if it is to receive financial support.

The importance of a mandate for IORs has been identified by Schmidt and Kochan (1977) and Hall et al. (1977). Hall et al. (1977, 1978) and Molnar and Rogers (1979) suggest that mandated relationships may lead to conflict, since organizations may be forced to interact even with domain dissensus, interpersonal animosities among members, and so on.

Mandated interactions do not guarantee that interactions will take place. Unless there is some sort of enforcement mechanism, organizations may ignore a mandate. Since mandates are typically associated with some type of resource flow and with monitoring, they usually do in fact serve as an important basis for interorganizational interactions. It is quite possible that an organization can receive contradictory mandates (Gardner and Snipe, 1970). This means that an organization will have to try to serve several mandates at one time along with its own orientations from an exchange perspective. It may seek to interact with one organization but be forced to interact with one or more other organizations. Again, this moves the analysis of interorganizational interactions still farther from a basis of pure rationality.

Mandated interactions should continue to receive attention in research and practice. Interorganizational interactions outside of the area of human services would appear to be frequently based on some sort of mandate. Governmental regulatory agencies are mandated to interact with business firms. City and county government agencies are mandated to interact with state and federal level agencies. While exchange considerations enter into the passage of laws and regulations through the process of lobbying and the give and take of policy formulation, the presence of a strong and enforced mandate leads to IORs of a different form than those which evolve from ongoing exchanges. Schwochan et al. (1988) found that mandated collective bargaining led to greater subunit power within organizations than was the case when mandated collective bargaining was not present.

In this section we have examined ad hoc, exchange, formalized agreement, and mandated bases of interorganizational interactions. Each basis has a different outcome. At the same time, all interorganizational interactions involve something passing between the organizations involved. We will now turn to a consideration of these resources which flow between organizations.

Resource Flows

Regardless of the environment, the situational factors, and the bases of interactions, interorganizational interactions have a content, and it is to this that we now turn. Exchange theory properly focuses on resource exchange, and we will examine resource interdependency among organizations. The flow of resources vary in their intensity, so that this quantitative aspect of interactions will be examined. We will then turn to the issue of joint programs, where organizations, in addition to exchanging resources, also engage in activities together.

Resource Interdependence   Situations in which two or more organizations are dependent upon one another for the resources each has access to or controls are the basis of resource interdependency. Resources take a variety of forms. Galaskiewicz and Marsden (1978) examined inflows and outflows of information, money, and social support in their interorganizational analysis. Molnar (1978) also identified information, but added other resources in terms of funds, facilities, and personnel. He also suggested that organizations that have intersecting domains tend to be more interdependent. Mulford (1980) adds equipment and meeting rooms to the list of resources which could be exchanged. Clients can also be seen to be a resource in this context (Boje and Whetten, 1981).

It has long been recognized that organizations are seldom capable of controlling all the resources they require (Levine and White, 1961; Litwak and Hylton, 1962). An interorganizational division of labor can develop in which the participating organizations specialize by providing a particular service in return for a particular resource they need (Aldrich, 1979). Each organization becomes dependent upon the other in this type of situation. Organizations tend to resist dependence and to attempt to make other organizations dependent upon them (Benson, 1975).

It is unclear what the direction of resource flows means in terms of interdependence. On one hand, a great outflow of some resource, such as money, could indicate great dependence, since the organization involved would appear to have to buy needed goods or services. On the other hand, money outflow may make other organizations more dependent upon the organization in question if this is their only source of funds.

Pennings (1980b) has identified three forms of interdependence. When there is *horizontal* interdependence, all members of an organization set compete with each other in obtaining resources and disposing of goods and services. In cases of *vertical* interdependence organizations interact at different stages of the production of goods or delivery of services. For example, in the juvenile justice system, police, courts, probation services, reformatories, and halfway houses are in a sequential order. Each organization jockeys for power, but the competition is less than in horizontal interdependence. *Symbiotic* interdependence occurs when organizations complement each other in the rendering of service to individual clients. Here there is minimal competition, especially when agreements regarding domain have been achieved.

Intensity   The level of resource investment required of the organizations involved in IORs determines the intensity of the relationship (Marrett, 1971; Aldrich, 1979). For service organizations, the higher the level of referrals, services provided, staff support, facilities, and other resources, the greater the intensity of the relationship. Implicit in the consideration of intensity is the question of the relative proportion of an organization's resources that are invested into the relationship. The higher the proportion, the more intense the relationship.

Van de Ven and Ferry (1980) emphasize the importance of information flows in the determination of intensity. In their view, information is an important commodity in an interaction and should be treated as distinct from other forms of resources. Van de Ven and Walker (1984) found that monetary transactions and client referrals entailed different patterns of interorganizational coordination. The nature of the resources involved must also be considered in terms of the intensity with which they are brought into a situation.

The more intense the relationship, the more important it is for the organizations involved. The relationships that any organization has vary in their intensity, from the casual to the all consuming. The former makes little difference, while the latter has the potential actually to consume the organization if all of its efforts involve interorganizational relationships and if these relationships use up all its resources.

Intensity is sometimes confused with or combined with the frequency of interactions. This is a bad mix, since frequent interactions can be casual, but a really intense interaction can be infrequent. For this reason, we will consider frequency in another context. Dyadic relationships, networks, and organizational sets can all vary in their degree of intensity. Interactions become most intense during crisis situations. For example, the tragic disappearance of a female student at my university led to intense and prolonged interaction between the campus police and the state police. Research on disasters (Drabek et al., 1981) reveals similarly intense interactions. In noncrisis situations, relationships will be less intense. The impact of intensity is both network wide and organization specific.

Joint Programs   Aiken and Hage (1968) and Mulford and Mulford (1980) have identified joint programs as a particular type of resource flow. Here the emphasis is not simply on resource flows in terms of interdependency, but on substantial resource commitment and collaboration. Aiken and Hage (1968) found that joint programs were of particular importance to the welfare and health organizations that they studied. They were more salient than client, personnel, or financial support flows. Joint programs were not "minor incidents" in the lives of the organizations. Some had been in existence for over 20 years (p. 919).

Aiken and Hage also found that joint programs tended to foster other joint programs, since the IORs grew in scope and depth.

Joint programs involve an investment of resources and an intense relationship. They also involve purposive actions in regard to some issue which is jointly confronted. Joint programs can involve a particular type of client or treatment program in the services sector or a new area of exploration in the area of raw materials, as in the case of joint ventures (Pfeffer and Nowak, 1976). The important difference between joint programs and other forms of interactions is that the actions are purposive and not just responsive to environmental pressures.

Transaction Forms

IORs are interaction processes between organizations and within networks and sets. In the analysis that follows, we will build on Marrett's identification (1971) and Aldrich's (1979) discussion of the critical dimensions of IORs. We will first note how the interactions can be structured and then turn to the transaction processes themselves.

Interaction Formalization We have already noted the fact that organizations can have formalized agreements among themselves which can govern their interrelationships. These agreements are in place prior to the succeeding interactions. There is another aspect of formalization that can serve to structure the interactions. This is the presence of an *intermediary* organization which serves to coordinate or control interorganizational interactions.

Warren (1967) analyzed Community Decision Organizations, and Mott (1968) studied a coordinating council, both of which represent the type of formalization under consideration here. Councils of churches, chambers of commerce, welfare boards, and other such mediating and coordinating organizations serve to structure the relationships among organizations. Van de Ven and Ferry (1980) suggest that the power of these formalizing agencies can be more or less binding, so that it is important to consider the degree of interaction formalization. In some cases, the intermediary organization's decisions are binding, while in other cases they are merely advisory. An example of this variation can be seen in Pfeffer and Long's (1977) analysis of organizations affected by the United Fund. They found that the power of the United Fund was inversely related to the capabilities of the member organizations obtaining funds from alternative sources. Those agencies which were highly dependent upon the United Fund would have their interactions more formalized and controlled than those with less dependence. Leblebici and Salancik (1982) found that the presence of an intermediary organization of the sort we have been discussing leads to stability of IORs.

Interaction Standardization Marrett (1971) and Aldrich (1979) identify two aspects of standardization. First is the degree to which the resources interchanged are standardized. If organizations agree to exchange particular types of clients or personnel, high standardization is present. Low standardization would occur when the units are heterogeneous. High standardization would result in more routinized interactions, with less time and energy devoted to sorting and classifying the units that are exchanged or transferred.

The second form of standardization involves the procedures used in the transactions. Low standardization would be represented by procedures based on a case-by-case decision process, while high standardization would be exemplified by similar procedures being used over a period of time. When high standardization is present, there are likely to be forms and checklists that are routinely filled out as the transaction occurs. Aldrich (1979) suggests the larger and more complex organizations are more likely to standardize their transactions than are smaller and less complex organizations. A good example of the variance in standardization is the assignment of academic credits for students transferring from a community college to a four-year college. A large public college or university is likely to have developed procedural standardization for determining transferable credits. The small private college would treat each transfer on a case-by-case basis. The credits themselves are examples of unit standardization.

Importance   IORs vary in their importance for the interacting organizations. Hall et al. (1977, 1978), Klonglan and Paulson (1971), and Schmidt and Kochan (1977) have focused on this dimension. The Hall et al. (1978) study found that the importance of interaction was a strong predictor of the frequency of interactions. The idea of importance contains two elements. The first is the importance of another organization to the work of a focal organization, while the second is the importance of the interaction itself. In either case, importance is a major contributor to the generation of IORs. Importance has been examined at the dyadic level and not at the set or network levels, but the pattern would appear to be the same. At the network level, if all mental health organizations in the network perceived that the other organizations and the interactions themselves were important, the interactions themselves would take place with greater frequency and intensity. Hall et al. (1977) reports that important interactions are likely to lead to formalized agreement among the organizations interacting.

Frequency   As noted, frequency of interaction and intensity are sometimes viewed synonymously. This is inappropriate, since frequency is a component of the transactions among organizations, while intensity is a component of the resource flow among organizations. While importance and frequency are also closely associated, there is not a necessary relationship between the processes. A once-a-year budget meeting may be more important than weekly casual contacts. In general, however, important relationships are frequent relationships. Hall et al. (1978) found that frequent interactions were related to high levels of both coordination and conflict. This suggests that frequent interactions tend to involve more elements of the organizations involved than do infrequent interactions. Marrett (1971), Aldrich (1979), and Van de Ven and Ferry (1980) all suggest that there is a strong linkage between frequency and intensity. Frequent interactions contribute to heightened resource flows. Interactions can have high or low frequency on the basis of voluntary exchange, formal agreements, or mandates.

Reciprocity   Reciprocity refers to the symmetry of the transactions among organizations. Resources can flow to both parties equally or in an imbalanced fashion. Baty, Evan, and Rothermel (1971) examined faculty personnel flows among graduate schools of business. They found that the flows were not reciprocal, with prestigious schools of business sending out more faculty members in the form of new Ph.D.s than they received. In this case, the lack of reciprocity contributed to the power of the sending schools, since the less powerful schools were dependent upon the more powerful. When there is mutual dependence, organizations will attempt to maintain reciprocal relationships.

Power   Of all the IOR transaction processes, power has received the most attention. Power in an interorganizational situation is equivalent to that in the intraorganizational situation—the ability of one party to have another party do what the other party would not otherwise do (Dahl, 1957). The power variable has been used in a variety of ways, and we will try to disentangle the various approaches that have been suggested.

One dominant theme is based on resources, with power being viewed as the possession of resources which enables an organization to use those resources to gain the compliance of others (Burt, 1977; Aldrich, 1979). Building on Emerson's (1962) work, which sees power as residing in dependency, analysts have argued that parties in a power relationship are tied to each other by the dependence of one party on the other, or perhaps by mutual dependence. Power lies in asymmetrical dependence.

Using Blau's (1964) work as a starting point, Aldrich (1979) examined the manner in which social service organization administrators deal with the power dependency issue. Four alternatives were suggested. First, an organization can build up its own resource base and thus reduce dependence. Second, the organization can seek alternative sources for needed resources, thus limiting dependency. Third, an organization can use coercive force to make the other organization surrender resources without complying with its demands. This is the conflict situation as exemplified by the strike. Finally, the organization can essentially withdraw from the situation by modifying its goals or technologies. If these alternatives are not available or are not chosen, dependency will continue, with the organization having less power than the organization with which it is interacting.

Halpert (1974), using a modification of French and Raven's (1968) analysis of power bases, identified expert, referent, reward, coercive, legal, and community power bases of interorganizational power. He saw possession of these power bases or resources as the source of organizational power in IOR transactions.

These approaches to IOR power discussed have been primarily applied to dyadic relationships. Network analysts have frequently substituted the notion of *centrality* for power in their research (see Alba, 1982). Centrality refers to the relative position of an organization in a network of organizations, with those more central being viewed as having more power (Boje and Whetten, 1981; Galaskiewicz, 1979). Information and resource flows can be traced in networks. In a totally decentralized network, there is equal participation by all organizations, with perfect symmetry or reciprocity and no power differences. As Aldrich

(1979) notes, this is a rare situation, since networks are typically integrated by a centrally located organization.

There is yet another aspect to IOR power. There are some IOR situations in which the issue of exchange is not a consideration and network centrality is determined in advance. This is the situation in which power relationships are determined in advance of any interactions. In a network of organizations in which all receive their resources from a central source, such as a government agency, the power relationships are predetermined. Some bargaining will occur, but the relationship is set in advance. Organizations that are designated as information clearinghouses would have a similar power role. As in the case of power within organizations, the present hierarchy of power must not be over-looked, although it has been by many interorganizational analysts.

Cooperation   Cooperation is a process in which organizations pursue their own goals and thus retain autonomy, while at the same time orienting their actions toward a common issue or outcome (Mulford, 1980; Warren, Rose, and Bergunder, 1974). We are distinguishing cooperation from coordination, since the latter process involves the pursuit of a common goal. Cooperation is typically viewed as a form of voluntary interaction (Maas, 1979) and would be found in instances of exchange- or voluntary-agreement–based relationships. Klonglan and Paulson (1971) note that cooperation can involve personnel interchange. Aiken and Hage (1968) viewed cooperation in terms of products and services for clients. The cooperation process involves a rather small investment on the art of the organizations involved, but it does mean that they have to take each other's actions into account.

Conflict   IOR conflict is an oppositional process in which one party attempts to block or thwart the activities of another party. As Galtung (1965) notes, conflict can occur at the individual and collective level and within and between social systems. For the analysis here, we are concerned with IOR conflict, be it interpersonal or collective in basis. Interpersonal conflict is relatively easy to understand. Collectively based conflict is more complex and refers to situations in which the organization as a whole is involved in the conflict. An example here is Sebring's analysis (1977) of university–state government interactions in which unsuccessful encounters in the past led to conflicts in the present.

Conflict can take several forms in IOR transactions. Some conflict is regulated, as in competition, while other conflicts take place outside of a regulatory base. As in the case of IOR processes, conflict can also be based on power differences or on domain disputes (Molnar and Rogers, 1979). It can also be based on ideological grounds. Halpert (1974) documents the manner in which some police agencies are in conflict with other social service organizations, primarily because of their differing philosophies.

The correlates of conflict are not well understood. A major reason for this is a pervasive belief that conflict is a process to be avoided. This belief appears to be misguided. Guetzkow (1966) and Assael, (1969), have suggested that conflict and its resolution can have long-run benefits for IORs. Zeitz (1980) argues that conflict is both system integrative and disintegrative. The resolution of old conflicts sets the stage for new conflicts in a dialectic manner. Hall, Clark, and Giordano (1979) found that conflict was related to interaction frequency and to interactions based on both formal agreements and mandates. They do not see agreements or mandates as the cause of conflicts, but rather interpret this relationship as being based on the fact that agreements and mandates are found in situations that are important to the parties involved. This study also found that conflict was related to power differences. While noting that resource acquisition can be an important source of conflict, the study found that conflict also existed between organizations which had very different resource bases, such as different levels of government, as when city agencies are in conflict with county agencies.

Conflict Resolution   Inasmuch as there are few Hundred Years Wars among organizations, it is safe to conclude that most conflicts are resolved. Van de Ven and Ferry (1980), drawing on earlier works by Blake and Mouton (1964), Lawrence and Lorsch (1967), Burke (1970), and Filley, House, and Kerr (1976) identified four conflict resolution techniques that take place at the IOR level. The issues can be ignored or avoided; the issues can be smoothed over by playing down differences and emphasizing common interests; the issues can be openly confronted with differences worked through as in the case of collective bargaining; or the issues can be submitted to some hierarchical power, either in the form of some party at a higher administrative level or an outside party which is given power over the situation.

Aldrich (1979) suggests two other alternatives—contracting or expanding the organizational boundary. Contraction involves removing the organization from some aspect of its domain and thus conflict resolution, while expansion permits an organization to encompass the conflicting other organization. Aldrich's suggestions are particularly relevant in the competitive situation. When an organization leaves a market, it is contracting; when it buys out a competitor, it is expanding its boundary.

Conflict resolution has been found to be a major contribution to coordination (Hall et al., 1978). It will be remembered that in this study conflict was based on interaction frequency and the importance of the interactions. These factors contribute to conflict, conflict resolution, *and* coordination. IORs are truly complex.

Coordination   Coordination has had an interesting role in IOR analyses. Probably most studies have had coordination as an explicit or implicit dependent variable, on the assumption that somehow coordination was good for any clients involved, could cut costs, and was good in its own right. That assumption is now under serious question.

Coordination involves a process of concerted decision making or action in which two or more organizations participate with some sort of deliberate adjustment to one another (Warren, Rose, and Bergunder, 1974). A key factor here is the idea that the transactions are deliberate and involve a goal which is collective. This is a major point of differentiation from cooperation. Aiken et al. (1975) subsume cooperation under coordination, but I prefer to keep the processes analytically distinct.

Gans and Horton (1975) identified two forms of coordination in social service organizations. *Administrative* coordination involves fiscal issues, personnel practices, and planning and programming. Joint budgeting and joint planning exemplified coordinated administrative practices. Coordinated *direct service* activities would involve such things as case conferences or a case coordinator. The coordination transaction process is complex in that administrative matters could be highly coordinated, with service coordination in a shambles.

In my view, coordination is a process and not an outcome of interorganizational relationships. It may or may not be desirable. Basing his comments on Warren et al.'s (1974) analysis of urban reform movements, Perrow (1979) makes the following comments in regard to coordination:

> What, then, about the lack of coordination? Little was needed; there was an overall consensus as to who should do what, a division of labor or of sectors, and new formal coordination mechanisms did not increase the efficiency of the agencies. As others have pointed out, coordination has costs associated with it, as well as presumed benefits, and there may be substantial gains with redundant, uncoordinated activity and substantial costs with coordination which eliminates back-up facilities. (p. 235)

The Warren et al. study also found that new agencies designed to enhance coordination and innovation actually accomplished little. We thus view coordination as one form of IOR transaction.

The forms of IOR transactions we have been discussing are largely drawn from research on human service organizations. Before considering the outcomes of IORs, the focus will now shift to a consideration of IORs in the private sector.

IORS IN THE PRIVATE SECTOR

Research on IORs in the private sector has a puzzling history. Business firms compete, and competition is clearly a form of IOR. Organizational theory has been surprisingly mute in regard to competition (an exception is Khandwalla, 1981). The framework that has been presented for dealing with human service organizations would appear applicable to the private sector, especially with the emphasis on resource flows. Aside from research on joint ventures, organizational theory has tended to ignore IOR and the private sector. A major exception here is in the area of interlocking boards of directors.

Director Interlocks

Interlocking boards of directors are situations in which members of the board of directors (or board of trustees) of one organization also serve on boards of other organizations. Interlocking boards of directors have been the subject of commentary and research for a long time. Pennings (1980b) notes that U.S. Supreme Court Justice Louis Brandeis warned in 1913 that such interlocks contain many evils, such as the suppression of competition. Pennings goes on to note that contemporary analyses of interlocks run the gamut from analyses of board interlocks as the means by which elites maintain societal control to sober scholarly analyses of the manner in which organizations attempt to control uncertainties by such interlocks.

The basic form of director interlock is the situation in which an officer or director of one organization is a member of the board of directors of another organization. Another form of interlock occurs when members of two organizations are on the board of a third organization (Burt, Christman, and Kilburn, 1980). This is illustrated in Figure 12–7.

Several phenomena are represented in Figure 12–7. Firestone Tire and Rubber Company owned eight establishments in the industries indicated. According to Burt (1980), these establishments were not randomly selected:

> they are, to varying extents, drawn from interdependent industries. The largest portion of supplies for the textile industry, for example, is purchased from the chemical industry, so it is to the advantage of Firestone's textile establishment to

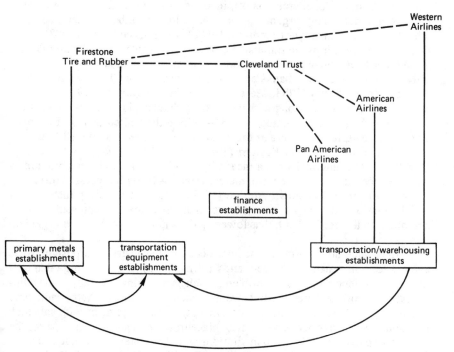

Note: Arrows represent market constraint, solid lines represent ownership, and dashed lines represent interlocking.

Source: Ronald S. Burt, Kenneth P. Christman, and Harold C. Kilburn, Jr. "Testing a Structural Theory of Corporate Co-optation: Interorganizational Directorate Ties as a Strategy for Avoiding Market Constraints on Profits," *American Sociological Review,* 45 (October 1980), 827.

FIGURE 12–7   Illustrating Three Types of Directorate Ties Involving Two Firestone Tire and Rubber Establishments in 1967

have transactions with Firestone's chemical establishment rather than being forced to deal on the open market. Similarly, the largest portion of supplies for the rubber industry is purchased from the chemical industry. Firestone's rubber establishment therefore benefits from its "inside" connection to Firestone's establishment in the chemical industry. (p. 564)

Organizations cannot purchase all organizations in their environments because of limited resources and federal merger restrictions. Interlocking boards of directors are a less direct way in which organizations can be linked. In Figure 12–7 Firestone and Western Airlines have direct interlocks with a member from Firestone on Western's board of directors and vice versa. Indirect interlocks are present through Cleveland Trust, a banking organization. Western Airlines is a classic example of organizational death, by the way. It was acquired by Delta Airlines, with its logo obliterated and all other visible signs no longer evident. Only some of its routes remain.

In the world of interlocking directorates, financial institutions are the dominant actors. Commercial banks, investment banks, and insurance companies are the most likely organizations to have their members on the boards of other types of organizations (Pennings, 1980b). Mariolis and Jones (1982) report that these relationships are quite stable over time. Mintz and Schwartz (1981) go so far as to conclude that the corporate system is dominated by only a handful of New York commercial banks and financial institutions. This has not always been the case. Roy's (1983; see also Mizruchi and Bunting, 1981) research indicates that railroads, along with the telegraph and coal industries, were at the core of interlocks for the period of 1886–1905 in the United States. Railroads were very powerful in that era as the nation industrialized and moved West.

Burt, Christman, and Kilburn (1980), Burt (1980, 1983), and Pennings (1980) note that interlocks are a means by which organizations can attempt to manage uncertainty in their environments. Interlocks provide access to resources and can influence decisions. Aldrich (1979) notes that there are instances in which interlock occurs because an organization demands representation on another organization's board, thus lowering the autonomy of the latter organization.

It is imperative to note that interlocks are *purposive*. Purposiveness is evident for both parties. Mizruchi and Stearns (1988) report that organizations that are experiencing financial problems, such as declining solvency and declining rates of profit seek out directors from financial institutions. At the same time financial firms "infiltrate" the decision-making structure of firms with solvency problems. These interlocks would take place in situations in which hope for the future was perceived. Financial institutions would not interlock with lost causes. Stearns and Mizruchi (1986), Richardson (1987), and Palmer et al. (1986) also find that interlocks tend to be reconstituted if they are broken. Breaks occur when a director dies or retires. Reconstitution is linked to ongoing resource dependencies.

In order to understand the consequences of interlocks of boards of directors, Pennings's (1980b, pp. 188–91) findings will be summarized (see also Burt, 1980). Of the 797 largest American business firms, only 62 have no interlocks with the remaining 735 firms. Financial firms are disproportionately represented in the interlocks. Interlocks are most common in concentrated industries where monopolies almost exist in the first place. Financial firms avoid interlocks with firms that appear risky, instead seeking interlocks with those that are not risky. Well-interlocked firms were found to have greater economic effectiveness. This was particularly the case with firms that rely on equity financing and which were capital intensive. The relationships between interlocks and economic effectiveness were strongest for effective organizations. Financial firms do not want to get involved with operations that they perceive as performing poorly. Pennings views these patterns of interlocks as persuasive attempts by financial firms to enhance their position with solvent firms that will be reliable customers for loans, bonds, and other forms of debt. It is a technique by which financial firms acquire good customers and by which the customers have access to financial resources. Burt (1983) views such interlocks as a device for managing competition to control uncertainty in corporate profits.

Pennings's findings are hardly radical, but they are in keeping with what we understand about the ways in which organizations seek to acquire resources and enhance their position in their environment. It should be stressed that organizations in the public sector engage in the same kinds of activities through boards of trustees, advisory boards, and the like. Zald (1970) demonstrated the importance of boards for the YMCA. An examination of the board of any college or university would reveal similar linkages into important segments of the organization's environments. Provan, Beyer, and Kruytbosch (1980) have shown the importance of board interlocks in the operation of the United Way.

Evidence slightly contrary to the positions of Pennings and Burt can be found in research carried out in the Minneapolis–St. Paul metropolitan area (Galaskiewicz et al., 1985). Contrary to Burt, these researchers did not find consistent patterns of interlock among firms that constrained each other across industries. Neither local sales nor labor markets affected the patterns of interlock. Galaskiewicz et al. do not conclude that Burt's interpretation is wrong, but that it may not work in a different local market situation.

Galaskiewicz et al. did find that social status within the community was important for interlocks. Socially elite individuals who were associated with large corporations were disproportionately represented on boards of directors. Firms tended to interlock with those of equal social standing. According to these Galaskiewicz et al. both "clout and grace" (p. 423) contributed to the densest interlocks. Economic clout and social grace made companies and people attractive to one another. The authors caution that there may be a regional influence on their findings.

Hage (1980, p. 95) believes that the actual power of boards of directors is quite limited in that their power is to ratify or defeat what the chief executive officer and his or her administration propose to do. Quite frequently, the executive officer and the administration have greater knowledge than members of the board and can thus control the situation. At the same time, boards of directors can remove top administrative officers (James and Soref, 1980; Bauer, 1981). The power of boards is a *variable* that can be determined only by empirical investigation.

Board interlocks have an additional basis which is independent of organizational rationality. Political sociologists have focused in on the social class factor and its relationship with interlocks. Based on Canadian evidence,

Ornstein (1984) concluded that corporate imperatives *and* class solidarity factors operate in interlocks. Kerbo and Della Fave (1983), using data from a U. S. Senate committee found that there is an "intercorporate complex" of major corporations, with banks in a central coordinating position which was short of control. They also found evidence for an inner group of the "corporate class" that provides the human linkages.

The social class argument has persuasive evidence in its behalf at the local level (Galaskiewicz et al., 1985; Palmer et al., 1986) and at the national level (Mintz and Schwartz, 1981; Useem, 1979, 1982, 1984; Domhoff and Dye, 1987) Clawson and Neustadtl (1989) analyzed the 1980 congressional elections. They found that corporate contributions to political action committees (PACs) for these elections were based on ideological conservatism. They conclude that interlocks are based on *classwide rational actions*. While it is hard to comprehend how classes can be more rational than organizations, the class argument is persuasive.

The class argument is especially persuasive if it is used in conjunction with an organizational perspective on interlocks. Mizruchi (1989) provides just that perspective. He examined some 1,596 dyads among 57 large manufacturing firms. He found that membership in the same primary industry or several similar industries, geographical proximity of corporate headquarters (but not plant locations), market constraints, and common relations with financial institutions (through stock ownership or directorate ties) were related to similarity of political behavior. He argues that *resource dependency* and social class explanations were operative.

Director interlocks are a means by which the resources that are important to organizations and their relationships flow between organizations. They can give an organization a competitive advantage through access to financing, information, and other resources.

OUTCOMES OF IOR

As might be expected, the outcomes of IOR are complex and difficult to measure. In the human services area, much of the research has been concerned with improved service delivery, which itself is difficult to conceptualize and measure. In a study of health care delivery with a focus on two hospitals, Milner (1980) found that service delivery was quite well coordinated through a complex system of formal and informal arrangements. One of the hospitals provided high-quality care to affluent patients, while the other provided lower-quality care to the poor. The interorganizational arrangements served to maintain this differentiation. IORs were thus effective, on one hand, but divisive, on the other.

The outcome issue is both simple and complex. Its simplicity is that it lies in the eyes and minds of the beholders. Van de Ven and Ferry (1980, p.327) have devised a simple set of questions to determine if other organizations have carried out their commitments, the relationships have been productive, and the time and effort spent in the relationships was worthwhile and to assess the degree of satisfaction with which relationships are viewed.

The complexity of the outcome issue is that there are multiple eyes and minds which can make this assessment. This is an identical problem with the issue of organizational effectiveness, which will be considered in the next chapter. The perceived effectiveness of interorganizational interactions can be assessed from the standpoint of participants within each organization, the organization as a whole, clients served or disserved, the community in which the interactions take place, or legislative or administrative decision makers who have jurisdiction over the particular dyads, sets, or networks in question. The outcome issue is thus one of political power, resource dependence, and moral choice. Outcomes which are good for one organization may be bad for another; clients may benefit, but the organizations may suffer; relationships may be cost effective, but damaging to organizations and clients. Analyses of IORs must keep these considerations in mind.

SUMMARY AND CONCLUSIONS

In this chapter we have attempted to provide an overview of the topic of IORs. We have identified the various forms of IORs, such as dyads, sets, and networks. We have also concerned ourselves with the level-of-analysis issue and have considered the difficulty in ordering the relationships among organizational, environmental, and IOR levels. We then presented a framework for analyzing IORs, beginning with general environmental considerations, then moving to specific situational factors, bases of interaction, resource flows, transaction forms, and, finally, outcomes. Whether or not this framework is useful or not will lie in its applicability.

Most of the research on which this analysis has been based was carried out in social service organizations, with the exception of the materials on director interlocks. We clearly need an expanded data base from a broader range of organizations. The analysis contained relatively little reference to the organizations involved in interactions. Little is actually known of this linkage. Aiken and Hage's work is among the few which have considered this issue and their data base is extremely limited, although Hage (1980) has attempted to extrapolate from this data base to some hypotheses regarding IORs. We also suffer from a shortage of information about the individuals involved in IOR interactions. There is some limited information on boundary spanners, but this role may actually be a peripheral one, with much greater importance found in the individuals who are on interlocking boards or those who interpret and decide upon the information brought by boundary spanners. There are important political and moral issues in regard to the power of interlocking directorates.

The area of IORs is thus one of great research potential. There is a general belief that the relationships are important, even though this has not yet been really demonstrated. There is also a general belief that IORs contribute to organizational effectiveness, the topic of the next chapter.

13

Organizational Effectiveness

In this chapter we deal with a topic that has been central to the entire analysis. We basically study organizations for two reasons. One is to understand how and why organizations are effective or ineffective. We may want to make them more or less effective from an economic, political, or moral perspective. It is now well recognized that the various parties concerned with any single organization can have contrasting and conflicting views on its effectiveness. We are not neutral about the organizations with which we deal as workers, clients, customers, or publics. I don't want to be abused by any organization, public or private. I also want the organizations in which I participate as a member to do well. Doing well is to be effective. My perspective on effectiveness, however, varies with my position in the organization. I see effectiveness differently as a faculty member from when I was a vice president of my university. I have different perspectives about the other organizations of which I am a part. I would like to see organized crime go out of existence, but I want to see our public schools thrive.

There is thus this practical and personal reason to study organizations. The second reason for studying organizations is more abstract. The ideal of organizational scholars is to develop organizational *theory*. In the next chapter we will evaluate several attempts to develop comprehensive organizational theories.

In this chapter our analysis essentially comes full circle. We began this book by considering some of the outcomes of organizations. We then examined structural characteristics, processes within organizations, and then organizational environments. In essence, the outcomes of structural arrangements, processes such as decision making and leadership, and dealing with the environment are designed to contribute to organizational effectiveness. Unfortunately, like organizations, organizational effectiveness is highly complex.

There have been several recent and generally excellent attempts to bring the literature on organizational effectiveness together (Cameron and Whetten, 1983; Zammuto, 1982). There are several competing models of effectiveness in the literature which have served as the bases for these analyses. In the present chapter, these models will be analyzed and their strengths and weaknesses highlighted. Inherent in the models and in the debates between the models is the idea that organizational effectiveness as a concept contains *contradictions*. With this in mind, a contradiction model of effectiveness will be developed, which is designed to encompass the insights that previous models have identified.

For practitioners and scholars who concentrate on organizational analysis, organizational effectiveness has been a dominant explicit and implicit point of departure. Benson (1977) suggests that this reflects the administrative-technical orientation of people who study organizations. They wish to find ways to adjust organizations to enhance effectiveness. Benson notes that while many studies deal with effectiveness in a direct and highly visible way, even those studies which do not focus on effectiveness tend to deal with it implicitly, as an underlying or background orientation.

Not everyone is concerned with organizational effectiveness in this manner. There are many important social issues which are basically attempts to prevent organizational effectiveness. Opponents of nuclear energy development and generation and of abortion are essentially against the effectiveness of the organizations that provide electricity and abortions. Ironically, the success of these oppositional efforts depends upon the effectiveness of the oppositional organizations.

The present analysis is an attempt to decompose the concept of organizational effectiveness and to expose and examine the contradictions inherent in the concept and its applications. The purpose is to provide a sounder basis for research, theory, and practice. It is hoped that the analysis will be more than administrative-technical and that it will be informative for individuals concerned with altering the directions that organizations take.

Before beginning the analysis, I will describe an organization that was highly effective, but now is slipping. The factors that contributed to its effectiveness are instructive. So too is the fact that it is slipping. The following is from the fourth edition of this book:

> The organization to be described is a small automobile dealership. It sells and services Saabs, Swedish cars of somewhat unique design and styling which are also quite expensive. By every indicator that is commonly used and by every effectiveness model that is currently in vogue, this is an effective organization. It makes a profit. It provides customers with good service at prices that are at times startlingly low. The workers have high morale and work diligently. The customers are happy, with most on a first-name basis with the owner of the dealership. The cars perform well and meet governmental safety and environmental protection criteria.
>
> What is the secret of success here? There actually appear to be several such secrets. In the first place, the organization is quite small, with no more than twenty individuals involved in sales, service, and clerical work. The head of the service department is also the owner and major salesperson. There seem to be no disputes

about what the appropriate goals of the organization are. Resources are apparently brought into the organization with little difficulty, since people either like Saabs or they do not, which makes for little intensive competition, especially since there are relatively few dealerships in the surrounding area. The various individuals and groups that are connected to the dealership as workers or customers appear to have compatible interests and there are few fights about overcharging or work being done that was not needed. There are no external pressures on the organization to change its policies. Although I have no direct evidence, it would appear that other organizations with which this one has contact would judge it to be quite effective, the only exception being organizations that are growth- or volume-oriented, who would view this operation as not aggressive enough.

This example contains many elements that will enter the later discussion. The organization's *goals* were being met. It was able to acquire and utilize sufficient *resources* to ensure organizational survival. Its *personnel* and *clientele* were satisfied. There was *agreement* among participants, within the organization at different levels in the organization and between members and nonmembers on what the organization was doing and how it was doing it. Finally, the organization was apparently serving the best interests of the *community*, since it provided a relatively fuel-efficient and safe automobile. On the latter point some might argue that the private automobile itself is socially harmful, but that argument can wait for a moment.

The fact that the past tense was used is meant to indicate that things have changed. Sales of Saabs have slipped. Personnel have left the organization because of low pay. Much of this is beyond the dealership's control, but inadequate pay is not. This example illustrates that effectiveness itself has elements that are in and out of organizational control.

The auto dealership example does contain the core points which must be considered in regard to effectiveness. These are the goals, resources, personnel, clientele, and community in which the organization is embedded. The basic point of this analysis is that *there are contradictions within and between these elements.*

The introduction of the notion of contradictions is not a new one in organizational analyses. Benson (1977) emphasizes dialectical processes in organizations. Heydebrand (1977) documents the fact that the very nature of organizations is one of contradiction, such as the activity of organizing versus organization itself or traditional hierarchical control versus new forms of control, such as professionalization. More recently, Cameron (1986) argued that effectiveness is a paradox, with both consensus and conflict in various conceptions of effectiveness.

AN ORIENTATION TOWARD EFFECTIVENESS

Before getting into the specifics of the contradiction model of effectiveness that is to be introduced here, it should be made clear that the approach to be taken forces the analysis of effectiveness away from attempts to conceive of *overall* organizational effectiveness. A contradiction model means the uncompromised acceptance of the fact that it is folly to try to conceptualize organizations as effective or ineffective (Campbell, 1977). This approach agrees with the urgings of Hannan and Freemen (1977b) and Kahn (1977) that effectiveness not be used as a scientific concept.

While there is agreement that effectiveness as an overall concept has little or no utility, it would be a major mistake to simply ignore issues and findings that have been developed in regard to effectiveness. This seeming paradox can be resolved if a contradiction model of effectiveness is used. Put very simply, a contradiction model of effectiveness will consider organizations to be more or less effective in regard to the variety of goals which they pursue, the variety of resources which they attempt to acquire, the variety of constituents inside and outside of the organization, and the variety of time frames by which effectiveness is judged. The idea of variety in goals, resources, and so on is key here, since it suggests that an organization can be effective in some aspects of its operations and less so on others.

The contradiction idea has its roots in the research project on organizations that deal with problem youths which was discussed in the previous chapter. It was found that these organizations had multiple and conflicting goals. One set of organizations in the study were juvenile detention centers. These organizations had the goals, among others, of "maintaining secure custody" and "providing healthy living arrangements." On the face of it, these are incompatible goals, since secure custody would be optimized by simply locking the youths in cells, which is hardly a healthy living arrangement. Other research, such as Kochan et al. (1976), has also pointed to the issue of multiple and conflicting goals.

The example of contradictory goals just noted above comes from the public sector. It is frequently believed that goals here are more amorphous and contradictory than those in the private sector. Unfortunately, the private sector picture is also one of contradictions. For example, the goal idea seems simple in the case of profit-making organizations. Indeed, much of the research on effectiveness has used this type of organization because of goal clarity. The seemingly readily quantifiable profit goal is not such a simple matter, however. It is confounded by such issues as the time perspective (long-run or short-run profits); the rate of profit (in terms of returns to investors); the important issue of survival and growth in a turbulent and unpredictable environment that might in the short run preclude profit making; the intrusion of other values, such as providing quality products or services or benefiting humankind; and the firm's comparative position vis-à-vis others in the same industry. Even the nature of profit itself has multiple meanings. It can involve return on stockholders' equity, return on total capital, sales growth, earnings-per-share growth, debt-to-equity ratio, and net profit margin. These are not well correlated (Forbes, 1973), which alone makes the idea of goals extremely complex.

The goal approach has another complication. We have already demonstrated the fact that organizational decisions and actions cannot be viewed from a rational model framework. Decisions that at one point in time appear to be rational turn out to be disastrous by events beyond organizational control.

In the pages that follow, we will present and evaluate the major models of effectiveness. Each makes a positive contribution to our understanding and contributes to the contradiction model.

MODELS OF ORGANIZATIONAL EFFECTIVENESS

The System-Resource Model

The choice of the system-resource model as the first effectiveness model to be examined is based on the fact that an extensive analysis of the environmental-organizational interface has been presented. This model was developed by Yuchtman and Seashore (1967; Seashore and Yuchtman, 1967) who begin by noting that variables concerning organizational effectiveness could be ordered into a hierarchy. At the top of the hierarchy is some ultimate criterion which can only be assessed over time. An example of such an ultimate criterion would be the optimum use of opportunities and resources found in the environment. In terms of the natural selection model, the ultimate criterion would be survival or death.

Next come penultimate criteria. According to Seashore and Yuchtman (1967), they have the following characteristics:

> They are relatively few in number; they are "output" or "results" criteria referring to things sought for their own value; they have trade-off value in relation to one another; they are in turn wholly caused by partially independent sets of lesser performance variables; their sum in some weighted mixture over time wholly determines the ultimate criterion. These criteria would be factorially independent of one another, although probably correlated in observed performance; also some of the component variables would be universal, others unique to certain classes of organizations. (pp. 378–79)

The next level of variables involve the subsidiary variables. These are many in number, some of which would refer to subgoals or means for achieving goals, while others would be in terms of organizational states or processes. The relationships among these variables would take many forms—positive and negative correlation, independence, causal, covarying, interacting, and so on. They would be related to the penultimate criteria in the form of being overlapping, but distinguishable subsets. These subsidiary variables would have short time frames and represent transitory states or processes within the organization.

Yuchtman and Seashore believed that the ultimate criterion was an unmeasurable construct and chose to focus in on the penultimate criteria. They then sought to investigate, through statistical testing,

1. Whether there is a set of penultimate performance variables, factorially pure, that account for much of the total variance in performances.
2. Whether the factors are strongly correlated with, and therefore potentially caused by, sets of subsidiary variables representing organizational states and processes, but not goals.
3. Whether the set of factors is constant across a number of similar organizations (not tested in the present analysis).
4. Whether this set of factors is constant over some span of time.

5. Whether the performance of a single organization is variable over time within the set of constant factors.

6. Whether the conceptual content of the factors suggest that some of them may be universal, others unique. (p. 380)

Yuchtman and Seashore had a unique data set with which to test their ideas. The data came from 75 independent insurance agencies in the United States. Data were available over an 11-year period, with three time periods used in the study. The nature of the insurance business is such that extensive records are kept, and Seashore and Yuchtman had some 200 variables with which to work, of which they utilized 76.

Based on a factor analysis, ten penultimate criteria were identified which accounted for about 70 percent of the total variance in performance. The factors were extremely stable over the 11-year period, even though the relationships among the factors varied at different time periods.

The factors did have different time frames, with some being very stable over time and others having cyclic or phasic effects. For example, three of the factors were extremely stable over the 11-year period. "Business volume" referred to issues such as agency work force, number of policies in force, and number of new sales. The stability is explained by the fact that once people are committed to buying life insurance, they tend to keep buying from the same agency. "Market penetration," or the extent to which the agency had captured a share of the local market, can be similarly viewed as success leading to success. "Business mix" referred to the presence of both large and small policies and individual and employee benefit policies. It was also linked to previous successes.

Three of the factors were much more time specific. These were the "youthfulness of the members," "productivity of new members," and "rate of manpower growth." Apparently these organizations would take in numbers of new young agents at one point in time and then not take many in during the next time period.

The rest of the factors were intermediate in their stability over time. These factors included "production costs," or measures of overhead expenses in regard to sales; "maintenance costs," or the costs involved in maintaining accounts; "management emphasis," or the managers' personal commission; and "member productivity," or the new business generated per agent. According to Seashore and Yuchtman, these internal performance criteria adjust somewhat over the shorter term in the interests of longer-term patterns.

Seashore and Yuchtman conclude that these findings lead to a definition of effectiveness of an organization as the *"ability to exploit its environment in the acquisition of scarce and valued resources to sustain its functioning"* (p. 393). Their reasoning is that while some of the penultimate criteria found could be construed as goals, such as business volume and market penetration, others, such as youthfulness of members or high proportion of new members, could not.

Another conclusion is that resource acquisition must be viewed as relative to the capacity of the environment. Some organizations operate in rich environments, while others act in poorer ones. They also note that their definition stresses the ability to utilize the environment, rather than maximum utilization of the environment, since maximum utilization could lead to the total depletion of resources.

Seashore and Yuchtman conclude their argument by noting that all of the penultimate criteria uncovered in their research probably could not be generalized to all organizations, but that some of them could be. They suggest that the systems-resource approach is preferable to the goal approach, since, in their view, imputing goals to organizations is teleological.

The Seashore-Yuchtman argument is persuasive. It does contain some problem areas, however. For instance, it is actually a question of semantics whether or not growth in business volume is viewed as only one form of resource acquisition or as a goal. The relatively stable penultimate criteria discussed by Seashore and Yuchtman can easily be viewed as goals or constraints on the decisions made by the insurance firms in question. The less stable criteria, such as youthfulness of members, could actually turn out to be predictor variables for these sorts of organizations. It is well known, for example, that young men and women who enter the life insurance sales occupation have good success at first, selling to relatives and friends. This would appear to be a means by which a goal, such as sales volume, could be achieved.

It should also be noted that resource acquisition does not just happen but is based on what the organization is attempting to achieve, namely, its goals. This is in line with our earlier discussion of decision making, in which decisions are made on the basis of perceived environmental conditions and organizational goals. It appears reasonable to argue that resources are seldom acquired just for their own sake but rather in reference to the paths selected by the power coalitions in the organization. Scott (1977, p. 67) suggests that Seashore and Yuchtman implicitly recognize this point when they suggest that criteria for determining effectiveness must be identified. Scott also suggests that the Seashore-Yuchtman formulation is overly narrow in that it only utilizes the interests of the organizational directors. In the case of insurance firms, potential customers could withhold resources, but there are many forms of organizations in which potential customers do not have this option. A more basic issue has been identified by Keeley (1984), who suggests that while survival of an organization may benefit some people, others might benefit from its dissolution.

Campbell (1977, p. 44) notes an additional problem with the kind of approach taken by Yuchtman and Seashore. While factor analysis is a fine methodological tool, it does not arrange the factors in the form of a hierarchy. Campbell is suggesting that some of the penultimate criteria may be more important than others, and thus that choices may have to be made among the criteria. In the case of the insurance firms, this could take the form of having to choose between increasing business volume or increasing market penetration. When stated in these terms, the argument moves awfully close to a goal-modeling format.

The Goal Model

The goal model of effectiveness is both simple and complex. In its simple version, effectiveness has been defined as the "degree to which (an organization) realizes its goals" (Etzioni, 1964, p. 8). Complexity occurs as soon as it is realized that most organizations have multiple and frequently conflicting goals. Kochan, Cummings, and Huber (1976) have pointed out that structural differentiation in organizations is related to goal diversity and goal incompatibility. Since most organizations do exhibit structural diversity, such multiplicity and incompatibility can almost be taken as a given for organizations. This makes the goal model difficult to use, but does not automatically destroy its utility.

Before dealing specifically with the model, some aspects of the nature of the goals should be noted. Goals involve intents and outcomes and serve as constraints on decision making. Organizational goals by definition are creations of individuals, singly or collectively. At the same time, the determination of a goal for collective action becomes a standard by which the collective action is judged. The collectively determined, commonly based goal seldom remains constant over time. New considerations imposed from without or within deflect the organization from its original goal, not only changing the activities of the organization, but also becoming part of the overall goal structure. The important point is that the goal of any organization is an abstraction distilled from the desires of members and pressures from the environment and internal system.

Thinking of goals as abstract values has the utility of indicating the reason why organizational members do not just act on their feelings or whims of a particular day. At the same time, it is a mistake to take as the abstraction the official goal statements of the organization. Perrow (1961) has analyzed this situation nicely. He notes that official goals are "the general purposes of the organization as put forth in the charter, annual reports, public statements by key executives and other authoritative pronouncements." Operative goals, on the other hand, "designate the ends sought through the actual operating policies of the organization; they tell us what the organization actually is trying to do, regardless of what the official goals say are the aims" (p. 855).

In one of the early studies in the tradition of modern organizational theory, Blau (1955) found that two employment agency units, which had the same official goals, actually were very different in what they really were attempting to accomplish. One unit was highly competitive, with members striving to outproduce each other in terms of the numbers of individuals placed. In the other unit, cooperation and quality of placement was stressed.

In discussing this point, Perrow notes (1961):

> Where operative goals provide the specific content of official goals, they reflect choices among competing values. They may be justified on the basis of an official goal, even though they may subvert another official goal. In one sense they are a means to official goals, but since the latter are vague or of high abstraction, the "means" become ends in themselves when the organization is the object of analysis. For example, where profit making is the announced goal, operative goals will specify whether quality or quantity is to be emphasized, whether profits are to be short run and risky or long run and stable, and will indicate the relative priority of diverse and somewhat conflicting ends of customer service, employee morale, competitive pricing, diversification, or liquidity. Decisions on all of these factors influence the nature of the organization and distinguish it from another with an identical official goal. (pp. 855–56)

Operative goals may be linked directly to official goals. At the same time, operative goals can develop which are unrelated to official goals. Perrow goes on to note:

> Unofficial operative goals, on the other hand, are tied more directly to group interests, and while they may support, be irrelevant to, or subvert official goals, they bear no necessary connection with them. An interest in a major supplier may dictate the policies of a corporate executive. The prestige that attaches to utilizing elaborate highspeed computers may dictate the reorganization of inventory and accounting departments. Racial prejudice may influence the selection procedures of an employment agency. The personal ambition of a hospital administrator may lead to community alliances and activities which bind the organization without enhancing its goal achievement. On the other hand, while the use of interns and residents as "cheap labor" may subvert the official goals of medical education, it may substantially further the official goal of providing a high quality of patient care. (p. 856)

Operative goals are thus a derivation of and distillation from official goals. They are developed and modified through ongoing interaction patterns within organizations. They are more than just the results of interpersonal interactions, however. They persist beyond the life of a particular interaction and become the standards by which the organization's actions are judged and around which decisions are made. Even though operative goals are developed in concrete interactions, they, like official goals, are abstractions, since they become standards by which actions and decisions are judged. (For additional discussion of these points, see Price 1972.)

The discussion of the development of operative goals suggests that goals change over time. There are three reasons for changes in the goals of organizations. First, organizations are in *direct* interaction with the environment through their IORs. Thompson and McEwen (1958) presented a framework for understanding goal shifts as a result of such interaction. Organizational goal setting is affected by competitive, bargaining, co-optative and coalitional relationships with the environment. Competition occurs when the rivalry between two organizations is mediated by a third party, as in the case of business firms competing for the same customers. Competition also occurs in the public sector as government agencies compete for a share of the tax dollar (Wildavsky, 1964). Competition affects the goal structure as the organization shapes its action to try to ensure continued support. In this regard, of course, the goal model can be seen to encompass at least some aspects of the systems resource model.

Bargaining also involves resources, but in a different manner. The organization is in direct interaction with suppliers, customers, and other organizations. In a bargaining situation, an organization has to "give" a little in order to get what it desires. Thompson and McEwen note the example of a university which bargains the right to name a building for a substantial gift to build the building. If the donor attaches strings to the gift, the university might alter its operative goals to get the money.

Co-optation is "the process of absorbing new elements into the leadership or policy-determining structure of an organization as a means of averting threats to its stability or existence" (Thompson and McEwen, 1958, p. 27). The classic study of co-optation is Selznick's (1966) analysis of the development of the Tennessee Valley Authority. The TVA shifted its emphases as segments of the community were brought into its decision-making system. Burt et al. (1980; Burt, 1983) have shown that business firms engage in co-optation as they engage in board interlocks in situations in which there are market constraints. Co-optation is a two-way street, of course, with both co-opters and co-optees being affected by the action.

Coalition is the actual combining of two or more organizations. This is the most extreme form "of environmental conditioning of organizational goals" (Thompson and McEwen, 1958, p. 28). In this case, the organizations in the coalition cannot set goals unilaterally.

Shifts in organizational goals as a result of direct interactions with other organizations in a focal organization's environment emphasize the importance of dealing with operative, rather than official goals. A reliance on just official goals would miss these sometimes subtle, sometimes dramatic shifts. This kind of analysis also indicates the importance of looking at organizational effectiveness over time, since a cross-sectional analysis might be done just prior to a significant shift and thus be essentially meaningless.

Goals can also change as a result of *internal* organizational changes. We have already noted the importance of power coalitions within organizations. These power coalitions can shift, sometimes as a result of external pressures, but also because of internal dynamics. Michels's (1949) classic study of the development of oligarchy in political parties and labor unions is illustrative of this. The goals of the rank and file tend to give way to those of the elites. Kanter and Brinkerhoff (1981; p. 322) see organizations as "battlegrounds for stakeholders, both inside and outside, who compete to influence the criteria for effectiveness so as to advance their own interests." Kanter and Brinkerhoff urge that a political model of organizations be used, which is quite appropriate for our consideration of goals.

Organizations may begin to emphasize goals which are easily quantifiable, at the expense of those which are not so easily quantified. Universities look at the number of faculty publications, rather than the more difficult to measure goal of classroom teaching; business firms look at output per worker, rather than "diligence, cooperation, punctuality, loyalty, and responsibility" (Gross, 1968, p. 295). If organizations do begin to emphasize that which is easily quantifiable, then there is a shift of goals in that direction. Jenkins (1977) notes that goal shifts are possible when there is slack in the organization and it is secure. He found that staff interactions guided by a new professional ideology and strong purposive commitments contributed to major and radical goal shifts within the National Council of Churches in the United States. He also suggests that threats to the organization's domain would probably lead to a more conservative stance.

The final source of goal shifts lies outside the organization and involves *indirect* pressures from the general environment. Economic conditions can become altered. Technological developments must be accommodated. Values shift. Organizational goals are adjusted to these environmental conditions. The classic study of this form of goal shift is Sills's (1957) analysis of the March of Dimes organization, which had been oriented around the treatment of individuals who suffered the crippling effects of polio. The development of safe vaccines, a technological development, essentially eliminated the need for the continued existence of the organization, until it shifted its goals to include other crippling diseases.

Another example of this form of goal shift can be seen among colleges and universities as the demographic composition of the population shifts. There is no longer a growing supply of young people, but there is of older people. Higher educational organizations are now including nontraditional students as major recruitment targets, with "seminars for seniors" and a wide array of continuing education programs. The demographic shifts are beyond the control of the organizations involved, as are the other sources of indirect pressure from the environment. Although organizations can try to influence values, manipulate the economy to their advantage, and keep up with technological developments, there are many situations that are simply beyond organizational control. At various times, the United States has faced shortages of gasoline. Organizations, even petroleum firms, have no control over the actions of oil producing nations. Thus, the environment can have an indirect, but still crucial, role in the determination of goal shifts.

Thus far, the analysis has suggested that organizations have multiple goals. These goals may be contradictory. They may also shift. We will now turn to a consideration of how goals can be used in analyzing effectiveness.

GOALS AND EFFECTIVENESS

As noted earlier, the most simple use of the goal model suggests that an organization is effective to the degree to which it achieves its goals. According to Campbell (1977):

> The goal-centered view makes a reasonably explicit assumption that the organiza-
> tion is in the hands of a rational set of decision makers who have in mind a set of
> goals that they wish to pursue. Further, these goals are few enough in number to
> be manageable and can be defined well enough to be understood. Given that goals
> can be thus identified, it should be possible to plan the best management strategies
> for attaining them. Within this orientation, the way to assess organizational
> effectiveness would be to develop criterion measures to assess how well the goals
> are being achieved.

Unfortunately, for organizations and those who analyze them, the matter is not that simple. Hannan and Freeman (1977b) have examined the goal model and have pinpointed some of the problems with its use. They begin their analysis by pointing out that it would be unsatisfactory to drop the goal concept totally, since goals are part of the defining characteristics of organizations. They go on to note, however, that a first and major difficulty with the goal approach is that there is likely to be a multiplicity of organizational goals. This occurs even among the publicly legitimated or official goals, as has already been noted. Hannan and Freeman comment: "Virtually all public agencies and bureaus have very many public goals. For example, the number and diversity of goals of agencies like the Department of Health, Education, and Welfare (HEW) and the Department of Commerce boggle the imagination" (pp. 111–12).

According to Hannan and Freeman, the second broad problem with goals involves their specificity (p. 113). Universities have the very general goals of advancing the store of useful knowledge; police agencies have the goal of protecting the public. These broad goals become much more specific in actual operations, with the more specific goals taking a variety of possible forms. For the police, for example, protecting the public could be approached from the standpoint of putting more officers on foot patrol, cracking down on prostitution, putting more officers in plainclothes operations, or making public relations statements. Within the organization, units can move into divergent directions which are consistent with the broader goal but which could interfere with each other.

The third problem with goals involves the temporal dimension (Hannan and Freeman, 1977b). They note:

> Should we consider the short run or the long run or both? The many published empirical studies that employ cross-sectional data on samples of organizations (see, for example, Lawrence and Lorsch, 1967) tacitly take the short-run perspective. Whether or not this is appropriate depends on the nature of the goals function for each organization. To the extent that the goals function stresses quick return on investment (as in many business ventures, disaster relief organizations, military field units, and so on) the short-run outcomes should be given highest priority. For those organizations that orient toward continued production (for example, many other types of business ventures, universities, research and development organizations, and so on) the year-to-year fluctuations in performance should be discounted and the average performance over longer periods emphasized. (p. 113)

Hannan and Freeman note that different levels in the hierarchy can employ different time frames, making the situation even more complex. They do not deal with the fact that different units within the same organization can also have different time frames as Lawrence and Lorsch (1967) found in their interdepartmental comparisons.

Hannan and Freeman suggest that the goal approach be retained in organizational analyses, by using goals in a manner similar to which individual preferences are used in microeconomics. They note that such preferences are not measured directly.

> Their role (more precisely, the role of hypotheses regarding preference functions or indifference curves) is to permit the formulation of testable hypotheses relating prices and consumer behavior.
>
> Many of the problems we have listed are also problems in the conceptualization and measurement of individual preferences. The point is that these difficulties do not impede the use of unmeasured preferences in the formulation of individual preference theories with strong empirical implications. The same could be true of organizational goals. Goals and environmental configurations together determine organizational behavior. We suggest treating goals as unmeasured causal variables and using propositions involving goals to derive falsifiable propositions relating environmental characteristics and organizational behavior. (p. 115)

As will be seen, in the contradiction model being developed here, we do not leave goals as unmeasured, but do attempt to deal with some of the issues raised in Hannan and Freeman's analysis.

Hannan and Freeman also deal with the second part of the goal model, which is organizational performance or output. Outcome assessment is difficult for several reasons. First is the time perspective used. An outcome that is successful for the short run could be disastrous for the long run. Another problem in outcome assessment involves "bounding systems" (Hannan and Freeman, 1977b, p. 116), or the problem in distinguishing the effects of events both inside and outside of the organization. The issue here is that it is very difficult to determine what activity within an organization contributes to some outcome. It is equally difficult to specify if this outcome is a result of organizational actions or the result of some external force. This point is not lost on organizational management. Bettman and Weitz (1983) report that corporate annual reports tend to attribute unfavorable outcomes to external, unstable, and uncontrollable causes. Favorable outcomes are attributed to actions taken by management. Closely related findings are reported by Staw, McKechnie, and Puffer (1983) in their analysis of letters to shareholders. These letters tend to be self-serving and attribute corporate performance to the actions taken by management. Interestingly, these letters appear to be convincing, since they are related to stock price increases. They are also related to the sale of stock by corporate management.

Hannan and Freeman note that the quality of the input of an organization affects the quality of the output. Many social service organizations, for example, select clients (inputs or external forces) who appear to have good chances of success in the treatment which the organization provides. More problematic clients are referred elsewhere or are simply passed around the social service system. This sort of situation makes the assessment of the outcome of the social service organization difficult, since it is difficult to disentangle organizational-versus-input effects.

The problem is made even more complicated by the fact that while both input quality and the contribution of units within organizations can be understood as contributors to performance, so too can the ability of the organization to control the quality of inputs. Control of environmental factors is an outcome of organizational actions. Organizations attempt to build up demands for their outputs. Success here means higher performance.

Hannan and Freeman conclude:

> Once we acknowledge that all these factors are subject to organizational strategy and action, we are faced with a serious methodological problem. All of the variables that appear in the conventional analyses are endogenous, that is, causally dependent on other variables in the model. For example, the quality of inputs may be a function of the expenditure on inputs, which is a function of output performance. If none of these factors is causally prior, or exogenous, it is extremely difficult to obtain unique estimates of any relevant causal effects in the system. In the technical language of econometrics, the system is underidentified. To remedy this situation one must make a considerable number of strong assumptions concerning the details of the causal structure. Unfortunately, the existing theories of

organizational performance (and effectiveness) do not provide a basis for these assumptions. (p. 122)

Hannan and Freeman conclude their argument by suggesting that effectiveness be dropped as a scientific concept, since comparisons across organizations cannot be made to construct and test abstract theories of organizations. They then suggest that effectiveness considerations remain valid in terms of engineering or social criticism. By this they mean that effectiveness can be used in the administrative technical sense by individuals interested in engineering or in managing organizations toward public or private goals. Social criticism can be accomplished by demonstrating that organizations are not doing what they claim to be doing or that they are not doing it well enough. In the contradiction model which will be developed here, the intent will be to permit effectiveness considerations to remain at the scientific level.

Scott (1977) has identified additional problems with the goal approach. He suggests that goals have been used in three ways in effectiveness analyses. First, they can be viewed as sources of incentives for organizational participants. Second, they can be approached as guides to participants' efforts. This is similar to the approach being taken here. The third aspect of goals is that "they provide criteria for identifying and appraising selected aspects of organizational functioning. In short, we must analytically distinguish between goals employed to motivate or direct participants' behavior, on the one hand, and goals used to set criteria for the evaluation of participants' or the entire organization's behavior, on the other" (p. 66). This distinction between goals for motivation and direction and goals for evaluative purposes is a useful one. Although we have emphasized the fact that goals must be incorporated into the decision-making framework, effectiveness concerns pull the analysis in the direction of the evaluative criteria side of the goal formulation.

There are additional problems with the goal model. Reimann (1975) has noted that the goal model of effectiveness contains the problem that an organization cannot be effective if this means attainment of all or most of its goals. Multiplicity and contradictions among goals must be recognized in any utilization of goals in effectiveness studies.

We have not dealt with the issue of who or which parties are to judge the performance of organizations in regard to goals. As will be developed in detail at a later point, the views of different organizational constituents can vary widely and should be considered, as they will be in the contradiction model. In the next section we will deal specifically with attempts to conceptualize effectiveness in terms of the satisfaction of organizational participants. One approach that has been promising, based on the goal model, has been to ask persons in superordinate positions about the effectiveness of organizational units which are subordinate to them. This approach is quite useful for performance assessments of organizational subunits. It also could be used in situations where organizations within a single political jurisdiction, such as state, county, or city organizations, are being examined. In reality, such effectiveness judgments are made at the time of budget allocations, but that process contains more than effectiveness considerations.

The approach of asking superordinates about the effectiveness of subordinates has been used with success by Mahoney and Weitzel (1969) and Duncan (1973). This approach has revealed the fact that even superordinates stress different goals. Mahoney and Weitzel note:

> General business managers tend to use productivity and efficient performance. These high-order criteria refer to measures of output, whereas lower-order criteria tend to refer to characteristics of the organization climate, supervisory style, and organizational capacity for performance. The research and development managers, on the other hand, use cooperative behavior, staff development, and reliable performance as high-order criteria; and efficiency, productivity, and output behavior as lower-order criteria. (p. 362)

Effectiveness thus lies in the eyes and minds of the beholders, with the important qualification that some beholders are more powerful than others. Before turning to an examination of participant-satisfaction approaches to effectiveness, which deal specifically with this issue, one final research finding regarding the goal model will conclude this section. Molnar and Rogers (1976) attempted to determine if measures of effectiveness from the goal model were related to measures of effectiveness from the systems-resource model. They found only weak relationships among the measures from the two approaches, suggesting again that effectiveness must be approached with full awareness of the contradictions inherent in organizations and in effectiveness.

Participant-Satisfaction Models

In this section we will examine models of effectiveness that, in various ways and at various levels, utilize individuals as the major frame of reference. The emphasis in these models is *not* satisfaction in terms of morale or some other psychological state of the individual. This is frequently a component of the goal model, seeing morale as just one of several goals. Rather, in these models the emphasis is on individual or group judgments about the quality of the organization.

Barnard (1938) set the tone for participant satisfaction models with his analysis of organizations as cooperative, incentive-distributing devices. "Individuals contributed their activities to organizations in return for incentives, the contribution of each in the pursuit of his particularistic ends being a contribution to the satisfaction of the ends of others. Barnard regarded the motives of the individuals participating in organizations as the critical determinants. Only if these were satisfied, could the organization continue to operate" (Georgiou, 1973, p. 300). Organizational success was not viewed in terms of goals being achieved, but rather through its capacity to survive through being able to gain enough contributions from the members by providing sufficient rewards or incentives.

Georgiou (1973), building on the work of Barnard, has developed what he labels as a "counter paradigm" to the goal model (see also Samuel, 1979). According to Georgiou:

Thus, the essential thrust of the counter paradigm is that the emergence of organizations, their structure of roles, division of labor, and distribution of power, as well as their maintenance, change, and dissolution can best be understood as outcomes of the complex exchanges between individuals pursuing a diversity of goals. Although the primary focus of interest lies in the behavior within organizations, and the impact of the environment on this, the reciprocal influence of the organization on the environment is also accommodated. Since not all of the incentives derived from the processes of organizational exchange are consumed within the interpersonal relations of the members organizational contributors gain resources with which they can influence the environment. (p. 308)

The implication of Georgiou's argument for effectiveness is that incentives within organizations must be adequate for maintaining the contributions of organizational members and must also contain a surplus for developing power capabilities for dealing with the environment. A basic problem with this argument is that it does not disclose how the incentives are brought into the organization in the first place. If a major incentive is money, this must be secured. To be sure, money is brought into the organization through exchanges with the environment, but it appears that the systems-resource approach or a goal model dealing with profit is necessary prior to considering individual inducements.

Cummings (1977) approaches effectiveness from a slightly different perspective. He states:

One possibly fruitful way to conceive of an organization and the processes that define it is as an instrument or an arena within which participants can engage in behavior they perceive as instrumental to their goals. From this perspective, an effective organization is one in which the *greatest percentage of participants* perceive themselves as free to use the organization and its subsystem as instruments for their own ends. It is also argued that the greater the degree of perceived organizational instrumentality by *each* participant, the more effective the organization. Thus, this definition of an effective organization is entirely psychological in perspective. It attempts to incorporate both the number of persons who see the organization as a key instrument in fulfilling their needs *and*, for each person, the degree to which the organization is so perceived. (pp. 59–60)

According to this approach, factors such as profitability, efficiency, and productivity are necessary conditions for organizational survival and not ends in themselves. The organization must acquire enough resources in order to permit it to be instrumental for its members. In a rather related approach, Steers (1977) argues that more effective organizations are those in which the members agree with the goals of the organization and thus work more consistently to achieve them.

Approaching organizational effectiveness from the perspective of individuals and their instrumental gains or their goals has three major problems. The first problem, which is particularly the case for Steers's approach, is that individuals have varying forms of linkages to the organizations of which they are a part. As Etzioni (1961, 1975) has demonstrated, people's involvement in organizations can be alienative, calculative, or moral. These different forms of involvement preclude the possibility of individual and goal congruence in many types of organizations. Continuing for a moment with a criticism of Steers's approach, it does not appear to be unfair to note that many personnel in most organizations are probably unaware of the organizations' official *or* operative goals, so that agreement becomes a moot point.

The more basic problem in these psychological formulations is that by focusing on instrumentality for individuals, the activities or operations of the organization as a whole, or by subunits, is missed. While the instrumentality approach is capable of being generalized across organizations, it misses the fact that organizational outputs do something in society. They are consumed, enjoyed, and are environmentally harmful. They affect other organizations and people in and out of other organizations as much as people within a focal organization. The psychological approach also downplays the reality of conflicts among goals and decisions that must be made in the face of environmental pressures. The problem is basically one of overlooking a major part of organizational reality. For example, Angle and Perry (1981) found a positive relationship between workers' commitment to the organization and such effectiveness indicators as adaptability, turnover, and tardiness. No such relationship was found with the effectiveness indicators of operating costs and absenteeism. By reducing effectiveness considerations to the individual level, the point is missed that there can be conflicts between desirable outcomes, such as lowered operating costs and lowered turnover.

A third problem with this form of individualistic approach is that it misses the fact that individuals outside the organization are affected by what organizations do. Stipak (1979), for example, found little relationship between objective service delivery indicators and citizen evaluation. Giordano (1976, 1977) found that the "clients" of a juvenile justice system network had clearly different views of the effectiveness of organizations such as the police, courts, and probation departments than the members of these agencies had. This is hardly surprising, of course, since the clients in this case were juveniles who had had trouble with the law. Nonetheless, a client perspective on effectiveness would seem to be a critical component of any comprehensive effectiveness analysis.

Keeley (1978, 1984) has tried to overcome the problems of just focusing on the reactions of internal organizational actors by proposing a "social justice" approach to effectiveness. Building on the work of Rawls (1971), Keeley suggests that a guiding principal for organizational evaluation might be "maximization of the least advantaged participants in a social system" (1978, p. 285). Keeley then proposes that this approach could be operationalized by minimizing the *regret* that participants experience in their interactions with the organization. Keeley's later work (1984) shifts to the idea of organizational harm, but retains the same flavor. He recognizes the difficulties associated with the actual application of this approach, but claims that this approach actually contains an optimization principle that goal models do not contain. It is possible to specify the manner in which group regret or harm can be minimized across organizations. It is not possible to specify how goal attainment can be optimized across organizations, given the diversity of goals.

Keeley concludes:

Finally, the social-justice model—specifically the minimization of regret principle—manages to balance participant interests in an ethical, yet pragmatic, fashion. It may seem perverse to focus on regretful organizational participants rather than on those, possibly more in number, who enjoy the outcomes of cooperative activity. But the point is that generally aversive system consequences ought not, and in the long run, probably will not be tolerated by some participants so that positive consequences can be produced for others. Systems that minimize the aversive consequences of interaction are, therefore, claimed to be more just as well as more stable in the long run. (1978, p. 290)

One can disagree with the practicality of Keeley's approach from the standpoint of the difficulties in determining levels of regret or harm for all system participants, but the point on ethicality is one that should remain fixed in effectiveness modeling.

Constraints, Goals, and Participants

Pennings and Goodman (1977) made a major contribution to the literature on effectiveness. They approach participants by introducing the concept of the *dominant coalition.* In order to show how Pennings and Goodman bring participants into effectiveness determination, it is necessary to trace their theoretical argument. Their approach is very similar to the contradiction model used in the present analysis.

Pennings and Goodman begin their argument by defining effectiveness: "Organizations are effective if relevant constraints can be satisfied and if organizational results approximate or exceed a set of referents for multiple goals" (p. 160).

The idea of constraints involves conditions or requirements that must be satisfied if an organization is to be effective. Constraints involve policies or procedures, set in advance. They guide decision making and behavior in the organizations. Examples of constraints are "maintaining market share at a certain percentage, maintaining quality at a certain level, and not doing business in foreign countries requiring political kickbacks" (p. 160).

Organizational goals refer to desired end states or objectives specified by the dominant coalition. Pennings and Goodman are explicit in their inclusion of multiple goals. Both constraints and goals are used in the assessment of effectiveness, but there are important differences between the two concepts. Goals receive special attention and concern from the dominant coalition. They are closely related to the motivations of the dominant coalition. Interestingly, goals and constraints can be on the same dimension or area of activity, but the difference lies in the attention paid by the dominant coalition. Pennings and Goodman state:

Whether achieving a particular quantity or quality level is a goal or constraint depends partially on which is more central to the organization's dominant coalition. For example, some U.S. universities emphasize the number of students enrolled as a constraint for quality of academic excellence, whereas other universities emphasize high enrollment but are constrained by the need of maintaining a minimum level of academic excellence. (p. 161)

A second difference between goals and constraints is that "goals may or may not approximate a referent, whereas constraints must be satisfied as a necessary condition of organizational effectiveness. Degrees (or the relative amount) of organizational effectiveness can be assessed by the degree to which a goal approximates or exceeds a referent" (p. 161). This is a complicated set of ideas and requires some discussion. Referents are the standards against which constraints and goals are weighed or evaluated. They involve the dominant coalition's standards of evaluation. Constraints must be met if an organization is to be effective, but just meeting the constraint does not mean effectiveness. Achieving a goal on top of the constraint is effectiveness. Pennings and Goodman use the example of a business firm that wants to increase its profits (a goal) and at the same time maintain the quality of service (a constraint). A failure in maintaining quality of service would contribute to ineffectiveness, but exceeding the quality of service standard would not lead to effectiveness. Only by increasing its profitability *and* maintaining the quality of service would the organization be effective. Effectiveness is based on the degree to which the goal is achieved.

Interestingly, Pennings and Goodman do not bring in resources as constraints. It would appear that the systems resource and goal models could be nicely joined in constraint-goal terminology. Certainly resources are required and the resource level required for operations is a constraint on the organization. This may be of the most appropriate usage of the systems-resource model, for example, *viewing resources as important constraints that must be satisfied before movements toward goals can be realized.*

Pennings and Goodman recognize the fact that there are multiple goals and constraints and that the time frame for these is not constant. They also recognize that for each constraint or goal there may be multiple referents. They do not note that different referents for a single goal or constraint may have contradictory elements, as will be demonstrated later. They do note that effectiveness must always be measured after the fact.

An important contribution of the Pennings–Goodman formulation is the recognition that organizations have internal and external constituencies (see also Katz and Kahn, 1978). These are the components of the dominant coalition that decides goals and determines constraints. Effectiveness criteria are defined by the dominant coalition on the basis of consensus agreements that are achieved. Consensus is achieved by negotiation among the parties involved. This is not a simple process, since the various constituencies themselves have differing and multidimensional preferences.

The process of achieving consensus has the effect of focusing attention on the goals, constraints, and referents. It also forces the dominant coalition to consider alternative arrangements among these elements, adjusting levels of constraints so that goals might be achieved, or altering goals in the face of constraints that cannot be adjusted. Pennings and Goodman view organizations as being made up of multiple constituencies that influence the setting of constraints, goals, and referents. The internal dominant coalition determines the forms and emphases that these take. According to Pennings and Goodman, "although constituencies may hold many referents and constraints with which to evaluate the organization, it is only to the extent to which these constraints and referents can be imposed on the organization that they become useful tools for assessing effectiveness" (p. 171).

There is an additional element that should be introduced at this point. Goals, constraints, and referents are determined by the dominant coalition. As the dominant coalition has changes in its composition that accompany power shifts or top leadership succession, goals, constraints, and referents will change. Cameron and Whetten (1981) and Zammuto (1982) have emphasized changes that take place over time in the perceptions of effectiveness and evolving constituent preferences. Goals, constraints, and referents are thus moving targets over time.

The approach to be taken in the contradiction model is quite similar to that of Pennings and Goodman. A major difference is the utilization of resources as constraints. Another important difference is that while the Pennings–Goodman formulation stresses consensus achieved in the dominant coalition, the contradiction model will not assume consensus. To be sure, decisions have to be made, but there may be times when the consensus that is achieved for a particular decision is so tenuous that it is very short lived, and the decision is soon reversed. The contradiction model stresses the fact that the various constituencies of an organization may have irreconcilable differences and that effectiveness for one party may be the opposite for another.

The Pennings–Goodman formulation is much more comprehensive than the other participant satisfaction models considered in this section. The importance they attribute to the consensus achieved through the dominant coalition led to its placement here. The placement here is also based on the importance given to the political process in effectiveness determination. Both systems-resource and goal modeling tend to imply rational decision making, with strategies adopted on the basis of how best to acquire resources or survive to maximize goal attainment. The present approach also assumes that decisions will be made on the basis of some degree of rationality, but tempered with the political facts of organizational life.

Social-Function Models

There is an additional approach to effectiveness to be considered which moves beyond participant satisfaction into the area of broad social functions. Social-function models are based on the issue of what organizations do to or for the society of which they are a part. Most representative of this approach is Parsons's (1960) analyses of organizations. According to Parsons, all social systems must solve four basic problems (pp. 183–86). The first is *adaptation*, or the accommodation of the system to the reality demands of the environment, coupled with the active transformation of the external situation. The second problem is *goal achievement*, or the defining of objectives and the mobilization of resources to obtain them. Third is *integration*, or establishing and organizing a set of relations among the member units of the system that serve to coordinate and unify them into a single entity. The last problem is *latency*, or the maintenance over time of the system's motivational and cultural patterns.

These "pattern variables" are designed to be applicable for all social systems. Organizations are part of the goal-achievement system of society. At the same time, organizations can be viewed as social systems in their own right and must deal with the four basic problems. Thus, in one sense, effectiveness can be conceptualized on the basis of how well these problems are resolved. Mulford et al. (1976–77) operationalized these problems and found that there were strong intercorrelations among them in terms of how well a set of non-economic organizations achieved integration, goal achievement, and so forth.

Parsons's approach has been criticized on several grounds. Blau and Scott (1962) suggest that his "extremely abstract conceptions yield a theoretical scheme devoid of a system of propositions from which specific hypotheses can be derived; in short that he has only developed a theoretical framework and not a substantive theory" (p. 40). Mouzelis (1967) notes that while some groups may be served by an organization, others may not—this is a basic problem of functional analysis. Conceptualizing and measuring societal functions served, while considering the interests of all parties involved, has thus far not been accomplished.

Despite these problems, interest in the societal functions served by organizations remains an issue. Perrow (1977) follows this tradition in an interesting manner. He first notes that most studies of effectiveness are what he calls the "variable analysis" type (p. 96). This type of study involves trying to isolate those variables which are somehow related to measures of effectiveness. This is in the administrative-technical tradition. In place of this form of analysis, Perrow suggests that analysts engage in two other types of effectiveness studies—"gross-malfunctioning analysis" and "revelatory analysis." Both involve the question of effectiveness for whom?

Gross-malfunctioning analysis is proposed as a method to isolate really poorly operating organizations with an eye toward improving their services or products. This is proposed as an alternative to the common practice of looking at high-performance organizations and trying to find the correlates of this high performance. Revelatory analysis deals more precisely with the effectiveness-for-whom question. Perrow views organizations as

> intentional human constructions but not necessarily rational systems guided by official goals; as bargaining arenas, rather than cooperative systems; as systems of power rather than crescive institutions reflecting cultural norms; and as resources for other organizations and groups rather than closed systems. If we define organizations, then, as intentional human constructions wherein people and groups compete for outputs of interest to them under conditions of unequal power, we have posed the issue of effectiveness quite differently than in the other two perspectives. We now have to ask, what does the organization produce? (p.101)

In answer to this question, Perrow notes that human service organizations, such as hospitals, prisons, schools, welfare organizations, and the like have outputs which are more critical than the services provided to clients. Employment opportunities, segregation and control of people who are thought to be deviant or of the wrong age to be part of society, business opportunities for legitimate business, and markets for organized crime are some of the major outputs of such social service organizations. Perrow believes that revelatory analysis would reveal what most managers know but social scientists cannot afford to acknowledge, namely, that complex social systems are greatly influenced by sheer chance, accident, luck; that most decisions are very ambiguous, preference orderings are incoherent and unstable, efforts at communication and understanding are often ineffective, subsystems are very loosely connected, and most attempts at social control are clumsy and unpredictable. (p. 103)

Perrow is suggesting two things here. First, organizations should not be analyzed with preconceived notions about what the function of the organization is. In a sense, he is calling for a recognition of both manifest and latent functions (Merton, 1957), although these terms are not used. He is also calling for an explicit recognition of the parties involved in organizational operations and their stake in the survival of the organization. The fact that different groups have different stakes suggests that an approach to organizations that looks at decisions and actions as a simple ordering around goals or environmental pressures is naive.

The effectiveness-for-whom issue is crucial in any effectiveness formulation. This is the contribution of those who view effectiveness from the societal function perspective. That different parties are affected in different ways by organizational actions should be clear. Actions that are successful in one direction may be unrelated to actions in another direction. Alexander and Buchholz (1978) have shown, for example, that corporate social responsibility is unrelated to the stock market performance of the corporations, even though a good financial performance may yield the reputation of social responsibility (McGuire et al., 1988). Efforts in one arena may have little impact in another.

If organizations are in a position to alter their social functions, they face environmental constraints. Child (1976) has pointed out, for example, that demands for greater participation in decision making on the part of workers are countered by the general trends toward growth, bureaucratization, and centralization.

THE CONTRADICTION MODEL

There is growing evidence that most organizational analysts are now realizing that effectiveness is a truly multifaceted phenomenon. For example, Campbell et al. (1974) found some *30* different criterion measures utilized in research on the topic. Cameron (1978), in research on colleges and universities, found that effectiveness is a "multidomain" phenomenon. He concludes:

Effectiveness in one domain may not necessarily relate to effectiveness in another domain. For example, maximizing the satisfaction and growth of individuals in an organization...may be negatively related to high levels of subunit output and coordination.... Specifically, publishing a large number of research reports may be a goal indicating a high level of effectiveness to faculty members (on an individual level) while indicating low effectiveness at the subunit or organizational level (e. g., poor teaching quality, little time with students, little personal attention for students, graduate student teaching instead of professors) to legislators and parents of undergraduates. (p. 625)

Cameron's point has a great deal of substantive validity. It is also quite close to the contradiction model. He does not deal with power differences among constituents or temporal shifts in environmental pressures as we will do here.

Another approach which is similar to the contradiction model is the "competing values" approach to effectiveness developed by Quinn and Rohrbaugh (1983). This is shown in Figure 13–1. Note that in addition to the horizontal axis of internal versus external focus and the vertical axis of control versus flexibility, there are also competing values on the diagonal axes, for example, human resource development versus productivity and stability versus growth. While it is hypothetically possible for an organization to have high values on each dimension, the more likely result is that an organization that is effective in terms of control will be less effective in terms of flexibility (Rohrbaugh, 1983).

Based on the evidence presented throughout this book and on the effectiveness models considered, the contradiction model can now be presented in a rather simple manner:

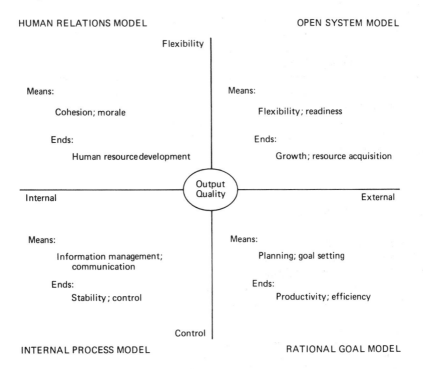

Source: John Rohrbaugh, "The Competing Values Approach: Innovation and Effectiveness in the Job Service," in Richard H. Hall and Robert E. Quinn (eds.) *Organizational Theory and Public Policy* (Beverly Hills, CA: Sage, 1983) p. 267.

FIGURE 13–1   A Summary of the Competing Value Sets and Effectiveness Models

1. Organizations face multiple and conflicting environmental constraints These constraints may be *imposed* on an organization; they may be *bargained* for, they may be *discovered*, or they may be *self-imposed* (Seashore, 1977). Imposed constraints are beyond organizational control. They involve our familiar environmental dimensions, such as legal or economic positions. To be sure, organizations lobby for legal and regulative advantage, but taxes and regulations are essentially imposed on organizations. This imposition is not just from government. A computer manufacturer which develops a new and improved computer with a new language is imposing this environment on users, since they must learn the new language—and install new equipment—if they are to stay "state of the art." Bargained constraints involve contractual agreements and competitive pressures in markets. Discovered constraints are cases in which an environmental constraint appears in an unanticipated manner, as when a coal company finds that its vein of ore runs out or a university finds that its costs for fuel have become so high that it must cut back on some other program. Self-imposed constraints involve the definitions of the environment that organizations utilize. For example, in a study of newspaper coverage of an oil spill, Molotch and Lester (1975) documented the fact that newspapers differed markedly in the amount of space given to the spill. Organizational policy thus defines the importance of environmental elements.

Regardless of the source of the constraints, their conflicting nature must be stressed, since efforts to deal with one constraint may operate against the meeting of another. Indeed, Gresov (1989) found that organizational units facing multiple contingencies are more prone to face design misfit and lower performance than those with more simple situations. As a general rule, the larger and more complex the organization, the greater the range and variety of constraints it will face. Organizations have to consider their environments, recognize and order the constraints that are confronted, and attempt to predict the consequences of their actions—all within the limitations on decision making and rationality we have considered.

2. Organizations have multiple and conflicting goals This point has probably been beaten to death, but one more pass might be useful. A case from my university—The State University of New York at Albany—is instructive here. The case involves a threatened budget cut, which is an annual occurrence that sometimes results in real cuts and sometimes does not. In the case I am describing, the threatened cuts were severe. Each vice president had to make up a list of "target" positions in his or her area. We know that decisions that are made in such situations are the result of power coalitions (Pfeffer and Salancik, 1974; Hills and Mahoney, 1978). At the same time, goals do not just disappear. Issues such as the emphasis on research, needs for the continued recruitment and retention of high-quality students and faculty to achieve the goal of being a high quality university, and reiterations of the importance of having a safe and attractive campus were voiced and were much more than rhetoric. When the cuts were made, they were based on goals *and* power coalitions. Both contained contractions that were played out in actions.

3. Organizations have multiple and conflicting internal and external constituencies The strict meaning of constituency is the people in a legislative district. Here the term refers to those people affected by an organization. They may be employees, members, customers, clients, or the public-at-large. The degree to which constituents are themselves organized varies widely. On the one hand, are organized groups, such as labor unions, nuclear power opponents, and PTAs. There are also spontaneous coalitions that form within organizations. On the other hand, are people affected by an organization that are completely unaware of each others' existence. There are also constituents who are affected by organizations who are unaware that they are being affected—some of Perrow's (1984) victims. In any event, we know that constituents are affected. They may or may not be considered in organizational decision making, and they may or may not themselves be organized. They must be part of any effectiveness consideration.

4. Organizations have multiple and conflicting time frames   We have already considered time frames in regard to goals. Hannan and Freeman (1977a) have some additional insights on time which are useful here:

> To the extent that the goals function stresses quick return on investment (as in many business ventures, disaster relief organizations, military field units, and so on) the short-run outcomes should be given the highest priority. For those organizations that orient toward continued production (for example, many other types of business ventures, universities, research and development organizations, and so on) the year-to-year fluctuations in performance should be discounted and the average performance over longer periods emphasized.
>
> The conceptual problem is that we do not know how organizations discount time. Two organizations with the same goals operating with the same structure in the same environment may place a very different emphasis on speed of return on investment. One organization may capitalize on some situations in a way that increases both the probability of quick favorable outcomes and the risk of long-term decline. The other may eschew the quick return in favor of the long-term security... the analyst must also know the premium placed on speed of return. (pp. 113–114)

There are also *intra*organizational variations in the time frame that is used (Lawrence and Lorsch, 1967). These differences occur between units and across levels on the vertical dimension.

The degree and mix of *environmental constraints* also varies over time. Constraints that were critical at one point in time may disappear as threats. New problems arise. Time also plays a role in terms of the history of an organization, since new organizations are more vulnerable. Similarly, organizations in industries or sectors that are declining face different problems than do those in growth industries or sectors.

The temporal dimension of effectiveness is essentially one of judgment. Decisions must be made in terms of the time frame of reference for analyzing goal attainment, the nature and phasing of environmental constraints, and the historical situation of the organization. Failing to recognize this can lead the analyst and practitioner to real problems. For the analyst, it is only a poor study; for the practitioner it is organizational decline or death.

We have considered contradictions in environmental constraints, goals, constituents, and time. These are the realities constructed in and for all organizations (Benson, 1977). They are the basis for judgment and action (Pfeffer, 1977). They lead to the conclusion that *no organization is effective*. Rather, organizations can be viewed as effective (or ineffective) to some degree in terms of specific constraints, goals, constituents, and time frames.

Some Applications   When considering the issue of applications from a contradiction model, the first conclusion that must be reached is that efforts to be effective must always involve less than total rationality. It is now a matter of faith in organizational theory that organizations do not optimize in their decision making, as the discussion of decision making has demonstrated.

The analysis presented here goes beyond these considerations and has emphasized the fact that there are compromises which must be made among pressing constraints, goals, constituents, and time frames. The ordering of the compromises is based on power relationships and coalitions within the organizations, coupled with external pressures. This is done within a framework of realization that if once an action is selected, others are not possible, particularly with constant or diminishing resources. Before considering these matters further, it is imperative that a relatively neglected topic be addressed—the fact that there are some constraints over which organizations can have no control.

Constraints Beyond Organizational Control   Organizations attempt to control those constraints which they perceive to be central to them. Devices such as industrial vertical integration, utilization of boards of directors, political intervention, and advertising are all efforts to reduce environmental uncertainty or shape the environment to the benefit of the organization. At the same time, some events are uncontrollable.

A simple example of this is the weather. If an organization is dependent upon particular weather patterns, it can do little in regard to the forces of nature. Cloud seeding has yet to become truly feasible, and no device has been developed to control the external temperature. Agricultural organizations are thus subject to droughts, floods, and prolonged hot or cold spells. Winter recreational organizations, such as ski resorts, suffer when there is no snow and when warm temperatures are present. A bad snow year can bring about the demise of some areas due to weather.

Organizations that are weather prone can engage in activities that minimize the influence of the forces of nature, such as building up reserves of food goods or making machine-made snow (even this does not work if the temperature is above freezing), but these organizations face a basically uncontrollable constraint.

More complex examples come in the forms of world political and economic shifts. As petroleum costs rise and supplies lessen, petroleum users are affected. While it can be argued that oil firms and some financial institutions are capable of controlling even these phases of their environments, this point seems exaggerated when the total scope of international political, economic, social, and military arrangements are considered. For the vast majority of private and public organizations, such control is out of the question. The organizations must be viewed simply as the recipient, though not necessarily passive, of externally derived forces.

There are other, less dramatic, forces than the sweep of world events that are important for organizations, but which they cannot control. These include such things as demographic patterns and local or regional economic developments. Colleges and universities, for example, are faced with a demographic situation over which they have no control.

Uncontrollable events and forces happen to organizations. They are part of the constraint package that is faced. What is important for the discussion here is that they cannot be manipulated. They are conditions to which organizations must adjust as they deal with other constraints, goals, constituents, and time frames.

Environmental Constraints That Are Potentially Manipulable

Organizations attempt to manipulate their environment. A major task of top management is enhancing the position of their organization in the environment. Analyses of interlocking corporate boards of directors have suggested that such interlocking can serve four major external functions (Aldrich, 1979, p. 297). The selection of directors can be a means by which financial, legal, or other information or expertise can be brought to the organization. Directors can also be selected with the intent of facilitating the organization's search for capital or other resources. This is the primary reason that bank officials are so heavily represented on the corporate boards across the array of business firms. Community leaders on the boards of hospitals or colleges serve to bring in the resource of legitimacy. Board composition can also serve a political function. The selection of the appropriate director can assist in coping with federal and state agencies, since the presence of politically powerful groups can serve to blunt vigorous governmental actions. Finally, board composition has been viewed as a means by which the interests of powerful external organizations are served, such as banks, insurance companies, or controlling blocks of family interests.

Interlocking directorates do not create certainty for the organizations involved. There is some evidence (Burt, Christman, and Kilburn, 1980; Pennings, 1980b) that certain patterns of interlocks may contribute to higher profitability for the organizations studied, but no claim has been made that the results of these analyses explain all of the variance in profit.

The fact that aspects of the environment are only potentially manipulable can be seen in Hirsch's (1975) analysis of the pharmaceutical and popular music industries. The pharmaceutical industry had great success in protecting itself from competition by securing the passage of state and federal legislation. It also was successful in getting organized medicine, through the American Medical Association, to permit the industry to advertise drugs by brand names, rather than by their generic name. Prescriptions were sold by brand, rather than compound. Hirsch found that the popular music (record) industry had a quite similar structure to begin with, but was unable to obtain protective legislation and exclusive rights to the profits possible whenever a song was played on the radio. The popular music industry lobbied and used other techniques to try to protect itself, but was unable to, and had severe problems as musical tastes changed along with the many other cultural changes in the 1960s. One industry was successful, while the other was not in manipulating its environment.

This is an area of uncertainty for organizations. If someone were to come up with a sure technique for controlling the environment, as the early and later monopolists have, every organization would adopt it. Antimonopoly laws are specifically designed to prevent environmental control. Organizations attempt to control as much as they legally can or as much as they can without being caught.

The discussion thus far has focused on the private sector. Public organizations also seek to control their environment. The public budgetary process is one in which resources are sought for organizational maintenance and growth. Public organizations send messages to their constituents and others. These messages are designed to protect the organization and further its interests. Altheide and Johnson (1980) conclude that this "propaganda" may be quite detrimental to the public in many instances.

In this section the argument has been that organizations engage in a variety of activities designed to manipulate their environment in their favor. Whether through interlocking boards of directors, purchasing suppliers, seeking to have favorable legislation passed, or through propaganda, the attempt is to manipulate the environment on behalf of the organization. These efforts only have the potential for success, since other organizations with other purposes are interacting with the same components of the environment. Organizations can be most sure of the consequences of their actions when the organization itself is considered.

Organizational Characteristics   Organizations have the capability of being structured and restructured in accordance with the outcomes of decision making and political processes within their own boundaries. Much of the thinking that has emerged from the contingency model (Lawrence and Lorsch, 1967) has dealt directly with this issue. The basic notion is that there are multiple organizational forms which are most likely to be successful, depending upon the situations which the organization is confronting (see Becker and Neuhauser, 1975, for an example of this kind of analysis, and Schoonhoven, 1981, for a methodological critique of the contingency approach). One of the major tasks of top management is to determine what the most appropriate organizational form is for various situations. It is not uncommon to find business firms in rapidly changing technological fields to have no formal tables of organization or organizational charts because the organization is in a constant change mode. Miller (1987) argues that there is a reciprocal relationship between strategy and structure.

Organizations are not completely flexible. Union contracts, custom, and laws mediate against total self-determination. Nonetheless, it is possible to structure or restructure organizations to bring about greater adaptability or rigidity or more or less participation in the decision-making process. The organizational form is the most subject to organizational control of all the factors affecting effectiveness that we have considered. Whether or not organizational form is most crucial for organizational effectiveness is unclear. It would appear that ultimate survival might well be a function of factors beyond organizational control (Whetten, 1980). The more controllable a particular situation is, perhaps the less important it is. It is quite clear that controlling the relevant environment, over time and across conditions, and structuring the organization to acquire sufficient resources and to pursue and move to accomplish major goals is a key to any consideration of effectiveness.

The purpose of this chapter has been to develop a perspective on effectiveness that is applicable across all types of organizations. As a parenthetical note, organizational *crime* has also been approached from the perspectives presented here. Building on the seminal works of Sutherland (1940, 1949) and later analyses by Clinard and Yeager (1980) and Ermann and Lundman (1982), a "contingency model of organizational crime" was developed by Finney and Lesieur (1982). This included the familiar concepts of performance emphasis, internal constraints, and legal and social environments.

SUMMARY AND CONCLUSIONS

This chapter has been an attempt to make some sense out of the critical area of organizational effectiveness. Conceptual and methodological contradictions in the analysis of effectiveness have been presented and a contradiction model was developed. The model contains key elements of the resource-acquisition and goals models and is an attempt to combine them in a manner which retains their key insights, but adds the important factor of inherent contradiction. Organizational effectiveness will remain as the major concern for organizational practitioners and analysts. Ignoring the contradictions will not advance knowledge or practice. Ignoring the fact that there are factors beyond organizational control or which are only potentially manipulable will also not contribute to theory or practice. It is only when theorists and practitioners realize the limited range of options open to organizations, as they confront constraints and mandates and attempt to move toward goal achievement and cope with the issues of multiple constituents and conflicting time frames, that both usable and theoretically interesting developments will take place.

In the next and final chapter we will consider organizational theory. It will be a short chapter, because many of the issues have already been considered in this chapter and throughout the analysis.

14

Organizational Theory

The objectives of this chapter are to examine some contemporary theories about organizations. The various theories to be considered permit us to see and understand different facets about organizations. The intent is not to advocate the superiority of any one theory. Indeed, the orientation here coincides with that of Neil Fligstein (1985) who notes that:

> each school of thought has tended to view its theory as a total causal explanation of organizational phenomena. This suggests that one of the central tasks in organizational theory is to reorient the field in such a way as to view competing theories as contributing to an understanding of organizational phenomena. (p. 377)

I do not intend to be a "paradigm warrior" (Aldrich, 1988). Thus, no single school of thought will be advanced as having the best explanations. There are an interesting set of debates surrounding some of the theories to be considered, and I will attempt to steer through these debates among the various warriors involved.

In the sections that follow, we will consider *five* alternative schools of thought about organizations. These schools of thought can be labeled theories, models, or perspectives, depending on the perspective of the analyst. Each and every one of the schools yields insights; none has been empirically verified as *the* explanation of organizational phenomena.

Before beginning the consideration of the alternative schools, I want to make it clear that the history of organizational theory will not be included in this analysis. Pugh (1966) and Clegg and Dunkerly (1980) can be used as useful resources for people interested in tracing the historical roots of contemporary organizational theory. Morgan (1986) and Pugh, Hickson, and Hinings (1985) also provide sound overviews of the history of organizational theory.

The approach taken here is inductive. Hage (1980) provides an excellent counterstrategy of deductive theorizing about organizations. The inductive approach permits us to build on the empirical research which has been summarized in earlier chapters. Indeed, the theories themselves have already been identified and critically evaluated at many earlier points.

The theories to be considered are grouped in a very similar manner as Pfeffer's (1982) overview and critique of organizational theory. Astley and Van de Ven (1983) have presented a somewhat similar set of distinctions among various schools of thought, but I prefer the Pfeffer categories. Pfeffer deals with theories which focus on individual, coalition, or subunit actions which will not be considered here. Our focus is on the *organizational* level of analysis. Pfeffer bases his analysis of organizational theories around the premises that are made in terms of perspectives on action that are taken. One such perspective sees organizational actions as externally constrained and controlled, and we will consider the *population ecology* and *resource dependence* models as Pfeffer does. At almost the opposite extreme are models of organizational action which see such actions as purposive and rational, with an emphasis on goal direction. Included in this category are the *rational contingency* model, which includes the Marxist or class twist to the traditional model and the *transaction cost* model which has developed out of the field of economics. A final perspective on action sees organizations as emergent from the values of organizational actors. This is the *institutional* approach to organizations. While Pfeffer includes other perspectives within his framework, the five approaches to be discussed here appear to have the greatest explanatory power.

THE POPULATION-ECOLOGY MODEL

The population-ecology model is associated with the works of Aldrich and Pfeffer (1976), Hannan and Freeman (1977b), Aldrich (1979), Kasarda and Bidwell (1984), Bidwell and Kasarda (1985), McKelvey (1982), McKelvey and Aldrich (1983), Carroll (1988), and Carroll and Hannan (1989). This approach "posits that environmental factors select those organizational characteristics that best fit the environment" (Aldrich and Pfeffer, 1976, p. 79.)

The population-ecology (sometimes known as the natural-selection model) approach was a major orientation in our consideration of organizational change and transformation. According to Aldrich and Pfeffer, the model differs from Campbell's (1969) analysis of systemic evolution in that no assumption of progression is made. The natural selection model does not assume that changes are necessarily in the direction of more complex or better organizations. The direction of change in organizations is simply toward a better fit with the environment.

According to Aldrich and Pfeffer, the population-ecology model does not deal with single organizational units, but is concerned with *forms* or *populations* of organizations. Organizational forms that have the appropriate fit with the environment are selected over those that do not fit or fit less appropriately.

Following Campbell, Aldrich and Pfeffer suggested that there are three stages in the natural-selection model. The first stage occurs when variations occur in organizational forms. These variations can be planned or unplanned. Once variations have taken place, the second stage, selection, occurs. The analogy here is to organic evolution in which some mutations work and others do not. Organizational forms that fit are selected over those that do not. The final stage is retention. The forms that are selected are "preserved, duplicated, or reproduced" (p. 81). Aldrich (1979) notes that retention takes place, in the contemporary situation, through devices such as business schools that train future organizational managers and executives. The training contains lessons learned from organizational forms that have been successful or selected. Studies in the population ecology mode have also focused on organizational foundings or births and on organizational mortality or death (Hannan and Freeman, 1988).

Organizational forms fill niches in the environment. Niches are "distinct combinations of resources and other constraints that are sufficient to support an organizational form" (Aldrich, 1979, p. 28). The notion of niches raises the fascinating possibility that there are unfilled niches "out there" just waiting for the right organizational form. Aldrich (p. 112) suggests that home video games and pocket electronic calculators were examples of unfilled niches being filled, but these are poor examples, since they are not organizational forms, but are simply consumer products. A better example of a once unfilled, but now filled, niche is the conglomorate corporation, in which a set of unrelated industries are brought together under a single ownership. This was a new organizational form that was selected by the environment as appropriate. Another example of a niche now filled is the fast-food restaurant form of organization.

Research on niches (Carroll, 1985; Freeman and Hannan, 1983) has shown that narrow niches tend to support organizations that are specialized, whereas wider niches are more supportive of more generalist organizations. In Carroll's research, for example, he found that narrow niches in terms of ethnic groups, neighborhoods, and religious and professional groups provided support for specialized newspapers. Freeman and Hannan's research involved restaurants with much the same results.

Aldrich and Pfeffer identify some problems with the population-ecology model. The sources of the original variations are not specified. Managerial processes within organizations are ignored. Inasmuch as only the successful organizational forms will survive in the long run, the processes by which the fit between the organization and the environment is achieved are ignored. The model also has the problem of being analogous to economic theories which assume perfect competition. Perfect competition does not exist in almost *all* instances.

Van de Ven (1979) provides some additional criticisms of this model as it was developed by Aldrich. Van de Ven suggests that the notion of "fit" between the environment and organizations is unclear. According to Van de Ven, Aldrich appears to use fit as either an *unquestioned axiom* or *inductive generalization* in a causal model that asserts that organizational environment determines structure because effective or surviving organizations adopt structures that fit their environmental niches relatively better than those that do not survive. To avoid a tautology, the proposition implicitly reduces to the hypothesis that organizational survival or effectiveness moderates the relationship between environment and structure (p. 323) italics in orginal.

This is interesting, because effectiveness is scarcely mentioned in the population-ecology modeling efforts. Van de Ven goes on to criticize the population-ecology model for drawing too heavily on analogies with biological systems. This biological analogy is ill-founded, since it does not deal with human decisions and motives. Ethical problems are ignored and the whole process is viewed as inevitable. Van de Ven notes that research on small groups has also dealt with the variation-selection-retention process without slipping to the biological analogy level.

Young (1988, 1989) has also severely criticized the population-ecology model, specifically the form presented by Hannan and Freeman, because of the reliance on biological theory. Freeman and Hannan (1989) believe that the population-ecology approach is well suited for viewing organizations as complex systems with limited flexibility, but Young argues that the approach may be only suited for a narrow range of organizational phenomena.

Van de Ven also criticizes the model because of its downplaying of strategic choices made on behalf of organizations. The variations in forms that occur have some source, and, according to Van de Ven, it is the strategic choices made within organizations. The idea of strategic choice will be incorporated in the present analysis at a later point.

There is another aspect of choice which is not considered in the population-ecology model. Grafton (1975) has noted that some federal agencies have been created as last-resort responses to socioeconomic or technological difficulties. These agencies fill a niche, to be sure, but the niche is defined by governmental decision makers.

There is an additional troublesome aspect of the population-ecology model. Organizations are not inert masses, even though they seem so at times. Even organizations that are seemingly inert have an impact by their very inertia, but this is not the point. The point is that organizations do things. They transform inputs into outputs. These outputs have an impact on the society. Individuals, groups, and other organizations respond to organizational outputs. We are harmed and benefited by organizational outputs. In this sense we are the environment of organizations. If we act toward organizations by support or opposition, and if we have power or can influence power holders, the environment responds to organizations. The population-ecology model tends to portray an image of an environment that is not filled with human actors, but is rather an unfeeling, uncaring, condition in which organizations must operate. Perrow (1979, p. 243) has also noted that the model removes power, conflict, disruption, and social class variables from the analysis of social processes. Carroll's (1988) anthology includes several papers which do in fact deal with institutional, cultural, and political forces, which suggests that population ecologists are paying heed to the criticisms.

These criticisms of the population ecology model are not intended to suggest that it has no utility. The utility of the model is primarily in two areas. As some sort of "ultimate test" of effectiveness, survival is a positive indication and organizational death a negative indication. The natural-selection model can thus give an historical perspective that other approaches do not. It does not work well, however, with large contemporary private and public organizations that are almost guaranteed survival for the short and even medium range of time (Aldrich and Pfeffer, 1976, p. 88). The natural-selection model is also useful as a sensitizing concept to the importance of environmental factors. If an organizational form is in a period of growth or decline, because of an expanding or shrinking niche, any model must take that into consideration. Medical technology in developed countries has now permitted many people to live until old age, with the infirmities that this brings. The organizational form of the hospital is inappropriate for the aging and ill individual who is not faced with a life-threatening emergency. The organizational form of the hospice appears to be filling the niche that was created. Evaluations of hospices will have to take the survival and growth potential into account.

Population-ecology theorists are very careful to note that their approach is concerned with organizational populations, rather than individual organizations. Unfortunately, many of the examples provided by theorists in support of the population-ecology approach have tended to be focused on individual organizations. Part of the difficulty has been semantic and part has been due to insufficient specification of the level of analysis being used. Carroll (1984) has provided a useful set of distinctions among levels of analysis. He notes that the organizational level can be used in terms of life-cycle processes among organizations. At the population-ecology level, the growth and decline of entire populations of organizations can be traced. Finally, there is the community ecology level. At this level populations of organizations that exist together within the same region can be examined. According to Astley (1985), the community population perspective permits an examination of similarities within a population of organizations and also permits analyses of between-population differences. Astley believes that a community ecology perspective has much more room for including factors such as opportunism and choice to be included in organizational analyses.

THE RESOURCE-DEPENDENCE MODEL

The population-ecology model downplays the role of organizational actors in determining the fate of organizations. Aldrich and Pfeffer (1976) suggest that there is an alternative model, which they label the resource-dependence model, which brings organizational decisions and actions back into consideration. Pfeffer and Salancik (1978) provide an important elaboration of the resource dependence argument. The discussion that follows relies heavily on Aldrich and Pfeffer's analysis, with some additions and extensions.

The resource-dependence model has strong ties to what has been labeled the political-economy model of organizations (Wamsley and Zald, 1973; Benson, 1975) and the dependence-exchange approach (Hasenfeld, 1972; Jacobs,

1974). The basic premise of the resource-dependence model is that decisions are made within organizations. These decisions are made within the internal political context of the organization. The decisions deal with environmental conditions faced by the organization (Schreyögg, 1980). Another important aspect of the model is that organizations attempt to deal *actively* with the environment. Organizations will attempt to manipulate the environment to their own advantage. Rather than being passive recipients of environmental forces, as the population-ecology model implies, organizations will make strategic decisions about adapting to the environment. Pfeffer and Salancik (1978) emphasize the role of management in this process. The earlier analysis of IORs is based heavily on resource-dependence theory.

The resource-dependence model begins with the assumption that no organization is able to generate all the various resources that it needs. Similarly, not every possible activity can be performed within an organization to make it self-sustaining. Both conditions mean that organizations must be dependent on the environment for resources. Even seemingly self-sustaining organizations, such as isolated monasteries, must recruit new members or they will go out of existence. The resources that are needed can be in the form of raw materials, finances, personnel, or services or production operations that the organization cannot or does not perform for itself. Resources would also include technological innovations (Marple, 1982). The sources of resources in the environment are other organizations, with the exception being farming and extractive industries which have the potential of owning the raw-material physical base. Even these organizations are dependent on other organizations for other resources. The fact that resources are obtained from other organizations means that the resource-dependence model can be thought of as an interorganizational resource-dependence model, since the resources come from other organizations.

Since the resource-dependence model portrays the organization as an active participant in its relationship with the environment, it also contains the idea that the administrators of organizations "manage their environments as well as their organizations, and the former activity may be as important, or even more important, than the latter" (Aldrich and Pfeffer, 1976, p. 83). This is what Parsons (1960) called the institutional level of operations, in which the organization is linked to the social structure by its top executives.

A key element of the resource-dependence model is *strategic choice* (Chandler, 1962; Child, 1972). This concept implies that a decision is made among a set of alternatives in regard to the strategy that the organization will utilize in its dealings with the environment. The assumption is that the environment does not force the organization into a situation in which no choice is possible. The organization is faced with a set of possible alternatives in dealing with the environment. Aldrich and Pfeffer note that the criteria by which choices are made and by which structures are determined are both important and problematic. There is not just one optimal structure or course of action. The resource-dependence model stresses the importance of internal power arrangements in the determination of the choices made. Both internal power arrangements and the demands of external groups are central to the decision-making process. The resource-dependence model does *not* include the idea of goals as part of the decision-making process.

As has been noted, the resource-dependence model suggests that organizations are, or attempt to be, active in affecting their environment. This contributes to the variation among organizations, since variations are the result of conscious, planned responses to environmental contingencies. Organizations attempt to absorb interdependence and uncertainty, either completely, as through merger (Pfeffer, 1972b), or partially, as through cooperation (Pfeffer, 1972a; Allen, 1974) or the movement or personnel among organizations (Pfeffer and Leblebici, 1973; Aldrich and Pfeffer, 1976, p. 87). The conglomorate corporation is a striking example of variation in organizational form brought about by strategic choice. It is also striking that the conglomorate form has recently been disappearing or selected out.

The resource-dependence model does deal with the selection process, which was central to the population-ecology model. Instead of viewing selection solely from the standpoint of the environment selecting appropriate organizational forms, the resource-dependence model considers the ways in which organizations interact with their environments to ensure that they survive and thrive. The environment is still the key factor, however. Aldrich and Pfeffer (p. 89) argue that the environment provides many of the constraints, uncertainties, and contingencies faced by organizations. As Hickson et al. (1971) have shown, organizational units that have the capability of dealing with constraints, uncertainties, and contingencies are those that obtain the most power within the organization. The power distribution within the organization is critical in determining the nature of the choices made, thus linking the environment to the choices made through the power process operating within the organization. The emphasis on power within the organization is a necessary one, since decisions are made in a political context. The resource-dependence model emphasizes interunit power differentials and tends to ignore hierarchical power differences. Hierarchical power differences must be considered in any analysis of strategic choice, since such differences can override interunit power struggles. It is quite possible that interunit power developments, as between marketing and production departments, have a crucial role in determining who rises in the hierarchy, but once the hierarchy is set, the power of the positions at the top of the organization would appear to be most central to the strategic decisions that are made. Regardless of the source of the power, of course, the strategic choices remain tied to environmental pressures. Again, it should be noted, the idea of goals is not included in this model in terms of decision making.

Aldrich and Pfeffer (1976), building on the work of Child (1972), note that there are three ways in which strategic choices operate in terms of the environment. The first is that decision makers in organizations do have autonomy. This autonomy is much greater than would be suggested by a strict adherence to environmental determinism. The autonomy of the decision makers is reflected in the fact that more than one kind of decision can be made about the environmental niche being occupied—more than one kind of structure is suitable for given environments. In addition, organizations can enter or leave niches. This is illustrated by the fact that business firms can decide to try new markets or abandon old ones. Similarly, many colleges and universities are attempting to expand their niches, obviously in the face of decreasing demand by traditional students, by offering more and more courses and programs designed for nontraditional, older students.

The second way in which strategic choices are made about the environment involves attempts to manipulate the environment itself. Business firms attempt to create a demand for their products; they may also enter into arrangements with other firms to regulate competition, legally or illegally. Operating through the political process, business firms may also secure the passage of tariffs or quotas to restrict competition from foreign firms. Organizations in the public sector do essentially the same thing when they expand or fight for the retention of their jurisdiction. Dunford (1987) suggests that organizations seek to reduce their dependency on other organizations. It is also to an organization's advantage to have other organizations dependent on it. Dunford notes that some organizations even suppress technological development, through manipulating patents, as a means of controlling resource dependence.

The third way in which the strategic choices are made about the environment is based on the fact that particular environmental conditions are perceived and evaluated differently by different people. This point is a crucial one that requires some elaboration. Organizational actors define reality in terms of their own background and values. Kanter (1977) has documented the manner in which recruitment policies for executives in a large business firm resulted in the firm's having executives of very homogeneous backgrounds. Kanter suggests that this permits the executives to have a great deal of trust in each other, since they will experience things in the same ways and, by implication, make the same kinds of decisions. The problem with such homogeneity, of course, is that the single point of view may be unable to detect errors.

The environment is perceived, interpreted, and evaluated by human actors within the organization. The perception becomes the reality, and environmental conditions are only important as they are perceived by organizational decision makers. Different actors can perceive the same phenomenon quite differently. The point here is that the environment is acted upon by organizational decision makers on the basis of their perceptions, interpretations, and evaluations. While there may be commonality because of homogeneity of background within an organization, and even this will not be perfect, there will not be commonality between organizations. Thus, different organizations will act differently toward the same environmental conditions, if the perceptions are different. In this regard, Starbuck (1976) has pointed out that the critical question is the extent to which organizational perceptions vary from objective indicators of environmental conditions.

Aldrich and Pfeffer correctly note that there are limitations on the range of choices which are available to organizational decision makers. There may be legal barriers which prevent an organization from moving into a particular area. Economic barriers also exist. Some projects may be too expensive. Markets can be so dominated by a few firms that it is impossible for a new, small firm to enter.

In addition to barriers that preclude certain decisions, decisions to attempt to alter the environment may not be possible for many organizations. Small organizations, for example, have much less power than do large organizations in terms of their capabilities of modifying their environments. A small state college has much less impact on the educational environment than does Harvard University.

The final aspect of the resource-dependence model is the manner in which the retention of organizational forms takes place. Aldrich and Pfeffer are less clear about the mechanisms that operate in regard to the resource-dependence model. However, they do suggest several mechanisms which organizations utilize that result in the retention of previously successful adaptations. In many ways, these retention mechanisms represent tactical decisions about how the organization is to operate once strategic decisions have been made.

One such retention device is *bureaucratization*. Organizations develop documentation and filing systems. Examples from the organizational past serve as precedents for the organizational present. The development of organizational policy serves the same function. Records and policies can provide the framework and content for decisions to be made. This provides continuity for the organization and ensures the past forms are retained. In addition, role specialization and standardization, with related job descriptions, also ensure the policies are followed. Another important characteristic of bureaucracy, advancement based on performance, also aids in continuity. If people are advanced up through the system, their experiences will be quite common and they will react in ways similar to the ways in which people have reacted in the past. Finally, the bureaucratic mechanism of a hierarchical structure also helps the retention process. The power of those at the top of the organization is viewed as legitimate. Authority is exercised and each decision is not questioned. As Perrow (1979) has noted, bureaucratization is probably the most efficient form of administration, and all organizations will move toward this form if they seek efficiency.

In addition to the organizational form of bureaucracy, persons entering an organization are continually *socialized* in formal and informal ways (Dornbusch, 1955). A major outcome of this socialization process is that "the culture of the organization is transmitted to new members" (p. 97). Part of the culture of the organization involves folk wisdom and operating "rules of thumb" that persist over time.

Finally, the *leadership* structure of organizations tends to be consistent over time. As has been noted, people are screened and filtered as they move to the top of organizations. The screening and filtering is done by people already at the top of the organization, and they are very likely to select people who are like themselves.

> Furthermore, since the promotion of leaders is based on their experience and expertise in dealing with critical organizational contingencies, to the extent that the definition of organizational uncertainties remains the same, similarity in leadership characteristics is further assured. Organizations that are marketing-oriented, such as consumer goods companies, may tend to promote people with sales or marketing experience, who because of similar backgrounds and socialization, will have fairly similar ideas about organizational policy. (Aldrich and Pfeffer, 1976, p. 98)

There are thus several mechanisms that ensure that organizational forms that have been successful will be retained. The thrust of the resource-dependence model is on the manner in which organizations deal with environmental contingencies.

Resource acquisition is a major activity of organizations and the resource-dependence model captures this, but it sidesteps the issue of goals. As will be seen shortly, I believe that this model must be augmented by a model that views organizational actions as also being goal based.

THE RATIONAL-CONTINGENCY MODEL

The resource-dependence model ignores goals, as does the population-ecology model. Both approaches appear to be counter to the reality of actual decision making. In the sections that follow, we will again consider the issue of goals, and then turn to the theory(ies) linked to a goal-based perspective.

The goal-based approach does not make assumptions about the rationality involved in decision making, nor does it take a simplistic view that organizations are only instruments designed to carry out goals. Rather, the approach adds goals back into the reasons that organizations act as they do. Goals are part of the culture of organizations and part of the mind sets of decision makers. Organizations, like the individuals who comprise them, are purposive creatures. The purposiveness can be overcome by external pressures, to be sure, and the organization may die or have to alter its operations drastically. The models which emphasize the environment are correct in pointing out the importance of the environment for the birth and death of organizations. They err, however, in departing totally from goal considerations.

It is now widely accepted (Lehman, 1988) that organizations have multiple and conflicting goals. This means that priorities among goals are problematic for organizations. Priorities are established by dominant coalitions within organizations. Pennings and Goodman (1977) conclude that the dominant coalition comprises a direct or indirect

> representation or cross-section of horizontal constituencies (that is, subunits) and vertical constituencies (such as employees, management, owners, or stockholders) with different and possibly competing expectations. Consensus about the importance of the various criteria of effectiveness is hypothesized to be a function of the relative weights that the various constituencies carry in the negotiated order which we call organization. Consensus among members of the dominant coalition can be employed as a vehicle for obtaining effectiveness data. For example, how important is market share versus employee satisfaction? What should be the trade-off between research and development, between teaching and research, between patient care, medical research, and physicians' education? And so on. The consensus of the coalition allows the identification of such effectiveness criteria. These criteria may have different degrees of importance for the different constituencies in the dominant coalition; but somehow the preferences and expectations are aggregated, combined, modified, adjusted, and shared by the members of the dominant coalition. By invoking the concept of dominant coalition it is possible to preserve the notion of organizations as rational decision making entities. (p. 152)

Pennings and Goodman's term "effectiveness criteria" has the same meaning, for the purposes here, as goals. Their emphasis on rationality is correct, but perhaps overstated. If we return for the moment to the environmental-based models, it can be seen that things happen around an organization which cannot be foreseen. And there may be competing external pressures *or* internal issues which cannot be rationally resolved because of their clearly contradictory nature. Nonetheless, the Pennings and Goodman approach is useful as a way of bringing goals back into the consideration of politics and decisions made by organizations.

The importance of goals should be approached from another standpoint. Simon (1964) argues that the idea of organizational goals is a reification, or a case of "treating it as a superindividual entity having an existence and behavior independent of the behavior of its members" (p. 2). The analysis here accepts such reification as necessary and correct. Interestingly, Simon then goes on to note:

> In the decision-making situations of real life, a course of action, to be acceptable, must satisfy a whole set of requirements, or constraints. Sometimes one of these requirements is singled out and referred to as the goal of the action. But the choice of one of the constraints, from many, to a large extent is arbitrary. For many purposes it is more meaningful to refer to the whole set of requirements as the (complex) goal of the action. This conclusion applies both to individual and organizational decision making. (p. 7)

Thus, to Simon and for our purposes here, goals are constraints for organizational decision making. So too are the environmental constraints discussed in the earlier sections. As a way of combining important elements from the perspectives of multiple and conflicting goals and environmental constraints, many analysts advocate the *rational-contingency* model.

The contingency idea has been developed from *contingency theory*. This theory emerged from Lawrence and Lorsch's (1967) seminal work. Later writers such as Galbraith (1973, 1977), Becker and Neuhauser (1975), and Negandhi and Reimann (1973a, b), developed the basic ideas further. Donaldson (1985) claims that contingency theory is a part of "normal science" (p. ix). His strong advocacy of contingency theory (see also Hinings, 1988) is based on his conclusion that empirical evidence strongly supports its utility—a point with which I agree.

According to Scott (1981, p. 114) contingency theory can be summarized in the following manner: *"The best way to organize depends on the nature of the environment to which the organization must relate"* (italics added). Thus, in Lawrence and Lorsch's study successful plastics firms were those that were differentiated to deal with an uncertain and changing environment, while beer bottle firms, with a less differentiated environment were less differentiated internally. For our purposes, goals would be equally as important as the environment.

Contingency theory has been heavily criticized as being tautological. It has also been criticized as not being a theory, since no explanation is made regarding why or how a best way to organize develops (Schoonhoven, 1981; Tosi and Slocum, 1984). Katz and Kahn (1978, p. 249) suggest that the idea of a best way to organize for a particular environment ignores political considerations, such as demands for collective bargaining, for a minimum wage, or for a union contract. Katz and Kahn note that high efficiency could be the result of paying low wages, inducing workers to work long hours, or to work harder. Pfeffer and Salancik (1978) have noted the importance of consumers and regulators for organizational operations. Despite these problems, contingency theory has become an important part of the literature on organizations (Schoonhoven, 1981; Donaldson, 1985).

When the idea of contingency is added to the notion of rationality, we have the rational-contingency model. Organizations are viewed as attempting to attain goals *and* deal with their environments, with the realization that there is not one best way to do so. Findings as diverse as Burt's (1983) on corporate philanthropy and Langston's (1984) analysis of the British pottery industry are supportive of this approach. In the case of corporate philanthropy, it was found that the proportion of business firms' net incomes contributed to charity covaried with the extent to which the firms were in sectors dependent upon consumption by individuals rather than other organizations. The organizations perceived charitable contributions as contributing to their profitability through their attempts to enhance their public relations image. In the British pottery example, bureaucratic elements were retained by the pottery firms because the bureaucratic elements increased profitablity. Langston implies that this can be interpreted in either a rational-contingency manner or as a Marxist, worker-control strategy.

The Marxian Twist

Marxist scholars have taken a very different perspective on rationality and rational-contingency approaches to organizations. According to Pfeffer (1982):

> Marxist analysis blends environmental determinism with rational, strategic choice. After all, Marx argued that the evolution of economic systems was inevitable and, in his analysis of social forces, saw the presence of certain inexorable historical trends.... Marxist analyses relevant to understanding organizations have proceeded from the premise of conscious, rational, strategic action taken on the part of the capitalist class and organizations controlled by that class. In this sense, it is an analysis quite consistent with other approaches presuming conscious, foresightful behavior. As Goldman (1980: 12) has noted, "The Marxist position sees a high degree of managerial consciousness and intentionality, even omnipotence, not only in technical decisions but also in ostensibly benign programs such as welfare work early in the Twentieth Century or the democratization experiments of the 1970's." (p. 163)

Pfeffer suggests that Marxian perspectives are useful in considering two important organizational issues. The first is that of worker control and the employment relationship. The second issue regards interorganizational relationships in the form of interlocking boards of directors, which are seen as an expression of "classwide rationality" as much as organizationally based rationality. Classwide rationality (Useem 1979, 1982; Moore, 1979) exists wherein elites seek to enhance and protect their position through their active participation in the governance of organizations.

There is mixed evidence in regard to the extent to which the worker control and deskilling of labor arguments can be supported. There is strong evidence in regard to the presence and role of interlocking boards of directors.

The Marxist approach suffers from the same problems that afflict the rational-contingency perspective more generally in that while outcomes are intendedly rational, there is no guarantee that they will be so. Just as goals may not be achieved and the environment not be effectively confronted, so too may worker control efforts and classwide rational actions be thwarted. Managers and directors cannot be assumed to be more rational and controlling in a Marxian analysis than they are in any other decision-making and implementation context. Nonetheless, as Pfeffer (1982) notes, the Marxian perspective is more successful than other approaches in linking organizational properties to the broad sweep of history.

It must be reiterated that the rational contingency model does *not* assume that rationality can necessarily be achieved, simply that it is attempted. Whether from a Marxist or non-Marxist perspective, the rational-contingency model views organizational actions as the result of choices made among a set of goals in an environmental context of constraints and opportunities (Drazin and Van de Ven, 1985).

THE TRANSACTION-COST MODEL

The transaction-cost model has developed out of the field of economics and has captured a great deal of attention among sociologists. This model is based primarily on the work of Oliver Williamson (1975, 1981, 1985; Williamson and Ouichi, 1981). The purpose of this model is to explain the existence and operation of organizations, particularly in the private sector.

The starting point for the model is the transaction or exchange of goods and services. It assumes that individuals will act in their own self-interests (the economist's rational "man"). Simple transactions happen in "on-the-spot" situations and are conducted in the free marketplace. Over history, simple markets became replaced by more complex and uncertain situations. The environment in which transactions take place became increasingly uncertain, and simple trust in relationships became more problematic. One consequence was the emergence of hierarchies or organizations.

It is important to note that Williamson takes a turn away from the route favored by most economists. By focusing on the costs of transactions, rather than production, Williamson introduces a new factor into the economics and sociology of organizations. As Scott (1987a, p. 148) notes:

> The typical neoclassical economic model conceived of firms as systems for managing production functions, with the primary decisions focused on the optimal mix of production factors—resources, labor, capital. In this model, variations in organizational structure are largely irrelevant. By contrast, the transaction costs perspective assumes that not the production but the exchange of goods and services

is critical, and it emphasizes the importance of the structures that govern these exchanges.

Organizations are seen as the response to uncertain environments. Included in these environments are potential exchange partners whose trustworthiness is unknown and who might behave in opportunistic ways. By bringing transactions under the hierarchy of the organization, behavior can be monitored through mechanisms such as direct supervision, auditing, and other control mechanisms. Behaviors come under the context of the employment contract. Transaction costs are thus reduced or at least controlled by the presence of the hierarchy. The logical extension here, of course, is that organizations would seek continued growth of control through the process of the formation of trusts and monopolies. This has indeed happened, and the role of government is thus introduced in the form of antitrust regulations.

Williamson does not claim that the transaction cost approach is the complete answer to all organizational phenomena. Indeed, in 1985 he notes (p. 18): "Given the complexity of the phenomena under review, transaction cost economics should often be used in addition to, rather than to the exclusion of, alternative approaches. Not every approach is equally instructive, however, and they are sometimes rival rather than complementary." Despite this caveat, Williamson continues to argue for the strong explanatory power of the transaction-costs approach.

As might be expected, the transaction-cost approach has raised the consciousness level of sociologists of organizations. Some have sought to attack the approach, while others have sought to incorporate it in their analyses of organizations. Typical of the latter category are Eccles and White (1988) who studied multiprofit-center firms. They note that there are transaction costs *within* firms, which may actually exceed the costs of external transactions. This is exemplified, in an entirely different setting, by the notion of indirect costs or overhead charged on grants and contracts made by government agencies to colleges and universities. The overhead charges can exceed the direct costs of the programs involved in some instances. Eccles and White do not believe that this negates Williamson but that their findings point to the fact that the traditional concerns of economists and sociologists cannot be isolated from each other, a point with which I agree completely.

In a study which does partially negate Williamson, Lazerson (1988) found that Italian small companies expanded through vertical and horizontal integration. The Italian firms created new small firms which they controlled. This replaces market relations in order to insulate themselves from competition. At the same time, they increase their dependence on markets by their intensified subcontracting. They create internal markets within the firms, but the important point is that hierarchies do not develop.

A different, but still critical, twist has been presented by Boisot and Child (1988) in their analysis of the reforms attempted by the People's Republic of China. In the early to mid-1980s, China attempted to introduce free enterprise in the form of markets—this is seen as a form of bureaucracy failure. This was not a complete success, because, according to Boisot and Child, the traditional patrimonial fief system continued to intrude into true market operations.

The most systematic attack on the transaction-cost approach is being developed by Granovetter (1985; see also Knapp, 1989). He criticizes the markets and hierarchies framework on the basis of his belief that economic transactions are actually embedded in social relationships. Granovetter develops the position that in modern societies, economic transactions are linked to trust that is, in turn, linked to social relationships, rather than economic relationships. Granovetter is continuing to develop his argument at the present time. The final outcome of his debate with Williamson will have to await future analyses.

The transaction-cost model, whether or not the costs are economic or social, is undoubtedly best used in combination with other explanations of organizational phenomena, as Williamson had noted earlier. This point is emphasized by Robins (1987) in his analysis of the transaction-cost approach. Robins concludes that the transaction-cost theory must be set within the framework of more general organizational theory and that transaction-cost theory has misread history. Robins concludes that transaction-cost theory can be used in combination with population-ecology, resource-dependency, and contingency theory.

There is a final study of relevance here (Waters, 1989). Instead of using markets as an alternative to bureaucratic organizations, Waters suggests that "collegiality" is an alternative to bureaucracy. Collegiality, as seen in the relationships among professionals, is another form of rationality of modern life.

My conclusion here is that the transaction-costs approach is a necessary addition to the theories discussed in the foregoing paragraphs. Regardless of whether transactions take place for social or economic reasons, and regardless of whether collegiality ranks with markets and hierarchies as a place where transactions can take place, the transaction-cost approach is important in that it informs us about the origins of organizations. Transaction-cost considerations then operate in conjunction with the theoretical perspectives which have been discussed.

THE INSTITUTIONAL MODEL

The final theoretical model to be considered is the institutional model. We first introduced this model in the discussion of organizational structure. This is a rapidly emerging approach to the understanding of organizational phenomena. It can best be appreciated in terms of the ways in which the model seeks to explain why organizations take the forms that they do. Much of the research here has been carried out in not-for-profit organizations with rather indeterminant technologies. DiMaggio and Powell (1983) argue that "institutional isomorphism" is now the dominant reason why such organizations assume the forms that they have. According to DiMaggio and Powell, Weber's original (1952, 1968) analysis of the driving force behind the move toward rationalization and bureaucratization was based on a capitalist market economy, with bureaucratization an "iron cage" in which humanity was bound since the process of bureaucratization was irreversible.

DiMaggio and Powell believe that major social changes have altered this situation to such a large extent that an alternative explanation is needed. Their analysis is based on the assumption that organizations exist in "fields" of other, similar organizations. They define an organizational field as follows:

> By organizational field, we mean those organizations that, in the aggregate, constitute a recognized area of institutional life: key suppliers, resource and product consumers, regulatory agencies and other organizations that produce similar services and products. The virtue of this unit of analysis is that it directs our attention not simply to competing firms, as does the population approach of Hannan and Freeman (1977b), or to networks of organizations that actually interact, as does the interorganizational network approach of Laumann et al. (1978), but to the totality of relevant actors. (p. 148)

According to this perspective, organizations are increasingly homogeneous within fields. Thus, public universities acquire a sameness, as do department stores, airlines, professional football teams, motor vehicle bureaus, and so on. DiMaggio and Powell cite three reasons for this isomorphism among organizations in a field. First, there are coercive forces from the environment, such as government regulations and cultural expectations which can impose standardization on organizations. Government regulations, for example, force restaurants (it is hoped) to maintain minimum health standards. As Meyer and Rowan (1977) have suggested, organizations take forms that are institutionalized and legitimated by the state.

DiMaggio and Powell also note that organizations mimic or model each other. This occurs as organizations face uncertainty and look for answers to their uncertainty in the ways in which other organizations in their field have faced similar uncertainties. Rowan (1982) argues, for example, that public schools add and subtract administrative positions in order to come into isomorphism with prevailing norms, values, and technical lore in their institutional environment. DiMaggio and Powell argue that large organizations tend to use a rather small number of consulting firms which "like Johnny Appleseeds, spread a few organizational models throughout the land" (p. 152). A very concrete example, noted by DiMaggio and Powell is the fact that Japan consciously modeled its courts, postal system, military, banking, and art education programs after Western models in the late nineteenth century. As DiMaggio and Powell note (p. 151):

> American corporations are now returning the compliment by implementing (their perceptions of) Japanese models to cope with thorny productivity and personnel problems in their own firms. The rapid proliferation of quality circles and quality-of-work-life issues in American firms is, at least in part, an attempt to model Japanese and European successes.

Prokesh (1985) in a *New York Times* article reports that business firms are establishing formal intelligence departments to keep tabs on competitors from home and abroad. One source is quoted as saying that "understanding your competitors' positions and how they might evolve is the essence of the strategic game." In DiMaggio and Powell's conceptualization, the field is more than simply competitors. The establishment of intelligence departments reflects the strong mimetic tendencies within organizations.

A third source of institutional isomorphism comes from normative pressures as the work force, and especially management, becomes more professionalized. Both professional training and the growth and elaboration of professional networks within organizational fields leads to a situation in which the managerial personnel in organizations in the same field are barely indistinguishable from one another. As people participate in trade and professional associations, their ideas tend to homogenize.

The institutional perspective thus views organizational design not as a rational process, but rather one of both external and internal pressures that lead organizations in a field to resemble each other over time. In this perspective strategic choices or attempts at member control would be viewed as coming from the institutional order in which an organization is embedded.

Institutional theory also places a strong emphasis on symbols. We were given a strong symbol of the place of institutional theory when *Administrative Science Quarterly* placed Scott's (1987b) theoretical review of institutional theory as its lead article. These placements are hardly accidental.

The work of DiMaggio and Powell (DiMaggio and Powell, 1983; Powell, 1985; DiMaggio, 1988) emphasizes the ways in which institutionalized practices are brought into organizations as noted. Organizations in the same field develop isomorphism as they exchange professional personnel and face common exigencies such as governmental policies.

An alternative institutional approach is associated with the works of Meyer, Scott, and Zucker (Meyer and Scott, 1983; Scott, 1987; Zucker, 1988). This approach contains a healthy dose of concern for environmental issues, but basically turns our attention more inward. The focus is on ways in which practices and patterns are given values and how interaction patterns and structures are legitimated. It is a grand extension of Berger and Luckmann's (1967) view that reality is socially constructed. Zucker's (1988) anthology provides an intellectually exciting view of organizations.

In this set of papers individual actors are viewed as having feelings and meanings. They are not narrow technocratic decision makers. Organizations are not shaped by the impersonal forces of technology or the demands of a relentless environment. Despite the attractiveness of this sort of formulation, I see four problems looming which could have serious consequences for institutional theory.

The first problem is potential tautological reasoning. This form of reasoning was a major contributor to the demise of functional theory within sociology. "A tautology is circular reasoning in which variables are defined in terms of each other, thus making causes and effects obscure and difficult to assess" (Turner and Maryanski, 1979, p. 124; see also Turner, 1979). This problem appears to creep into DiMaggio's analysis when he notes (1988):

> Put simply, the argument of this section is that institutionalization is a product of the political efforts of actors to accomplish their ends and that the success of an institutionalization project and the form that the resulting institution takes depend

on the relative power of actors who support, oppose, or otherwise strive to influence it. I refer to the politics of institutionalization as *structural* because they follow an internal logic of contradiction, such that the success of an institutionalization process creates new sets of legitimated actors who, in the course of pursuing distinct interests, tend to delegitimate and deinstitutionalize aspects of the organizational form to which they owe their own autonomy and legitimacy. Central to this line of argument is an apparent paradox rooted in the two senses in which the term *institutionalization* is used. Institutionalization as an *outcome* places organizational structures and practices beyond the reach of interest and politics. By contrast, institutionalization as a *process* is profoundly political and reflects the relative power of organized interests and the actors who mobilize around them (italics in original). (p. 13)

If this is not tautological reasoning, it is uncomfortably close to it. This quotation also contains the seeds of a problem which will be noted later—the tendency to bring all organizational phenomena under the institutional label. This problem also plagued the functionalists.

The second problem is that institutional theory has paid almost no attention to what is institutionalized and what is not. This can be seen in the weirdly ironic case of Talcott Parsons. Parsons wrote fairly extensively about organizations and even specified the *institutional* level of analysis (Parsons, 1960). This is not even mentioned in Scott's (1987b), DiMaggio's (1988), or Zucker's (1988) works. This is not a call to go back to Parsons, but rather empirical evidence that not everything that says institutional is institutionalized.

This is a critical problem. There is a tendency to apply institutional theory in an ex post facto manner. This can be done in an almost mystical manner. Ideas and practices come and go for no reason other than institutionalization. It would appear that in reality, some performance criteria are applied in assessing the success of a practice. The adoption of structures or practices is much more than institutionalized whim.

The third problem is essentially ontological. The prime interest rate and changes in it are very real to borrowing organizations, the number of 18-year-olds is very real to college administrators, and the number of 21-year-olds is very real for brewers. Institutional theory can be very useful at this point. Individual and collective organizational myths develop about the meanings of these realities. This point has been very well demonstrated. The danger, however, is in making the reality that was the source of the myth into the myth itself.

The final problem is overextension. There is a tendency, as noted earlier, to apply institutional theory to a vast array of situations and organizations. DiMaggio and Powell (1983) were careful to hypothesize that institutional effects were more likely in situations of indeterminant technology and ambiguous goals. Zucker (1988, p. xix) clearly recognizes the importance and applicability of the resource-dependence theory. DiMaggio's most recent (1988) paper pays direct attention to the political process.

Despite these problems, it would appear that institutional theory is the darling of the 1990s. In the long run, however, its attractiveness may be its own undoing.

SUMMARY AND CONCLUSION

I have summarized the major contemporary theoretical approaches to understanding organizations. None of the explanations is capable of standing on its own, despite what some of the advocates might argue. Each has its special insights and applicabilities.

As organizational research moves into the 1990s, there is widespread acceptance of the need to apply these theories *in combination*, rather than as competing explanations. Fligstein's (1985) research is an exemplar here, as is that by Pfeffer and Davis-Blake (1987), Hamilton and Biggart (1988), and Singh et al. (1986). These researchers do not test theories against each other. Rather, they seek to explain the largest amount of variance that they can.

It is almost common sense to realize that organizations must acquire resources as they simultaneously seek to achieve their goals and keep up with their competitors. There appears to be a strong sentiment among organizational theorists that the time has come to cease being "paradigm warriors" (Aldrich, 1988) and instead seek fuller explanations through combining perspectives. As this is done, theoretical growth will be evident. We may even be able to move toward the elusive goal of specifying which theoretical explanations work in which settings and thus have truly meaningful explanations of organizations. This book has been an effort in that direction.

REFERENCES

Abbott, Andrew (1989). "The New Occupational Structure: What Are the Questions?" *Work and Occupations*, 16, No. 3 (August), 273–91.

Aiken, Michael, and Jerald Hage (1966). "Organizational Alienation: A Comparative Analysis." *American Sociological Review*, 31, No. 4 (August), 497–507.

———, and ——— (1968). "Organizational Interdependence and Interorganizational Structure." *American Sociological Review*, 33, No. 6 (December), 912–30.

Aiken, Michael, Robert Dewar, Nancy Ditomaso, Jerald Hage, and Gerald Zeitz (1975). *Coordinating Human Services*. San Francisco: Jossey-Bass.

Alba, Richard D. (1982). "Taking Stock of Network Analysis: A Decade's Results." In *Research in the Sociology of Organizations: A Research Annual,* ed. Samuel B. Bacharach. Greenwich, CT: JAI Press.

Aldrich, Howard E. (1971). "Organizational Boundaries and Interorganizational Conflict." *Human Relations*, 24 (Fall), 279–87.

——— (1972a). "Technology and Organizational Structure: A Reexamination of the Findings of the Aston Group." *Administrative Science Quarterly*, 17, No. 1 (March), 26–43.

——— (1972b). "Reply to Hilton: Seduced and Abandoned." *Administrative Science Quarterly*, 17, No. 1 (March), 55–57.

——— (1974). "The Environment as a Network of Organizations: Theoretical and Methodological Implications." Paper presented at the International Sociological Association Meetings, Toronto.

——— (1979). *Organizations and Environments*. Englewood Cliffs, NJ: Prentice Hall.

——— (1988). "Paradigm Warriors: Donaldson Versus the Critics of Organization Theory." *Organization Studies*, 9, No. 1, 18–25.

————, and Jeffrey Pfeffer (1976). "Environments of Organizations." *Annual Review of Sociology,* Vol. 2. Palo Alto, CA: Annual Review.

————, and David Whetten (1981). "Organization-Sets, Action-Sets, and Networks: Making the Most of Simplicity." In *Handbook of Organizational Design,* Vol. 1, eds. Paul C. Nystrom and William H. Starbuck. New York: Oxford University Press.

Alexander, Ernest R. (1974). "Decision Making and Organizational Adaptation: A Proposed Model." Eighth World Congress of Sociology, Toronto.

———— (1979). "The Design of Alternatives in Organizational Contexts." *Administrative Science Quarterly,* 24, No. 3 (September), 382–404.

Alexander, Gordon J., and Roger A. Buchholz (1978). "Corporate Social Responsibility and Stock Market Performance." *Academy of Management Journal,* 21, No. 3 (September), 479–86.

Allen, Michael Patrick (1974). "The Structure of Interorganizational Elite Cooptation: Interlocking Corporate Directorates." *American Sociological Review* 39, No. 3 (June), 393–96.

———— (1976). "Management Control in the Large Corporation: Comment on Zeitlin." *American Journal of Sociology,* 81, No. 4 (January), 885–94.

————, Sharon K. Panian, and Roy E. Lotz (1979). "Managerial Succession and Organizational Performance: A Recalcitrant Problem Revisited." *Administrative Science Quarterly,* 24, No. 2 (June), 167–80.

————, and Sharon K. Panian (1982). "Power, Performance, and Succession in the Large Corporation." *Administrative Science Quarterly,* 27 (December), 538–47.

Altheide, David L., and John M. Johnson (1980). *Bureaucratic Propaganda.* Boston: Allyn & Bacon.

Alutto, Joseph, and James A. Belasco (1972). "A Typology for Participation in Organizational Decision Making." *Administrative Science Quarterly,* 17, No. 1 (March), 117–25.

Alvarez, Rudolfo, Kenneth G. Lutterman, and Associates (1979). *Discrimination in Organizations.* San Francisco: Jossey-Bass.

Anderson, Paul A. (1983). "Decision Making by Objection and the Cuban Missile Crisis." *Administrative Science Quarterly,* 28 (June), 201–22.

√Angle, Harold L., and James L. Perry (1981). "An Empirical Assessment of Organizational Commitment and Organizational Effectiveness." *Administrative Science Quarterly,* 26, No. 1 (March), 1–14.

Antonio, Robert J. (1979). "Domination and Production in Bureaucracy." *American Sociological Review,* 44, No. 6 (December), 895–912.

Argote, Linda (1982). "Input Uncertainty and Organizational Coordination in Hospital Emergency Units." *Administrative Science Quarterly,* 27, No. 3 (September), 420–34.

Agranoff R., and A. Pattahas (1979). *Dimensions of Services Integration: Service Delivery, Program Linkages, Policy Management, Organizational Structure.* Human Services Monograph Series 13, Project SHARE, DHEW Publication No. 02-76-130, Washington, DC: U.S. Government Printing Office.

Argyris, Chris (1969). "On the Effectiveness of Research and Development Organizations." *American Scientist,* 56, No. 4 (July), 344–55.

———— (1972). *The Applicability of Organizational Sociology.* London: Cambridge University Press.

———— (1973). "Personality and Organization Theory Revisited." *Administrative Science Quarterly*, 18, No. 2 (June), 141–67.

Aronowitz, Stanley (1973). *False Promises*. New York: McGraw-Hill.

Asher, Hanna, and Jonathan Z. Shapiro (1988). "Managing Centrality: A Note on Hackman's Resource Allocation Theory." *Administrative Science Quarterly*, 33, No. 2 (June), 275–83.

Assael, Henry (1969). "Constructive Role of Interorganizational Conflict." *Administrative Science Quarterly*, 14, No. 4 (December), 573–82.

Astley, W. Graham (1985). "The Two Ecologies: Population and Community Perspectives on Organizational Evolution." *Administrative Science Quarterly*, 30 (June), 224–41.

————, and Andrew H. Van de Ven (1983). "Central Perspectives and Debates in Organizations Theory." *Administrative Science Quarterly*, 28 (June), 245–73.

Athanassaides, John C. (1974). "On Investigation of Some Communication Patterns of Female Subordinates in Hierarchical Organizations." *Human Relations*, 27, No. 2 (March), 195–209.

Attewell, Paul (1987). "The De-skilling Controversy." *Work and Occupations*, 14, No. 3 (August), 323–46.

Azumi, Koya, and Charles J. McMillan (1974). *Subjective and Objective Measures of Organizational Structure*. New York: American Sociological Association.

Bacharach, Peter, and Morton S. Baratz (1962). "The Two Faces of Power." *American Political Science Review*, 56, No. 6 (December), 947–52.

Bacharach, Samuel B., and Edward J. Lawler (1980). *Power and Politics in Organizations*. San Francisco: Jossey-Bass.

Baldridge, J. Victor, and Robert A. Burnham (1975). "Organizational Innovation: Individual, Organizational, and Environmental Impacts." *Administrative Science Quarterly*, 20, No. 2 (June), 165–76.

Bales, Robert F. (1953). "The Equilibrium Problem in Small Groups." In *Working Paper in Theory of Action*, eds. Talcott Parsons, Robert F. Bales, and Edward Shils. New York: The Free Press.

————, and Philip E. Slater (1955). "Role Differentiation in Small Decision Making Groups." In *Family Socialization and Interaction Processes*, eds. Talcott Parsons and Robert Bales. New York: The Free Press.

Barnard, Chester I. (1938). *The Function of the Executive*. Cambridge, MA: Harvard University Press.

Baron, James N. (1984). "Organizational Perspectives on Stratification." In *Annual Review of Sociology*, Vol. 10, ed. Ralph Turner. Palo Alto, CA: Annual Review.

————, Alison Davis-Blake, and William T. Bielby (1986). "The Structure of Opportunity: How Promotion Ladders Vary Within and Among Organizations." *Administrative Science Quarterly*, 31, No. 2 (June), 248–73.

————, P. Devereaux Jennings, and Frank R. Dobbin (1988). "Mission Control? The Development of Personnel Systems in U.S. Industry." *American Sociological Review*, 53, No. 4 (August), 497–514.

————, and William T. Bielby (1980). "Bringing the Firms Back in: Stratification, Segmentation and the Organization of Work." *American Sociological Review*, 45, No. 5 (October), 737–65.

————, and ———— (1984). "The Organization of Work in a Segmented Economy." *American Sociological Review*, 49 (August), 454–73.

Barton, Allen H. (1961). *Organizational Measurement*. Princeton, NJ: College Entrance Examination Board.

Bass, Bernard M. (1985). *Leadership and Performance Beyond Expectations*. New York: Free Press.

Baty, Gordon, Wiliam Evan, and Terry Rothermel (1971). "Personnel Flows as Interorganizational Relations." *Administrative Science Quarterly*, 16, No. 4 (December), 430–43.

Bauer, Douglas (1981). "Why Big Business Is Firing the Boss." *The New York Times Magazine* (March 8), 22–25, 79–91.

Bavelas, Alex (1950). "Communication Patterns in Task Oriented Groups." *Journal of the Acoustic Society of America*, 22, No. 6 (November), 725–30.

Becker, Selwyn W., and Duncan Neuhauser (1975). *The Efficient Organization*. New York: Elsevier.

Benson, J. Kenneth (1975). "The Interlocking Network as a Political Economy." *Administrative Science Quarterly*, 20, No. 2 (June), 229–49.

——— (1977). "Innovation and Crisis in Organizational Analysis." *Sociological Quarterly*, 18, No. 1 (Winter), 3–16.

———, Joseph T. Kunce, Charles A. Thompson, and David L. Allen (1973). *Coordinating Human Services*. Columbia: University of Missouri, Regional Rehabilitation Institute.

Berger, Peter and Thomas Luckmann (1967). *The Social Construction of Reality*, Garden City, NY: Anchor.

Berle, Adolph A., and Gardiner C. Means (1932). *The Modern Corporation and Private Property*. New York: Macmillan.

Bettman, James R., and Barton A. Weitz (1983). "Attributions in the Board Room: Causal Reasoning in Corporate Annual Reports." *Administrative Science Quarterly*, 28 (June), 165–83.

Beyer, Janice M. (1981). "Ideologies, Values, and Decision Making in Organizations." In *Handbook of Organizational Design*, Vol. 2, pp. 166–202, eds. Paul C. Nystrom and William H. Starbuck. New York: Oxford University Press.

———, and Harrison M. Trice (1979). "A Reexamination of the Relations Between Size and Various Components of Organizational Complexity." *Administrative Science Quarterly*, No. 1 (March), 48–64.

Bidwell, Charles E., and John D. Kasarda (1985). *The Organization and Its Ecosystem: A Theory of Structuring in Organizations*. Greenwich, CT: JAI Press.

Bierstedt, Robert (1950). "An Analysis of Social Power." *American Sociological Review*, 15, No. 6 (December), 730–38.

Biggart, Nicole Woolsey (1977). "The Creative-Destructive Process of Organizational Change: The Case of the Post Office." *Administrative Science Quarterly*, No. 7 (September), 410–26.

———, and Gary G. Hamilton (1984). "The Power of Obedience." *Administrative Science Quarterly*, 29 (December), 540–49.

Bills, David (1987). "Costs, Commitment, and Rewards: Factors Influencing the Design and Implementation of Internal Labor Markets." *Administrative Science Quarterly*, 32, No. 2 (June), 202–21.

Birnbaum, Phillip H., and Gilbert Y. Y. Wong (1985). "Organizational Structure of Multinational Banks from a Culture-Free Perspective." *Administrative Science Quarterly*, 30, No. 3 (June), 262–77.

Blake, Richard R., and Jane S. Mouton (1964). *The Managerial Grid*. Houston: Gulf.

Blau, Judith R., and Richard D. Alba (1982). "Empowering Nets of Participation." *Administrative Science Quarterly*, 27 (September), 363–79.

———, and William McKinley (1979). "Ideas, Complexity, and Innovation." *Administrative Science Quarterly*, 24, No. 2 (June), 200–19.

———, and Gordana Rabrenovic (1989). "Dominant Concerns and Interorganizational Relations." San Francisco: Annual Meetings, American Sociological Association/Department of Sociology, University of North Carolina, Chapel Hill.

Blau, Peter M. (1955). *The Dynamics of Bureaucracy*. Chicago: University of Chicago Press.

——— (1964). *Exchange and Power in Social Life*. New York: John Wiley.

——— (1968). "The Hierarchy of Authority in Organizations." *American Journal of Sociology*, 73, No. 4 (January), 453–67.

——— (1970). "Decentralization in Bureaucracies." In *Power in Organizations*, ed. Mayer N. Zald. Nashville, TN: Vanderbilt University Press.

——— (1972). "Interdependence and Hierarchy in Organizations." *Social Science Research*, 1, No. 1 (April), 1–24.

——— (1973). *The Organization of Academic Work*. New York: John Wiley.

——— (1974). *On the Nature of Organizations*. New York: John Wiley.

———, Wolf Heydebrand, and Robert E. Stauffer (1966). "The Structure of Small Bureaucracies." *American Sociological Review*, 31, No. 2 (April), 179–91.

———, and Richard A. Schoenherr (1971). *The Structure of Organizations*. New York: Basic Books.

———, and W. Richard Scott (1962). *Formal Organizations*. San Francisco: Chandler.

Blauner, Robert (1964). *Alienation and Freedom*. Chicago: University of Chicago Press.

Boddewyn, John (1974). "External Affairs: A Corporate Function in Search of Conceptualization and Theory." *Organization and Administrative Sciences*, 5, No. 1 (Spring), 67–106.

Boeker, Warren (1989). "The Development and Institutionalization of Subunit Power in Organizations." *Administrative Science Quarterly*, 34, No. 3 (September), 388–410.

Boisot, Max, and John Child (1988). "The Iron Law of Fiefs: Bureaucratic Failure and Problem of Governance in the Chinese Economic Reforms." *Administrative Science Quarterly*, 33, No. 4 (December), 507–27.

Boje, David M., and David A. Whetten (1981). "Effects of Organizational Strategies and Contextual Constraints on Centrality and Attributions of Influence in Interorganizational Networks." *Administrative Science Quarterly*, 26 (September), 378–95.

Boulding, Kenneth E. (1964). "A Pure Theory of Conflict Applied to Organizations." In *Power and Conflict in Organizations*, ed. Robert L. Kahn and Elise Boulding. New York: Basic Books.

Bozeman, Barry (1987). "*All Organizations Are Public: Bridging Public and Private Organizational Theories*". San Francisco: Jossey-Bass.

Brass, Daniel J. (1984). "Being in the Right Place: A Structural Analysis of Individual Influence in an Organization." *Administrative Science Quarterly*, 29, No. 3 (August), 518–39.

Braverman, Harry (1974). *Labor and Monopoly Capital: The Degradation of Work in the Twentieth Century*. New York: Monthly Review Press.

Brewer, John (1971). "Flow of Communication, Expert Qualifications, and Organizational Authority Structure." *American Sociological Review*, 36, No. 3 (June), 475–84.

Brinkerhoff, Merlin B. (1972). "Hierarchical Status, Contingencies, and the Administrative Staff Conference." *Administrative Science Quarterly*, 17, No. 3 (September), 395–407.

Broskowski, Anthony (1980). "Literature Review on Interorganizational Relationships and Their Relevance to Health and Mental Health Coordination." Tampa, FL: Northside Community Mental Health Center (final report), NIMH Contract #278-00300P.

Brown, M. Craig (1982). "Administrative Succession and Organizational Performance: The Succession Effect." *Administrative Science Quarterly*, 27 (March), 1–16.

Brown, John L., and Rodney Schneck (1979). "A Structural Comparison Between Canadian and American Industrial Organizations." *Administrative Science Quarterly*, 24, No. 1 (March), 24–47.

Brown, Richard Harvey (1978). "Bureaucracy as Praxis: Toward a Political Phenomenology of Formal Organizations." *Administrative Science Quarterly*, 23, No. 3 (September), 365–82.

Bucher, Rue (1970). "Social Process and Power in a Medical School." In *Power in Organizations*, ed. Mayer N. Zald. Nashville, TN: Vanderbilt University Press.

Burke, John P. (1986). *Bureaucratic Responsibility*. Baltimore: Johns Hopkins University Press.

Burke, Ronald J. (1970). "Methods of Resolving Superior-Subordinate Conflict: The Constructive Use of Subordinate Differences and Disagreements." *Organizational Behavior and Human Performance*, 5, No. 4 (July), 393–411.

Burns, Tom (1967). "The Comparative Study of Organizations." In *Methods of Organizational Research*, ed. Victor H. Vroom. Pittsburgh: University of Pittsburgh Press.

———, and G. M. Stalker (1961). *The Management of Innovation*. London: Tavistock.

Burrell, Gibson, and Gareth Morgan (1979). *Sociological Paradigms and Organizational Analysis*. London: Heinemann.

Burt, Ronald S. (1977). "Power in a Social Typology." *Social Science Research*, 6 (Winter), 1–83.

——— (1980). "Cooptive Corporate Action Networks: A Reconsideration of Interlocking Directorates Involving American Manufacturing." *Administrative Science Quarterly*, 25, No. 4 (December), 557–82.

——— (1983). "Corporate Philanthropy as a Cooptive Process." *Social Forces*, 62 (May), 419–49.

——— (1988). "The Stability of American Markets." *American Journal of Sociology*, 94, No. 2 (September), 356–95.

———, Kenneth P. Christman, and Harold C. Kilburn, Jr. (1980). "Testing a Structural Theory of Corporate Cooptation: Interorganizational Directorate Ties as a Strategy for Avoiding Market Constraints on Projects." *American Sociological Review*, 45, No. 5 (October), 821–41.

Cameron, Kim (1978). "Measuring Organizational Effectiveness in Institutions of Higher Education." *Administrative Science Quarterly*, 23, No. 4 (December), 604–32.

——— (1986). "Effectiveness as Paradox." *Management Science*, 32 (May), 539–53.

————, and David A. Whetten (1981). "Perceptions of Organizational Effectiveness over Organizational Life Cycles." *Administrative Science Quarterly*, 26 (December), 524–44.

————, and ———— (1983). *Organizational Effectiveness: A Comparison of Multiple Models*. New York: Academic Press.

————, Myung U. Kim, and David A. Whetten (1987). "Organizational Effects of Decline and Turbulence." *Administrative Science Quarterly*, 32, No. 2 (June), 222–40.

Campbell, Donald (1969). "Variation and Selective Retention in Socio-Cultural Evolution." *General Systems: Yearbook of the Society for General Systems Research*, 16, 69–85.

Campbell, John P. (1977). "On the Nature of Organizational Effectiveness." In *New Perspectives on Organizational Effectiveness*, eds. Paul S. Goodman and Johannes M. Pennings. San Francisco: Jossey-Bass.

————, et al. (1974). *The Measurement of Organizational Effectiveness*. Final Report, Navy Personnel Research and Development Center Contrast N00022-73-C-0023. Minneapolis: Personnel Decisions.

Caplow, Theodore (1964). *Principles of Organization*. New York: Harcourt Brace Jovanovich.

———— (1983). *Managing Any Organization*. New York: Holt, Rinehart and Winston.

Caragonne, P. (1978). "Service Integration: Where Do We Stand?" Paper prepared for the 39th National Conference on Public Administration (April), Phoenix, AZ.

Carper, William B., and William E. Snizek (1980). "The Nature and Types of Organizational Taxonomies: An Overview." *Academy of Management Review*, 5, No. 1 (January), 65–75.

Carroll, Glenn R. (1984). "Organizational Ecology." *Annual Review of Sociology* Vol. 10. Palo Alto, CA: Annual Reviews.

———— (1984). "Dynamics of Publisher Succession in Newspaper Organizations." *Administrative Science Quarterly*, 29 (March), 93–113.

———— (1985). "Concentration and Specialization: Dynamics of Niche Width in Populations of Organizations." *American Journal of Sociology*, 90 (May), 1262–83.

————, ed. (1988). *Ecological Models of Organizations*. Cambridge, MA: Ballinger.

————, and Jacques Delacroix (1982). "Organizational Mortality in the Newspaper of Argentina and Ireland: An Ecological Approach." *Administrative Science Quarterly*, 27, No. 2 (June), 169–98.

————, and Michael T. Hannan (1989). "Density Dependence in the Evolution of Populations of Newspaper Organizations." *American Sociological Review*, 54, No. 4 (August), 524–41.

————, and Yangchung Paul Huo (1986). "Organizational Task and Institutional Environments in Ecological Perspective: Findings from the Local Newspaper Industry." *American Journal of Sociology*, 91, No. 4 (January), 838–73.

Carstensen, Fred B., and Richard Hume Werking (1983). "The Process of Bureaucratization in the U.S. State Department and the Vesting of Economic Interests: Toward Clearer Thinking and Better History." *Administrative Science Quarterly*, 28 (March), 56–60.

Cartwright, Dorwin (1965). "Influence, Leadership, and Control." In *Handbook of Organizations*, pp. 1–47, ed. James G. March. Chicago: Rand McNally.

Cartwright, Dorwin, and A. Zander (1968). "Motivational Processes in Groups: Introduction." In *Group Dynamics*, 3rd ed., ed. D. Cartwright and A. Zander, New York: Harper & Row.

Champagne, Anthony, Marian Neef, and Stuart Nagel (1981). "Laws, Organizations, and the Judiciary." In *Handbook of Organizational Design*, Vol. 1, eds. Paul C. Nystrom and William H. Starbuck. New York: Oxford University Press.

Chandler, A. D., Jr. (1962). *Strategy and Structure*. Cambridge, MA: MIT Press.

Child, John (1972). "Organizational Structure, Environment, and Performance: The Role of Strategic Choice." *Sociology*, 6, No. 1 (January), 1–22.

—— (1973). "Strategies of Control; and Organizational Behavior." *Administrative Science Quarterly*, 18, No. 1 (March), 1–17.

—— (1976). "Participation, Organization, and Social Cohesion." *Human Relations*, 29, No. 5 (May), 429–51.

——, and Alfred Kieser (1981). "Development of Organization over Time." In. *Handbook of Organizational Design*, Vol. 1, eds. Paul C. Nystrom and William H. Starbuck. New York: Oxford University Press.

——, and Roger Mansfield (1972). "Technology, Size and Organizational Structure." *Sociology*, 6, No. 3 (September), 369–93.

Christenson, James A., James G. Hougland, Jr., Thomas W. Ilvento, and Jon M. Shepard (1988). "The 'Organization Man' and the Community: The Impact of Organizational Norms and Personal Values on Community Participation and Transfers." *Social Forces*, 66, No. 3 (March), 808–26.

Clark, John P. (1988). "Presidential Address on the Importance of Our Understanding Organizational Conflict." *The Sociological Quarterly*, 29, No. 2 (Summer), 149–61.

Clawson, Dan (1980). *Bureaucracy and the Labor Process: The Transformation of U.S. Industry, 1860–1920*. New York: Monthly Review Press.

——, and Alan Neustadtl (1989). "Interlocks, PACs and Corporate Conservatism." *American Journal of Sociology*, 94, No. 4 (January), 749–73.

Clegg, Stewart (1981). "Organization and Control." *Administrative Science Quarterly*, 26 (December), 545–62.

——, and David Dunkerley (1980). *Organization, Class, and Control*. London: Routledge and Kegan Paul.

Clinard, Marshall B., and Peter Yeager (1980). *Corporate Crime*. New York: The Free Press.

Cohen, Michael D., James G. March, and Johan P. Olsen (1972). "A Garbage Can Model of Organizational Choice." *Administrative Science Quarterly*, 17, No. 1 (March), 1–25.

Cohen, Stephen S., and John Zysman (1988). "Manufacturing Innovation and American Industrial Competitiveness." *Science*, 239 (4 March), 1110–15.

Coleman, James S. (1974). *Power and the Structure of Society*. New York: W. W. Norton.

Comstock, Donald, and W. Richard Scott (1977). "Technology and the Structure of Subunits: Distinguishing Individual and Work Group Effects." *Administrative Science Quarterly*, 22, No. 2 (June), 177–202.

Conaty, Joseph, Hoda Mahmoudi, and George A. Miller (1983). "Social Structure and Bureaucracy: A Comparison of Organizations in the United States and Pre-revolutionary Iran." *Organization Studies*, 4, No. 2, 105–28.

Cook, Karen S. (1977). "Exchange and Power in Networks of Interorganizational Relations." *Sociological Quarterly*, 18, No. 1 (Winter), 62–82.

Cornfield, Daniel B. (1983). "Chances of Layoff in a Corporation: A Case Study." *Administrative Science Quarterly*, 28, No. 4 (December), 503–20.

Corwin, Ronald (1973). *Reform and Organizational Survival: The Teacher Corps as an Instrument of Educational Change.* New York: John Wiley & Sons.

Coser, Lewis (1956). *The Functions of Social Conflict.* New York: The Free Press.

———— (1967). *Continuities in the Study of Social Conflict.* New York: The Free Press.

Craig, John G., and Edward Gross (1970). "The Forum Theory of Organizational Democracy: Structural Guarantee as Time Related Variables." *American Sociological Review*, 35, No. 1 (February), 19–33.

Crittenden, Ann (1978). "Philanthropy, The Business of the Not-so-Idle Rich." *The New York Times* (July 23), Section F, pp. 3–5.

Crozier, Michael (1964). *The Bureaucratic Phenomenon.* Chicago: University of Chicago Press.

———— (1973). *The Stalled Society*, trans. Rupert Sawyer. New York: Viking Press.

Cummings, Larry L. (1977). "The Emergence of the Instrumental Organization." In *New Perspectives on Organizational Effectiveness*, eds. Paul S. Goodman and Johannes M. Pennings. San Francisco: Jossey-Bass.

Daft, Richard L., and Selwin W. Becker (1978). *Innovation in Organizations: Innovation Adoption in School Organizations.* New York: Elsevier.

Daft, Richard L., and Patricia J. Bradshaw (1980). "The Process of Horizontal Differentiation: Two Models." *Administrative Science Quarterly*, 25, No. 3 (September), 441–56.

Daft, Richard L., and Norman B. Macintosh (1981). "A Tentative Exploration into the Amount and Equivocality of Information Processing in Organizational Work Units." *Administrative Science Quarterly*, 26 (June), 207–24.

Dahl, Robert (1957). "The Concept of Power." *Behavioral Science*, 2, No. 3 (July), 201–15.

Dahrendorf, Ralf (1959). *Class and Class Conflict in Industrial Society.* London: Routledge and Kegan Paul.

Dalton, Melville (1959). *Men Who Manage.* New York: John Wiley.

Damanpour, Fariborz, and William M. Evan (1984). "Organizational Innovation and Performance: The Problems of 'Organizational Lag.'" *Administrative Science Quarterly*, 29 (September), 392–409.

Danet, Barbara (1981). "Client-Organization Relationships." In *Handbook of Organizational Design*, Vol. 2, eds. Paul C. Nystrom and William H. Starbuck. New York: Oxford University Press.

Delacroix, Jacques, and Glenn R. Carroll (1983). "Organizational Foundings: An Ecological Study of the Newspaper Industries of Argentina and Ireland." *Administrative Science Quarterly*, 28 (June), 274–91.

Dess, Gregory G., and Donald W. Beard (1984). "Dimensions of Organizational Task Environment." *Administrative Science Quarterly*, 29 (March), 52–73.

Dewar, Robert D., and Jerald Hage (1978). "Size, Technology, Complexity and Structural Differentiation: Toward a Theoretical Synthesis." *Administrative Science Quarterly*, 23, No. 1 (March), 111–36.

Dewar, Robert D., David A. Whetten, and David Boje (1980). "An Examination of the Reliability and Validity of the Aiken and Hage Scales of Utilization, Formalization, and Task Routineness." *Administrative Science Quarterly*, 25, No. 1 (March), 120–28.

DiMaggio, Paul J. (1988). "Interest and Agency in Institutional Theory." In *Institutional Patterns and Organizations: Culture and Environment*, ed. Lynne G. Zucker. Cambridge, MA: Ballinger.

———, and Walter W. Powell (1983). "The Iron Cage Revisited: Institutional Isomorphism and Collective Rationality in Organizational Fields." *American Sociological Review*, 48 (April), 147–60.

Domhoff, G. William, and Thomas R. Dye eds. (1987). Power Elites and Organizations. Newbury Park, CA: Sage.

Donaldson, Lex (1985). In *Defense of Organizational Theory: A Reply to the Critics*. Cambridge: Cambridge University Press.

———, and Malcolm Warner (1974). "Bureaucratic and Electoral Control in Occupational Interest Associations." *Sociology*, 8, No. 1 (January), 47–59.

Dornbusch, Sanford M. (1955). "The Military Academy as an Assimilating Institution." *Social Forces*, 33, No. 4 (May), 316–21.

———, and W. Richard Scott (1975). *Evaluation and the Exercise of Authority*. New York: Basic Books.

Downs, Anthony (1967). *Inside Bureaucracy*. Boston: Little, Brown.

Downs, George W., Jr., and Lawrence B. Mohr (1976). "Conceptual Issues in the Study of Innovation." *Administrative Science Quarterly*, 21, No. 4 (December), 700–14.

Drabek, Thomas E., Harriet L. Tamminga, Thomas S. Kilijanek, and Christopher R. Adams (1981). *Managing Multiorganizational Emergency Responses: Emergent Search and Rescue Networks in Natural Disaster and Remote Area Settings*. Boulder: Institute of Behavioral Science, University of Colorado.

Drazin, Robert, and Andrew H. Van de Ven (1985). "Alternative Forms of Fit in Contingency Theory." *Administrative Science Quarterly*, 30, No. 4 (December), 514–39.

DuBick, Michael A. (1978). "The Organizational Structure of Newspapers in Relation to Their Metropolitan Environments." *Administrative Science Quarterly*, 23, No. 3 (September), 418–33.

Dubin, Robert (1965). "Supervision and Productivity: Empirical Findings and Theoretical Considerations." In *Leadership and Productivity*, eds. Robert Dubin, George Homans, Floyd Mann, and Delbert Miller. San Francisco: Chandler.

Dunbar, Roger L. M., and Nikolai Wasilewski (1985). "Regulating External Threats in the Cigarette Industry." *Administrative Science Quarterly*, 30, No. 4 (December), 540–59.

Duncan, Robert B. (1972). "Characteristics of Organizational Environments and Perceived Environmental Uncertainty." *Administrative Science Quarterly*, 17, No. 3 (September), 313–27.

——— (1973). "Multiple Decision-Making Structures in Adapting to Environmental Uncertainty: The Impact on ORganizational Effectiveness." *Human Relations*, 26, No. 3 (June), 273–91.

Dunford, Richard (1987). "The Suppression of Technology as a Strategy for Controlling Resource Dependence." *Administrative Science Quarterly*, 32, No. 4 (December), 512–25.

Eccles, Robert G., and Harrison C. White (1988). "Price and Authority in Inter-Profit Center Transactions." *American Journal of Sociology*, 94 Supplement, S17–S51.

Edström, Anders, Bent Högbert, and Lars Erik Norbäk (1984). "Alternative Explanations of Interorganizational Cooperation: The Case of Joint Programs and Joint Ventures in Sweden." *Organization Studies*, 5, 147–68.

Edwards, Richard C. (1975). "The Social Relations of Production in the Firm and Labor Market Structure." *Politics and Society*, 5, 83–108.

——— (1979). *Contested Terrain*. New York: Basic Books.

Egelhoff, William G. (1982). "Strategy and Structure in Multinational Corporations: An Information Processing Approach." *Administrative Science Quarterly*, 27, No. 3 (September), 435–58.

Eitzen, D. Stanley, and Norman R. Yetman (1972). "Managerial Change, Longevity and Organizational Effectiveness." *Administrative Science Quarterly*, 17, No. 1 (March), 110–18.

Emerson, Richard M. (1962). "Power-Dependence Relations." *American Sociological Review*, 27, No. 1 (February), 31–40.

Emery, F. E., and E. L. Trist (1965). "The Causal Texture of Organizational Environments." *Human Relations*, 18, No. 1 (February), 21–32.

Enz, Cathy A. (1988). "The Role of Value Congruence in Intraorganizational Power." *Administrative Science Quarterly*, 33, No. 2 (June), 284–304.

——— (1989). "The Measurement of Perceived Intraorganizational Power: A Multi-Respondent Perspective." *Organizational Studies*, 10, No. 2, 241–51.

Ermann, M. David, and Richard J. Lundman (1982). *Corporate and Governmental Deviance: Problems of Organizational Behavior in Contemporary Society*, 2nd ed. New York: Oxford University Press.

Etzioni, Amitai (1961). *A Comparative Analysis of Complex Organizations*. New York: The Free Press.

——— (1964). *Modern Organizations*. Englewood Cliffs, NJ: Prentice Hall.

——— (1965). "Dual Leadership in Complex Organizations." *American Sociological Review*, 30, No. 5 (October), 688–98.

——— (1968). *The Active Society: A Theory of Societal and Political Processes*. New York: The Free Press.

——— (1975). *A Comparative Analysis of Complex Organizations*, rev. ed. New York: The Free Press.

Evan, William (1966). "The Organization Set: Toward a Theory of Interorganizational Relations." In *Approaches to Organizational Design*, ed. James Thompson, Pittsburgh: University of Pittsburgh Press.

Farberman, Harvey A. (1975). "A Criminogenic Market Structure: The Automobile Industry." *The Sociological Quarterly*, 16, No. 4 (Autumn), 438–57.

Feldman, Martha S., and James G. March (1981). "Information in Organizations as Signal and Symbol." *Administrative Science Quarterly*, 26 (June), 171–86.

Fennell, Mary C. (1980). "The Effects of Environmental Characteristics on the Structure of Hospital Clusters." *Administrative Science Quarterly*, 29, No. 3 (September), 489–510.

Fiedler, Fred E. (1967). *A Theory of Leadership Effectiveness*. New York: McGraw-Hill.

——— (1972). "The Effects of Leadership Training and Experience: A Contingency Model Explanation." *Administrative Science Quarterly*, 17, No. 4 (December), 453–70.

———, and J. E. Garcia (1987). *New Approaches to Leadership: Cognitive Resources and Organizational Performance*. New York: John Wiley.

——, and M. M. Chemers (1982). *Improving Leader Effectiveness: The Leader Match Concept*, 2nd ed. New York: John Wiley.

Filley, Alan C., and Robert J. House (1969). *Managerial Processes and Organizational Behavior*. Glenview, IL: Scott, Foresman.

——, ——, and Steven Kerr (1976). *Managerial Process and Organizational Behavior*. Glenview, IL: Scott, Foresman.

Finney, Henry C., and Henry R. Lesieur (1982). "A Contingency Theory of Organizational Crime." In *Research in the Sociology of Organizations*, Vol. 1, ed. Samuel B. Bacharach. Greenwich, CT: JAI Press.

Fligstein, Neil (1985). "The Spread of the Multidivisional Form Among Large Firms." *American Sociological Review*, 50 (June), 377–91.

—— (1987). "The Intraorganizational Power Struggle: Rise of Financial Personnel to Top Leadership in Large Corporations, 1919–1979." *American Sociological Review*, 52, No. 1 (February), 44–58.

Fombrun, Charles J. (1986). "Structural Dynamics Within and Between Organizations." *Administrative Science Quarterly*, 31, No. 3 (September), 403–21.

Forbes Magazine (1973). "The Numbers Game: The Larger the Company, the More Understanding the Accountant?" 112, No. 1 (July), 33–35.

Form, William (1980). "Resolving Ideological Issues on the Division of Labor." In *Sociological Theory and Research: A Critical Appraisal*, pp. 110–55, ed. Hubert M. Blalock, Jr. New York: Free Press.

Freeman, John H. (1973). "Environment, Technology, and the Administrative Intensity of Manufacturing Organizations." *American Sociological Review*, 38, No. 5 (December), 750–63.

—— (1979). "Going to the Well: School District Administrative Intensity and Environmental Constraints." *Administrative Science Quarterly*, 24, No. 1 (March), 119–33.

——, and Michael T. Hannon (1983). "Niche Width and the Dynamics of Organizational Populations." *American Journal of Sociology*, 88 (May), 1116–45.

——, Glenn Carroll, and Michael Hannan (1983). "The Liability of Newness: Age-Dependence in Organizational Death Rates." *American Sociological Review*, 48 (October), 692–710.

——, and Michael T. Hannan (1989). "Setting the Record Straight: Rebuttal to Young." *American Journal of Sociology*, 95, No. 3 (September), 425–39.

Freidson, Eliot (1973). *The Professions and Their Prospects*. Beverly Hills, CA: Sage.

French, John R. P., and Bertram Raven (1968). "The Bases of Social Power." In *Group Dynamics*, 3rd ed., eds. Dorwin Cartwright and Alvin Zander. New York: Harper & Row.

Frost, Peter J., Larry F. Moore, Meryl Reis Louis, Craig C. Lundberg, and Joanne Martin (eds.) (1985). *Organizational Culture*. Beverly Hills, CA: Sage.

Galaskiewicz, Joseph (1979). "The Structure of Community Organizational Networks." *Social Forces*, 57, No. 4 (June), 1346–64.

—— (1985). "Interorganizational Relations." *Annual Review of Sociology*, Vol. 11 Palo Alto, CA: Annual Reviews.

——, and Karl R. Krohn (1984). "Positions, Roles, and Dependencies in a Community Interorganizational System." *The Sociological Quarterly*, 25, No. 4, (Autumn), 527–50.

——, and Peter J. Marsden (1978). "Interorganizational Resources Networks: Formal Patterns of Overlap." *Social Science Research*, 7, No. 2 (June), 89–107.

————, and Deborah Shatin (1981). "Leadership and Networking Among Neighborhood Human Service Organizations." *Administrative Science Quarterly*, 26 (September), 434–48.

————, and Stanley Wasserman (1989). "Mimetic Processes Within an Inter-organizational Field." *Administrative Science Quarterly*, 34, No. 3 (September), 454–79.

————, Stanley Wasserman, Barbara Rauschenbach, Wolfgang Bielefeld, and Patti Mullaney (1985). "The Influence of Corporate Power, Social Status, and Market Position on Corporate Interlocks in a Regional Network." *Social Forces*, 64 (December), 403–31.

Galbraith, Jay (1973). *Designing Complex Organizations*. REading, MA: Addison-Wesley.

———— (1977). *Organization Design*. Reading, MA: Addison-Wesley.

Galbraith, John Kenneth (1974). "The U.S. Economy Is Not a Free Market Economy." *Forbes*, 113, No. 10 (May), 99.

Galtung, Johan (1965). "Institutionalized Conflict Resolution: A Theoretical Paradigm." *Journal of Peace Research*, 2, No. 4, 348–96.

Gamoran, Adam, and Robert Dreeben (1986). "Coupling and Control in Educational Organizations." *Administrative Science Quarterly*, 31, No. 4 (December), 612–32.

Gamson, William, and Norman Scotch (1964). "Scapegoating in Baseball." *American Journal of Sociology*, 70, No. 1 (July), 69–72.

Gans, Sheldon P., and Gerald T. Horton (1975). *Integration of Human Services: The State and Municipal Levels*. New York: Praeger.

Gardner, Elmer A., and James N. Snipe (1970). "Toward the Coordination and Integration of Personal Health Services." *American Journal of Public Health*, 60, No. 11 (November), 2068–78.

Geeraerts, Guy (1984). "The Effects of Ownership on the Organization Structure in Small Firms." *Administrative Science Quarterly*, 29, No. 2 (June), 232–37.

Georgiou, Petro (1973). "The Goal Paradigm and Notes Toward a Counter Paradigm." *Administrative Science Quarterly*, 18, No. 3 (September), 291–310.

Gilb, Corinne Lathrop (1981). "Public or Private Governments." In *Handbook of Organizational Design*, Vol. 2, pp. 464–91. eds. Paul C. Nystrom and William H. Starbuck. New York: Oxford University Press.

Giordano, Peggy C. (1974). "The Juvenile Justice System: The Client Perspective." Ph.D. dissertation, University of Minnesota, Minneapolis.

———— (1976). "The Sense of Injustice: An Analysis of Juveniles' Reaction to the Justice System." *Criminology*, 14, No. 1 (May), 93–112.

———— (1977). "The Clients Perspective in Agency Evaluation." *Social Work*, 22, No. 1 (January), 34–39.

Glisson, Charles A. (1978). "Dependence of Technological Routinizations on Structural Variables in Human Service Organizations." *Administrative Science Quarterly*, 23, No. 3 (September), 383–95.

Goffman, Irving (1959). *The Presentation of Self in Everyday Life*. Garden City, NY: Doubleday.

Goldman, Paul (1980). "The Marxist Analysis of Organizations: Values, Theories, and Research." Unpublished manuscript, Department of Sociology, University of Oregon.

————, and Donald R. Van Houton (1977). "Managerial Strategies and the Worker: A Marxist Analysis of Bureaucracy." *The Sociological Quarterly*, 18 (Winter), 108–25.

Gooding, Richard C., and John A. Wagner III (1985). "A Meta-Analytic Review of the Relationship Between Size and Performance: The Productivity and Efficiency of Organizations and Their Subunits." *Administrative Science Quarterly*, 30, No. 4 (December), 462–81.

Goodman, Paul, and Johannes Pennings, eds. (1977). *New Perspectives on Organizations' Effectiveness*. San Francisco: Jossey-Bass.

Gordon, Gerald, and Selwyn Becker (1964). "Careers, Organizational Size and Succession." *American Journal of Sociology*, 70, No. 2 (September), 216–22.

Gouldner, Alvin, ed. (1950). *Studies in Leadership*. New York: Harper & Row.

———— (1954). *Patterns of Industrial Bureaucracy*. New York: The Free Press.

Grafton, Carl (1975). "The Creation of Federal Agencies." *Administration and Society*, 7, No. 3 (November), 328–65.

Grandoci, Anna (1984). "A Perscriptive Contingency View of Organizational Decision Making." *Administrative Science Quarterly*, 29 (June), 192–209.

Granovetter, Mark (1973). "The Strength of Weak Ties." *American Journal of Sociology*, 78, No. 6 (May), 1360–80.

———— (1984). "Small Is Bountiful: Labor Markets and Establishment Size." *American Sociological Review*, 49, No. 3 (June), 323–34.

———— (1985). "Economic Action and Social Structure: The Problem of Embeddedness." *American Journal of Sociology*, 91, No. 4 (November), 481–510.

Gresov, Christopher (1989). "Exploring Fit and Misfit with Multiple Contingencies." *Administrative Science Quarterly*, 34, No. 3 (September), 431–53.

Gross, Edward (1968). "Universities as Organizations: A Research Approach." *American Sociological Review*, 33, No. 4 (August), 518–43.

Grusky, Oscar (1961). "Corporate Size, Bureaucratization, and Managerial Succession." *American Journal of Sociology*, 67, No. 3 (November), 355–59.

———— (1963). "Managerial Succession and Organizational Effectiveness." *American Journal of Sociology*, 69, No. 1 (July), 21–31.

———— (1964). "Reply." *American Journal of Sociology*, 70, No. 1 (July), 72–76.

———— (1970). "The Effects of Succession: A Comparative Study of Military and Business Organization." In *The Sociology of Organizations*, eds. Oscar Grusky and George Miller. New York: The Free Press.

Guest, Robert (1962). "Managerial Succession in Complex Organizations." *American Journal of Sociology*, 68, No. 1 (July), 47–54.

Guetzkow, Harold (1965). "Communications in Organizations." In *Handbook of Organizations*, ed. James G. March. Chicago: Rand McNally.

———— (1966). "Relations Among Organizations." In *Studies in Behavior in Organizations: A Research Symposium*, ed. R. V. Bowers. Athens: University of Georgia Press.

Gusfield, Joseph R. (1955). "Social Structure and Moral Reform: A Study of the Woman's Christian Temperance Union." *American Journal of Sociology*, 61, No. 3 (November), 221–32.

———— (1963). *Symbolic Crusade*. Urbana: University of Illinois Press.

Haas, J. Eugene, Richard H. Hall, and Norman J. Johnson (1966). "Toward an Empirically Derived Taxonomy of Organizations." In *Studies on Behavior in Organizations*, ed. Raymond V. Bowers. Athens: University of Georgia Press.

Hage, Jerald (1965). "An Axiomatic Theory of Organizations." *Administrative Science Quarterly*, 10, No. 3 (December), 289–320.

—— (1974). *Communications and Organizational Control*. New York: John Wiley.

—— (1980). *Theories of Organizations*. New York: John Wiley.

——, and Michael Aiken (1967a). "Relationship of Centralization to Other Structural Properties." *Administrative Science Quarterly*, 12, No. 1 (June), 72–91.

——, and —— (1967b). "Program Change and Organizational Properties." *American Journal of Sociology*, 72, No. 5 (March), 503–19.

——, and —— (1969). "Routine Technology, Social Structure, and Organizational Goals." *Administrative Science Quarterly*, 14, No. 3 (September), 366–77.

——, and —— (1970). *Social Change in Complex Organizations*. New York: Random House.

——, Michael Aiken, and Cora Bagley Marrett (1971). "Organizational Structure and Communications." *American Sociological Review*, 36, No. 1 (October), 860–71.

——, and Robert Dewar (1973). "Elite Values Versus Organizational Structure in Predicting Innovation." *Administrative Science Quarterly*, 18, No. 3 (September), 279–90.

Hall, Richard H. (1962). "Intraorganizational Structural Variation: Application of the Bureaucratic Model." *Administrative Science Quarterly*, 7, No. 3 (December), 295–308.

—— (1963). "The Concept of Bureaucracy." *American Journal of Sociology*, 69, No. 1 (July), 32–40.

—— (1968). "Professionalization and Bureaucratization." *American Sociological Review*, 33, No. 2 (February), 92–104.

—— (1975). *Occupations and the Social Structure*, 2nd ed. Englewood Cliffs, NJ: Prentice Hall.

—— (1981). "Technological Policies and Their Consequences." In *Handbook of Organizational Design*, Vol. 2, pp. 320–35. eds. Paul C. Nystrom and William H. Starbuck. New York: Oxford University Press.

—— (1986). *The Dimensions of Work*. Beverly Hills, CA: Sage.

—— (1987). *Organizations: Structures, Processes, and Outcomes*, 4th ed. Englewood Cliffs, NJ: Prentice Hall.

——, and Charles R. Tittle (1966). "Bureaucracy and Its Correlates." *American Journal of Sociology*, 72, No. 3 (November), 267–72.

——, and Weiman Xu (forthcoming). "Run Silent, Run Deep: A Note on the Ever Pervasive Influence of Cultural Dirrerences on Organizations in the Far East." *Organization Studies*.

——, John P. Clark, and Peggy C. Giordano (1979). "The Extent and Correlates of Interorganizational Conflict." Albany, NY: SUNY-Albany.

——, John P. Clark, Peggy Giordano, Paul Johnson, and Martha Van Roekel (1977). "Patterns of Interorganizational Relationships." *Administrative Science Quarterly*, 22, No. 3 (September), 457–74.

——, ——, ——, ——, and —— (1978). "Interorganizational Coordination in the Delivery of Human Services." In *Organization and Environment: Theory, Issues, and Reality*, ed. Lucien Karpik. Beverly Hills, CA: Sage.

————, J. Eugene Haas, and Norman Johnson (1967a). "An Examiniation of Blau-Scott and Etzioni Typologies." *Administrative Science Quarterly*, 12, No. 2 (June), 118–39.

————, ————, and ———— (1967b). "Organizational Size, Complexity, and Formalization." *American Sociological Review*, 32, No. 6 (December), 903–12.

————, ————, and ———— (1972). "Reply to Weldon." *Administrative Science Quarterly*, 17, No. 1 (March), 79–80.

Halpert, Burton P. (1974). *An Empirical Study of the Relationship Between Power, Conflict, and Cooperation on the Interorganizational Level.* Doctoral dissertation, Department of Sociology, University of Minnesota, Minneapolis.

———— (1982). "Antecedents." In *Interorganizational Coordination: Theory, Research, and Implementation,* eds. David L. Rogers and David A. Whetten and Associates. Ames: Iowa State University Press.

Hambrick, Donald C. (1981). "Environment, Strategy and Power Within Top Management Teams." *Administrative Science Quarterly*, 26 (June), 253–76.

————, and Richard A. D'Aveni (1988). "Large Corporate Failures as Downward Spirals." *Administrative Science Quarterly*, 33, No. 1 (March), 1–23.

Hamilton, Gary L., and Nicole Woolsey Biggart (1988). "Market, Culture, and Authority: A Comparative Analysis of Management and Organization in the Far East." *American Journal of Sociology*, 94, Supplement S52–S94.

Hannan, Michael T., and John H. Freeman (1977a). "Obstacles to Comparative Studies." In *New Perspective on Organizational Effectiveness,* eds. Paul S. Goodman and Johannes Pennings. San Francisco: Jossey-Bass.

————, and ———— (1977b). "The Population Ecology of Organizations." *American Journal of Sociology*, 82 (March), 929–64.

———— (1984). "Structural Inertia and Organizational Change." *American Sociological Review*, 49 (April), 149–64.

————, and John Freeman (1987). "The Ecology of Organizational Founding: American Labor Unions, 1836–1985." *American Journal of Sociology*, 92, No. 4 (January), 910–43.

————, and ———— (1988). "The Ecology of Organizational Mortality: American Labor Unions, 1836–1985." *American Journal of Sociology* 94, No. 1 (July) 25–52.

Harris, Stanley G., and Robert I. Sutton (1986). "Functions of Parting Ceremonies in Dying Organizations." *Academy of Management Journal*, 29, No. 1 (March), 5–30.

Hart, David K., and William G. Scott (1975). "The Organizational Imperative." *Administration and Society*, 7, No. 3 (November), 259–85.

Hasenfeld, Yeheskel (1972). "People Processing Organizations: An Exchange Approach." *American Sociological Review*, 37, No. 3 (June), 256–63.

Hawley, Amos H. (1968). "Human Ecology." In *International Encyclopedia of the Social Sciences*, ed. D. L. Sills. New York: Macmillan.

Hawley, W. E., and L. D. Rogers (1974). *Improving the Quality of Urban Management.* Beverly Hills, CA: Sage.

Hayes, Robert H., and William J. Abernathy (1980). "Managing Our Way to Economic Decline." *Harvard Business Review*, 58, No. 1 (July–August), 67–77.

Hedberg, Bo (1981). "How Organizations Learn and Unlearn." In *Handbook of Organizational Design*, Vol. 2, eds. Paul C. Nystrom and William H. Starbuck. New York: Oxford University Press.

Heilbroner, Robert (1974). "Nobody Talks About Busting General Motors in 500 Companies." *Forbes*, 113, No. 9 (May), 61.

Heise, David R. (1972). "How Do I Know My Data? Let Me Count the Ways." *Administrative Science Quarterly*, 17, No. 1 (March), 58–61.

Heller, Frank A. (1973). "Leadership Decision Making and Contingency Theory." *Industrial Relations*, 12, No. 2 (May), 183–99.

———, Pieter Drenth, Paul Coopman, and Veljko Rus (1988). *Decisions in Organizations: A Three Country Comparison*. Newbury Park, CA: Sage.

Helmich, Donald, and Warren B. Brown (1972). "Succession Type and Organizational Change in the Corporate Enterprise." *Administrative Science Quarterly*, 17, No. 3 (September), 371–81.

Heydebrand, Wolf V. (1973). *Comparative Organizations: The Results of Empirical Research*. Englewood Cliffs, NJ: Prentice Hall.

——— (1977). "Organizational Contradictions in Public Bureaucracies: Toward a Marxian Theory of Organiztions." *The Sociological Quarterly*, 18, No. 1 (Winter), 83–107.

Hicks, Alexander, Roger Friedland, and Edwin Johnson (1978). "Class Power and State Policy: The Case of Large Business Corporations, Labor Unions, and Governmental Redistribution in the American States." *American Sociological Review*, 43, No. 3 (June), 302–15.

Hickson, David J. (1987). "Decision Making at the Top of Organization." *Annual Review of Sociology*, Vol. 13, pp. 165–93. Palo Alto, CA: Annual Reviews.

———, Derek S. Pugh, and Diana C. Pheysey (1969). "Operational Technology and Organizational Structure: An Empirical Reappraisal." *Administrative Science Quarterly*, 14, No. 3 (September), 378–97.

———, C. R. Hinings, C. A. Lee, R. E. Schneck, and J. M. Pennings (1971). " A 'Strategic Contingencies' Theory of Interorganizational Power." *Administrative Science Quarterly*, 16, No. 2 (June), 216–29.

———, C. R. Hinings, C. J. McMillan, and J. P. Schwitter (1974). "The Culture Free Context of Organizational Structure: A Tri-National Comparison." *Sociology*, 8, No. 1 (January), 59–80.

———, J. Butler, D. Cray, G. R. Mallory, and D. C. Wilson (1986). *Top Decisions: Strategic Decision Making in Organizations*. San Francisco: Jossey-Bass.

Hills, Frederick S., and Thomas A. Mahoney (1978). "University Budgets and Organizational Decision Making." *Administrative Science Quarterly*, 23, No. 3 (September), 454–65.

Hilton, Gordon (1972). "Causal Inference Analysis: A Seductive Process." *Administrative Science Quarterly*, 17, No. 1 (March), 44–54.

Hinings, C. R. (1988). "Defending Organizaional Theory: A British View from North America." *Organization Studies* 9, No. 1, 2–7.

Hirsch, Paul M. (1975). "Organizational Effectiveness and the Institutional Environment." *Administrative Science Quarterly*, 20, No. 3 (September), 327–44.

Hirschhorn, Larry (1985). "On Technological Catastrophe." *Science*, 28, No. 4701 (17 May), 846–47.

Hirschman, Albert O. (1972). *Exit, Voice, and Loyalty*. Cambridge, MA: Harvard University Press.

Hochschild, Arlie Russell (1983). *The Managed Heart: Commercialization of Human Feeling*. Berkeley and Los Angeles: University of California Press.

Hofstede, Geert H. (1972). *Budget Control and the Autonomy of Organizational Units.* Proceedings of the First International Sociological Conference on Participation and Self-management, Zagreb, Yugoslavia.

Holden, Constance (1980). "Innovation—Japan Races Ahead as U.S. Falters." *Science,* 210, No. 4471 (November), 751–54.

Hollander, Edwin P., and James W. Julian (1969). "Contemporary Trends in the Analysis of Leadership Processes." *Psychological Bulletin,* 71, No. 5 (May), 387–97.

Hougland, James G., Jon M. Shepard, and James R. Wood (1979). "Discrepancies in Perceived Organizational Control: Their Decrease and Importance in Local Churches." *The Sociological Quarterly,* 20, No. 1 (Winter), 63–76.

———, and James R. Wood (1980). "Control in Organizations and Commitment of Members." *Social Forces,* 59, No. 1 (September), 85–105.

Hrebeniak, Lawrence G., and William F. Joyce (1985). "Organizational Adaptation: Strategic Choice and Environmental Determinism." *Administrative Science Quarterly,* 30 (September), 336–49.

Hsu, Cheng-Kuang, Robert M. Marsh, and Hiroshi Mannari (1983). "An Examination of the Determinants of Organizational Structure." *American Journal of Sociology,* 88, No. 5 (March), 975–96.

Inkson, J., Derek S. Pugh, and David J. Hickson (1970). "Organizational Context and Structure: An Abbreviated Replication." *Administrative Science Quarterly,* 15, No. 3 (September), 318–29.

Jackall, Robert (1988). *Moral Mazes: The World of Corporate Managers.* New York: Oxford University Press.

Jacobs, David (1974). "Dependency and Vulnerability: An Exchange Approach to the Control of Organizations." *Administrative Science Quarterly,* 19, No. 1 (March), 45–59.

——— (1987). "Business Resources and Taxation: A Cross-sectional Examination of the Relationship Between Economic Organization and Public Policy." *The Sociological Quarterly,* 28, No. 4 (Winter), 437–54.

——— (1988). "Corporate Economic Power and the State: A Longitudinal Assessment of Two Explanations." *American Journal of Sociology,* 93, No. 4 (January), 852–81.

Jackson, Susan E., and Jame E. Dutton (1988). "Discerning Threats and Opportunities." *Administrative Science Quarterly,* 33, No. 3 (September), 370–87.

James, David R., and Michael Soref (1981). "Profit Constraints on Managerial Autonomy: Managerial Theory and the Unmaking of the Corporate President." *American Sociological Review,* 46, No. 1 (February), 1–18.

Janowitz, Morris (1969). *Institution Building in Urban Education.* New York: Russell Sage Foundation.

Jenkins, J. Craig (1977). "Radical Transformation of Organizational Goals." *Administrative Science Quarterly,* 22, No. 4 (December), 568–86.

Jermier, John M., and Leslie J. Berkes (1979). "Leader Behavior in a Police Command Bureaucracy: A Closer Look at the Quasi-Military Model." *Administrative Science Quarterly,* 24, No. 1 (March), 1–23.

John, D. (1977). *Managing the Human Service System: What Have We Learned from Services Integration?* Project SHARE Monograph Series. Rockville, MD: National Institute of Mental Health.

Julian, Joseph (1966). "Compliance Patterns and Communication Blocks in Complex Organizations." *American Sociological Review,* 31, No. 3 (June), 382–89.

Jurkovich, Ray (1974). "A Core Typology of Organizational Environments." *Administrative Science Quarterly*, 19, No. 3 (September), 380–89.

Kahn, Robert L. (1977). "Organizational Effectiveness: An Overview." In *New Perspectives on Organizational Effectiveness*, eds. Paul S. Goodman and Johannes M. Pennings. San Francisco: Jossey-Bass.

———, Donald M. Wolfe, Robert P. Quinn, J. Diedrick Snoek, and Robert A. Rosenthal (1964). *Organizational Stress: Studies in Role Conflict and Ambiguity*. New York: John Wiley.

Kalleberg, Arne (1983). "Work and Stratification: Structural Perspectives." *Work and Occupations, 10, No. 3 (August), 251–59.*

———, and Ivar Berg (1987). *Work and Industry: Structures, Markets, and Processes.* New York: Plenum.

Kanter, Rosabeth Moss (1977). *Men and Women of the Corporation.* New York: Basic Books.

———, and Derick Brinkerhoff (1981). "Organizaional Performance: Recent Developments in Measurement." *Annual Review of Sociology*, 7, 321–49.

Kaplan, Abraham (1964). "Power in Perspective." In *Power and Conflict in Organizations*, eds. Robert L. Kahn and Elise Boulding. New York: Basic Books.

Kasarda, John D., and Charles E. Bidwell (1984). "A Human Ecological Theory of Organizational Structuring." In *Sociological Human Ecology: Contemporary Issues and Applications*, eds. Michael Micklin and Harvey M. Choldin. Boulder, CO: Westview Press.

Katz, Daniel (1964). "Approaches to Managing Conflict." In *Power and Conflict in Organizations*, ed. Robert L. Kahn and Elise Boulding. New York: Basic Books.

———, Barbara A. Gutek, Robert L. Kahn, and Eugenia Barton (1975). *Bureaucratic Encounters.* Ann Arbor, MI: Institute for Social Research.

———, and Robert L. Kahn (1966). *The Social Psychology of Organizations*, rev. ed. New York: John Wiley & Sons.

——— (1978). *The Sociology Psychology of Organizations*, rev. ed. New York: John Wiley & Sons.

Katz, Ralph (1982). "The Effects of Group Longevity on Project Communication and Performance." *Administrative Science Quarterly*, 27 (March), 81–104.

Kaufman, Herbert (1971). *The Limits of Organizational Change.* University: University of Alabama Press.

Keegan, Warren J. (1974). "Multinational Scanning: A Study of the Information Sources Utilized by Headquarters Ececutives in Multinational Companies." *Administrative Science Quarterly*, 19, No. 3 (September), 411–21.

Keeley, Michael (1978). "A Social Justice Approach to Organizational Evaluation." *Administrative Science Quarterly*, 23, No. 2 (June), 272–92.

——— (1984). "Impartiality and Participant-Interest Theories of Organizational Effectiveness." *Administrative Science Quarterly*, 29 (March) 1–12.

Kerbo, Harold R., and L. Richard Della Fave (1983). "Corporate Linkage and Control of the Corporate Economy: New Evidence and a Reinterpretation." *The Sociological Quarterly*, 24 (Spring), 201–18.

Khandwalla, Pradip N. (1972). "Environment and Its Impact on the Organization." *International Studies of Management and Organization*, 2, No. 3 (Fall), 297–313.

——— (1981). "Properties of Competing Organizations." In *Organizational Design*, Vol. 1, eds. Paul C. Nystrom and William H. Starbuck. New York: Oxford University Press.

Kimberly, John R. (1975). "Environmental Constraints and Organizational Structure: A Comparative Analysis of Rehabilitation Organizations." *Administrative Science Quarterly*, 20, No. 1 (March), 1–19.

———— (1976). "Organizational Size and the Structuralist Perspective: A Review Critique, and Proposal." *Administrative Science Quarterly*, 21, No. 4 (December), 577–97.

———— (1979). "Issues in the Creation of Organizations: Initiation, Innovation, and Institutionalization." *Academy of Management Journal*, 22 (September), 437–57.

———— (1980). "Initiation, Innovation, and Institutionalization in the Creation Process." In *The Organizational Life Cycle*, ed. John R. Kimberly and Robert H. Miles and Associates. San Francisco: Jossey-Bass.

———— (1981). "Managerial Innovation." In *Handbook of Organizational Design*, Vol. 1, eds. Paul C. Nystrom and William H. Starbuck. NY: Oxford University Press.

————, and Robert A. Miles and Associates (1980). *The Organizational Life Cycle*. San Francisco: Jossey-Bass.

————, and Robert E. Quinn (1984). "The Challenge of Transition Management." In *Managing Organizational Transitions*, eds. John R. Kimberly and Robert E. Quinn. Homewood, IL: Richard D. Irwin.

Klatzky, Sheila (1970a). "The Relationship of Organizational Size to Complexity and Coordination." *Administrative Science Quarterly*, 15, No. 4 (December), 428–38.

———— (1970b). "Organizational Inequality: The Case of Public Employment Agency." *American Journal of Sociology*, 76, No. 3 (November), 474–91.

Klauss, Rudi, and Bernard M. Bass (1982). *Interpersonal Communication in Organizations*. New York: Academic Press.

Klonglan, Gerald E., and Steven K. Paulson (1971). *Coordinating Health Organizations: The Problem of Cigarette Smoking*. Final report submitted to the National Clearinghouse for Smoking and Health, United States Public Health Service.

————, Richard D. Warren, Judy M. Winkelpleck, and Steven K. Paulson (1976). "Interorganizational Measurement in the Social Services Sector: Differences by Hierarchical Level." *Administrative Science Quarterly*, 21, No. 4 (December), 675–87.

Knapp, Tim (1989). "Hierarchies and Control: A New Interpretation and Reevaluation of Oliver Williamson's Markets and Hierarchies Story." *The Sociological Quarterly*, 30, No. 3, 425–40.

Knoke, David and David Prensky (1984). "What Relevance Do Organizational Theories Have for Voluntary Organizations." *Social Science Quarterly*, 65, No. 1 (March), 3–20.

Kochan, Thomas A., Larry C. Cummings, and George P. Huber (1976). "Operationalizing the Concepts of Goals and Goal Incompatibility in Organizational Behavior Research." *Human Relations*, 29, No. 6 (June), 527–44.

————, George P. Huber, and Larry C. Cummings (1975). "Determinants of Interorganizational Conflict in Collective Bargaining in the Public Sector." *Administrative Science Quarterly*, 20, No. 1 (March), 10–23.

Kohn, Melvin (1971). "Bureaucratic Man: A Portrait and Interpretation." *American Sociological Review*, 36, No. 3 (June), 461–74.

————, and Carmi Schooler (1973). "Occupational Experience and Psychological Functioning: An Assessment of Reciprocal Effects." *American Sociological Review*, 38, No. 1 (February), 97–118.

——— (1978). "The Reciprocal Effects of Substantive Complexity of Work and Intellectual Flexibility: A Longitudinal Assessment." *American Journal of Sociology*, 84, No. 1 (July), 1–23.

——— (1982). "Job Conditions and Personality: A Logitudinal Assessment of the Reciprocal Effects." *American Journal of Sociology*, 87, No. 6 (May), 1257–86.

Kornhauser, William (1963). *Scientists in Industry*. Berkeley: University of California Press.

Kralewski, John E., Laura Pitt, and Deborah Shatin (1985). "Structural Characteristics of Medical Practice Groups." *Administrative Science Quarterly*, 30, No. 1 (March), 34–45.

Kriesberg, Louis (1962). "Careers, Organizational Size and Succession." *American Journal of Sociology*, 68, No. 3 (November), 355–59.

——— (1964). "Reply." *American Journal of Sociology*, 70, No. 2 (September), 223.

Lachman,, Ran (1989). "Power from What? A Reexamination of Its Relationship with Structural Conditions." *Administrative Science Quarterly*, 34, No. 2 (June), 231–51.

Lammers, Cornelius J. (1967). "Power and Participation in Decision Making." *American Journal of Sociology*, 73, No. 2 (September), 201–16.

——— (1975). "Self-management and Participation: Two Concepts of Democratization in Organizations." *Organization and Administrative Sciences*, 5, No. 4 (Winter), 35–53.

——— (1981). "Contributions of Organizational Sociology." Part II: "Contributions to Organizational Theory and Practice—A Liberal View." *Organization Studies*, 2, No. 4, 361–76.

Langston, John (1984). "The Ecological Theory of Bureaucracy: The Case of Josiah Wedgwood and the British Pottery Industry." *Administrative Science Quarterly*, 29 (September), 330–54.

Laumann, Edward O., Joseph Galaskiewicz, and Peter Marsden (1978). "Community Structure as Interorganizational Linkage." *Annual Review of Sociology*, 4, 455–84.

———, and David Knoke (1987). *The Organizational State: Social Choice in National Policy Domains*. Madison: University of Wisconsin Press.

———, ———, and Yong-Hak Kim (1985). "An Organizational Approach to State Policy Formation: A Comparative Study of Engery and Health Domains." *American Sociological Review*, 50, No. 2 (February), 1–19.

Lawler, Edward E., and Layman W. Porter (1967). "The Effect of Performance on Job Satisfaction." *Industrial Relations*, 7, No. 1 (October), 20–28.

Lawrence, Paul R., and Jay W. Lorsch (1967). *Organization and Environment*. Cambridge, MA: Harvard University Press.

Lazarsfeld, Paul S., and Herbert Menzel (1961). "On the Relationship Between Individual and Collective Properties." In *Complex Organizations: A Sociological Reader*, ed. Amitai Etzioni. New York: Holt, Rinehart and Winston.

Lazerson, Mark H. (1988). "Organizational Growth of Small Firms: An Outcome of Markets and Hierarchies?" *American Sociological Review* 53, No. 3 (June) 330–42.

Leavitt, Harold J. (1951). "The Effects of Certain Communications Patterns on Group Performance." *Journal of Abnormal and Social Psychology*, 46, No. 1 (January), 38–50.

Leblebici, Huseyin, and Gerald Salancik (1982). "Stability in Interorganizational Exchanges: Rulemaking Processes of the Chicago Board of Trade." *Administrative Science Quarterly*, 27, (June), 227–42.

————, and ———— (1981). "Effects of Environmental Uncertainty on Information and Decision Processes in Banks." *Administrative Science Quarterly*, 26 (December), 578–96.

Lehman, Edward W. (1988). "The Theory of the State Versus the State of Theory." *American Sociological Review* 53, No. 6 (December), 807–23.

Leifer, Richard, and George P. Huber (1977). "Relations Among Perceived Environmental Uncertainty, Organizational Structure, and Boundary Spanning Behavior." *Administrative Science Quarterly*, 22, No. 2 (June), 235–47.

Levine, Adeline Gordon (1982). *Love Canal: Science, Politics, and People.* Lexington, MA: D. C. Heath.

Levine, Sol, and Paul E. White (1961). "Exchange as a Conceptual Framework for the Study of Interorganizational Relationships." *Administrative Science Quarterly*, 5, No. 1 (March), 583–610.

————, ————, and Benjamin D. Paul (1963). "Community Interorganizational Problems in Providing Medical Care and Social Services." *American Journal of Public Health*, 53, No. 8, (August), 1183–95.

Levinthal, Daniel A., and Mark Fichman (1988). "Dynamics of Interorganizational Attachments: Auditor-Client Relationships." *Administrative Science Quarterly* 33, No. 3 (September), 345–69.

Levitt, Barbara, and Clifford Nuss (1989). "The Lid on the Garbage Can: Institutional Constraints on Decision Making in the Technical Core of College-Text Publishers." *Administrative Science Quarterly*, 34, No. 2 (June), 190–207.

Lieberson, Stanley, and James F. O'Connor (1972). "Leadership and Organizational Performance: A Study of Large Corporations." *American Sociological Review*, 37, No. 2 (April), 117–30.

Lincoln, James R., and Gerald Zeitz (1980). "Organizational Properties from Aggregate Data." *American Sociological Review*, 45 (June), 391–405.

————, Mitsuyo Hanada, and Kerry McBride (1986). "Organizational Structures in Japanese and U.S. Manufacturing." *Administrative Science Quarterly*, 31, No. 3 (September), 338–64.

————, Jon Olson, and Mitsuyo Hanada (1978). "Cultural Effects on Organizational Structure: The Case of Japanese Firms in the United States." *American Sociological Review*, 43, No. 3 (December), 829–47.

Lipset, Seymour Martin (1960). *Agrarian Socialism.* Berkeley and Los Angeles: University of California Press.

————, Martin A. Trow, and James S. Coleman (1956). *Union Democracy.* New York: The Free Press.

Lipsky, Michael (1982). *Street Level Bureaucracy: Dilemmas of the Individual in Public Service.* New York: Russell Sage Foundation.

Litwak, Eugene (1961). "Models of Organizations Which Permit Conflict." *American Journal of Sociology*, 76, No. 2 (September), 177–84.

————, and Lydia Hylton (1962). "Interorganizational Analysis: A Hypothesis on Coordinating Agencies." *Administrative Science Quarterly*, 6, No. 1 (March), 395–420.

Long, J. Scott, and Robert McGinnis (1981). "Organizational Context and Scientific Productivity." *American Sociological Review*, 46, No. 4 (August), 422–42.

Lorsch, Jay W. and John J. Morse (1974). *Organizations and Their Members: A Contingency Approach.* New York: Harper and Row.

Maas, Meridean Leone (1979). "A Formal Theory of Organizational Power." Doctoral dissertation, Department of Sociology, Iowa State University, Ames.

Mahoney, Thomas A., Peter Frost, Norman F. Crandall, and William Weitzel (1972). "The Conditioning Influence of Organizational Size on Managerial Practice." *Organizational Behavior and Human Performance*, 8, No. 2 (October), 230–41.

Mahoney, Thomas A., and William Weitzel (1969). "Managerial Models of Organizational Effectiveness." *Administrative Science Quarterly*, 14, No. 3 (September), 357–65.

Manns, Curtis L, and James G. March (1978). "Financial Adversity, Internal Competition, and Curricular Change in a University." *Administrative Science Quarterly*, 23, No. 4 (December), 541–52.

Mansfield, Roger (1973). "Bureaucracy and Centralization: An Examination of Organizational Structure." *Administrative Science Quarterly*, 18, No. 4 (December), 77–88.

March, James G. (1981). "Footnotes to Organizational Change." *Administrative Science Quarterly*, 26 (December), 563–77.

———, and Herbert A. Simon (1958). *Organizations*. New York: John Wiley.

Marglin, Stephen A. (1974). "What Do Bosses Do? The Origins and Functions of Hierarchy in Capitalist Production." *The Review of Radical Political Economics*, 6, No. 2 (Summer), 60–112.

Mariolis, Peter, and Maria H. Jones (1982). "Centrality in Corporate Interlock Networks: Reliability and Stability." *Administrative Science Quarterly*, 27 (December), 571–84.

Marple, David (1982). "Technological Innovation and Organizational Survival: A Population Ecology Study of Nineteenth Century American Railroads." *The Sociological Quarterly*, 23 (Winter), 107–16.

Marrett, Cora Bagley (1971). "On the Specification of Interorganizational Dimensions." *Sociology and Social Research*, 56, No. 1 (October), 83–99.

——— (1980). "Influences on the Rise of New Organizations: The Formation of Women's Medical Societies." *Administrative Science Quarterly*, 25 (June), 185–199.

Marsh, Robert M., and Hiroshi Mannari (1980). "Technological Implications Theory: A Japanese Test." *Organization Studies*, 1, No. 2, 161–83.

———, and ——— (1981). "Technology and Size as Determinants of the Organizational Structure of Japanese Factories." *Administrative Science Quarterly*, 26, No. 1 (March), 32–57.

Martin, Patricia Yancey (1979). "Size in Residential Service Organizations." *The Sociological Quarterly*, 20, No. 4 (Autumn), 569–79.

Masuch, Michael, and Perry LaPotin (1989). "Beyond Garbage Cans: An AI Model of Organizational Choice." *Administrative Science Quarterly*, 34, No. 1 (March), 38–67.

Maurice, Marc, Francoise, Sellier, and Jean-Jacques Silvestre (1980). "The Search of a Societal Effect in the Production of Company Hierarchy: A Comparison Between France and Germany." Paper translated from *Revue Francoise de Sociologie* (June 1979).

———, Arndt Sorge, and Malcolm Warner (1980). "Societal Differences in Organizing Manufacturing Units: A Comparison of France, West Germany and Great Britain." *Organization Studies*, 1, 59–86.

McCaffrey, David P. (1982). *OSHA and the Politics of Health Regulation.* New York: Plenum.

McGuire, Jean B., Alison Sundgren, and Thomas Schneeweis (1988). "Corporate Social Responsibility and Firm Financial Performance." *Academy of Management Journal*, 31, No. 4 (December), 854–72.

McKelvey, Bill (1975). "Guidelines for the Empirical Classification of Organizations." *Administrative Science Quarterly*, 20, No. 4 (December), 509–25.

———— (1978). "Organizational Systematics: Taxonomic Lessons from Biology." *Management Science*, 24, No. 13 (September), 1428–40.

———— (1982). *Organizational Systematics: Taxonomy, Evolution, Classification.* Berkeley and Los Angeles: University of California Press.

————, and Howard Aldrich (1983). "Populations, Natural Selection, and Applied Organizational Science." *Administrative Science Quarterly*, 28 (March), 101–28.

McKinley, William (1987). "Complexity and Administrative Intensity: The Case of Declining Organizations." *Administrative Science Quarterly*, 32, No. 1 (March), 81–105.

McMillan, Charles J. (1973). "Corporations Without Citizenship: The Emergence of Multinational Enterprise." In *People and Organizations*, ed. Graeme Soloman and Kenneth Thompsons. London: Longman Group.

————, David J. Hickson, C. R. Hinings, and R. E. Schneck (1973). "The Structure of Work Organizations Across Societies." *Academy of Management Journal*, 16, No. 4 (December), 555–69.

McNeil, Kenneth (1978). "Understanding Organizational Power: Building on the Weberian Legacy." *Administrative Science Quarterly*, 23, No. 1 (March), 65–90.

————, and Richard E. Miller (1980). "The Profitability of Consumer Protection: Warranty Policy in the Auto Industry." *Administrative Science Quarterly*, 25, No. 3 (September), 407–27.

————, and Edmond Minihan (1977). "Regulation of Medical Devices and Organizational Behavior in Hospitals." *Administrative Science Quarterly*, 22, No. 3 (September), 475–90.

Mechanic, David (1962). "Sources of Power of Lower Participants in Complex Organizations." *Administrative Science Quarterly*, 7, No. 3 (December), 349–64.

Meindl, James R., Sanford B. Ehrlich, and Janet M. Dukerich (1985). "The Romance of Leadership." *Administrative Science Quarterly*, 30 (March), 78–102.

Merton, Robert K. (1957). *Social Theory and Social Structure.* Glencoe, IL: Free Press.

Metcalf, J. L. (1976). "Organizational Strategies and Interorganizational Networks." *Human Relations*, 29, No. 4 (April), 327–43.

Meyer, Alan D. (1982). "Adapting to Environmental Jolts." *Administrative Science Quarterly*, 27 (December), 515–37.

Meyer, John W., and Brian Rowan (1977). "Institutionalized Organizations: Formal Structure as Myth and Ceremony." *American Journal of Sociology*, 83, No. 2 (September), 340–63.

————, and W. Richard Scott (1983). *Organizational Environments: Ritual and Rationality.* Beverly Hills, CA: Sage.

————, ————, and David Strang (1987). "Centralization, Fragmentation, and School District Complexity." *Administrative Science Quarterly*, 32, No. 2 (June), 186–201.

Meyer, Marshall W. (1968a). "Automation and Bureaucratic Structure." *American Journal of Sociology*, 74, No. 3 (November), 256–64.

———— (1968b). "Two Authority Structures of Bureaucratic Organization." *Administrative Science Quarterly*, 13, No. 2 (September), 211–18.

———— (1971). "Some Constraints in Analyzing Data on Organizational Structures." *American Sociological Review*, 36, No. 1 (April), 294–97.

———— (1975). "Leadership and Organizational Structure." *American Journal of Sociology*, 81, No. 3 (November), 514–42.

————, and Associates (1978). *Environments and Organizations*. San Francisco: Jossey-Bass.

————, and M. Craig Brown (1977). "The Process of Bureaucratization." *American Journal of Sociology*, 83, No. 2 (September), 364–85.

————, and Lynn G. Zucker (1989). *Permanently Failing Organizations*. Newbury Park, CA: Sage.

Michels, Robert (1949). *Political Parties*. New York: Free Press.

Miles, Raymond E., Charles C. Snow, and Jeffrey Pfeffer (1974). "Organization Environment: Concepts and Issues." *Industrial Relations*, 13, No. 3 (October), 244–64.

Mileti, Dennis S., David S. Gillespie, and J. Eugene Haas (1977). "Size and Structure in Complex Organizations." *Social Forces*, 56, No. 2 (September), 208–17.

Milgrom, Paul, and John Roberts (1988). "An Economic Approach to Influence Activities in Organizations." *American Journal of Sociology*, 94, (Supplement), S154–S179.

Miller, Danny (1987). "Strategy Making on Structure: Analysis and Implications for Performance." *Academy of Management Journal*, 30, No. 1 (March), 7–32.

————, and Peter H. Friesen (1984). *Organizations: A Quantum View*. Englewood Cliffs, NJ: Prentice Hall.

————, and Cornelia Droge (1986). "Psychological and Traditional Determinants of Structure." *Administrative Science Quarterly*, 31, No. 4 (December), 539–60.

Miller, George A. (1967). "Professionals in Bureaucracy, Alienation Among Industrial Scientists and Engineers." *American Sociological Review*, 32, No. 5 (October), 755–68.

Milner, Murray, Jr. (1980). *Unequal Care: A Case Study of Interorganizational Relations in Health Care*. New York: Columbia University Press.

Miner, Anne S. (1987). "Idiosyncratic Jobs in Formalized Organizations." *Administrative Science Quarterly*, 32, No. 3 (September), 327–51.

Mintz, Beth, and Michael Schwartz (1981). "Interlocking Directorates and Interest Group Formation." *American Sociological Review*, 46 (December), 951–69.

Mintzberg, Henry (1979). *The Structuring of Organizations*. Englewood Cliffs, NJ: Prentice Hall.

———— (1983). *Power in and Around Organizations*. Englewood Cliffs, NJ: Prentice Hall.

Mitroff, Ian I., and Ralph H. Kilmann (1984). *Corporate Tragedies: Product Tampering, Sabotage, and Other Catastrophes*. New York: Praeger.

Mizruchi, Mark S. (1989). "Similarity of Political Behavior Among Large American Corporations." *American Journal of Sociology*, 95, No. 2 (September), 401–24.

————, and David Bunting (1981). "Influence in Corporate Networks: An Examination of Four Measures." *Administrative Science Quarterly*, 26 (September), 475–89.

———, and Linda Brewster Stearns (1988). "A Longitudinal Study of the Formation of Interlocking Directorates." *Administrative Science Quarterly*, 33, No. 2 (June), 194–210.

Moch, Michael K. (1976). "Structure and Organizational Resource Allocation." *Administrative Science Quarterly*, 21, No. 4 (December), 661–74.

———, and Edward V. Morse (1977). "Size, Centralization, and Organizational Adoption of Innovation." *American Sociological Review*, 43, No. 5 (October), 716–25.

Mohr, Lawrence B. (1971). "Organizational Technology and Organizational Structure." *Administrative Science Quarterly*, 16, No. 4 (December), 444–51.

——— (1973). "The Concept of Organizational Goal." *American Political Science Review*, 67, No. 2 (June), 470–81.

Molnar, Joseph. (1978). "Comparative Organizational Properties and Interorganizational Interdependence." *Sociology and Social Research*, 63, No. 1 (October), 24–48.

———, and David L. Rogers (1976). "Organizational Effectiveness: An Empirical Comparison of the Goal and System Resource Approaches." *The Sociological Quarterly*, 17, No. 3 (Summer), 401–13.

———, and ——— (1979). "A Comparative Model of Interorganizational Conflict." *Administrative Science Quarterly*, 24, No. 3 (September), 405–24.

Molotch, Harvey, and Marilyn Lester (1975). "Accidental News: The Great Oil Spill as Local Occurrence and National Event." *American Journal of Sociology*, 81, No. 2 (September), 235–60.

Moore, Gwen (1979). "The Structure of a National Elite Network." *American Sociological Review*, 44 (October), 673–92.

Morgan, Gareth (1986). *Images of Organizations*. Beverly Hills, CA: Sage.

Morris, Robin (1972). "Is the Corporate Economy a Corporate State?" *The American Economic Review*, 62, No. 1 (March), 103–19.

Morrissey, Joseph P., Richard H. Hall, and Michael L. Lindsey (1981). *Interorganizational Relations: A Sourcebook of Measures for Mental Health Programs*, Special Projects Research Unit. Albany: New York State Office of Mental Health.

Mott, Basil J. F. (1968). *Anatomy of a Coordinating Council*. Pittsburgh: University of Pittsburgh Press.

Mouzelis, Nicos P. (1967). *Organization and Bureaucracy: An Analysis of Modern Theories*. Chicago: Aldine.

Mulder, Mauk, and Henke Wilke (1970). "Participation and Power Equalization." *Organizational Behavior and Human Performance*, 5, No. 5 (September), 430–48.

Mulford, Charles L. (1980). "Dyadic Properties as Correlates of Exchange and Conflict Between Organizations." Unpublished paper, Department of Sociology, Iowa State University, Ames.

——— (1984). *Interorganizational Relations: Implications for Community Development*. New York: Human Sciences Press.

———, and Mary Ann Mulford (1980). "Interdependence and Intraorganizational Structure for Voluntary Organizations." *Journal of Voluntary Action Research*, 9, Nos. 1–4, 20–34.

———, Gerald E. Klonglan, Richard D. Warren, and Janet B. Padgitt (1976–77). "A Multidimensional Evaluation of Effectiveness in a Non-Economic Organization." *Organization and Administrative Sciences*, 7, No. 4 (Winter), 125–43.

Nagi, Saad Z. (1974). "Gate-Keeping Decisions in Service Organizations: When Validity Fails." *Human Organization*, 33, No. 1 (Spring), 47–58.

Needleman, Martin L., and Carolyn Needleman (1979). "Organizational Crime: Two Models of Criminogenesis." *The Sociological Quarterly*, 20, No. 4 (Autumn), 517–28.

Negandhi, Anant R., and Bernard C. Reimann (1972). "A Contingency Theory of Organization Re-examined in the Context of a Developing Country." *Academy of Management Journal*, 15, No. 2 (June), 137–46.

———(1973a). "Correlates of Decentralization: Closed and Open System Perspectives." *Academy of Management Journal*, 16, No. 4 (December), 570–82.

——— (1973b). "Task Environment, Decentralization and Organizational Effectiveness." *Human Relations*, 26, No. 2 (April), 203–14.

Nelson, Joel I. (1966). "Clique Contacts and Family Orientations." *American Sociological Review*, 31, No. 5 (October), 663–72.

New York Times (1981). (April 27), Section A, p. 8, Col. 3.

Nutt, Paul C. (1984). "Types of Organizational Decision Processes." *Administrative Science Quarterly*, 29, (September), 414–50.

Olsen, Johan P. (1981). "Integrated Organizational Participation in Government." In *Handbook of Organizational Design*, Vol. 1, eds. Paul C. Nystrom and William H. Starbuck. New York: Oxford University Press.

O'Reilly, Charles A., III, and Karlene H. Roberts (1974). "Information Filtration in Organizations: Three Experiments." *Organizational Behavior and Human Performance*, 11, No. 2 (April), 253–65.

Organ, Dennis W., and Charles N. Greene (1981). "The Effects of Formalization on Professional Involvement: A Compensatory Process." *Administrative Science Quarterly*, 26, No. 2 (June), 237–52.

Ornstein, Michael (1984). "Interlocking Directorates in Canada: Intercorporate or Class Alliance?" *Administrative Science Quarterly*, 29 (June), 210–37.

Ott, J. Steven (1989). *The Organizational Culture Perspective*. Chicago: Dorsey.

Ouchi, William G. (1977). "The Relationship Between Organizational Structure and Organizational Control." *Administrative Science Quarterly*, 22, No. 1 (March), 95–113.

———, and Alfred M. Jaeger (1978). "Social Structure and Organizational Type," in *Environments and Organizations*, ed. Marshall W. Meyer and Associates. San Francisco: Jossey-Bass.

———, and Jerry B. Johnson (1978). "Types of Organizational Control and Their Relation to Emotional Well-being." *Administrative Science Quarterly*, 23, No. 2 (June), 293–317.

———, and Mary Ann Maguire (1975). "Organizational Control: Two Functions." *Administrative Science Quarterly*, 20, No. 4 (December), 559–69.

Palmer, Donald, Roger Friedland, and Jitendra V. Singh (1986). "The Ties That Bind: Organizational and Class Bases of Stability in a Corporate Interlock Network." *American Sociological Review*, 51, No. 6 (December), 781–96.

———, Roger Friedland, P. Devereaux Jennings, and Melanie E. Powers (1987). "The Economics and Politics of Structure: The Multidivisional Form and the Large U.S. Corporation." *Administrative Science Quarterly*, 32, No. 1 (March), 25–48.

Parsons, Talcott (1960). *Structure and Process in Modern Society*. New York: The Free Press.

Pascale, Richard (1985). "The Paradox of 'Corporate Culture': Reconciling Ourselves to Socialization." *California Management Review*, 27, (Winter), 26–41.

Pearson, Jessica S. (1978). "Organizational Response to Occupational Injury and Disease: The Case of the Uranium Industry." *Social Forces*, 57, No. 1 (September), 23–41.

Pennings, Johannes M. (1973). "Measures of Organizational Structure: A Methodological Note." *American Journal of Sociology*, 79, No. 3 (November), 686–704.

—— (1980a). "Environmental Influences on the Creation Process." In *The Organizational Life Cycle*, eds. John R. Kimberly and Robert H. Miles and Associates. San Francisco: Jossey-Bass.

—— (1980b). *Interlocking Directorates*. San Francisco: Jossey-Bass.

—— (1982). "Organizational Birth Frequencies: An Empirical Investigation." *Administrative Science Quarterly*, 27 (March), 120–44.

——, and Paul S. Goodman (1977). "Toward a Workable Framework." In *New Perspectives on Organizational Effectiveness*, eds. S. Goodman and Johannes M. Pennings. San Francisco: Jossey-Bass.

Perrow, Charles (1961). "The Analysis of Goals in Complex Organizations." *American Sociological Review*, 26, No. 6 (December), 688–99.

—— (1967). "A Framework for the Comparative Analysis of Organizations." *American Sociological Review*, 32, No. 2 (April), 194–208.

—— (1970a). "Departmental Power and Perspective in Industrial Firms." In *Power in Organizations*, ed. Mayer N. Zald. Nashville, TN: Vanderbilt University Press.

—— (1970b). *Organizational Analysis*. Belmont, CA: Wadsworth.

—— (1977). "Three Types of Effectiveness Studies." In *New Perspectives on Organizational Effectiveness*, eds. Paul S. Goodman and Johannes M. Pennings. San Francisco: Jossey-Bass.

—— (1979). *Complex Organizations: A Critical Essay*, 2nd ed. Glenview: IL: Scott, Foresman.

—— (1983). "The Organizational Context of Human Factors Engineering." *Administrative Science Quarterly*, 28 (December), 521–41.

—— (1984). *Normal Accidents: Living with High-Risk Technologies*. New York: Basic Books.

Perrucci, Robert, and Marc Pilisuk (1970). "Leaders and Ruling Elites: The Interorganizational Bases of Community Power." *American Sociological Review*, 35, No. 6 (December), 1040–57.

Peter, Laurence J., and Raymond Hull (1969). *The Peter Principle*. New York: William Brown.

Peters, Thomas J., and Robert H. Waterman, Jr. (1982). *In Search of Excellence: Lessons from America's Best-Run Companies*. New York: Harper & Row.

Peterson, Richard A. (1970). "Some Consequences of Differentiation." In *Power in Organizations*, ed. Mayer N. Zald. Nashville, TN: Vanderbilt University Press.

—— (1981). "Entrepreneurship and Organization." In *Handbook of Organizational Design*, Vol. 1, eds. Paul C. Nystrom and William H. Starbuck. New York: Oxford University Press.

Pfeffer, Jeffrey (1972a). "Merger as a Response to Organizational Interdependence." *Administrative Science Quarterly*, 17, No. 3 (September), 328–94.

—— (1972b). "Size and Composition of Corporate Boards of Directors." *Administrative Science Quarterly*, 17, No. 2 (June), 218–28.

—— (1977). "Power and Resource Allocation in Organizations." In *New Directions in Organizational Behavior*, eds. Barry Staw and Gerald Salancik. Chicago: St. Clair Press.

———— (1978). "The Micropolitics of Organizations." In *Environments and Organizations*, eds. Marshall W. Meyer and Associates. San Francisco: Jossey-Bass.

———— (1981). *Power in Organizations*. Marshfield, MA: Pitman.

———— (1982). *Organizations and Organization Theory*. Boston: Pitman.

———— (1983). "Organizational Demograhy." In *Research in Organizational Behavior*, Vol. 5, eds. L. L. Cummings and Barry M. Staw. Greenwich, CT: JAI Press.

————, and Yinon Cohen (1984). "Determinants of Internal Labor Markets in Organizations." *Administrative Science Quarterly*, 29, No. 4 (December), 550–72.

————, and Husein Leblebici (1973). "The Effect of Competition on Some Dimensions of Organizational Structure." *Social Forces*, 52, No. 2 (December), 268–79.

————, and Anthony Long (1977). "Resource Allocation in United Funds: Examination of Power and Dependence." *Social Forces*, 55, No. 3 (March), 776–90.

————, and William L. Moore (1980). "Average Tenure of Academic Department Heads: The Effects of Paradigm, Size, and Departmental Demography." *Administrative Science Quarterly*, 25, No. 3 (September), 387–406.

————, and Phillip Nowak (1976). "Joint Ventures and Interorganizational Dependence." *Administrative Science Quarterly*, 21, No. 3 (September), 398–418.

————, and Gerald R. Salancik (1974). "Organizational Decision Making as a Political Process: The Case of a University Budget." *Administrative Science Quarterly*, 19, No. 2 (June), 135–51.

————, and Gerald R. Salancik (1978). *The External Control of Organizations: A Resource Dependence Perspective*. New York: Harper & Row.

————, Gerald R. Salancik, and Huseyin Leblebici (1978). "Uncertainty and Social Influence in Organizational Decision Making." In *Environments and Organizations*, eds. Marshall W. Meyer and Associates. San Francisco: Jossey-Bass.

————, and Alison Davis-Blake (1987). "The Effect of the Proportion of Women on Salaries: The Case of College Administrators." *Administrative Science Quarterly*, 32, No. 1 (March), 1–24.

Pinder, Craig C., and Larry F. Moore (1979). "The Resurrection of Taxonomy to Aid the Development of Middle Range Theories of Organizational Behavior." *Administrative Science Quarterly*, 24, No. 1 (March), 99–118.

Pinfield, Lawrence T. (1986). "A Field Evaluation of Perspectives on Organizational Decision Making." *Administrative Science Quarterly*, 33, No. 3 (September), 365–88.

Pondy, Louis R. (1967). "Organizational Conflict: Concepts and Models." *Administrative Science Quarterly*, 12, No. 1 (September), 296–320.

———— (1969). "Varieties of Organizational Conflict." *Administrative Science Quarterly*, 14, No. 4 (December), 499–505.

———— (1970). "Toward a Theory of Internal Resource Allocation." In *Power in Organizations*, ed. Mayer N. Zald. Nashville, TN: Vanderbilt University Press.

Powell, Walter W. (1985). *Getting into Print*. Chicago: University of Chicago Press.

Price, James L. (1968). *Organizational Effectiveness: An Inventory of Propositions*. Homewood, IL: Richard D. Irwin.

———— (1972). *Handbook of Organizational Measurement*. Lexington, MA: D. C. Heath.

————, and Charles W. Mueller (1986). *Handbook of Organizational Measurement*. Marshfield, MA: Pitman.

Priest, T. B., and Robert A. Rothman (1985). "Lawyers in Corporate Chief Executive Positions: A Historical Analysis of Careers." *Work and Occupations*, 12 (May), 131–46.

Prokesh, Steven E. (1985). *The New York Times*, CXXXV (October, 28), Section D, p. 1.

Provan, Keith G., Janice M. Beyer, and Carlos Kruytbosch (1980). "Environmental Linkages and Power in Resource-Dependence Relations Between Organizations." *Administrative Science Quarterly*. 25, No. 2 (June), 200–25.

Pugh, Derek S. (1966). "Modern Organization Theory: A Psychological and Sociological Study." *Psychological Bulletin*, 66, No. 21 (October), 235–51.

―――― (1969). "The Context of Organizational Structures." *Administrative Science Quarterly*, 14, No. 1 (March), 91–114.

――――, David J. Hickson, and C. R. Hinings (1969). "An Empirical Taxonomy of Work Organizations." *Administrative Science Quarterly*, 14, No. 1 (March), 115–26.

――――, David J. Hickson, and C. R. Hinings, eds. (1985). *Writers on Organizations*. Beverly Hills, CA: Sage.

――――, D. J. Hickson, C. R. Hinings, and C. Turner (1968). "Dimensions of Organizational Structure." *Administrative Science Quarterly*, 13, No. 1 (June), 65–105.

――――, David J. Hickson, C. R. Hinings, K. M. Lupton, K. M. McDonald, C. Turner, and T. Lupton (1963). "A Conceptual Scheme for Organizational Analysis." *Administrative Science Quarterly*, 8, No. 3 (December), 289–315.

Quinn, Robert E. (1977). "Coping with Cupid: The Formation, Impact, and Management of Romantic Relationships in Organizations." *Administrative Science Quarterly*, 22, No. 1 (March), 30–45.

――――, and John Rohrbaugh (1983). "A Spatial Model of Effectiveness Criteria: Towards a Competing Values Approach to Organizational Analysis." *Management Science*, 29, (March), 363–77.

Raelin, Joseph A. (1982). "A Policy Output Model of Interorganizational Relations." *Organization Studies*, 3, 243–67.

Rahim, M. Afzahur (1986). *Managing Conflict in Organizations*. New York: Praeger.

―――― (1989). *Managing Conflict: An Interdisciplinary Approach*. New York: Praeger.

Ranson, Stewart, Bob Hinings, and Royster Greenwood (1980). "The Structuring of Organizational Structures." *Administrative Science Quarterly*, 25, No. 2 (March), 1–17.

Raphael, Edna (1967). "The Anderson Wharton Hypothesis in Local Unions: A Comparative Study." *American Sociological Review*, 32, No. 5 (October), 768–86.

Rawls, J. (1971). *A Theory of Justice*. Cambridge, MA: Harvard University Press.

Reid, William J. (1969). "Inter-organizational Coordination in Social Welfare: A Theoretical Approach to Analysis and Intervention." In *Readings in Community Organization Practice*, eds. Ralph M. Kramer and Henry Spect. Englewood Cliffs, NJ: Prentice Hall.

Reimann, Bernard C. (1975). "Organizational Effectiveness and Management's Public Values: A Canonical Analysis." *Academy of Management Journal*, 18, No. 2 (June), 224–41.

Reinganum, Marc R. (1985). "The Effect of Executive Succession on Stockholder Wealth." *Administrative Science Quarterly*, 30 (March), 46–60.

Reve, Torger, and Louis W. Stern (1979). "Interorganizational Relations in Marketing Channels." *Academy of Management Review*, 4, No. 3 (July), 405–16.

Richardson, R. Jack (1987). "Directorship Interlocks and Corporate Profitability." *Administrative Science Quarterly*, 32, No. 3 (September), 367–86.

Ritzer, George (1989). "The Permanently New Economy: The Case for Reviving Economic Sociology." *Work and Occupations*, 16, No. 3 (August), 243–72.

———, and David Walczak (1986). *Working: Conflict and Change*. Englewood Cliffs, NJ: Prentice Hall.

Robbins, Stephen P. (1974). *Managing Organizational Conflict: A Nontraditional Approach*. Englewood Cliffs, NJ: Prentice Hall.

Roberts, Karlene H., Charles L. Hulin, and Denise M. Rousseau (1978). *Developing an Interdisciplinary Science of Organizations*. San Francisco: Jossey-Bass.

Robins, James A. (1987). "Organizational Economics: Notes on the Transaction Cost Theory in the Study of Organizations." *Administrative Science Quarterly*, 32, No. 1 (March), 68–86.

Rogers, David L. (1974). "Toward a Scale of Interorganizational Relations Among Public Agencies." *Sociology and Social Research*, 59, No. 1 (October), 61–70.

Rohrbaugh, John (1983). "The Competing Values Approach: Innovation and Effectiveness in the Job Service." In *Organizational Theory and Public Policy*, eds. Richard H. Hall and Robert E. Quinn. Beverly Hills, CA: Sage.

Romanelli, Elaine (1989). "Environments and Strategies of Organization Startup: Effects on Early Survival." *Administrative Science Quarterly*, 34, No. 3 (September), 369–87.

Rosenbaum, James E. (1979). "Organizational Career Mobility: Promotion Chances in a Corporation During Periods of Growth and Contraction." *American Journal of Sociology*, 85, No. 1 (July), 21–48.

Rosner, M., B. Kovacic, A. S. Tannenbaum, M. Vianello, and G. Weiser (1973). "Worker Participation and Influence in Five Countries." *Industrial Relations*, 12, No. 2 (May), 200–12.

Rosow, Jerome M., ed. (1974). *The Worker and the Job: Coping with Change*. Englewood Cliffs, NJ: Prentice Hall.

Rothschild, Joyce, and J. Allen Whitt (1986). The Cooperative Workplace: Potentials and Dilemmas of Organizational Democracy and Participation. New York: Cambridge University Press.

Rothschild-Whitt, Joyce (1979). "The Collectivist Organization: An Alternative to Rational Bureaucratic Models." *American Sociological Review*, 44, No. 4 (August), 519.

Roy, William G. (1981). "The Process of Bureaucratization of the U. S. State Department and the Vesting of Economic Interests, 1886–1905." *Administrative Science Quarterly*, 26, No. 3 (September), 419–33.

——— (1983a). "Toward Clearer Thinking: A Reply." *Administrative Science Quarterly*, 28, No. 1 (March), 61–64.

——— (1983b). "The Unfolding of the Interlocking Directorate Structure of the United States." *American Sociological Review*, 48 (April), 248–57.

Rowan, Brian (1982). "Organizational Structure and the Institutional Environment: The Case of Public Schools." *Administrative Science Quarterly*, 27 (June), 259–79.

Rubin, I. (1979). "Loose Structure, Retrenchment and Adaptability in the University." Paper presented at the Midwest Sociological Society meetings, Minneapolis.

Rus, Veljko (1972). "The Limits of Organized Participation." In *Proceedings of the First International Conference on Participation and Self-management*, Vol 2. Zagreb, Yugoslavia.

———— (1980). "Positive and Negative Power: Thoughts on the Dialectic of Power." *Organization Studies*, 1, 3–19.

Rushing, William A. (1968). "Hardness of Material as Related to Division of Labor in Manufacturing Industries." *Administrative Science Quarterly*, 13, No. 2 (September), 224–45.

Sabel, Charles F. (1982). *Work and Politics*. New York: Cambridge University Press.

Salancik, Gerald R., and James R. Mindl (1984). "Corporate Attributions as Strategic Illusions of Management Control." *Administrative Science Quarterly*, 29 (June), 238–54.

————, and Jeffrey Pfeffer (1977). "Constraints on Administrator Discretion: The Limited Influence of Mayors on City Budgets." *Urban Affairs Quarterly*, 12, No. 4 (June), 475–98.

————, and ———— (1974). "The Bases and Use of Power in Organizational Decision Making: The Case of a University." *Administrative Science Quarterly*, 19, No. 4 (December), 453–73.

Samuel, Yitzhak (1979). "An Exchange and Power Approach to the Concept of Organizational Effectiveness." Department of Sociology and Anthropology, Tel Aviv University, Israel.

Sanford, R. Nevitt (1964). "Individual Conflict and Organizational Interaction." In *Power and Conflict in Organizations*, eds. Robert L. Kahn and Elise Boulding. New York: Basic Books.

Scheff, Thomas J. (1961). "Control over Policy by Attendants in a Mental Hospital." *Journal of Health and Human Behavior*, 2, No. 2 (Summer), 93–105.

Schermerhorn, John R., Jr. (1975). "Determinants of Interorganizational Cooperation." *Academy of Management Journal*, 18, No. 4 (December), 846–56.

Schmidt, Stuart M., and Thomas A. Kochan (1972). "Conflict: Toward Conceptual Clarity." *Administrative Science Quarterly*, 17, No. 3 (September), 371–81.

————, and ———— (1977). "Interorganizational Relationships: Patterns and Motivations." *Administrative Science Quarterly*, 22, No. 2 (June), 220–34.

Schneider, Susan C. (1989). "Strategy Formulation: The Impact of National Culture." *Organization Studies*, 10, No. 2, 149–68.

Schollhammer, Hans (1971). "Organization Structures of Multinational Corporations." *Academy of Management Journal*, 14, No. 3 (September), 345–65.

Schoonhoven, Claudia Bird (1981). "Problems with Contingency Theory: Testing Assumptions Hidden Within the Language of Contingency 'Theory.'" *Administrative Science Quarterly*, 26 (September), 349–77.

Schreyögg, Georg (1980). "Contingency and Choice in Organization Theory." *Organization Studies*, 1, No. 4, 305–26.

Schwochan, Susan, Peter Fenilee, and John Thomas Delaney (1988). "The Resource Allocation Effects of Mandated Relationships." *Administrative Science Quarterly*, 33, No. 3 (September), 418–37.

Scott, W. Richard (1964). "Theory of Organizations." In *Handbook of Modern Sociology*, ed. Robert E. L. Farris. Chicago: Rand McNally.

⸺ (1977). "Effectiveness of Organizational Effectiveness Studies." In *New Perspectives on Organizational Effectiveness*, eds. Paul S. Goodman and Johannes M. Pennings. San Francisco: Jossey-Bass.

⸺ (1981). *Organizations: Rational, Natural, and Open Systems*. Englewood Cliffs, NJ: Prentice Hall.

⸺ (1983). "Introduction: From Technology to Environment." In *Organizational Environments: Ritual and Rationality*, eds. John W. Meyer and W. Richard Scott. Beverly Hills, CA: Sage.

⸺ (1987a). *Organizations: Rational, Natural, and Open Systems*, 2nd ed. Englewood Cliffs, NJ: Prentice Hall.

⸺ (1987b). "The Adolescence of Institutional Theory." *Administrative Science Quarterly*, 32, No. 4 (December), 493–511.

⸺, and Bruce L. Black, eds. (1986). *The Organization of Mental Health Services: Societal and Community Systems*. Beverly Hills, CA: Sage.

Seashore, Stanley E. (1977). "An Elastic and Expandable Viewpoint." In *New Perspectives on Organizational Effectiveness*, eds. Paul S. Goodman and J. M. Pennings. San Francisco: Jossey-Bass.

⸺, and Ephraim Yuchtman (1967). "Factorial Analysis of Organizational Performance." *Administrative Science Quarterly*, 12, No. 3 (December), 377–95.

Sebring, Robert H. (1977). "Health Councils as a Strategy for Community Change." *Journal of the Community Development Society*, 18, No. 1 (Spring), 74–85.

Seiler, Lauren H., and Gene F. Summers (1979). "Corporate Involvement in Community Affairs." *The Sociological Quarterly*, No. 3 (Summer), 375–86.

Selznick, Philip (1957). *Leadership in Administration*. New York: Harper & Row.

⸺ (1960). *The Organizational Weapon*. New York: The Free Press.

⸺ (1966). *TVA and the Grass Roots*, Harper Torchbook, ed. New York: Harper & Row.

Shenkar, Oded (1984). "Is Bureaucracy Inevitable: The Chinese Experience." *Organizational Studies*, 5, No. 4, 289–308.

Shrum, Wesley, and Robert Wuthnow (1988). "Reputational Status of Organizations in Technical Systems." *American Journal of Sociology*, 93, No. 4 (January), 882–912.

Sills, David L. (1957). *The Volunteers*. New York: Free Press.

Silverman, David (1957). *Models of Men, Social and Rational*. New York: John Wiley.

⸺ (1971). *The Theory of Organizations: A Sociological Framework*. New York: Basic Books.

Simmel, George (1902). "The Number of Members as Determining the Sociological Form of the Group II." *American Journal of Sociology*, 8, No. 2 (September), 158–96.

Simon, Herbert (1957). *Administrative Behavior*. New York: The Free Press.

Simon, Herbert A. (1964). "On the Concept of Organizational Goal." *Administrative Science Quarterly*, 9, No. 1 (June), 1–22.

Simpson, Richard L. (1969). "Vertical and Horizontal Communication in Formal Organizations." *Administrative Science Quarterly*, 14, No. 3 (September), 188–96.

Singh, Jitendra V., David J. Tucker, and Robert J. House (1986). "Organizational Legitimacy and the Liability of Newness." *Administrative Science Quarterly*, 31, No. 2 (June), 171–93.

Smith, Kenwyn (1989). "The Movement of Conflict in Organizations: The Joint Dynamics of Splitting and Triangulation." *Administrative Science Quarterly*, 34 (March), 1–20.

Smith, Mark, and Michael C. White (1987). "Strategy, CEO Specialization and Succession." *Administrative Science Quarterly*, 32, No. 2 (June), 263–80.

Snow, Charles C., and Lawrence G. Hrebiniak (1980). "Strategy, Distinctive Competence and Organizational Performance." *Administrative Science Quarterly*, 25, No. 2 (June), 317–36.

Spenner, Kenneth (1979). "Temporal Changes in Work Content." *American Sociological Review*, 44 (December), 965–75.

———— (1983). "Deciphering Prometheus: Temporal Changes in the Skill Level of Work." *American Sociological Review*, 48, (December), 824–37.

Staber, Udo, and Howard Aldrich (1983). "Trade Association Stability and Public Policy." In *Organizational Theory and Public Policy*, eds. Richard H. Hall and Robert E. Quinn. Beverly Hills, CA: Sage.

Starbuck, William H. (1976). "Organizations and Their Environments." In *Handbook of Industrial and Organizational Psychology*, ed. Marvin D. Dunnette. Chicago: Rand McNally.

———— (1983). "Organizations as Action Generators." *American Sociological Review*, 48, (February), 91–102.

————, and Paul C. Nystrom (1981). "Designing and Understanding Organizations." In *Handbook of Organizational Design*, Vol. 1, eds. Paul C. Nystrom and William H. Starbuck. New York: Oxford University Press.

Staw, Barry M. (1982). "Counterforces to Change." In *Change in Organizations: New Perspectives on Theory, Research, and Practice*, eds. Paul S. Goodman and Associates. San Francisco: Jossey-Bass.

————, and Eugene Szwajkowski (1975). "The Scarcity-Munificence Component of Organizational Environments and the Commission of Illegal Acts." *Administrative Science Quarterly*, 20, No. 3 (September), 345–54.

————, Lance E. Sandelands, and Jane E. Dutton (1981). "Threat-Rigidity Effects in Organizational Behavior: A Multilevel Approach." *Administrative Science Quarterly* 26 (December), 501–24.

————, Pamela I. McKechnie, and Sheila M. Puffer (1983). "The Justification of Organizational Performance." *Administrative Science Quarterly*, 28 (December), 582–600.

————, and Jerry Ross (1989). "Understanding Behavior in Escalation Situations." *Science*, 246, (13 October), 216–20.

Stearns, Linda Brewster, and Mark S. Mizruchi (1986). "Broken-Tie Reconstitution and the Functions of Interorganizational Interlocks: A Reexamination." *Administrative Science Quarterly*, 31, No. 4 (December), 522–38.

Stearns, Timothy M., Alan N. Hoffman, and Jan B. Heide (1987). "Performance of Commercial Television Stations as an Outcome of Interorganizational Linkages and Environmental Conditions." *Academy of Management Journal*, 30, No. 1 (March), 71–90.

Steckmest, Francis W. (1982). *Corporate Performance: The Key to Public Trust*. New York: McGraw-Hill.

Steers, R. M. (1977). *Organizational Effectiveness: A Behavioral View*. Pacific Palisades, CA: Goodyear.

Stern, Robert N. (1981). "Competitive Influences on the Interorganizational Regulation of College Athletics." *Administrative Science Quarterly*, 26, No. 1 (March), 15–32.

Stewman, Shelby (1986). "Demographic Models of Internal Labor Markets." *Administrative Science Quarterly*, 31, No. 2 (June), 212–47.

Stinchcombe, Arthur L. (1959). "Bureaucratic and Craft Administration of Productions." *Administrative Science Quarterly*, 4, No. 2 (September), 168–87.

——— (1965). "Organizations and Social Structure." In *Handbook of Organizations*, ed. James G. March. Chicago: Rand McNally.

Stipak, B. (1979). "Citizen Satisfaction with Urban Services: Potential Misuse as a Performance Indicator." *Public Administration Review*, 39, No. 1 (January), 46–52.

Stogdill, Ralph (1974). *Handbook of Leadership: A Survey of Theory and Research*. New York: The Free Press.

Stolzenberg, Ross M. (1978). "Bringing the Boss Back in: Employer Size, Employee Schooling and Socioeconomic Achievement." *American Sociological Review*, 43, No. 6 (December), 813–28.

Stone, Katherine (1973). "The Origins of Job Structures in the Steel Industry." *Radical America*, 7, 17–66.

Sutherland, Edwin H. (1940). "White-Collar Criminality." *American Sociological Review*, 5 (February), 1–12.

——— (1949). *White Collar Crime*. New York: Holt, Rinehart and Winston.

Sutton, Robert I. (1987). "The Process of Organizational Death: Disbanding and Reconnecting." *Administrative Science Quarterly*, 32, No. 4 (December), 542–69.

Swigert, Victoria Lynn, and Ronald A. Farrell (1980–81). "Corporate Homicide: Definitional Processes in the Creation of Deviance." *Law and Society Review*, 15, No. 1 (Fall), 163–82.

Tannenbaum, Arnold S. (1968). *Control in Organizations*. New York: McGraw-Hill.

———, Bogdan Kovacic, Menochen Rosner, Mino Vianello, and George Wieser (1974). *Hierarchy in Organizations*. San Francisco: Jossey-Bass.

———, and Tamas Rozgonyi (1986). *Authority and Reward in Organizations: An International Research*. Ann Arbor, MI: Survey Research Center.

Taylor, Frederick W. (1911). *The Principles of Scientific Management*. New York: Harper & Row.

Taylor, James C. (1971). "Some Effects of Technology in Organizational Change." *Human Relations*, 24, No. 2 (April), 105–23.

Terkel, Studs (1974). *Working*. New York: Pantheon Books.

Terreberry, Shirley (1968). "The Evolution of Organizational Environments." *Administrative Science Quarterly*, 12, No. 4 (March), 590–613.

Thomas, Alan Berkeley (1988). "Does Leadership Make a Difference to Organizational Performance?" *Administrative Science Quarterly*, 33, No. 3 (September), 388–400.

Thompson, James D. (1967). *Organizations in Action*. New York: McGraw-Hill.

———, and William McEwen (1958). "Organizational Goals and Environment: Goalsetting as an Interaction Process." *American Sociological Review*, 23, No. 1 (February), 23–31.

Thompson, Victor (1961). *Modern Organizations*. New York: Alfred A. Knopf.

Tolbert, Pamela S. (1985). "Institutional Environments and Resource Dependence: Sources of Administrative Structure in Institutions of Higher Education." *Administrative Science Quarterly*, 30 (March), 1–13.

———, and Lynne G. Zucker (1983). "Institutional Sources of Change in the Formal Structure of Organizations: The Diffusion of Civil Service Reforms, 1880–1935." *Administrative Science Quarterly*, 28 (March), 22–39.

Tosi, Henry L., Jr., and John W. Slocum, Jr. (1984). "Contingency Theory: Some Suggested Directions." *Journal of Management*, 10 (Spring), 9–26.

Toynbee, Arnold (1974). "As I See It." *Forbes*, 113, No. 7 (April), 68.

Tracy, Philips, and Koya Azumi (1976). "Determinants of Administrative Control: A Test of a Theory with Japanese Factories." *American Sociological Review*, 41, No. 1 (February), 80–94.

Turk, Herman (1973). "Comparative Urban Structure from an Interorganizational Perspective." *Administrative Science Quarterly*, 18, No. 1 (March), 37–55.

Turner, Jonathan H. (1979). *The Structure of Social Theory*, rev. ed. Homewood, IL: Dorsey.

———, and Alexandra Maryanski (1979). *Functionalism*. Menlo Park, CA: Benjamin/Cumming.

Tushman, Michael L., and Phillip Anderson (1986). "Technological Discontinuities and Organizational Environments." *Administrative Science Quarterly*, 31, No. 3 (September), 439–65.

Useem, Michael (1979). "The Social Organization of the American Business Elite and Participation of Corporate Directors in the Governance of American Institutions." *American Sociological Review*, 44, No. 4 (August), 553–72.

——— (1982). "Classwide Rationality in the Politics of Managers and Directors of Large Corporations in the United States and Great Britain." *Administrative Science Quarterly*, 27 (June), 199–226.

——— (1984). *The Inner Circle*. New York: Oxford University Press.

Van De Ven, Andrew H. (1979). "Howard E. Aldrich: Organizations and Environments." *Administrative Science Quarterly*, 24, No. 2 (June), 320–26.

——— (1983). "Review of Thomas B. Peters and Robert H. Waterman, Jr., *In Search of Excellence: Lessons from America's Best-Run Companies*" (New York: Harper & Row 1982), in *Administrative Science Quarterly*, 28, No. 4 (December), 621–22.

———, and Andre L. Delbecq, and Richard Koenig, Jr. (1976). "Determinants of Coordination Modes Within Organizations." *American Sociological Review*, 41, No. 2 (April), 322–38.

———, and Diane L. Ferry (1980). *Measuring and Assessing Organizations*. New York: John Wiley.

———, and Gordon Walker (1984). "The Dynamics of Interorganizational Coordination." *Administrative Science Quarterly*, 29, No. 4 (December), 598–621.

Van Houten, Donald R. (1987). "The Political Economy and Technical Control of Work Humanization in Sweden During the 1970s and 1980s." *Work and Occupations*, 14, No. 4 (November), 483–513.

Vaughan, Diane (1983). *Controlling Unlawful Organizational Behavior: Social Structure and Corporate Misconduct*. Chicago: University of Chicago Press.

Waegel, William B., M. David Ermann, and Alan M. Horowitz (1981). "Organizational Responses to Imputations of Deviance." *The Sociological Quarterly*, 22, No. 1 (Winter), 43–55.

Wager, L. Wesley (1972). "Organizational 'Linking-Pins': Hierarchical Status and Communicative Roles in Interlevel Conferences." *Human Relations*, 25, No. 4 (September), 307–26.

Walsh, Kieron, Bob Hinings, Royster Greenwood, and Stewart Ransom (1981). "Power and Advantage in Organizations." *Organization Studies*, 2, 131–52.

Wamsley, Garry L. (1970). "Power and the Crisis of the Universities." In *Power in Organizations*, ed. Mayer N. Zald. Nashville: University of Tennessee Press.

———, and Mayer N. Zald (1973). *The Political Economy of Public Organizations*. Lexington, MA: D. C. Heath.

Warren, Roland (1967). "The Interorganizational Field as a Focus for Investigation." *Administrative Science Quarterly*, 12, No. 3 (December), 396–419.

———, Stephen Rose, and Ann Bergunder (1974). *The Structure of Urban Reform*. Lexington, MA: D. C. Heath.

Warriner, Charles K. (1956). "Groups Are Real: A Reaffirmation." *American Sociological Review*, 21, No. 9 (October), 549–54.

——— (1979). "Empirical Taxonomics of Organizations: Problematics in Their Development." Lawrence: University of Kansas.

——— (1980). "Organizational Types: Notes on the 'Organizational Species' Concept." Lawrence: Department of Sociology, University of Kansas.

———, Richard H. Hall, and Bill McKelvey (1981). "The Comparative Description of Organizations: A Research Note and Invitation." *Organizational Studies*, 2, No. 2 (April).

Waters, Malcom (1989). "Collegiality, Bureaucratization, and Professionalization: a Weberian Analysis." *American Journal of Sociology*, 94, No. 5 (March), 945–72.

Weber, Max (1947). *The Theory of Social and Economic Organization*, trans. A. M. Parsons and T. Parsons. New York: The Free Press.

——— (1952). *The Protestant Ethic and the Spirit of Capitalism*. New York: Scribners.

——— (1968). *Economy and Society: An Outline of Interpretive Sociology*. New York: Bedminster.

Weick, Karl (1976). "Educational Organizations as Loosely Coupled Systems." *Administrative Science Quarterly*, 21, No. 1 (March), 1–19.

——— (1979). *The Social Psychology of Organizing*, 2nd ed. Reading, MA: Addison-Wesley.

Weiner, Nan (1977). "Situational and Leadership Influence on Organizational Performance." Columbus: College of Administrative Science, The Ohio State University.

Weisbrod, Burton A. (1989). "Rewarding Performance That Is Hard to Measure: The Private Nonprofit Sector." *Science*, 244 (May), 541–46.

Weitzel, William, and Ellen Jonsson (1989). "Decline in Organizations: A Literature Integration and Extension." *Administrative Science Quarterly*, 34, No. 1 (March), 91–109.

Weldon, Peter D. (1972). "An Examination of the Blau-Scott and Etzioni Typologies: A Critique." *Administrative Science Quarterly*, 17, No. 1 (March), 76–78.

Whetten, David A. (1978). "Coping with Incompatible Expectations: An Integrated View of Role Conflict." *Administrative Science Quarterly*, 23, No. 2 (June), 254–71.

——— (1980). "Sources, Responses and Effects of Organizational Decline." In *The Organizational Life Cycle*, eds. John R. Kimberly and Robert H. Miles and Associates. San Francisco: Jossey-Bass.

White, Harrison (1971). *System Models of Mobility in Organizations*. Cambridge, MA: Harvard University Press.

Wiewel, Wim, and Albert Hunter (1985). "The Interorganizational Network as a Resource: A Comparative Case Study on Organizational Genesis." *Administrative Science Quarterly*, 30, No. 4 (December), 482–96.

Wildavsky, Aaron (1964). *The Politics of the Budgetary Process*. Boston: Little, Brown.

Wilensky, Harold (1967). *Organizational Intelligence: Knowledge and Policy in Government and Industry*. New York: Basic Books.

Williamson, Oliver E. (1975). *Markets and Hierarchies: Analysis and Antitrust Implications*. New York: Free Press.

———— (1981). "The Economics of Organizations: The Transaction Cost Approach." *American Journal of Sociology*, 87 (November), 548–77.

———— (1985). *The Economic Institutions of Capitalism*. New York: The Free Press.

————, and William G. Ouichi (1981). "The Markets and Hierarchies Program of Research: Origins, Implications, Prospects." In *Perspectives on Organizational Design and Behavior*, eds. Andrew H. Van de Ven and William E. Joyce. New York: Wiley-Interscience.

Withey, Michael, and William H. Cooper (1989). "Predicting Exit, Voice, Loyalty, and Neglect." *Administrative Science Quarterly*, 34, No. 4 (December), 521–39.

Wood, James R. (1975). "Legitimate Control and Organizational Transcendance." *Social Forces*, 54, No. 1 (September), 199–211.

———— (1981). *Leadership in Voluntary Organizations: The Controversy over Social Action in Protestant Churches*. New Brunswick, NJ: Rutgers University Press.

Woodward, Joan (1958). *Management and Technology*. London: Her Majesty's Stationery Office.

———— (1965). *Industrial Organizations: Theory and Practice*. London: Oxford University Press.

Work in America (1973). Prepared under auspices of W. E. Upjohn Institute, Cambridge, MA: MIT Press.

Wright, Eric Olin (1978). *Class, Crisis, and the State*. London: New Left Books.

———— (1979). *Class Structure and Income Determination*. New York: Academic Press.

Yarmolinsky, Adam (1975). "Institutional Paralysis." *Daedalus*, 104, No. 1 (Winter), 61–67.

Yeager, Peter C. (1982). "Review to Francis W. Steckmest, *Corporate Performance: The Key to Public Trust*" (New York: McGraw-Hill), *Contemporary Sociology*, 11, No. 6 (November), 747–48.

Young, Ruth C. (1988). "Is Population Ecology a Useful Paradigm for the Study of Organizations?" *American Journal of Sociology*, 94, No. 1 (July), 1–24.

———— (1989). "Reply to Freeman and Hannan and Brittain and Wholey." *American Journal of Sociology*, 95, No. 2 (September), 445–46.

Yuchtman, Ephraim, and Stanley Seashore (1967). "A System Resource Approach to Organizational Effectiveness." *American Sociological Review*, 32, No. 6 (December), 891–903.

Yukl, Gary A. (1981). *Leadership in Organizations*. Englewood Cliffs, NJ: Prentice Hall.

———— (1989). *Leadership in Organizations*, 2nd ed. Englewood Cliffs, NJ: Prentice Hall.

Zald, Mayer N. (1969). "The Structure of Society and Social Service Integration." *Social Science Quarterly*, 50, No. 3 (December), 567–77.

———— ed. (1970). *Organizational Change: The Political Economy of the YMCA*. Chicago: University of Chicago Press.

Zalkind, Sheldon, and Timothy W. Costello (1962). "Perceptions: Some Recent Research and Implications for Administration." *Administrative Science Quarterly*, 7, No. 2 (September), 218–35.

Zaltman, Gerald, Robert Duncan, and Jonny Holbek (1973). *Innovations and Organizations.* New York: Wiley-Interscience.

Zammuto, Raymond F. (1982). *Assessing Organizational Effectiveness.* Albany: State University of New York Press.

Zeitlin, Maurice (1974). "Corporate Ownership and Control: The Large Corporation and the Capitalist Class." *American Journal of Sociology*, 79, No. 5 (March), 1073–119.

———— (1976). "In Class Theory of the Large Corporation: Response to Others." *American Journal of Sociology*, 81, No. 4 (January), 894–903.

Zeitz, Gerald (1980). "Interorganizational Dialectics." *Administrative Science Quarterly*, 25, No. 1 (March), 72–78.

———— (1983). "Structural and Individual Determinants of Organizational Morale and Satisfaction." *Social Forces*, 61, No. 4 (June), 1088–1108.

———— (1984). "Bureaucratic Role Characteristics and Member Affective Response in Organizations." *The Sociological Quarterly*, 25, No. 3 (Summer), 301–18.

Zucker, Lynne G. (1977). "The Role of Institutionalization in Cultural Persistence." *American Sociological Review*, 42 (October), 726–43.

———— ed. (1988). *Institutional Patterns and Organizations: Culture and Environment.* Cambridge, MA: Ballinger.

Zwerman, William L. (1970). *New Perspectives on Organization Theory.* Westport, CT: Greenwood.

INDEX

Author index

Abbott, A., **16**
Abernathy, W.J., 27
Adams, C.R., 232
Aiken, M., 53, 60–62, 64, 65, 66, 67, 71, 77, 78, 92, 128, 173, 196, 224, 232, 236, 237
Alba, R.D., 180, 235
Aldrich, H.E., 12, 79, 89, 90, 122, 128, 131, 164, 187, 188, 189, 210, 216, 217, 223, 224, 226, 229, 231, 232, 233, 234, 235, 237, 240, 270, 273, 274–75, 277, 278, 279, 281, 291
Alexander, E.R., 159, 161
Alexander, G.J., 265
Allen, M.P., 112, 147, 149, 151, 279
Altheide, D.L., 13, 271
Alutto, J., 160
Alvarez, R., 10
Anderson, P.A., 159, 188
Angle, H.L., 260
Antonio, R.J., 11–12
Argote, L., 60
Argranoff, R., 227
Argyris, C., 89, 93, 115
Aronowitz, S., 3
Asher, H., 120
Assael, H., 236
Astley, W.G., 274, 277
Athanassaides, J.C., 168
Attewell, P., 104
Azumi, K., 50

Bacharach, P., **161**
Bacharach, S.B., 82, 110, 111–12, 112–13, 116, 160
Baldridge, J.V., 61, 196
Bales, R.F., 137
Baratz, M.S., 161
Barnard, C.I., 29, 164, 258
Baron, J.N., 9, 44, 62, 104, 132
Barton, A.H., 36
Barton, E., 8, 9
Bass, B.M., 151, 165
Baty, G., 235
Bauer, D., 148, 241
Bavelas, A., 176
Beard, D.W., 212
Becker, S.W., 145, 197, 271, 283
Belasco, J.A., 160
Bennis, W., 140
Benson, J.K., 32, 33, 68, 183, 226, 229, 231, 245, 246, 269, 277

Berg, I., 34
Berger, P., 289
Bergunder, A., 217, 236, 237, 238
Berkes, L.J., 141
Berle, A.A., 12, 151
Bettman, J.R., 256–57
Beyer, J.M., 94, 160, 213, 221, 241
Bidwell, C.E., 187, 188, 274
Bielby, W.T., 9, 44, 62
Bielefeld, W., 241, 242
Bierstedt, R., 109
Biggart, N.W., 99, 106, 111, 186, 291
Bills, D., 62, 104
Birnbaum, P.H., 99
Blake, R.R., 237
Blau, J.R., 37, 94, 180
Blau, P.M., 30, 33, 40, 49, 53, 60, 65–66, 70, 72, 74, 76, 83, 85, 88, 94, 109, 126, 172–73, 177, 235, 251, 264
Blauner, R., 90
Boddewyn, J., 214
Boeker, W., 120
Boisot, M., 286
Boje, D.M., 50, 65, 225, 226, 227, 231, 235
Boulding, K.E., 129–30
Bozeman, B., 43
Bradshaw, P.J., 95
Brass, D.J., 76
Braverman, H., 103
Brewer, J., 173
Brinkerhoff, D., 253
Brinkerhoff, M.B., 172
Broskowski, A., 227
Brown, J.L., 97
Brown, M.C., 68, 97, 147, 148, 203
Brown, R.H., 27
Brown, W.B., 149
Bucher, R., 110
Buchholz, R.A., 265
Bunting, D., 240
Burke, J.P., 27
Burke, R.J., 237
Burnham, R.A., 61, 196
Burns, T., 38, 39, 40, 58, 79, 86, 90
Burrell, G., 36, 68
Burt, R.S., 12, 206, 207, 235, 239, 240, 241, 253, 270, 284
Butler, J., 155

Cameron, K., **191, 245, 246, 263, 265**
Campbell, D., 274
Campbell, J.P., 250, 254, 265
Caplow, T., 101, 217, 227
Caragonne, P., 227
Carper, W.B., 41, 43

Carroll, G.R., 86–87, 149, 187, 190, 192, 206, 274, 275, 276, 277
Carstensen, F.B., 13, 215
Cartwright, D., 140
Champagne, A., 13, 205
Chandler, A.D. Jr., 101, 103, 278
Chemers, M.M., 142
Child, J., 26, 74, 77, 82, 88, 93, 102, 183, 189, 265, 278, 279, 286
Christenson, J.A., 11
Christman, K.P., 12, 239, 240, 253, 270
Clark, J.P., 126–27, 132, 221, 223, 226, 229, 230, 234, 237
Clawson, D., 104, 242
Clegg, S., 25–26, 34, 40–41, 63, 68, 106, 121, 164, 273
Clinard, M.B., 14, 15, 272
Cohen, M.D., 159
Cohen, S.S., 26–27
Cohen, Y., 9
Coleman, J.S., 16, 30, 152
Comstock, D., 77, 92
Conaty, J., 99
Cook, K.S., 217, 226, 228–29
Cooper, W.H., 9
Coopman, P., 154
Cornfield, D.B., 62
Corwin, R., 196
Coser, L., 131
Costello, T.W., 167–69
Craig, J.G., 122
Crandall, N.F., 89
Cray, D., 155
Crittenden, A., 11
Crozier, M., 26, 55–56, 68, 116–17
Cummings, L.C., 129, 251
Cummings, L.L., 259

Daft, R.L., 95, 165, 166, 197
Dahl, R., 109, 235
Dahrendorf, R., 128
Dalton, M., 113, 115–16
Damanpour, F., 194
Danet, B., 3
D'Aveni, R.A., 191, 192, 193
Davis-Blake, A., 62, 291
Delacroix, J., 86–87, 187, 190, 192, 206
Delaney, J.T., 230–31
Delbecq, A.L., 78, 94
Della Fave, L.R., 132, 242
Dess, G.G., 212
Dewar, R.D., 50, 54, 65, 94, 95, 173, 196, 237
DiMaggio, P.J., 104–5, 287–88, 289, 290
Ditomaso, N., 237
Dobbin, F.R., 62, 104
Domhoff, G.W., 242
Donaldson, L., 88, 283, 284
Dornbusch, S.M., 67, 76, 77, 112, 281
Downs, A., 179–80
Downs, G.W. Jr., 192
Drabek, T.E., 232

Drazin, R., 106, 285
Dreeben, R., 80
Drenth, P., 154
Droge, C., 103
DuBick, M.A., 96
Dubin, R., 141
Dukerich, J.M., 135, 136
Dunbar, R.L.M., 210, 214
Duncan, R.B., 157, 194, 197, 213, 258
Dunford, R., 280
Dunkerly, D., 25–26, 34, 40–41, 63, 68, 121, 164, 273
Dutton, J.E., 157, 201
Dye, T.R., 242

Eccles, R.G., 286
Edström, A., 228
Edwards, R.C., 103, 104
Egelhoff, W.G., 25
Ehrlich, S.B., 135, 136
Eitzen, D.S., 147
Emerson, R.M., 109, 235
Emery, F.E., 90, 224
Enz, C.A., 113, 120
Ermann, M.D., 16, 272
Etzioni, A., 26, 30, 40, 112, 125–26, 135, 137, 251, 259
Evan, W.M., 194, 217, 235

Farberman, H.A., 15
Farrell, R.A., 16
Feldman, M.S., 167
Fenilee, P., 230–31
Fennell, M.C., 96, 199–200
Ferry, D.L., 74, 217, 218, 225, 226, 227, 229, 232, 233, 234, 237, 242
Fichman, M., 229
Fiedler, F.E., 142
Filley, A.C., 140–42, 237
Finney, H.C., 272
Fligstein, N., 106, 111, 117, 273, 291
Fombrun, C.J., 85
Form, W., 104
Freeman, J.H., 97, 105, 184, 187, 200, 207, 214, 254–55, 256–57, 268, 274, 275, 276, 288
French, J.R.P., 112, 235
Friedland, R., 13, 103, 240, 242
Friesen, P.H., 41–42
Frost, P.J., 68, 89, 169

Galaskiewicz, J., 11, 105, 217, 223, 224, 225, 227, 228, 231, 235, 241, 242, 288
Galbraith, J.K., 150, 283
Galtung, J., 236
Gamoran, A., 80
Gamson, W., 147
Gans, S.P., 238
Garcia, J.E., 142
Gardner, E.A., 230
Geeraerts, G., 90

Georgiou, P., 258–59
Gilb, C.L., 65
Gillespie, D.S., 88
Giordano, P.C., 8, 221, 223, 226, 229, 230, 234, 237, 260
Glisson, C.A., 68, 94
Goffman, I., 68
Goldman, P., 103, 284
Gooding, R.C., 89
Goodman, P.S., 102, 261–62, 282
Gordon, G., 145
Gouldner, A., 121, 136, 137, 143–45
Grafton, C., 276
Grandoci, A., 159–60
Granovetter, M., 3, 43, 90, 227, 287
Greene, C.N., 74
Greenwood, R., 74, 85, 95, 97, 102, 121
Gresov, C., 201, 267
Gross, E., 122, 253
Grusky, O., 121, 145, 146, 147, 148
Guest, R., 121, 143–45
Guetzkow, H., 177, 236
Gusfield, J.R., 21
Gutek, B.A., 8, 9

Haas, J.E., **40, 41, 42, 53–54, 55, 88, 89**
Hage, J., 9, 32, 53, 54, 60–62, 64, 65, 66, 67, 71, 72, 74, 77, 78, 86, 92, 94, 95, 115, 128, 155, 156, 160, 173, 175, 176, 180, 183, 186, 194, 196, 197, 224, 232, 236, 237, 241, 274
Hall, R.H., 2, 3, 14, 17, 40, 41, 42, 43, 53–54, 55, 72, 73, 74, 86, 89, 93, 99, 132, 197, 221, 223, 226, 229, 230, 234, 237
Halpert, B.P., 225, 227, 230, 235, 236
Hambrick, D.C., 120, 191, 192, 193
Hamilton, G.G., 111
Hamilton, G.L., 99, 106, 291
Hanada, M., 98, 99
Hannan, M.T., 105, 184, 187, 190, 254–55, 256–57, 268, 274, 275, 276, 288
Harris, S.G., 192
Hart, D.K., 2
Hasenfeld, Y., 277
Hawley, A.H., 199
Hawley, W.E., 79
Hayes, R.H., 27
Hedberg, B., 184
Heide, J.B., 223
Heilbroner, R., 25
Heise, D.R., 89–90
Heller, F.A., 154, 160
Helmich, D., 149
Heydebrand, W.V., 30, 32, 49, 82, 88, 173, 246
Hicks, A., 13
Hickson, D.J., 41, 42, 54, 65, 67, 88, 92, 119, 120, 154, 155, 161, 274, 279
Hills, F.S., 120, 160, 267
Hilton, G., 89
Hinings, B., 74, 85, 95, 97, 102, 121

Hinings, C.R., 41, 42, 54, 65, 67, 88, 120, 274, 279, 283
Hirsch, P.M., 214, 270
Hirschhorn, L., 14
Hirschman, A.O., 9
Hochschild, A.R., 9, 33–34
Hoffman, A.N., 223
Hofstede, G.H., 78
Högbert, B., 228
Holbek, J., 194, 197
Holden, C., 197
Hollander, E.P., 138
Horowitz, A.M., 16
Horton, G.T., 238
Hougland, J.G. Jr., 11, 126
House, R.J., 140–42, 189, 190, 237, 291
Hrebiniak, L.G., 214
Hsu, C-K., 80
Huber, G.P., 97, 129, 213, 251
Hulin, C.L., 37, 168
Hull, R., 173
Hunter, A., 187
Huo, Y.P., 187
Hylton, L., 217, 225, 231

Iacocca, L., 140
Ilvento, T.W., 11
Inkson, J., 88

Jackall, R., 27, 114
Jackson, S.E., 157
Jacobs, D., 206, 214, 229, 277–78
Jaeger, A.M., 98
James, D.R., 151, 241
Janowitz, M., 24
Jenkins, J.C., 253
Jennings, P.D., 62, 103, 104
Jermier, J.M., 141
John, D., 227
Johnson, E., 13
Johnson, J.B., 98
Johnson, J.M., 13, 271
Johnson, N.J., 40, 41, 42, 53–54, 55, 89
Johnson, P., 221, 223, 226, 229, 230, 234
Jones, M.H., 240
Jonsson, E., 191
Julian, J.W., 138
Jurkovich, R., 212

Kahn, R.L., **8, 9, 32, 34, 38, 102, 136, 164, 166, 170, 171, 174, 177, 178, 185, 262, 283–84**
Kalleberg, A., 9, 34
Kanter, R.M., 10, 164–65, 169, 180, 253, 280
Kaplan, A., 109
Kasarda, J.D., 187, 188, 274
Katz, D., 8, 9, 32, 38, 102, 127, 129, 136, 164, 166, 170, 171, 174, 177, 178, 185, 262, 283–84
Katz, R., 181
Kaufman, H., 184, 185

Keegan, W.J., 157
Keeley, M., 250, 260–61
Kerbo, H.R., 132, 242
Kerr, S., 237
Khandwalla, P.N., 79, 96, 214, 238
Kieser, A., 183, 189
Kilburn, H.C. Jr., 12, 239, 240, 253, 270
Kilijanek, T.S., 232
Kilmann, R.H., 14
Kim, M.Y., 191
Kim, Y-H., 13
Kimberly, J.R., 35, 87, 182, 187–90, 192, 201
Klatzky, S., 88, 207
Klauss, R., 165
Klonglan, G.E., 221, 225, 234, 236
Klonglan, R.D.W., 264
Knapp, T., 287
Knoke, D., 13, 26, 45, 46
Kochan, T.A., 129, 221, 226, 229, 230, 251
Koenig, R. Jr., 78, 94
Kohn, M., 3, 8, 17
Kornhauser, W., 70
Kovacic, B., 80, 81, 126
Kralewski, J.E., 76
Kriesberg, L., 145
Krohn, K.R., 11, 217
Kruytbosch, C., 213, 221, 241

Lachman, R., 120
Lammers, C.J., 27, 82, 118
Langston, J., 284
LaPotin, P., 159
Laumann, E.O., 13, 26, 105, 288
Lawler, E.E., 141
Lawler, E.J., 82, 110, 111–13, 116, 160
Lawrence, P.R., 57, 58–59, 79, 86, 90, 92, 132, 204, 237, 255, 268, 271, 283
Lazarsfeld, P.S., 36
Lazerson, M.H., 286
Leavitt, H.J., 176
Leblebici, H., 79, 96, 160, 200–201, 214, 233, 279
Lee, C.A., 279
Lehman, E.W., 282
Leifer, R., 97, 213
Lesieur, H.R., 272
Lester, M., 267
Levine, A.G., 15, 45
Levine, S., 225, 226, 228, 231
Levinthal, D.A., 229
Levitt, B., 160
Lieberson, S., 150–51
Lincoln, J.R., 37, 50, 78, 98, 99
Lindsey, M.L., 223
Lipset, S.M., 22–23, 152
Lipsky, M., 64
Litwak, E., 66, 86, 217, 225, 231
Long, A., 121, 233
Long, J.C., 9
Lorsch, J.W., 3, 57, 58–59, 79, 86, 90, 92, 132, 204, 237, 255, 268, 271, 283

Lotz, R.E., 147
Louis, M.R., 68, 169
Luckmann, T., 289
Lundberg, C.C., 68, 169
Lundman, R.J., 272
Lupton, K.M., 88
Lupton, T., 88
Lutterman, K.G., 10

Maas, M.L., 227, 236
McBride, K., 99
McCaffrey, D.P., 206
McDonald, K.M., 88
McEwen, W., 252, 253
McGinnis, R., 9
McGuire, J.B., 265
Macintosh, N.B., 165, 166
McKechnie, P.I., 256
McKelvey, B., 38, 39, 41–42, 43, 183, 187, 188, 274
McKinley, W., 60, 94
McMillan, C.J., 25, 50, 88, 120
McNeil, K., 197, 200, 215
Maguire, M.A., 78
Mahmoudi, H., 99
Mahoney, T.A., 89, 120, 160, 258, 267
Mallory, G.R., 155
Mannari, H., 80, 94, 99
Manns, C.L., 197
Mansfield, R., 76, 88, 93
March, J.G., 28, 159, 167, 190, 197
March, R.M., 80
Marglin, S.A., 82, 103
Mariolis, P., 240
Marple, D., 278
Marrett, C.B., 173, 187, 229, 232, 233, 234
Marsden, P.J., 105, 231, 288
Marsh, R.M., 94, 99
Martin, J., 68, 169
Martin, P.Y., 88
Maryanski, A., 289
Masuch, M., 159
Maurice, M., 99
Means, G.C., 12, 151
Mechanic, D., 122, 123
Meindl, J.R., 135, 136
Melcher, A.L., 75
Menzel, H., 36
Merton, R.K., 69, 217, 265
Metcalf, J.L., 222
Meyer, A.D., 201
Meyer, J.W., 96, 98, 105, 186, 288, 289
Meyer, M.W., 54, 68, 88, 93, 97, 148, 189, 203, 213
Michels, R., 120, 152, 253
Miles, R.A., 35, 182
Miles, R.E., 10, 102, 157
Mileti, D.S., 88
Milgrom, P., 160
Miller, D., 41–42, 103, 107, 271
Miller, G.A., 71, 99

Miller, R.E., 200
Milner, M. Jr., 242
Mindl, J.R., 150
Miner, A.S., 8
Minihan, E., 197
Mintz, B., 132, 240, 242
Mintzberg, H., 41, 108, 116
Mitroff, I.I., 14
Mizruchi, M.S., 240, 242
Moch, M.K., 196
Mohr, L.B., 92, 192
Molnar, J., 226, 230, 231, 236, 258
Molotch, H., 267
Moore, G., 284
Moore, L.F., 41, 43, 68, 169
Moore, W.L., 148
Morgan, G., 36, 68, 108–9, 127, 163, 169, 274
Morris, R., 15–16
Morrissey, J.P., 223
Morse, E.V., 196
Morse, J.J., 3
Mott, B.J.F., 233
Mouton, J.S., 237
Mouzelis, N.P., 116, 117, 264
Mueller, C.W., 50, 163
Mulder, M., 126
Mulford, C.L., 217, 226, 231, 232, 236, 264
Mulford, M.A., 232
Mullaney, P., 241, 242

Nagel, S., 13, 205
Nagi, S.Z., 213
Needleman, C., 14
Needleman, M.L., 14
Neef, M., 13, 205
Negandhi, A.R., 79, 283
Neuhauser, D., 271, 283
Neustadtl, A., 242
Norbäk, L.E., 228
Nowak, P., 210, 219, 233
Nuss, C., 160
Nutt, P.C., 160
Nystrom, P.C., 90, 100–101, 187, 192

O'Connor, J.F., 150–51
Olsen, J.P., 159
Olson, J., 98
O'Reilly, C.A. III., 172
Organ, D.W., 74
Ornstein, M., 132, 241–42
Ott, J.S., 169
Ouchi, W.G., 77, 78, 94, 98, 285

Padgitt, J.B., 264
Palmer, D., 103, 240, 242
Panian, S.K., 112, 147, 149
Parsons, T., 39, 171, 263, 278, 290
Pascale, R., 169
Pattahas, A., 227
Paul, B.D., 225, 226
Paulson, S.K., 221, 225, 234, 236

Pearson, J.S., 200
Pennings, J.M., 50, 65, 102, 187, 206, 231, 238, 240, 261–62, 270, 279, 282
Perrow, C., 14, 21–22, 38, 64, 66, 86, 90, 91, 92, 104, 110, 117, 118, 137, 165, 204, 215, 238, 251–52, 264, 268, 276, 281
Perrucci, R., 11
Perry, J.L., 260
Peter, L.J., 173
Peters, T.J., 101
Peterson, R.A., 121, 190
Pfeffer, J., 9, 10, 37, 62, 79, 83, 95, 96, 102, 116, 120, 121, 132, 148, 150, 157, 160, 184, 208, 210, 214, 215, 219, 233, 267, 269, 274–75, 277, 278, 279, 281, 284, 285, 291
Pheysey, D.C., 88, 92, 119
Pilisuk, M., 11
Pinder, C.C., 41, 43
Pinfield, L.T., 158
Pitt, L., 76
Pondy, L.R., 121, 131
Porter, L.W., 141
Powell, W.W., 104–5, 287–88, 289, 290
Powers, M.E., 103
Prensky, D., 45, 46
Price, J.L., 50, 53, 163, 252
Priest, T.B., 111, 205
Prokesh, S.E., 105, 288
Provan, K.G., 213, 221, 241
Puffer, S.M., 256
Pugh, D.S., 41, 42, 54, 65, 67, 88, 92, 119, 273, 274

Quinn, R.E., 69, 187–90, 266
Quinn, R.P., 34

Rabrenovic, G., 37
Raelin, J.A., 230
Rahim, M.A., 131
Ranson, S., 74, 85, 95, 97, 102, 121
Raphael, E., 55
Rauschenbach, B., 241, 242
Raven, B., 112, 235
Rawls, J., 260
Reid, W.J., 227
Reimann, B.C., 79, 257, 283
Reinganum, M.R., 149
Reve, T., 223
Richardson, R.J., 240
Ritzer, G., 3, 52
Robbins, S.P., 128
Roberts, J., 160
Roberts, K.H., 37, 168, 172
Robins, J.A., 287
Roekel, M.V., 221, 223, 226, 229, 230, 234
Rogers, D.L., 225, 230, 236, 258
Rogers, L.D., 79
Rohrbaugh, J., 266
Romanelli, E., 187
Rose, S., 217, 236, 237, 238

Rosenbaum, J.E., 9
Rosenthal, R.A., 34
Rosner, M., 80, 81, 126
Rosow, J.M., 3
Ross, J., 155
Rothermel, T., 235
Rothman, R.A., 111, 205
Rothschild, J., 44, 45
Rothschild-Whitt, J., 45
Rousseau, D.M., 37, 168
Rowan, B., 98, 105, 186, 288
Roy, W.G., 13, 215, 240
Rozgonyi, T., 80
Rubin, I., 79
Rus, V., 80, 132, 154

Sabel, C.F., **104, 127**
Salancik, G.R., 102, 120, 150, 160, 200–201,
    215, 233, 267, 277, 278, 284
Samuel, Y., 258
Sandelands, L.E., 201
Sanford, R.N., 127
Scheff, T.J., 122
Schermerhorn, J.R. Jr., 227
Schmidt, S.M., 129, 221, 226, 229, 230
Schneck, R.E., 97, 279
Schneeweis, T., 265
Schneider, S.C., 100, 209
Schoenherr, R.A., 53, 60, 66, 76, 83, 88, 94
Schollhammer, H., 98
Schooler, C., 3, 8, 17
Schoonhoven, C.B., 271, 283, 284
Schreyögg, G., 100, 278
Schwartz, M., 132, 240, 242
Schwitter, J.P., 88, 120
Schwochan, S., 230–31
Scotch, N., 147
Scott, W.G., 2
Scott, W.R., 30–31, 40, 67, 70, 76, 77, 92, 96,
    111, 112, 127, 172–73, 177, 250, 257,
    264, 283, 285, 289, 290
Seashore, S.E., 248–50, 267
Sebring, R.H., 236
Seiler, L.H., 10
Selznick, P., 18–20, 80, 136, 253
Shapiro, J.Z., 120
Shatin, D., 76, 224, 225
Shenkar, O., 16
Shepard, J.M., 11, 126
Shrum, W., 223
Sills, D.L., 253
Silverman, D., 68, 128
Simmel, G., 36
Simon, H.A., 28, 31, 33, 102, 159, 283
Simpson, R.L., 174
Singh, J.V., 189, 190, 240, 242, 291
Slater, P.E., 137
Slocum, J.W. Jr., 283
Smith, K., 129–30
Smith, M., 150
Snipe, J.N., 230

Snizek, W.E., 41, 43
Snoek, J.D., 34
Snow, C.C., 10, 102, 157, 214
Soref, M., 151, 241
Sorge, A., 99
Spenner, K., 104
Staber, U., 189
Stalker, G.M., 58, 79, 86, 90
Starbuck, W.H., 90, 100–101, 159, 187, 192,
    213, 280
Stauffer, R.E., 88, 173
Staw, B.M., 155, 184, 201, 256
Stearns, L.B., 240
Stearns, T.M., 223
Steckmest, F.W., 27
Steers, R.M., 259
Stern, L.W., 223
Stern, R.N., 216
Stewman, S., 62
Stinchcombe, A.L., 52, 86, 201, 202–3
Stipak, B., 260
Stogdill, R., 136
Stolzenberg, R.M., 9
Stone, K., 103
Strang, D., 96
Summers, G.F., 10
Sundgren, A., 265
Sutherland, E.H., 14, 15, 272
Sutton, R.I., 192
Swigert, V.L., 16
Szawjkowski, E., 201

Tamminga, H.L., **232**
Tannenbaum, A.S., 80, 81, 119, 126, 152
Taylor, F.W., 104
Taylor, J.C., 78
Terkel, S., 3
Terreberry, S., 224
Thomas, A.B., 150
Thompson, J.D., 32, 90, 91, 102, 155–56, 183,
    229, 252, 253
Thompson, V., 70
Tittle, C.R., 89
Tolbert, P.S., 106, 186
Tosi, H.L. Jr., 283
Toynbee, A., 25
Trice, H.M., 94
Trist, E.L., 90, 224
Trow, M.A., 152
Trump, D., 140
Tucker, D.J., 189, 190, 291
Turk, H., 217, 224
Turner, C., 54, 65, 88
Turner, J.H., 289
Tushman, M.L., 188

Useem, M., **13, 132, 215, 242, 284**

Van de Ven, A.H., **74, 78, 94, 101, 106, 217,**
    218, 225, 226, 227, 229, 232, 233, 234,
    237, 242, 274, 275–76, 285

Van Houten, D.R., 103, 106
Vaughan, D., 15
Vianello, M., 80, 81, 126

Waegel, W.B., 16
Wager, L.W., 168
Wagner, J.A. III., 89
Walczak, D., 52
Walker, G., 229, 232
Wamsley, G.L., 110, 277
Warner, M., 88, 99
Warren, R.D., 217, 221, 225, 233, 236, 237, 238
Warriner, C.K., 32, 36, 39, 41, 43
Wasilewski, N., 210, 214
Wasserman, S., 223, 241, 242
Waterman, R.H. Jr., 101
Waters, M., 287
Weber, M., 28–29, 86, 104–5, 109, 111, 112, 287
Weick, K., 79, 155, 198, 214
Weiner, N., 150
Weisbrod, B.A., 44
Weiser, G., 126
Weitz, B.A., 256–57
Weitzel, W., 89, 191, 258
Weldon, P.D., 40
Werking, R.H., 13, 215
Whetten, D.A., 50, 65, 79, 191, 200, 217, 225, 226, 227, 231, 235, 245, 263, 272
White, H.C., 34, 286
White, M.C., 150
White, P.E., 225, 226, 228, 231
Whitt, J.A., 44, 45

Wieser, G., 80, 81
Wiewel, W., 187
Wildavsky, A., 207, 252
Wilensky, H., 165, 172
Wilke, H., 126
Williamson, O.E., 285
Wilson, D.C., 155
Winkelpleck, J.M., 221, 225
Withey, M., 9
Wolfe, D.M., 34
Wong, G.Y.Y., 99
Wood, J.R., 126
Woodward, J., 90
Wright, E.O., 9
Wuthnow, R., 223

Xu, W., 99

Yarmolinsky, A., 79
Yeager, P.C., 14, 15, 27, 272
Yetman, N.R., 147
Young, R.C., 276
Yuchtman, E., 248–50
Yukl, G.A., 135, 138, 139

Zald, M.N., 121, 241, 277

Zalkind, S., 167–69
Zaltman, G., 194, 197
Zammuto, R.F., 245, 263
Zeitlin, M., 12, 151
Zeitz, G., 37, 50, 74, 78, 236, 237
Zucker, L.G., 186, 189, 289, 290
Zysman, J., 26–27

Subject index

Accidents, "normal," 14
Action set, 217
Actors, organizations as, 35–37
Adaptation, 189, 263
Ad hoc bases of interorganizational relation-
    ships, 228
Adhocracy, 41
Administrative innovation, 194
Advanced technology, 78
Adversity, innovation in periods of, 197
Affirmative action policies, 10
Alienation, 3, 71–72, 81
All-channel communication system, 177
Analytic dimensions of environment, 210–13
Anarchic decision making, 158
Appeals, socioemotional, 140–41
Approval-gaining devices, 173
Associational leaders, 152
Authoritarian (task) leadership style, 140
Authority, 40, 54, 111–12. *See also* Power
Authority leakage, 15
Autocracies, 108
Autocratic leadership, 141
Autonomous unit of large organizations, 32–33
Awareness of interorganizational relationships,
    225
"Axiomatic" theory of horizontal complexity,
    53

Bargaining, 252
Baseball teams, managerial succession and,
    146–47
Behavior. *See* Individual
Beneficiary, classification based on, 40–41
Bias in communication, 180
Births, organizational, 186–87, 206
Blacks, discrimination against, 4–7, 10
Boards of directors, 12–13, 217, 228, 238–42,
    284–85
Bolshevik revolution, 19, 20
Boundaries, organizational, 31
Boundary spanners, 180, 213
Bounded rationality, 102, 104, 159
Bounding systems, 256
Brandeis, Louis, 238
Budgetary controls, 78
Bureaucracy, bureaucratization, 11–12, 41, 66,
    72–74, 86, 108, 110, 281, 287
Bureaucratic personality, 69

Bureaupathic behavior, 70
Bureautic behavior, 70
Business Roundtable, 27

Capacity of environment, 210, 224, 249–50
Cause-and-effect knowledge, 157–58
Centrality, 76, 235
Centralization, organizational, 49, 74–83
  decentralization vs., 75–76, 77, 79
  definitions of, 74–75
  environmental relations and, 78–80
  formalization and, 65–66
  forms of, 75
  macropolitical considerations and, 80–82
  micropolitical considerations and, 82–83
  outcomes of, 83
  size and, 76
  technology and, 77–78
Change, organizational, 182–98
  defined, 183
  environmental vs. goal-based, 183, 186–87, 252–54
  innovation, 193–96
  internal, 17, 253
  nature of, 182–85
  potential for, 183–85
  process, 185–98
  resistance to, 22–24, 184–85
Change, social, 1–2, 17–24
Change agent, organization as, 17–22
Charismatic authority, 112
Chief executive officers, 111, 149–50
Circle pattern of communication, 176, 177
Civil service system, 24
Class, social, 241–42
Classification of organizations, 37–47
Client, individual as, 8–9
Client-advocacy organizations, 8
Cliques, 115–16
Coalitions, 115–16, 253
  dominant, 102–3, 261–63, 282
  of interest groups, 160
Codetermination, 109
Collective perception of communications, 175
Collegiality, 287
Commitment, involvement and, 126
Common sense typology, 39
Commonweal organizations, 40
Communication, 72, 163–81
  conflict from imperfect, 128
  from external sources, 179–81
  horizontal, 174–77
  importance of, 164–67
  individual factors in, 167–69
  networks of, 176–77
  organizational factors in, 169–74
  problems, 166, 177–79
  vertical, 169–74
Community, organizational outcomes for, 10–11
Competence, dominant, 43

"Competing values" approach to effectiveness, 266
Competition, 79, 96, 189, 207–8, 252, 280
Complexity, environmental, 224
Complexity, organizational, 49, 50–62, 94–95
  additional correlates of, 60–62
  coordination and control, 57–60
  intraorganizational variations in, 51–52
  as a variable, 52–55
  variance of elements of, 55–57
Compliance, 40, 125–27
Concentration-dispersion, environmental, 211, 224
Configuration, 54
Conflict, 127–31
  bases of, 127–29
  communications between subunits and, 176
  interorganizational, 236–37
  management-worker, 9
  organization set and, 218, 221
  outcomes of, 131
  professional-organizational, 73
  situation of, 129–31
  society and, 132
  See also Power
Conflict resolution, 59, 130–31, 237
Consensus-dissensus, domain, 211, 226
Consensus in dominant coalition, 262–63
Conservatism, 22–24, 185
Constituencies, 189, 262, 267–68
Constraints
  environmental, 150–51, 267, 268, 269–71, 283
  organizational, 261–63
Consumer organizations, 8
Context
  individual productivity and, 9
  leadership succession and, 149
  organizational structure and, 87–100
Contingency approach to organizational structure, 60
Contingency theory, 214, 271, 272, 283–84
  rational, 274, 282–85
Contradiction model of organizational effectiveness, 32, 245, 246–47, 265–72
Control
  competition and, 79
  complexity and, 57–60
  of environment, 214–15
  importance of communication for, 164–65
  See also Centralization, organizational; Formalization
Cooperation
  interorganizational, 236
  organization set and, 218, 221
Co-optation, 18–19, 252–53
Coordination
  competition and, 79
  complexity and, 57–60
  hierarchy and, 173–74
  interorganizational, 237–38

Corporate group, 29
Corporations
    harmful social impacts of, 14–15
    interlocking directorates, 12–13, 132, 217,
        228, 238–42, 284–85
    multinational, 24–26, 98, 99
    social responsibility of, 27
Costs, transaction, 274, 285–87
Coupling, loose, 79–80, 214
Crime, organizational, 14–15, 16, 62, 201, 206,
    272
Cultural conditions, 209–10, 223
Cultural Revolution in People's Republic of
    China, 16
Culture, organizational structure and, 98–100,
    209
Customer, individual as, 8–9

Data collection methodologies, 36–37
Death, organizational, 190–93, 206, 240
Decentralization, 75–76, 77, 79
Decision making, 154–61
    co-optation and, 18–19
    environmental uncertainty and, 201
    good vs. bad, 161
    importance of communication for, 164–65
    levels of decisions, 95
    organizational factors influencing, 35–36
    participation in, 78, 160–61
    power and, 155, 160–61
    rationality in, 159–60
    resource-dependence model and, 274, 277–82
    strategic, 154–61
    strategic choice, 101–6, 278–80
    See also Leadership
Decision-making rights, 75
Decline, organizational, 191–93
Delegation, 76, 77
Democracy, direct vs. representative, 109
Democratic organizations, 44
Demographic conditions, 184, 208
Density
    environmental, 190
    organizational, 203
Dependency, 116–18
    localized dependence, 227
    in power relationship, 109–10
    resource, 242, 274, 277–82
Design, organizational, 100–106, 289
Deskilling of labor, 104
Determinist perspective, 36
Development, environment and, 201–3
Differentiation, 94
    cliques and, 116
    horizontal, 52–54, 61
    internal, 32
    organizational size and, 88
    vertical, 54, 61
    See also Complexity, organizational
Diffusion, 188
Direct democracy, 109

Directives, organizational, 77
Directorates, interlocking, 12–13, 132, 217,
    228, 238–42, 284–85
Disasters, technologically related, 14
Discrimination, 4–7, 10
Dispersion-concentration, environmental, 211,
    224
Distortion, 166, 175, 178
Distressed innovation, 194
Divisionalized form, 41
Division of labor, 54
Domain claims, 213
Domain consensus-dissensus, 211, 226
Dominance, environmental, 44
Dominant coalition, 102–3, 261–63, 282
Dominant competence, 43
Downward communication, 170–71
Dual leadership, 137, 152
Dual rationality, 161
Dyadic interorganizational relationship, 217,
    218, 220

Ecological conditions, 208–9
Ecological perspective on change, 187–90
Ecology-population model, 274–77
Economic conditions, 9, 206–8
Education, 17, 34, 53, 202
Effectiveness, organizational, 59–60, 244–72
    constraints and participants in, 261–63
    contradiction model of, 32, 245, 246–47,
        265–72
    definitions, 249, 250–51, 261
    goal model of, 250–54, 257–58
    goals and, 254–65
    managerial succession and, 146–47
    orientation toward, 246–47
    participant-satisfaction models of, 258–61
    social-function models of, 263–65
    systems-resource model of, 248–50, 262
Elite, bureaucracy, 12
Elite values, 196–97
Employee, individual as, 2–8
Employment, patterns of, 2–7, 10
Energy policy, 13–14
Entrepreneurism, 190
Environment, 199–215
    capacity of, 210, 224, 249–50
    centralization and, 78–80
    complexity and, 58
    constraints from, 150–51, 267, 268, 269–71,
        283
    control of, 214–15
    defined, 199
    development and, 201–3
    dimensions of, 203–13, 223–24
    ecological perspective on change and, 187–90
    "friendly" vs. "hostile," 96
    goal shifts and, 253–54
    impact of, 214–15
    innovation and, 197
    organizational change and, 183, 186–87

Environment *(cont.)*
  organizational impact on, 11–16
  organizational structure and, 95–98, 99
  perception of, 97, 213–14, 280
  physical, 31–32
  research on, 199–203
  resource-dependence model and, 277–82
  social, 32, 187
  uncertainty in, 201, 240
Environmental dominance, 44
Environmental jolt, 201
Escalation situations, 155
Ethics, 27
Evaluation, centralized vs. decentralized, 76
Exchange basis for interorganizational relation-
    ships, 228–29
Existence, struggle for, 188
Expectations, 35
  role, 34
Expertise, power of, 115, 122

Factor analysis, 249, 250
Family ownership, 12, 149–50
Feedback, 170–71, 180
Field, organizational, 105, 288
Field of conflict, 129, 130
Filtering process, 179
Firm internal labor markets (FILMs), 34, 62
Flexibility, ideational, 17
Foreign control, effects of, 97
Foreign policy, 13
Formalization, 49, 62–74, 94
  centralization of power and, 65–66
  interaction, 233
  of interorganizational agreements, 229–30
  maximal, 63
  measures and definitions of, 64–65
  minimal, 64
  organization set and, 218, 220
  outcomes for individuals, 68–70
  program change and, 61, 66
  reactions to, 70–74
  technology and, 66–68
  tradition and, 68
Foundings, organizational, 186–87, 206
Frequency of interaction, 218, 219, 234
Functional conflict, 127–28

"Garbage can" model of decision making, 159
Gate keepers, 213
Gateway innovations, 195
Geographical proximity, 226–27
Goal model of organizational effectiveness,
    250–54, 257–58
Goals, organizational, 31
  constraints vs., 261–63
  decision making and, 158
  effectiveness and, 254–65
  indoctrination into, 171
  multiple and conflicting, 267, 282–83
  nature of, 251–52

organizational structure and, 251
  time frames and, 255, 268–69
  uses of, 257
Government organizations, 13, 15, 18, 23–24,
    97, 186, 187
Gross malfunctioning analysis, 264
Growth, organizational, 15–16

Halo effect, 168
Harm to society, organizational potential for,
    14–15
Health policy, 13–14
Hierarchical conflict, 128
Hierarchical differentiation, 54, 61
Hierarchy, upward communication and,
    171–74.
  See also Power; Structure, organizational
Homogeneity-heterogeneity, environmental,
    210–11, 224
Horizontal communication, 174–77
Horizontal differentiation, 52–54, 61
Horizontal interdependence, 231–32
Horizontal power relationships, 113–18,
    127–28
Hostile corporate takeovers, 193

Ideational flexibility, 17
Ideographic approach, 36
Ideology, 80–82, 226
Incentive-distributing devices, organizations
    as, 258–59
Individual, 2–10, 29, 33–34
  categories of, 9–10
  as client or customer, 8–9
  communication and, 167–69
  economic factors and, 9
  as employee, 2–8
  outcomes of formalization for, 68–70
Indoctrination of subordinates, 171
Influence, authority vs., 111–12
Information, decision making and, 157–58.
  See also Communication
Information processing in organizations,
    165–66
Innovation, 61, 193–96
  See also Change, organizational
In Search of Excellence (Peters and Water-
    man), 101
Insider vs. outsider, successor as, 144, 148–49
Instability-stability, environmental, 79, 211,
    224
Institutional environment, 187
Institutional level of organization, 171
Institutional model (institutional isomorphism),
    104–6, 274, 287–90
Integration, 59, 263
Integrative organization, 39
Intelligence departments, 105, 288–89
Intensity of interorganizational relationship,
    232
Intensive technology, 91

Interaction frequency, 218, 219, 234
Interdepartmental power, 116–18
Interdependence, 94, 231–32
Interest groups, coalitions of, 160
Interlocking directorates, 12–13, 132, 217, 228, 238–42, 284–85
Intermediary organizations, 233
Internal differentiation, 32
Internal labor markets, 34, 62
Internal organizational changes, 17, 253
Internal politics, 82–83, 102
Interorganizational networks, 217–18
Interorganizational power, 132
Interorganizational relationships (IOR), 11, 216–43, 252, 284–85
    environment and, 222, 223–24
    forms and levels of, 217–23
    outcomes of, 242–43
    in private sector, 238–42
    reasons for, 228–31
    resource flows and, 231–33
    situational factors in, 225–28
    transaction forms in, 233–38
Interorganizational set, 217, 218
Interpersonal ties, awareness of, 225
Interpretation, 179
Involvement, 126–27, 259–60
Isomorphism, institutional, 104–6, 274, 287–90

Japanese governmental policies, 197
Japanese vs. American firms, 98
Job codification, alienation and, 71–72
Job instruction, 170
Joint programs, 61–62, 232–33
Joint ventures, 210, 219–20, 233

Knowledge, cause-and-effect, 157–58
Knowledge technology, 92, 93

Labor markets, internal, 34, 62
Labor unions, 13, 152
Latency, 263
Lateral communication, 174–77
Layoff process, 62
Leadership, 134–53, 281
    components of, 137–39
    constraints on, 150–51
    dual, 137, 152
    functions of, 136–37
    motivation in, 151
    nature of, 135–40
    outcomes of, 140–52
    power vs., 135–36
    styles of, 140–42
    succession of, 143–51
    in voluntary organizations, 152–53
    See also Decision making
Leakage, authority, 15
Legal authority, 112
Legal conditions, 204–5, 223
Legal entity, organization as, 16

Life cycles, organizational, 182–83, 186–93
Line-staff relationships, 113–14
Linkage, interorganizational. See Interorganizational relationships (IOR)
Literacy, 202
Localized dependence, 227
Long-linked technology, 91
Loose coupling, 79–80, 214
Love Canal, 15, 20
Lower participants, power of, 122–23

Machine bureaucracy, 41
Macropolitics of organization, 80–82
Management
    participative, 78, 80–82, 160–61
    scientific, 104
    subunit size and, 89
Management-worker conflict, 9
Managerial level of organization, 171
Managing Any Organization (Caplow), 101
Mandated relationships, 230–31
Market power, 44
Marxist analysis, 81, 103–4, 284–85
Materials technology, 92
Matrixlike systems, 180
Mechanical organization, 86
Mediating technology, 91
Mediation, 130–31
Meetings, 180
Mergers, 193
Methodologies, data collection, 36–37
Micropolitics of organization, 82–83
Military-industrial complex, 217
Mimetic tendencies, 105, 288–89
Money economy, 202
Moral issues, 27
Motivations of leaders, 151
Multinational corporations, 24–26, 98, 99
"Multi" organizations, 32
Multiple organizational forms, 86
Mutual benefit organizations, 40
Mutual dependency, 109–10

National Football League, coach succession in, 147
Natural-selection model, 188, 274–77
Networks
    communications, 176–77
    interorganizational, 217–18
Niches, 188–89, 275, 279–80
Nominalist position, 36
Nomothetic approach, 36
Nondecision, 161
Nonprogrammed innovation, 194
Norms, 35, 209–10

Objectives. See Goals, organizational
Occupations, 2–7
Official goals, 251, 252
Oligarchy, 152
Omission, 177, 178

Operations technology, 92–93
Operative goals, 251–52
Organic organization, 86
Organization(s), 1–27
  characteristics related to innovation, 196–98
  definitions of, 28–33
  as determinant of actions, 34
  as "enacting" entity, 198
  as legal entity, 16
  reality of, 33–37, 280
  reasons to study, 1–2, 26–27, 244
  social organization and, 30
  types of, 37–47, 50
  variables for classifying, 43–45
Organizational analysis, 2
Organizational levels, communication across,
  171
Organizational set, 217, 218–23
Organizational structure. *See* Structure, organizational
Organizational theory, 26–27, 273–91
  institutional model, 104–6, 274, 287–90
  population-ecology model, 274–77
  rational contingency model, 274, 282–85
  resource-dependence model, 242, 274,
    277–82
  transactions cost model, 274, 285–87
Organizational weapon, 19–20, 21
Organization and Environment (Lawrence and
  Lorsch), 57
Outcomes of organizations, 1–27
  for community, 10–11
  for individual, 2–10, 29, 33–34
  social change, 1–2, 17–24
  across societies, 24–26
  for society, 11–16
Outsider vs. insider, successor as, 144, 148–49
Overload, 178–79

**Pairwise interorganizational relationship,
  217, 218, 220**
Parent organizations, 80
Participant-satisfaction models of organizational effectiveness, 258–61
Participative management, 78, 80–82, 160–61
Pattern-maintenance organization, 39
Patterns of Industrial Bureaucracy (Gouldner),
  143–45
Peaceableness, conflict resolution through,
  130
Perception
  collective, of communications, 175
  of environment, 97, 213–14, 280
  process of, 167–69
Perceptual defense, 168
Performance, leadership succession and,
  143–45, 150
  See also Effectiveness, organizational
Permanently Failing Organizations (Meyer
  and Zucker), 189
Personality, bureaucratic, 69

Personnel turnover, 185–86
Physical environment, 31–32
Policy
  government, 13–14, 97, 197
  organizational, 75
Political base of society, 203
Political conditions, 205–6
Political organization, 39
Politics
  centralization and, 80–82
  internal, 82–83, 102
  leadership succession and, 149–50
Population-ecology model, 274–77
Populations of organizations, 43
Power, 108–33
  act of, 111
  amount of, 118–19
  authority vs., 111
  bases and sources of, 112–13
  of boards of directors, 241
  decision making and, 155, 160–61
  distribution of, 65–66, 119–21
  external factors affecting, 121–22
  interorganizational, 235–36
  leadership vs., 135–36
  local power structures, 11
  in lower participants, 122–23
  market, 44
  nature of, 109–13
  of organizations, 22
  outcomes of, 125–33
  reality of organization and, 34
  relationships of, 108–11, 113–18, 127–28
  resource-dependence model and, 279
  strategic choice and, 102–3
  types of, 111–12, 125–26
  in voluntary organizations, 122
  See also Centralization, organizational; Conflict; Leadership
Praxis, 30
Procedures and practices, communicating, 170
Production organization, 39
Productivity, 9, 141
Professional bureaucracy, 41
Professional-organizational relationships,
  114–15
Professionals, professionalization, 70–74, 78,
  106, 173, 176, 289
Profit vs. nonprofit organizations, 44
Program change, 61, 66
Programmed innovation, 194
Project groups, 180–81
Projection, 168
Proximity, geographical, 226–27
Public leaders, 152
Publicness of organization, 43–44
Public organizations, 271

Queuing, 178

Race, employment and, 4–7

Rational contingency model, 274, 282–85
Rationale for task, communicating, 170
Rationality
    bounded, 102, 104, 159
    in decision making, 159–60
    dual, 161
Raw materials, organizational structure and,
    91–92
Realist position, 36
Reality of organizations, 33–37, 280
Reasoning, tautological, 289–90
Reciprocity, 235
Redundancy, 179–80
Referents, 262, 263
Regulations, 230, 286
Reifications, goals as, 31
Representative democracy, 109
Resistance to change, 22–24, 184–85
Resource(s)
    allocation system, 121
    development and, 201–2
    exchange of, 229
    standardization of, 233–34
    system-resource model, 248–50, 262
Resource-dependence model, 242, 274, 277–82
Resource flows, 231–33
Resource interdependency, 231–32
Responsibility, organizational, 16, 27
Retention, 188, 275, 281–82
Revelatory analysis, 264–65
Revolution, social change through, 19–20, 22
Reward system for professionals, 114–15
Ritual scapegoating no-way casualty theory,
    147
Rockefeller family, 12
Role expectations, 34
Roman bureaucracy, 11–12
Routinization, degree of, 66–68, 78, 92–94
Rules. *See* Formalization

Satisfaction, indicators of, 141
Scapegoating, ritual, 147
Scientific management, 104
Selection, 275
Self-management, 82
Service organizations, 40
Sex, employment patterns by, 4–7
Simple structure, 41
Situation, interorganizational relationships and,
    225–28
Situational approach to leadership, 138
Size, organizational, 15–16, 43
    centralization and, 76
    interorganizational relationships and, 227–28
    organizational structure and, 87–90, 94–95
    rate of succession and, 145–46
    technology and, 92–93
Social change, 1–2, 17–24
    internal organizational change and, 17
    organizational resistance to, 22–24
    organizations as agents of, 17–22

Social environment, 32, 187
Social-function models of organizational effec-
    tiveness, 263–65
Socialization, 281
"Social justice" approach to effectiveness,
    260–61
Social organization, 30
Social relationships, 29
Social responsibility, 27
Social status, interlocking directorate and,
    241–42
Social stratification, 9
Society, organizations and, 11–16, 24–26,
    131–32
Socioemotional appeals, 140–41
Solution-centeredness of decision making, 160
Spatial dispersion, 55, 56
Specialization, 53, 54, 65
Stability, environmental, 79, 211, 224
Staff-line relationships, 113–14
Standards, standardization, 65, 73, 233–34
State University of New York (SUNY), 48–49
Stereotyping, 168, 169, 173
Strategic choice, 101–6, 278–80
Strategic decision making, 154–61
Structure, organizational, 48–107
    centralization, 49, 74–83
    communication and, 164
    complexity, 49, 50–62, 94–95
    contextual factors in, 87–100
    culture and, 98–100, 209
    defined, 85
    design factors in, 100–106
    effectiveness and, 271–72
    formalization, 49, 62–74, 94
    functions of, 85
    goals and, 251
    leadership succession and, 148–49
    strategic choice factor in, 101–6
    variations in, 86
Structured decision making, 158
Subunits, communication between and within,
    174–76
Succession, leadership, 143–51
Support, societal, 21–22
Supportive leadership style, 140–42
Symbiotic interdependence, 232
Symbols, 289
Systematics, 43
"Systemic obstacles" to change, 185
Systems-resource model of organizational
    effectiveness, 248–50, 262

Takeovers, hostile, 193
Task-oriented communications, 174–75
Tautological reasoning, 289–90
Taxonomies, organizational, 41–43
Technical conditions, 204–5
Technical level of organization, 171
Technocracies, 108–9
Technological innovation, 193, 194

Technology, 223
  advanced, 78
  centralization and, 77–78
  components of, 92–93
  development of organizational form and,
    203
  disasters and, 14
  formalization and, 66–68
  organizational structure and, 90–95
  typology, 90–91
Tennessee Valley Authority (TVA), 18–19
Time frames, 255, 268–69
Tradition, formalization and, 68
Traditional authority, 112
Training, 33–34, 71
Traits, leadership, 137
Transaction forms, interorganizational, 233–38
Transactions cost model, 274, 285–87
Transformations, organizational, 187–90
Turbulence, environmental, 211–13, 224
Turnover, personnel, 185–86
Typologies of organizations, 37–41

Uncertainty, 78, 94, 116–18, 119–20, 165,
    201, 240

Unions, 13, 152
U.S. presidency, succession in, 148
U.S. State Department, 13
U.S. Supreme Court, 205
Upward communication, 171–74, 177
Urbanization, 202

"Vacancy chains," 34
Values, 196–97, 209–10, 266
Variable analysis, 264
Variation, purposeful or blind, 188
Vertical communication, 169–74
Vertical differentiation, 54, 61
Vertical interdependence, 231–32
Voluntarism, 36
Voluntary organizations, 45–47, 50, 122, 126,
    152–53

Weapon, organizational, 19–20, 21
Wheel pattern of communication, 176, 177
Women, discrimination against, 4–7, 10
Women's Christian Temperance Union, 21
Work
  individual reactions to, 3–8
  patterns of, 17